Wages, School Quality,
and Employment Demand

IZA Prize in Labor Economics Series

Since 2002, the Institute for the Study of Labor (IZA) has awarded the annual IZA Prize in Labor Economics for outstanding contributions to policy-relevant labor market research and methodological progress in this sub-discipline of economic science. The IZA Prize is the only international science prize awarded exclusively to labor economists. This special focus acknowledges the global significance of high-quality basic research in labor economics and sound policy advice based on these research findings. As issues of employment and unemployment are among the most urgent challenges of our time, labor economists have an important task and responsibility. The IZA Prize in Labor Economics is today considered one of the most prestigious international awards in the field. It aims to stimulate further research on topics that have enormous implications for our future. All prize-winners contribute a volume to the IZA Prize in Labor Economics Series published by Oxford University Press, which has been established to provide an overview of the laureates' most significant findings.

The IZA Prize in Labor Economics has become an integral part of the institute's manifold activities to promote progress in labor market research. Based on nominations submitted by the IZA Research Fellows, a high-ranking IZA Prize Committee selects the prize-winner. In conjunction with the Award Ceremony the IZA Prize Conference brings together a number of renowned experts to discuss topical labor market issues.

It is not by coincidence that the IZA Prize in Labor Economics Series is published by Oxford University Press. This well-reputed publishing house has shown a great interest in the project from the very beginning as this exclusive series perfectly complements their range of publications. We gratefully acknowledge their excellent cooperation.

1L. F. Jimmermann

Klaus F. Zimmermann, IZA Director

Winners of the IZA Prize in Labor Economics

2010	Francine D. Blau (Cornell University)
2009	Richard A. Easterlin (University of Southern California)
2008	Richard Layard (London School of Economics)
	Stephen J. Nickell (Nuffield College)
2007	Richard B. Freeman (Harvard University)
2006	David Card (University of California, Berkeley)
	Alan B. Krueger (Princeton University)
2005	Dale T. Mortensen (Northwestern University)
	Christopher A. Pissarides (London School of Economics)
2004	Edward P. Lazear (Stanford University)
2003	Orley C. Ashenfelter (Princeton University)
2002	Jacob Mincer (Columbia University)

Alan B. Krueger – David Card
2006 IZA Prize Laureates

Wages, School Quality, and Employment Demand

David Card and Alan B. Krueger

Edited by
Randall K. Q. Akee
Klaus F. Zimmermann

OXFORD
UNIVERSITY PRESS

OXFORD
UNIVERSITY PRESS

Great Clarendon Street, Oxford, OX2 6DP,
United Kingdom

Oxford University Press is a department of the University of Oxford.
It furthers the University's objective of excellence in research, scholarship,
and education by publishing worldwide. Oxford is a registered trade mark of
Oxford University Press in the UK and in certain other countries

© IZA, 2011

The moral rights of the authors have been asserted

First published 2011
First published in paperback 2016

Published in the United States of America by Oxford University Press
198 Madison Avenue, New York, NY 10016, United States of America

British Library Cataloguing in Publication Data
Data available

Library of Congress Cataloging in Publication Data
Data available

ISBN 978-0-19-969338-2 (Hbk.)
ISBN 978-0-19-877995-7 (Pbk.)

Award Statement
of the IZA Prize Committee

The IZA Prize in Labor Economics 2006 is awarded to the outstanding and highly productive U.S. labor economists David Card (University of California, Berkeley) and Alan Krueger (Princeton University). Their work has crucially shaped the research agenda in labor economics and has certainly raised the standards for empirical research in applied economics. Their studies are directed towards the analysis of policy-relevant issues, and their research findings continue to have a substantial impact on the debate of labor market policy and education policy around the globe. David Card and Alan Krueger have become a leading authority with regard to policy advice based on sound econometric research.

Card and Krueger share an instinct for finding the right kind of exogenous variation and collecting the relevant data from which reliable inferences can be drawn. With a remarkable sense for using the appropriate dose of sophisticated econometric techniques, they have unearthed intriguing facts from existing data or from appropriate natural experiments that would have otherwise remained in obscurity. Many of their findings spurred substantial debates and inspired much subsequent work. Often challenging the conventional views of the profession, their surprising new results were at times received with skepticism and critical distance. But David Card and Alan Krueger convinced many skeptics by their in-depth analyses that are based on carefully designed research strategies and reflect their expert knowledge on the details of the data they use. Card and Krueger's work abounds with key methodological contributions on instrumental variable estimation, measurement error, regression-discontinuity methods, or the use of "natural experiments." Card and Krueger have greatly promoted the quasi-experimental approach to causal modeling as a transparent scientific methodology. Their studies, which contain several brilliant examples of "natural experiments," have fueled the quest for and the use of natural experiments in a large economics literature that followed.

Their research centers on estimating the effects of schooling and institutional factors on labor market outcomes. Jointly, individually, and with various co-authors, they have made several seminal contributions that have greatly advanced our understanding of the factors that determine the wage structure and shape inequality. Krueger's article with Lawrence Summers on inter-industry wage differentials, which is still one of the most widely cited works in labor economics, indicated that part of the observed inter-industry wage differentials reflects noncompetitive rents. Since the start of his career, Alan Krueger has recognized the importance of institutions such as unions, work councils, and implicit contracts for labor market outcomes and argued that employment relationships are too complex to be adequately described in the traditional competitive framework. Similarly, David Card's work on unions and collective bargaining highlights the impact of institutions on the determination of wages, employment, and consequently inequality. He showed, for example, that unions compress wage distributions by raising wages of workers with lower observed skills disproportionately, carefully taking account of measurement error in reported union status and the possibility that better workers select into unionized jobs. In other influential work on the effects of immigration on wages and employment of natives, Card showed that immigration has virtually no adverse effects on the labor market prospects of less-skilled workers. In a famous study, Card creatively exploits a sudden large-scale immigration of Cubans to Miami as a natural experiment. The influx of Cubans known as the Mariel boat lift increased supply in the Miami labor market by about 7 percent between May and September 1980 but was unrelated to local labor market conditions. By comparing labor market outcomes in Miami to those of various other similar cities, Card answers the counterfactual question of how wages and unemployment would have been in the Miami labor market if the immigrants had not come.

David Card and Alan Krueger have much advanced the human capital literature. Several other well-known studies, which Alan Krueger co-authored with various scholars, develop innovative estimation techniques, propose novel instruments, or exploit unique data sets in order to get unbiased estimates of the returns to schooling. David Card ingeniously structured the literature by formulating a general model that sheds light on the econometric issues involved in the estimation of the returns to schooling when schooling decisions are endogenous. In earlier work he had devised an econometric methodology together with Thomas Lemieux, which makes it possible to evaluate the extent to which changes in returns to observed and unobserved skills can account for changes in wage differentials.

In a sequence of joint studies, Card and Krueger have assessed how school quality determines labor market outcomes. While the previous literature had provided ambiguous results and concluded that there is no relation between school quality and test scores, Card and Krueger shifted the discussion away from student achievement tests to labor market outcomes. Their studies have structured the way we should think about the effects of improvements in schooling quality and how we should assess its impact econometrically. Evaluating various dimensions and measures of school quality, such as student–teacher ratios, average term length, or annual teacher pay, they documented evidence for a causal positive relation between the quality of schooling and economic returns to education. They provided evidence that those who were educated in states with better school quality enjoyed higher returns to their educational investments later in their lives. Krueger's subsequent studies on the effects of class size and on the returns to attending a more selective college substantiate these results. Their work on schooling quality impressively highlights the role of human capital policy for reducing inequality.

Card and Krueger's joint work on the economics of the minimum wage reflects their originality and style of doing empirical research. It is also a prime example of their impact on the economics profession and on the political debate, as it demonstrates how their controversial research findings shook mainstream economics and instigated heated debates among economists and policymakers. As is true for most of their work, their studies on the effects of the minimum wage have inspired much subsequent research that has eventually led to a better understanding of the functioning of labor markets.

In a sequence of studies, which are collected in their book Myth and Measurement: The New Economics of the Minimum Wage, they assembled empirical evidence from various labor markets, different periods, and different states showing no indication that higher minimum wages – contrary to the predictions of the traditional labor market model – reduce employment in the U.S. In one of their most famous joint studies, they surveyed 410 fast-food restaurants in New Jersey and Pennsylvania before and after the minimum wage was raised by about 20 percent in New Jersey, but not in its neighboring state. By comparing outcomes before and after the policy change within and across states, they evaluate the effects of the minimum wage change. This excellent example of using "natural experiments" to make causal inferences illustrates the power of the quasi-experimental approach as a transparent empirical strategy in labor economics. This has inspired original data collection and the search for exogenous variation generated by natural experiments in a large economics literature that followed.

The influence of Card and Krueger's work is also felt in many other fields of economic science. Their style of doing empirical research has become a role model for research methodology across the economics profession. The IZA Prize 2006 honors the work of two scholars who have given great momentum and research spirit to the field.

George A. Akerlof   University of California, Berkeley

Armin Falk   IZA; University of Bonn

Richard Portes   Centre for Economic Policy Research (CEPR)

Joseph E. Stiglitz   Columbia University, New York

Klaus F. Zimmermann   IZA; University of Bonn

Contents

Contents

Contents

I
Ingenuity and Creativity – David Card and Alan Krueger

Randall K. Q. Akee and Klaus F. Zimmermann

David Card and Alan B. Krueger were jointly awarded the 2006 IZA Prize in Labor Economics. The IZA Prize honors individuals who have made profound contributions to the field of labor economics. Previous winners of the IZA Prize include Jacob Mincer, Orley Ashenfelter, Edward Lazear, Dale Mortensen, and Christopher Pissarides. These past winners have contributed to the field of labor economics by undertaking pioneering research on topics such as human capital investments, on-the-job learning, female labor supply decisions, trade union membership, program evaluation methodologies, compensation schemes and worker productivity, personnel economics, and the development of search and matching models for a variety of markets. David Card and Alan Krueger join this esteemed group of economists for their exceptional work in labor economics.

It is difficult to overstate the contributions of these two scholars. Their work has spanned large and important spaces in labor economics: unemployment, minimum wages, migration, measurement error, unionization, wage differentials among various groups in the U.S., labor demand, social insurance and technological change. The citation count for their papers in the Social Sciences Citation Index shows the phenomenal extent of their reach in the economics profession. It is clear that in a discipline where most papers are seldom cited, the Card and Krueger papers (both their joint and independent papers) stand out for their influence; indeed, their 1992 *Journal of Political Economy* paper has been cited over 300 times.

Beyond their research and influence within specific subject areas, Card and Krueger have been extremely influential in econometrics methodology as well; they were at the forefront of employing an "experimental" approach in their research design and implementation. Both of these prize winners have made significant methodological contributions on instrumental variable estimation, measurement error, regression-discontinuity methods in addition to the use of "natural" experiments.

The authors have served in various editorial capacities at some of the most esteemed economics journals such as the American Economic Review, Econometrica, Quarterly Journal of Economics, Journal of the European Economics Association, Journal of Labor Economics, Journal of Economic Perspectives and Economic Letters. Both Card and Krueger have been IZA Research Fellows since the formative years of the institute; Card joined in 1999, while Krueger followed in 2000.

One of the most important themes of Card's and Krueger's work is their examination of the determinants of labor market outcomes. Their most prolific areas of research on these determinants have been on the role of human capital investment and institutions. They have explored this theme in a variety of areas in labor economics. For instance, their work has shown that observed wage differences across different industries cannot simply be explained by standard models of competitive markets. Instead, the role of unions, implicit contracts and other institutional factors may affect wages both within and between industries.

Another institutional factor that Card and Krueger have explored in-depth is the minimum wage in the U.S. Increases in minimum wages, at least from a standard theoretical standpoint, should have adverse consequences for employment in affected areas – especially for the low-skilled. Card and Krueger investigated the role of this particular labor market institution on the employment outcomes for low-skilled individuals in a variety of settings. In one of their most famous papers, Card and Krueger compare employment outcomes for low-skilled individuals in New Jersey and Pennsylvania in similar industries after New Jersey increases its minimum wage by about 20 percent (Card and Krueger 1994, Chapter 6 in this volume). Their research indicates that there is no evidence for a decrease in employment and even a slight increase in employment numbers. They conclude that the wage increase was merely passed on to customers in the fast-food industry. These results are a further example that the standard models of competitive markets do not fully explain all employment outcomes; alternative models such as a monopsonistic market might be a better fit in this case.

This particular line of research has sparked significant controversy in the U.S. amongst other researchers. For instance, IZA Research Fellow David Neumark and William Wascher (2000) have called into question the data and instead use administrative payroll data to show a contrary result. Kennan (1995) argues that Card and Krueger may have been a little too forceful in their conclusions regarding the non-negative effects of an increase in the minimum wage. Specifically, he calls into question whether a more representative industry could be found. Card and Krueger (2000, Chapter 7 in this volume) follow up their initial work with a larger data set using administrative data and are able to confirm their earlier findings. In this particular debate, IZA has taken the stance that minimum wages are not necessary nor are they desirable in Germany. Given the existence of extensive social welfare and assistance programs already, both on a scale and scope that do not exist in the United States, IZA has opposed the establishment of minimum wages in Germany (see e.g. IZA Compact 2002, 2008; Zimmermann et al. 2009).

Card and Krueger explored another important determinant of labor market outcomes – the human capital investment and the returns to that investment. Specifically, they have explored the effects of the quality of human capital investment on labor market outcomes. The papers on the effect of school quality changed the focus of the debate from student achievement in school to actual labor market outcomes. In their research, the authors employed relatively novel methodologies and data sets. This overlaps with IZA work in the area of school quality. For instance, IZA now houses the OECD Programme for International Student Assessment (PISA) data sets for use by researchers.

In his research, Krueger (1999, Chapter 4 in this volume) used the novel Tennessee Star data which is one of the first examples of randomized experiments in labor economics (certainly it is the first for class size). In their research on the differences in school spending between North and South Carolina, the authors provide the data and the historical background information which determined demographic differences across the two US states several generations previously (Card and Krueger 1996, Chapter 3 in this volume). This information is crucial in establishing the plausibility of the "natural" experiment between these two states. Their exposition here is an important primer for others who have employed the use of "natural" experiments in their own work subsequently. From this research, the authors find that more spending on school quality is an important determinant of the long-run return to education for children.

The work of Card and Krueger fits nicely with the mission and spirit of the Institute for the Study of Labor. Over its more than ten years of existence, IZA has constantly striven to position itself at the intersection of sound academic research on labor economics and policymaking. Card and Krueger's research in the areas of school quality, wage inequality, the role of unions and changes in minimum wages have important implications for policymakers in not only the United States, but Europe as well. These issues have advanced to the center of the policy debates in the past few decades within the European Union as newer member states seek admission. The issues of differential skills and schooling, assimilation policies, and minimum wages and social protection legislation are important topics for all European countries individually and collectively.

For example, the effect of new immigrants on the employment outcomes of natives is an important topic in Europe with free migration between European Union member states. In an influential paper, David Card examined the effect of an influx of new immigrants to Miami on the employment of natives. Utilizing a natural experiment, Card (1990, Chapter 8 in this volume) finds that the exogenous increase in Cuban immigrants due to the Mariel boatlift did not adversely affect employment in Miami. Card's research on this topic is especially important in the European context, where citizens of newly admitted EU-member states have the right of free entry into other EU states and anti-immigrant fears run high.

David Card was an early advocate for program evaluation in Germany. He helped initiate the debate on labor market program evaluation in meetings in Berlin approaching the German Ministry of Labor with other IZA officials. As a result of these efforts, IZA has developed an entire research area and produced an influential book on this topic (Schmidt et al. 2001). IZA has since then played an important role in helping to establish a program evaluation tradition in German research and policymaking, which had a long-lasting effect on labor market reforms undertaken in the Schröder Federal Government after 2005. Beyond intensive policy advice to policy makers such as Chancellor Gerhard Schröder, Economics and Labor Minister Wolfgang Clement and the Head of the Nuremberg Employment Agency Florian Gerster, IZA, was also publicly and influentially advocating for the reforms (Zimmermann 2003, 2006). As a consequence, there is now some substantial evidence on the effectiveness of labor policy measures in Germany drawing from the findings of a growing research community (Eichhorst and Zimmermann 2007).

Alan Krueger has served in various capacities in the U.S. federal government. In the Clinton Administration, he served as the Chief Economist to the U.S. Department of Labor from 1994 to 1995. Currently, Krueger has taken the position of Assistant Secretary for Economic Policy and Chief Economist of the U.S. Treasury Department.

Card and Krueger's research agenda which explores human capital investment and labor market institutions on labor market outcomes has an enduring legacy. Their inspiring ingenuity and research efforts have provided important foundational findings that continue to be relevant for labor economists. The influential IZA Discussion Paper Series contains many papers that were directly inspired by Card and Krueger's research. Card and Krueger pioneered the exploration of these topics primarily in the United States; European researchers have taken up their efforts in the European context and have provided valuable insight into policy debates occurring in Europe and around the world.

This book has four parts and contains some of Card and Krueger's most influential papers on the topics of school quality, earnings differentials, and minimum wages. Part II, the first main part, focuses on school quality and the differences in wages across groups in the U.S. A brief introduction written by the two authors provides insight into the four chapters in this section and the responses and critiques from other academics. The authors position their research in the historical context and discuss the novelty of their approach in determining the effect of school quality on earnings. The authors exploit several natural experiments which make it possible to improve upon previous research efforts where the nature of causality was difficult to isolate.

The second main part of the book, Part III, focuses on the effect of changes in minimum wages on employment and wage setting. A brief introduction to this part once again provides unique insight into the evolution of this research agenda by the authors. They mention their motivation and the particular events which provided the impetus to undertake the particular look at minimum wage effects on low-skilled employment demand. The authors also discuss the response to their results which showed no effect on increases in minimum wages on the employment levels of the low-skilled in affected areas. A final chapter in this section examines the role of fixed-wage union contracts when unexpected aggregate price shocks occur. In this setting, the author finds that real wages are negatively related to employment as the standard model would predict.

Finally, the book concludes with Part IV, on thoughts about the research process and important lessons learned. The authors emphasize the importance of high quality data, well-specified survey design and sound economic models to guide the research endeavor. Card and Krueger thus deal with an issue of vital importance for economic science. In a joint effort with other economic research institutes, IZA has also demanded better data access for independent research in Germany for many years – and eventually was successful. Today, IZA runs its own International Data Service Center (IDSC), which provides a wide range of data services including documentation of data sets as well as controlled remote data processing (http://idsc.iza.org/).

The IDSC meets the data and technology needs of IZA's resident research community, the various global and virtual IZA research communities (such as its fellow and affiliate networks) and the research community at large. Owing to this ideal environment, the IDSC is exceptionally well connected to the research community. As a result, the center continuously receives feedback and suggestions which it turns into innovative data products for the analysis and documentation of scientifically relevant data. The IDSC thereby continuously develops its competence and expertise in data support, data access and data services for labor economists – thus in some sense following the example of David Card and Alan Krueger.

II

School Quality, Earnings, and Black–White Wage Differences

Introduction

Schooling is a critical determinant of labor market success. Workers with an elementary education earn substantially less than those who have completed secondary schooling, while those with a bachelor's degree can expect to earn 30–40 percent more *per year* than secondary school graduates. Many prestigious occupations – engineering, law, and medicine, for example – are only open to people with advanced degrees. In most modern economies the earnings advantages associated with formal schooling have risen substantially over the past two decades, as new technologies and increasing international trade have transformed the structure of jobs.

Human capital theory, as developed by Jacob Mincer, Gary Becker, and others, interprets the wage premium earned by people with more education as an economic "return" to the investment of time and resources during their years of formal schooling. In this framework more *intensive* schooling, provided by more highly skilled teachers in schools with fewer pupils per teacher, would be expected to yield *higher* returns later in life. The human capital investment perspective also suggests an important lasting effect of policies like segregated schooling that lead to lower schooling investments for some groups relative to others.

Chapters 2, 3, and 4, written in the 1990s, address the connection between school quality and students' earnings later in life. Although a number of economists had explored similar ground in the 1960s and early 1970s, the paucity of data on the quality of schooling experienced by different individuals, coupled with a shift in interest away from education-related topics, led to a long hiatus in the school quality literature. Several developments in the 1980s helped push the analysis of school quality back to the center stage in empirical labor economics. One was the remarkable surge in education-related wage differentials that began early in the decade. A second was growing concern over perceived "failures" in the public school systems of many countries, including the United States and the United Kingdom. A third factor was the increasing awareness of the value of research designs that build on so-called natural experiments to provide credible estimates of important but controversial effects, like the return to school quality.

The research presented in these chapters represented a response to all three challenges. We began by posing a simple question: Could we draw a causal link from the quality of the schools attended by people born in different states at different times to their earnings later in life? We conjectured that the changes in the quality of the school system in a state could be treated as a series of natural experiments that were effectively exogenous to the children in a given cohort. We then developed a simple econometric approach to isolate the shifts in the return to education experienced by different cohorts of individuals from different states. A guiding principle in our approach was the observation that a change in school quality should affect the payoff per year *of schooling attended.* We also assumed that a rise in school quality could induce people to stay in school longer, providing an additional source of benefit to students later in life.

Our initial focus, summarized in Chapter 2, was on the earnings of white men. Whites are the largest demographic group in the labor market, and men have relatively high employment rates, so we were able to sidestep concerns over small sample sizes and selective labor market participation. We found a robust, statistically significant relationship, between state-wide measures of school quality – specifically, the pupil–teacher ratio, average term length, and the relative pay of teachers – and the rate of return to education experienced by students educated in that state. Indeed, we concluded that the economic returns to school quality were high enough to "pay back" the initial investment costs, even taking account of the delay between early childhood, when schooling investment are made, and adulthood, when the returns to these investments are realized.

Chapter 3 presents a complementary analysis of returns to school quality for African Americans, focusing on men educated in the segregated southern states prior to 1965. One of the motivations for this study is the extraordinary range of variation in school quality experienced by black students in different southern states. For example, schools for black students in South Carolina had roughly 65 pupils per teacher in the period around World War I, while at the same time in Missouri the ratio was approximately 35. By the mid-1960s pupil-teacher ratios for black student in both states were in the 25–30 range. The earnings effects of such large differences are likely to be apparent even in the presence of measurement errors and minor biases in the econometric specification.

A second motivation for studying the returns to schooling for southern-born blacks is that school spending in the segregated South was mainly decided by *white* politicians. Arguably, cross-state differences in the levels and trends in school quality for black students were *not* attributable to changes in the incomes or attitudes of black families that could have led to higher earnings for their children even in the absence of improved school quality. Finally, by studying the link between school quality and earnings for southern-born blacks we were able to place a quantitative bound on the importance of segregated schooling in explaining the trends in the relative earnings of African Americans over the period from 1960 to 1980.

The results from our study provided strong confirmation that the intensity of schooling investment affects the return to schooling. Perhaps more importantly, we concluded that changes in school quality could explain most of the convergence in rates of return to schooling earned by southern-born blacks relative to southern-born whites between cohorts born in the 1910s and those born in the 1940s. These changes in turn accounted for about one-fifth of the closing of the overall black-white earnings gap between 1960 and 1980.

The conclusion from these two chapters that school quality matters for the subsequent earnings of students has led to continuing controversy. Some critics challenged our basic research design, which linked state-wide *average* quality measures to the labor market outcomes of people educated in the state. Others criticized the details of our econometric strategy for isolating the component of earnings that could be attributed to school quality in the individual's state of birth. Chapter 4 presents a partial response to these criticisms. In this chapter we review the basic human capital investment model that provided an underpinning for the analysis in our original studies, and comment on the previous and subsequent literature. We note that most, but by no means all, studies in the literature have found a significantly positive relationship between school quality and earnings. We also consider in some detail a simple "case study" of black and white men from two southern states – North and South Carolina – which provided dramatically different relative resources to black schools in the pre-World War II period, but which converged to a common level by 1970. The results provide a clear illustration of the importance of trends in school quality in explaining trends in both the relative education and relative earnings of blacks versus whites.

Though we believe that the labor market provides the ultimate standard for judging the value of investments in school quality, such judgments are only feasible long after the investments have been made. Shorter term assessments are usually made using standardized tests, on the assumption that test scores are a valid measure of "human capital." While many researchers have attempted to use observational research designs to evaluate the effects of school quality on test scores, such studies face a critical obstacle. In contrast to the historical situation, where states offered widely varying levels of school quality, in most current settings there is so little exogenous variation in school quality that even carefully designed studies are likely to be seriously compromised. For example, many schools provide additional resources to under-performing students. Such compensatory allocation systems induce a strong negative correlation between school quality and test scores that is very hard to control in an observational study.

It is widely acknowledged that the most scientifically reliable way to overcome the biases that arise in observational settings is via a randomized controlled test. Chapter 5 (written by Alan Krueger) presents a detailed analysis of the first large scale randomized evaluation of school quality: the Tennessee Star experiment, conducted in the late 1980s to test the effect of smaller class sizes on the academic achievement of elementary school children. This experiment involved 11,600 students at 80 different schools, and provides uniquely valuable information on the impacts of class size reductions on student test scores.

Consistent with the findings in Chapters 2 and 3 based on historical comparisons, the results from the Star experiment show that children in relatively small classes (13–17 students) have higher achievement than those in "regular" classes (22–25 students). Though it is difficult to extrapolate test score gains for young children to long-run earnings impacts, a translation based on available evidence linking cognitive scores to labor market rewards suggests that the impact of small classes may be large enough to "pay back" the investment costs of the intervention.

1

Does School Quality Matter? Returns to Education and the Characteristics of Public Schools in the United States

Beginning with the highly influential Coleman report (Coleman et al. 1966), researchers have found little, if any, association between the quality of schools and student achievement on standardized tests (for example Hanushek 1986). On the basis of these findings, it is widely argued that increases in public school funding have few important benefits for students. This conclusion, although politically popular, contradicts two other strands of evidence on the quality of schooling. On one hand, the small number of studies that have directly correlated school quality and earnings have found a significantly positive relationship between them (Welch 1966; Morgan and Sirageldin 1968; Johnson and Stafford 1973; Wachtel 1976; Rizzuto and Wachtel 1980). On the other hand, much of the gain in black–white relative earnings over the past century has been attributed to growth in the relative quality of black schooling (Welch 1967, 1973a, 1973b; Freeman 1976; Smith and Welch 1989).

There are several possible explanations for the conflicting evidence. Studies of earnings and school quality typically focus on the

This chapter is a revised version of: Card, D., Krueger, A. (1992). Does School Quality Matter: Returns to Education and the Characteristics of Public Schools in the United States, in: Journal of Political Economy 100, 1–40, © University of Chicago Press, 1992, reprinted by permission of the University of Chicago Press. The authors are grateful to Michael Boozer and Dean Hyslop for outstanding research assistance, and have also benefited from the comments of Richard Freeman, Claudia Goldin, Jean Grossman, James Heckman, Lawrence Katz, Robert Margo, Sherwin Rosen, an anonymous referee, and seminar participants at several institutions. Financial support from the Princeton Industrial Relations Section is gratefully acknowledged.

correlation between school characteristics (such as per capita expenditure) and the average earnings of students educated in a school district. One can easily argue that family background variables affect both education expenditures and labor market earnings. In this case, the correlation of school quality and earnings is potentially spurious. From the opposite perspective, one can argue that test scores are an imperfect measure of school performance. Indeed, although earnings and test scores are correlated, they are by no means identical.[1] Factors that affect subsequent labor market achievement may have a much smaller impact on test scores. Furthermore, the relation between school quality and test scores at the eighth or twelfth grade fails to capture any effects of school quality on subsequent learning.

This chapter presents an extensive analysis of the relation between earnings and school quality for cohorts of men born between 1920 and 1949. We use the relatively large samples available from the 1980 census to estimate rates of return to education by state of birth and cohort. We then relate rates of return to schooling to objective measures of school quality, including pupil/teacher ratios, relative wages of teachers, and the length of the school term.[2]

Our procedures overcome at least some of the objections to earlier studies of earnings and school quality. First, our statistical models include unrestricted state of birth effects and therefore control for any differences in the mean earnings of men born in different states. To the extent that differences in family characteristics raise or lower earnings for all levels of schooling attainment, our estimated rates of return are purged of any effects of differential family background. Second, we control for systematic differences in the returns to education associated with an individual's current region of residence. We thereby eliminate relative supply or demand effects that raise or lower the returns to education in different parts of the country. Finally, in much of our analysis we incorporate permanent state-specific effects in the return to education and use only the within-state variation among consecutive cohorts to identify the effects of school quality on the returns to education.

Our results indicate that there is substantial variation in the rate of return to education across individuals born in different states and at different times. Much of this variation is associated with differences in the quality of schooling. We find that rates of return are higher for individuals who attended schools with lower pupil/teacher ratios and higher relative teacher salaries. For example, our estimates suggest that a decrease in the pupil/teacher ratio by five students is associated with a 0.4-percentage-point increase in the rate of return to schooling. Similarly, a 10 percent increase in teachers' pay is associated with a 0.1-percentage-point increase in the rate of return to schooling. We also find that returns are linked to higher education among teachers. Controlling for measures of school quality, however, we find no evidence that returns to education are related to the income or schooling levels of the parents' generation.

Our main focus is on the relation between school quality and the rate of return to education. Changes in the slope of the earnings–schooling relation, however, do not necessarily raise average earnings. For example, the earnings gains of better-educated workers may come at the expense of the less educated. On the other hand, changes in the quality of schooling may affect the average level of education as well as the marginal return to added years of schooling. To address these issues we present some simple "reduced-form" evidence on the relationship between school quality and the mean levels of education and earnings. Controlling for any permanent differences across individuals born in different states, we find significant positive effects of school quality on both the average years of schooling and mean earnings of students. The reduced-form results suggest that increases in school quality affect subsequent earnings by increasing the number of years of completed education and by increasing the return to each year of schooling.

1.1. An Empirical Framework for Modeling Returns to Schooling

Our goal is to relate the returns to education earned by individuals educated in different states to the characteristics of the public school system during the time they attended school. To fix ideas it is useful to assume that individuals attend school in their state of birth and to ignore private schooling. (The effects of these simplifications are explored below.) Let y_{ijkc} represent the logarithm of weekly earnings for individual i, born in state j in cohort c and currently living in state k of region r, and let E_{ijkc} represent the years of education completed by individual i. Suppose that earnings are determined by an equation of the form

(1) $$y_{ijkc} = \delta_{jc} + \mu_{kc} + X_{ijkc}\,\beta_c + E_{ijkc} \cdot (\gamma_{jc} + \rho_{rc}) + \epsilon_{ijkc},$$

where δ_{jc} represents a (cohort-specific) fixed effect for each state of birth, μ_{kc} represents a (cohort-specific) fixed effect for each state of residence, X_{ijkc} represents a set of measured covariates (years of labor market experience, marital status, and an indicator for whether i lives in a standard metropolitan statistical area [SMSA]), and ϵ_{ijkc} represents a stochastic error term. Equation (1) assumes a linear specification of the return to education, consisting of two components: a cohort and state of birth effect (γ_{jc}) and a cohort and region of residence effect (ρ_{rc}).[3] These components allow observed rates of return to schooling to vary because of differences in the return to education across different regional labor markets (i.e., variation in ρ_{rc}) and because of differences in the rate of return to education earned by individuals in a given state of birth and cohort group in *any* labor market (i.e., variation in γ_{jc}).

Notice that when we include interactions between state of birth dummies and education and another set of interactions between region of residence dummies and education, the state of birth-specific contribution to the return to education is identified by individuals who are educated in one state and move to another region. *It is the shift in the return to education attributable to schooling in a particular state that we seek to explain by differences in school quality across states and over time.*

Specifically, we hypothesize that the state of birth components in the return to education depend on the quality of the public schools, and possibly on a set of state-specific constants:

$$(2) \qquad \gamma_{jc} = a_j + Q_{jc}b,$$

where Q_{jc} is a vector of measures of the quality of the education system in state j during the time that cohort c attended school. In this specification any permanent differences in the returns to education arising, for example, from differences in the distributions of ability across states are absorbed by the state of birth effects (a_j) in (2).

Under these assumptions, the effects of a particular measure of education quality can be obtained in one step by estimating a log-linear earnings function that includes state of birth effects, state of residence effects, interactions of region of residence with education, and interactions of education with state of birth effects and the quality measures for state j and cohort c. However, we prefer to proceed in two steps: first, estimating the average rate of return to education for individuals born in cohort c in state j, controlling for state of birth, state of residence, and any regional differences in the return to education; and then using a second-step regression to relate the estimated rates of return (by cohort and state of birth) to the quality variables.

The two-step procedure has several important advantages. In the first place, it provides a convenient reduction of the data and allows us to illustrate the diversity in the returns to education and their relation to measures of school quality. A two-step procedure also facilitates extremely general models of the earnings function (1), including models with cohort-specific state of birth and state of residence effects, and models with permanent state of birth effects in the return to education. In addition, we can incorporate a simple correction for the interstate mobility of children. A disadvantage of the two-step procedure is that cohorts must be defined fairly broadly to obtain reliable estimates of the state- and cohort-specific returns to education. In the analysis below we use 10-year intervals of births. This aggregation eliminates any within-cohort variation in school quality or the returns to education and leads to some efficiency loss. Since individuals are assigned the mean levels of school quality for their state of birth and cohort, however, aggregation does not introduce classical measurement error into the quality measures (see Griliches 1986, p. 1478).

1.1.1. Functional Form

The assumption of a linear relation between schooling and (log) earnings is widely used in applied studies of earnings and is often found to perform as well as or better than simple alternatives (e.g. Heckman and Polachek 1974). However, most studies pool samples of individuals from different states and birth cohorts with no allowance for regional or cohort differences in returns. It is conceivable that the log earnings–schooling relation is approximately linear in pooled samples but is nonlinear for particular subsamples. It is also conceivable that changes in the quality of public schooling shift the returns to elementary or secondary education more (or less) than the returns to college. If so, then the specification of the return to education function should allow for kinks at 12 years of education.

In an effort to obtain some simple evidence on these issues, we estimated a series of unrestricted earnings-schooling models using narrowly defined subsamples of individuals in the 1980 census. These models include a complete set of dummy variables for 0–20 years of education, as well as controls for potential labor market experience, marital status, state of residence, and residence in an SMSA.[4] Figure 1.1 graphs the estimated return to education relationships for six of the subsamples: three cohorts of white men born in Alabama or Georgia (1920–29, 1930–39, and 1940–49) and three cohorts of white men born in California. Figure 1.2 graphs the estimated return to education relationships (together with their standard error bounds) for national samples of white men in the same three cohorts.

Figure 1.1

Wages vs. Schooling, by Cohort and State of Birth:

a) White Men Born in Alabama or Georgia

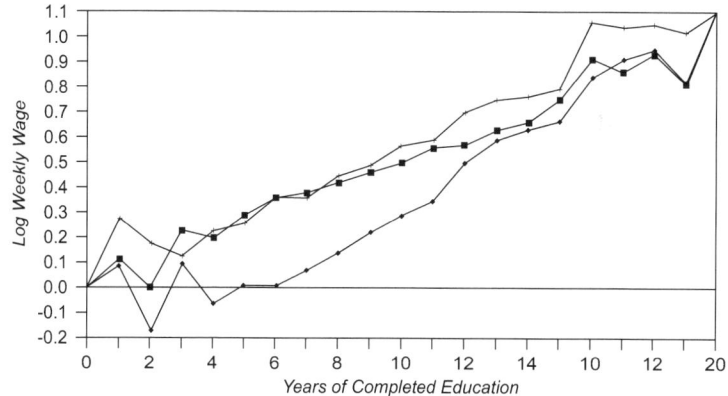

b) White Men Born in California

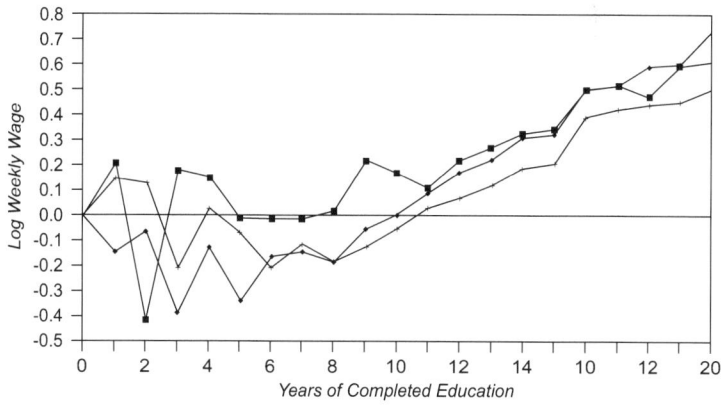

Figure 1.2

Return to Single Years of Education

a) White Men Born 1920–1929, Nationwide

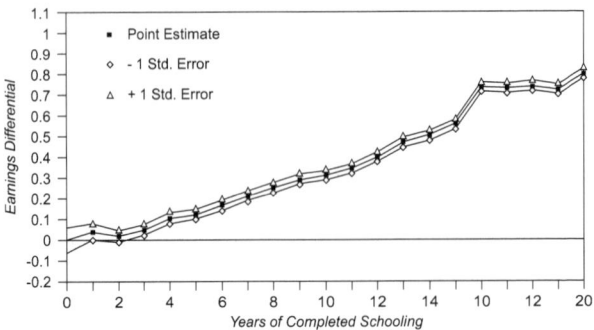

b) White Men Born 1930–1939, Nationwide

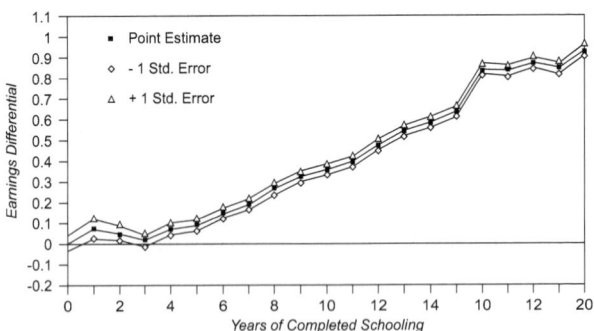

c) White Men Born 1940–1949, Nationwide

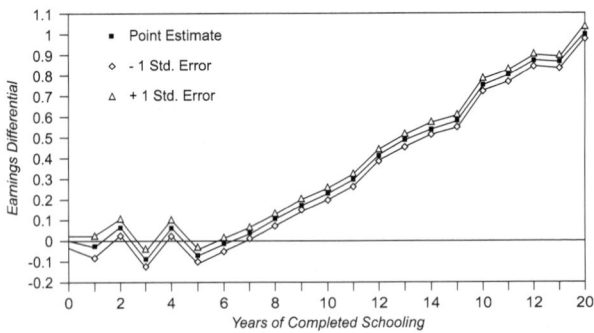

The figures illustrate three general findings. First, for a particular cohort and state of birth group, the earnings–education relation is approximately log-linear for levels of education above a minimum threshold. Although there is some evidence of a college graduation effect, departures from log-linearity above the threshold level are small. Second, the threshold varies widely across states and over time within states. It is relatively low for older cohorts and for individuals from states with lower average educational attainment. This phenomenon is also evident in the national samples in Figure 1.2: the threshold is at approximately 2 years of education for men born between 1920 and 1929, at 3 years of education for those born during 1930–1939, and at 5 years for those born in 1940–1949. Third, the rate of return to education (for years of education above the threshold level) is higher for later cohorts.

The positive correlation between the average educational attainment of a state of birth and cohort group and the kink or threshold point in their return to education function led us to investigate the determinants of this threshold more carefully. For each of 13 larger states (or pairs of contiguous states) and each of three 10-year birth cohorts, we first estimated a nonparametric version of the return to education function (using 20 unrestricted dummy variables) and found the approximate threshold point in the return to education relation. We then compared this point to various percentiles of the education distribution in each state-cohort group. This comparison led us to a simple empirical relation: across different cohorts and states of birth and different race groups, the threshold point corresponds approximately to the grade level attained by the second percentile of the education distribution of workers. For example, a simple linear regression of the estimated threshold point on the grade attained by the second percentile of the education distribution has an estimated coefficient of 0.88 with an estimated standard error of 0.13 and an R^2 of .57.[5]

Given the pattern of the nonparametric estimates of the return to education function for the larger states, in the remainder of the chapter we concentrate on measuring the return to education for years of schooling above the second percentile of the education distribution of an individual's state of birth and cohort. Specifically, we replace an individual's completed education by the following linear spline: $\min\{E_{ijkc} - T_{jc}, 0\}$, where T_{jc} is the second percentile of the education distribution for men born in state j in cohort c. We present some evidence on the effects of ignoring the threshold in Section 1.3.3. Since only 2 percent of those in the sample have levels of education below the threshold point, the estimated rates of return to years of education above the threshold turn out to be quite similar to the estimated returns from a conventional log-linear earnings-schooling model.

1.2. Measures of the Quality of Public Schooling

Since the late nineteenth century the U.S. Office of Education has published a regular summary of the characteristics of the public school systems in each state. These data are available on a semiannual basis from 1918 to 1958 in the *Biennial Survey of Education* and annually since 1960 in the *Digest of Education Statistics*. The Office of Education tabulates the results of questionnaires sent to the state offices of education inquiring about statewide enrollment, revenues, number of teaching positions, length of school term, average teacher salaries, and other variables.

The *Biennial Survey of Education* is a rich source of information on the average characteristics of public schools in different states at different points in time. From the available data we have assembled information on three main characteristics: the ratio of enrolled students to instructional staff in the state (pupil/teacher ratio), the average length of the school term (term length), and average annual teacher salaries (see Appendix A for more information). We hypothesize that increases in term length increase the amount of material covered in a school year and thereby increase the economic value of additional years of schooling. We similarly hypothesize that reductions in the pupil/teacher ratio improve the quality of classroom instruction and lead to higher returns for each year of completed education. Finally, we hypothesize that higher teacher salaries enable schools to attract and retain more qualified and highly motivated teachers, leading to improved classroom instruction and higher returns to education.

Several previous authors, including Morgan and Sirageldin (1968), Johnson and Stafford (1973), Wachtel (1976), and Rizzuto and Wachtel (1980), have used total expenditures per pupil as an index of school quality. We suspect that the quality of education is more directly linked to indexes of pupil/teacher ratios and teacher salaries than to total expenditures per pupil, and indeed this is suggested by the results in Welch (1966). Nevertheless, roughly 60 percent of total education expenditures go for instructional salaries. Since the per capita expenditure on instructional salaries is simply the ratio of the average teacher wage to the pupil/teacher ratio, differences in teacher salaries and pupil/teacher ratios account for a majority of the variation in total expenditures per pupil.

Given geographic differences in the cost of living and in the level of alternative wages available to potential teachers, it seems unlikely that the level of teacher wages is an adequate index of teacher quality in different states. We have therefore normalized teacher wages in each state by the level of average wages in the state. We use average weekly earnings of employees covered by the social security system to adjust wage rates from 1940 onward. Prior to 1940, we use a regional wage rate for workers on federal construction projects to normalize average teacher salaries. The comparison wage series are index-linked between 1940 and 1944 as described in Appendix A. In view of the changing coverage of the social security wage index and given the necessity of index-linking disparate wage series, we have chosen to remove the trend in average relative teacher salaries during our sample period. Specifically, we divide the relative teacher wage in each state by the national average of this ratio in the same year. This procedure eliminates any time-series variability in the average value of relative teacher salaries, while preserving the interstate variation in relative teacher wages at a point in time.

A summary of these three measures of school quality is presented in Table 1.1. We report statewide averages of the quality measures for three cohorts of students: those born between 1920 and 1929, those born between 1930 and 1939, and those born between 1940 and 1949. The averages for a cohort assume that each person attends public school for 12 years and that the number of individuals born per year in any cohort is constant. By assuming 12 years of education, we measure the *potential* quality of the schooling available to individuals in a particular cohort and abstract from the possible endogeneity of school quality and average schooling. Nevertheless, when the averages are computed using individual-specific years of education for the men in each cohort, the quality measures are virtually identical.

The data in Table 1.1 show substantial variation in education "quality" across states. For the 1920–1929 birth cohort, pupil/teacher ratios range from 20 (in the Dakotas, Montana, and Wyoming) to over 35 (in Arkansas, Mississippi, and North Carolina). Average term lengths for this cohort range from 139 days (in Mississippi) to over 180 days (in the middle-Atlantic states). Similarly, relative teacher wages range

Table 1.1

Average of School Quality Variables for Cohorts Born in 1920–1929, 1930–1939, and 1940–1949 (Black and White Students Combined)

	Pupil/teacher ratio			Term length (days)			Relative teacher wage		
	1920-29	1930-39	1940-49	1920-29	1930-39	1940-49	1920-29	1930-39	1940-49
Alabama	35.9	31.7	29.1	150	168	176	.73	.81	.90
Arizona	30.8	28.6	26.4	169	169	170	1.05	1.13	1.11
Arkansas	36.3	32.3	29.1	151	165	173	.65	.75	.86
California	28.0	29.7	27.2	177	176	177	1.30	1.27	1.17
Colorado	24.9	24.1	24.1	174	175	177	.95	.98	.95
Connecticut	29.6	25.2	24.2	182	181	180	1.11	1.09	1.07
Delaware	27.3	24.4	22.5	183	182	180	1.13	1.05	1.01
Florida	30.4	26.5	26.1	166	175	180	.96	1.06	1.15
Georgia	34.8	30.2	28.4	154	173	180	.75	.80	.93
Idaho	26.0	26.5	26.0	170	173	174	.84	.92	.92
Illinois	28.1	24.9	24.3	184	187	184	1.06	1.02	1.00
Indiana	30.0	28.3	27.2	169	171	175	.96	.99	1.00
Iowa	21.7	20.8	20.5	176	177	179	.79	.85	.85
Kansas	21.3	20.5	21.1	171	171	174	.76	.82	.89
Kentucky	33.4	29.7	27.4	159	165	172	.75	.76	.76
Louisiana	33.7	29.8	27.2	161	173	179	.78	.96	1.04
Maine	25.9	25.0	23.8	178	179	181	.73	.76	.82
Maryland	32.8	30.4	26.7	187	185	182	1.20	1.22	1.19
Massachusetts	27.8	25.2	23.4	179	178	177	1.32	1.26	1.12
Michigan	28.6	27.5	25.6	180	180	180	.89	.91	.91
Minnesota	25.0	24.0	23.5	175	173	174	.89	.97	1.00
Mississippi	37.6	34.4	31.4	139	154	168	.65	.66	.78
Missouri	27.7	27.1	26.6	177	180	182	.86	.86	.87
Montana	20.1	19.7	20.0	176	177	179	.80	.96	.96
Nebraska	21.0	19.0	19.4	177	177	177	.70	.76	.84
Nevada	22.7	24.3	24.9	175	176	178	.92	.97	.96
New Hampshire	25.1	23.5	23.8	177	176	177	1.07	1.03	1.02
New Jersey	28.2	24.1	22.9	186	183	181	1.31	1.14	1.02

Table 1.1 (continued)

Average of School Quality Variables for Cohorts Born in 1920–1929, 1930–1939, and 1940–1949 (Black and White Students Combined)

	Pupil/teacher ratio			Term length (days)			Relative teacher wage		
	1920-29	1930-39	1940-49	1920-29	1930-39	1940-49	1920-29	1930-39	1940-49
New Mexico	28.5	29.1	26.0	176	179	180	.92	1.11	1.13
New York	27.6	25.7	32.2	184	182	181	1.54	1.30	1.13
North Carolina	35.8	31.9	28.8	161	175	180	.95	1.09	1.12
North Dakota	18.4	17.7	17.9	175	172	177	.67	.76	.81
Ohio	29.4	27.4	26.4	179	179	177	1.03	.97	.93
Oklahoma	32.1	27.0	25.6	172	176	176	.74	.87	.92
Oregon	24.7	24.5	23.0	172	176	179	.90	.97	1.02
Pennsylvania	31.4	27.2	25.4	181	182	182	1.17	1.08	1.05
Rhode Island	27.8	25.0	23.9	180	180	180	1.23	1.20	1.17
South Carolina	34.2	29.9	28.7	154	171	179	.89	.89	.92
South Dakota	17.7	16.6	17.6	174	175	177	.72	.81	.82
Tennessee	32.8	29.9	28.8	164	170	176	.78	.80	.88
Texas	29.3	27.2	25.7	164	173	175	.75	.92	1.01
Utah	31.0	29.2	27.8	172	174	176	.91	1.07	1.06
Vermont	23.5	22.7	22.6	175	173	173	.74	.84	.91
Virginia	32.9	29.3	26.7	182	179	180	.81	.89	.96
Washington	30.8	29.0	25.4	180	178	178	1.05	1.11	1.05
West Virginia	27.2	27.3	26.8	171	174	174	.85	.84	.77
Wisconsin	25.7	24.0	23.3	179	179	178	.94	.94	.94
Wyoming	20.3	21.5	21.4	175	175	177	.83	.91	.98
District of Columbia	30.8	28.5	27.4	178	176	178	1.85	1.54	1.28

Note: Cohort averages are formed under the assumption of 12 years of elementary and secondary education. See Appendix A for sources.

from 0.75 or lower (in many southern states) to over 1.25 (in many northeastern states). As one might expect, the interstate variation in our measures of education quality is much lower for the later cohorts. This is particularly true of the term length variable, which falls in a narrow range for individuals born in the latest cohort.

The trends in school quality during our sample period vary widely across states. Most of the southern states show uniform improvements in quality. Other states, such as Michigan and Missouri, show almost no change in the quality variables, and some states show declines in certain dimensions of quality. The differences are most pronounced in relative teacher wages. For example, teachers in Alabama and Georgia show strong relative wage gains, and teachers in Massachusetts, New Jersey, and New York show relative wage losses during our sample period.

1.3. Returns to Education by Cohort and State of Birth for White Men

In this section we present estimates of the average rates of return to education for white men born in the 48 mainland states and the District of Columbia between 1920 and 1949. We divide the samples of men born in these states into three 10-year birth cohorts and obtain estimated rates of return for 147 separate state and cohort groups. We then perform a second-step analysis of the relation between rates of return to schooling and the school quality measures in Table 1.1. We explore the effects of some other characteristics of the school systems in each state and contrast these to the effects of some measures of family background. We also discuss the results of a simple correction for the measurement error induced by the interstate mobility of children. Finally, we present a brief analysis of the rates of return to education obtained from models that ignore the minimum thresholds highlighted in Figures 1.1 and 1.2.

1.3.1. Rates of Return to Education by State and Cohort

Our estimated rates of return to education are obtained from three cohort-specific regressions fitted to individual data on log weekly earnings for 1979. The data samples are taken from the 5 percent Public-Use A Sample of the 1980 census (see Appendix B for details).

Following the specification of equation (1), the explanatory variables in each regression include a set of 50 indicator variables for an individual's current state of residence, a set of 48 indicator variables for an individual's state of birth, and controls for potential experience and its square, marital status, and residence within an SMSA. To control for differences in the rate of return to education across different labor markets in the country, the models also include interactions between nine current region of residence dummies and completed education.[6] Finally, the models include state of birth-specific interactions with individual education, where, as described in Section 1.1., individual education is modeled as the maximum of zero and years of education over and above the second percentile of the education distribution in an individual's state of birth and cohort. These interactions are interpreted as estimates of the rate of return to education for individuals from a particular cohort and state.

The estimated rates of return, together with their estimated sampling errors, are presented in Table 1.2. The lower panel of the table reports the weighted means and standard deviations of the estimated returns across the 49 states, together with their correlations with the three cohort-specific quality measures. Despite the fact that the estimates are obtained from highly parameterized models (there are 158 explanatory variables in the regression equation for each cohort), the estimates are relatively precise, with standard errors in the range of 0.1–0.3 percent for most states. As the patterns in Figures 1.1 and 1.2 suggest, average rates of return to education are much lower for older workers: 5.1 percent per year for the oldest cohort (age 50–59 in 1979) versus 7.4 percent for the youngest cohort (age 30–39 in1979). The interstate dispersion in returns (corrected for sampling error) shows the opposite trend, being largest for the oldest cohort and smallest for the youngest.

The correlations in the lower panel of Table 1.2 suggest that returns to education are significantly related to all three measures of school quality. The connection is illustrated in Figure 1.3, which plots the rate of return for each state of birth (for the 1920–1929 cohort) against the relative teacher wage in the state. We have divided the states into three groups, on the basis of the pupil/teacher ratio, and denoted states in each group by a different symbol. The pattern of the plot suggests that returns are higher among states with lower pupil/ teacher ratios when teacher wages are controlled for, and higher among states with higher relative teacher pay when the pupil/teacher ratio is controlled for.

Does School Quality Matter?

Figure 1.3

Relative Teacher Wage vs. Return to School, with High, Low and Medium Pupil/Teacher Ratio Indicated

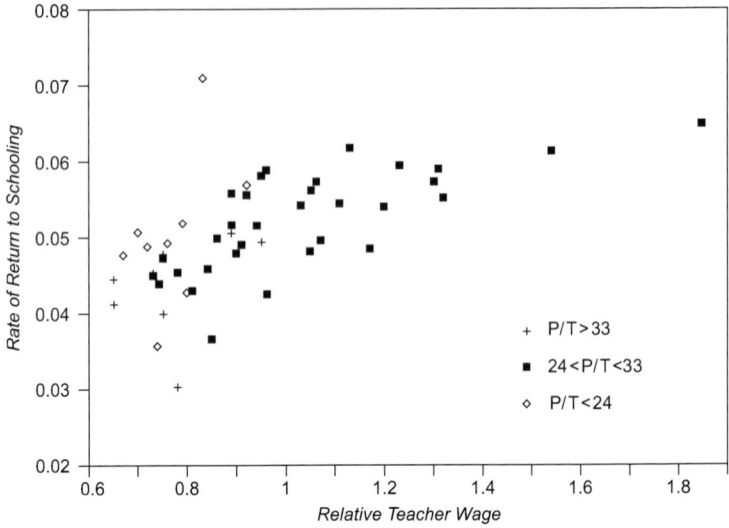

Figure 1.4

Change in Returns vs. Change in Pupil/Teacher Ratio, 1940s Cohort Minus 1920s Cohort

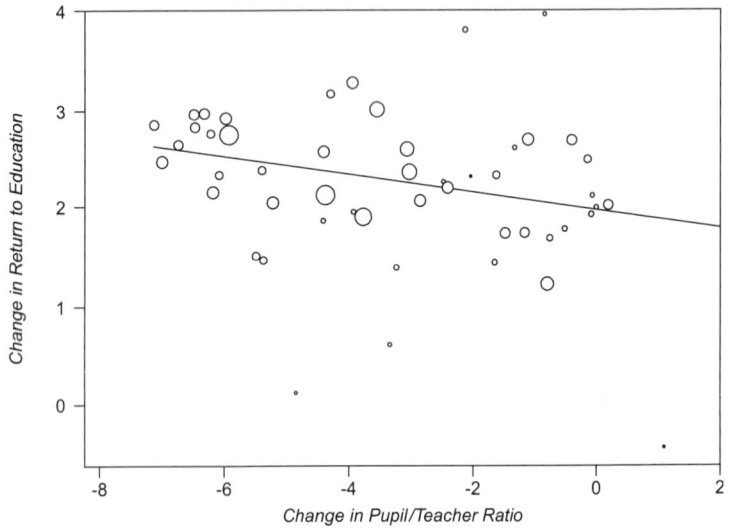

Table 1.2

Estimated Returns to Education by State and Cohort:
White Males Born in 1920–1949

State	Estimated return for cohort born in:		
	1920–1929	1930–1939	1940–1949
Alabama	4.52	6.08	7.15
	(.22)	(.21)	(.20)
Arizona	5.62	7.15	7.47
	(.49)	(.50)	(.42)
Arkansas	4.44	5.60	7.28
	(.23)	(.23)	(.23)
California	5.76	6.20	6.96
	(.21)	(.19)	(.13)
Colorado	5.82	6.22	7.49
	(.34)	(.33)	(.29)
Connecticut	5.46	7.14	7.83
	(.28)	(.28)	(.23)
Delaware	6.19	7.07	6.31
	(.76)	(.76)	(.58)
Florida	4.25	6.07	7.40
	(.33)	(.30)	(.23)
Georgia	4.76	6.14	7.71
	(.21)	(.21)	(.19)
Idaho	4.58	5.40	6.57
	(.50)	(.43)	(.39)
Illinois	5.74	6.91	7.63
	(.15)	(.14)	(.12)
Indiana	5.89	6.98	7.95
	(.22)	(.20)	(.16)
Iowa	5.19	6.02	6.92
	(.24)	(.23)	(.21)
Kansas	4.92	5.90	7.40
	(.27)	(.26)	(.24)
Kentucky	3.99	5.59	6.90
	(.19)	(.18)	(.16)
Louisiana	3.02	4.78	5.84
	(.27)	(.25)	(.22)
Maine	4.49	6.63	8.29
	(.40)	(.36)	(.33)
Maryland	5.41	5.99	7.74
	(.28)	(.27)	(.22)
Massachusetts	5.54	7.21	8.10
	(.22)	(.22)	(.18)
Michigan	5.59	6.64	8.17
	(.18)	(.16)	(.14)
Minnesota	5.17	6.09	6.89
	(.23)	(.22)	(.20)
Mississippi	4.12	5.67	6.87
	(.29)	(.27)	(.24)
Missouri	4.99	6.32	7.68
	(.20)	(.19)	(.17)
Montana	4.27	4.82	6.39
	(.48)	(.46)	(.42)
Nebraska	5.06	6.43	7.38
	(.31)	(.30)	(.29)
Nevada	5.69	6.64	7.24
	(1.20)	(1.00)	(.75)

Does School Quality Matter?

Table 1.2 (continued)

Estimated Returns to Education by State and Cohort:
White Males Born in 1920–1949

	Estimated return for cohort born in:		
State	1920–1929	1930–1939	1940–1949
New Hampshire	4.96	6.12	7.57
	(.52)	(.50)	(.43)
New Jersey	5.91	7.49	7.95
	(.20)	(.20)	(.16)
New Mexico	5.56	5.84	7.80
	(.47)	(.42)	(.38)
New York	6.16	7.18	8.28
	(.13)	(.12)	(.10)
North Carolina	4.94	5.93	7.40
	(.19)	(.19)	(.17)
North Dakota	4.76	5.17	6.53
	(.38)	(.36)	(.38)
Ohio	5.43	6.86	7.78
	(.16)	(.15)	(.12)
Oklahoma	4.39	5.72	7.34
	(.22)	(.22)	(.22)
Oregon	4.79	5.26	6.23
	(.42)	(.40)	(.29)
Pennsylvania	4.87	6.26	7.61
	(.13)	(.13)	(.11)
Rhode Island	5.96	6.62	7.90
	(.41)	(.40)	(.33)
South Carolina	5.05	5.76	6.56
	(.28)	(.27)	(.22)
South Dakota	4.87	5.68	6.79
	(.41)	(.39)	(.39)
Tennessee	4.53	6.62	7.80
	(.20)	(.19)	(.18)
Texas	4.73	5.93	7.72
	(.16)	(.15)	(.14)
Utah	4.90	5.56	6.28
	(.44)	(.39)	(.34)
Vermont	3.57	6.82	7.54
	(.55)	(.53)	(.48)
Virginia	4.29	5.54	6.44
	(.21)	(.20)	(.17)
Washington	4.82	5.46	6.28
	(.34)	(.30)	(.23)
West Virginia	3.66	5.25	6.34
	(.23)	(.21)	(.20)
Wisconsin	5.17	6.10	7.37
	(.21)	(.20)	(.18)
Wyoming	7.10	4.99	6.65
	(.69)	(.65)	(.59)
District of Columbia	6.54	6.07	7.14
	(.63)	(.54)	(.38)
Mean over all states	5.07	6.27	7.44
Standard deviation	.65	.58	.56
Correlation with:			
Pupil/teacher ratio	-.36	-.23	-.19
Term length	.62	.51	.35
Relative teacher wage	.71	.51	.25

Note: Column entries are estimated rates of return to education, based on samples of the 1980 census. The estimated standard deviation of returns is adjusted for the expected contribution of sampling variability. Standard errors are in parentheses.

A second illustration of the relation between school quality and returns to education is provided by Figure 1.4, which plots the intrastate *change* in the return to education between the 1920–1929 and the 1940–1949 cohorts against the corresponding *change* in the cohort average pupil/teacher ratio. As implied by the sampling errors in Table 1.2, the intercohort changes in the returns to education are imprecisely estimated for some of the smaller states. We have therefore plotted each state observation with a circle that is proportional to the inverse sampling variance of the estimated change in returns. We have also plotted the weighted-least-squares regression line (weighted by the inverse sampling variance of the change in the estimated return) relating the intrastate changes in returns to the corresponding changes in the pupil/teacher ratio. The figure indicates that rates of return to education rose more quickly between the 1920–1929 cohort and the 1940–1949 cohort in states that experienced a larger reduction in pupil/ teacher ratios.

1.3.2. Rates of Return and the Quality of Schools

Table 1.3 presents estimation results for a series of regression models fitted to the estimated rates of return presented in Table 1.2. The models are estimated by weighted least squares, using as weights the inverse sampling variances of the estimated returns.[7] The first set of models, in columns 1–5, excludes any state-specific information other than the measured quality variables; the second set, in columns 6–11, includes a set of 49 unrestricted state effects. These models therefore rely on the within-state covariation between rates of return to education and measured school quality to estimate the effect of the quality variables.

The model in column 1 includes only dummy variables for the second and third cohorts. These two variables alone explain 71 percent of the (weighted) variance in the returns to education.[8] The estimated coefficients show significantly higher returns for the later cohorts: approximately 1.2 percent per decade. The three quality variables are introduced individually into the regression model in columns 2–4 and jointly in column 5. Individually, all three variables are strongly correlated with returns to education, with t-statistics of -3.3, 7.0, and 7.2 for the pupil/teacher ratio, term length, and the relative teacher wage, respectively. When the three quality variables are entered jointly, however, the effects of term length and the pupil/teacher ratio are smaller and less precisely determined, presumably as a result of the multicollinearity among the quality variables.

The models with state effects lead to conclusions broadly similar to those of the models in columns 1–5, although the estimated coefficient of the pupil/teacher ratio is larger in absolute value when state effects are included, and the estimated coefficients of the other two quality measures are smaller. When the three quality variables are included jointly (in column 10), the estimated coefficient of the term length variable falls to zero. Evidently, only two dimensions of school quality can be identified in the data once state-specific effects are included.[9]

The magnitudes of the estimated school quality coefficients suggest a quantitatively important effect of school quality on the return to education. For example, the estimates in column 10 show that a decrease in the pupil/teacher ratio by 10 students is associated with a 0.9 percent increase in the return to years of schooling above the threshold level. If the threshold is 8 years of schooling (and is unaffected by the change in school quality), this reduction in the pupil/ teacher ratio will raise the earnings of high school graduates by 3.6 percent. A 30 percent increase in relative teacher salaries is similarly predicted to raise the rate of return to education by roughly 0.3 percent, and the earnings of high school graduates by 1.2 percent (again, if the threshold level of education is constant at 8 years).

Despite the joint significance of the quality variables, they explain relatively little of the intercohort trend in returns to education. When the models in columns 5 and 1 are compared, for example, the quality measures explain only 12 percent of the increased return to education between the earliest and the middle cohorts, and 6 percent of the increase between the middle and latest cohorts. In the models with state effects, the quality variables explain more of the intercohort trend in returns to education: about 20 percent of the increase between the 1920–29 cohort and the 1930–39 cohort, and 10 percent of the increase between the 1930–39 and 1940–49 cohort. Nevertheless, the cohort dummies are highly significant, and their omission leads to a substantial overstatement of the quality effects. For example, when the cohort effects are excluded in column 11, the coefficient of the pupil/teacher variable rises to -50.1.

The higher average rates of return for younger workers do not necessarily reflect true cohort effects. If there is any relation between age and the return to education, the estimated cohort dummies in Table

Table 1.3

Determinants of the Return to Education (Dependent Variable: Percentage Return to Education)

Independent variable	Excluding state effects					Including 49 state effects					
	(1)	(2)	(3)	(4)	(5)	(6)	(7)	(8)	(9)	(10)	(11)
1. Pupil/teacher ratio (/100)	—	-5.37	—	—	-2.38	—	-9.52	—	—	-9.35	-50.06
		(1.62)			(1.64)		(2.81)			(3.18)	(3.74)
2. Term length (hundreds of days)	—	—	4.57	—	1.93	—	—	-2.16	—	-.02	-1.91
			(.67)		(.94)			(.70)		(.99)	(.93)
3. Relative teacher wage	—	—	—	1.86	1.35	—	—	—	.99	.97	1.28
				(.26)	(.33)				(.35)	(.44)	(.87)
4. Dummy for born 1930–1939	1.21	1.07	1.03	1.20	1.07	1.21	.98	1.13	1.21	.98	—
	(.14)	(.14)	(.12)	(.12)	(.12)	(.07)	(.10)	(.07)	(.07)	(.09)	
5. Dummy for born 1940–1949	2.37	2.16	2.13	2.35	2.16	2.35	1.98	2.24	2.36	1.99	—
	(.13)	(.14)	(.12)	(.11)	(.12)	(.07)	(.12)	(.07)	(.06)	(.12)	
6. R^2	.71	.72	.78	.78	.80	.95	.96	.95	.95	.96	.83

Note: Sample size is 147. Mean and standard deviation of the dependent variable are 6.421 and 1.161, respectively. Equations are weighted by the inverse sampling variances of the dependent variable. Models in cols. 1–5 include an intercept. Standard errors are in parentheses.

1.3 confound cohort and age effects. To provide some crude evidence on the relative importance of age and cohort effects, we used the 1970 census to estimate rates of return to education for our two older cohorts 10 years earlier. The following table shows the estimated rates of return for the two cohorts in 1970 and 1980:

Cohort	Year	
	1970	1980
1920–1929	6.73	5.04
1930–1939	7.44	6.25

If we assume that the 1930–1939 cohort had the same (or only slightly better) quality schooling as the earlier cohort, these data indicate an overall decline in the average return to education between 1970 and 1980 of at least 0.50 percent (when the 6.73 percent return for the 1920–1929 cohort in 1970 is compared to the 6.25 percent return for the 1930–1939 cohort in 1980). With this estimate of the relative period effect, the implied age effects indicate a 1.2-percentage-point decline in the return to education between the ages of 40–49 and 50–59 and a 0.7-percentage-point decline between ages 30–39 and 40–49. Together with our finding that school quality variables explain relatively little of the cohort effects, these results suggest that most of the higher return to education observed for younger workers in the 1980 cross section is attributable to age effects.

Finally, we note that the estimated state effects in Table 1.3 are highly significant. For example, a comparison of the models in columns 5 and 10 leads to a χ^2 statistic of 642 for the joint significance of the state effects (with 48 degrees of freedom). This suggests that some important state-specific determinants of the return to education are missing from our analysis. Examination of the estimated state effects indicates that returns to education are relatively low (when measured quality is controlled for) for men born in the south and in the north central/northwest regions and relatively high in the midwest and northeast.

A finding of relatively low returns for white men from the southern states may be somewhat surprising, given that the quality measures in our analysis refer to the entire school system in each state. States that operated segregated school systems before 1954 typically had lower pupil/teacher ratios, longer term lengths, and higher teacher salaries in white schools than in black schools (see Chapter 2). As a result, average quality measures based on total student enrollments *understate* the quality of the white schools in these states. Nevertheless, when a dummy variable for the segregated states is added to the model in column 5 of Table 1.3, it has an estimated coefficient of -0.41 (with a standard error of 0.13). Furthermore, when the segregated states are stratified into those with 20 percent or higher black enrollment and those with less than 20 percent black enrollment, the returns to education are even lower in the states with higher black enrollments (0.42 percent vs. 0.31 percent lower in states with less than 20 percent black enrollment). These findings are inconsistent with a simple mismeasurement hypothesis for the quality of white schools in the south. Rather, they suggest that other dimensions of quality were significantly lower in the South or that other characteristics of the southern states affect the returns to education.

1.3.3. Other Characteristics of Schools and States

We have analyzed the effects of several other school and state-level characteristics on the returns to education. Table 1.4 summarizes our main findings. In each case we have included the three basic measures of school quality as well as state-specific fixed effects. To preview the results, we find that the estimated coefficients of the school quality variables are largely unaffected by the addition of controls for other characteristics, including characteristics of teachers, average income in the state, educational attainment, and characteristics of private schools.

Columns 1–3 of Table 1.4 address the effect of family background characteristics on the return to education. A number of previous studies (including Coleman et al. 1966) have found a strong association between family background factors, such as parental education and income, and student performance on standardized tests. If these family background characteristics are correlated with school quality and if these characteristics change substantially over time within states (so they are not absorbed by the state fixed effects), our estimates of the effect of school quality may be confounded by the effect of family background variables.

Although the census lacks direct information on the education of individuals' parents, we can at least partially control for differences in parental education by including the median level of education among adults who lived in the state when the men in our sample at-

Table 1.4

Additional Determinants of the Return to Education: White Men (Dependent Variable: Percentage Return to Education, Fixed-effects Estimates)

	Regression										
	1	2	3	4	5	6	7	8	9	10	11
1. Pupil/teacher ratio (/100)	-9.67 (3.16)	-9.36 (3.21)	-9.77 (3.20)	-9.33 (3.10)	-9.81 (3.06)	-9.80 (2.98)	-8.42 (3.54)	-10.62 (3.22)	-9.23 (3.23)	-9.77 (3.20)	-8.82 (3.51)
2. Term length (hundreds of days)	-.51 (1.03)	-.04 (1.12)	-.65 (1.17)	-.98 (1.05)	-.40 (.97)	-1.26 (1.01)	-.08 (1.00)	-1.04 (1.13)	.06 (1.04)	-.35 (1.04)	-1.09 (1.25)
3. Relative teacher wage	1.22 (.47)	.95 (.57)	1.13 (.58)	.86 (.43)	1.05 (.44)	1.05 (.43)	.86 (.48)	1.12 (.44)	1.00 (.47)	.80 (.47)	1.52 (.61)
4. Median education of parents' generation	-.18 (.11)	—	-.18 (.11)	—	—	—	—	—	—	—	.38 (.13)
5. Log real per capita income of parents' generation	—	.18 (.52)	.13 (.51)	—	—	—	—	—	—	—	-.50 (.53)
6. Fraction male teachers	—	—	—	-3.36 (1.39)	—	-3.46 (1.43)	—	—	—	—	-2.98 (1.73)
7. Mean years of education of teachers	—	—	—	—	.33 (.13)	.38 (.13)	—	—	—	—	.38 (.13)
8. Mean years of experience of teachers	—	—	—	—	.03 (.03)	.02	—	—	—	—	.02
9. Fraction high school grads in cohort	—	—	—	—	—	—	.89 (1.48)	—	—	—	.93 (1.52)
10. Fraction college grads in cohort	—	—	—	—	—	—	—	-3.86 (2.11)	—	—	-1.38 (2.34)
11. Fraction of enrollment in private schools	—	—	—	—	—	—	—	—	.71 (2.69)	—	1.51 (2.62)
12. Weighted gap between pupil/teacher ratio in Catholic and public schools	—	—	—	—	—	—	—	—	—	-6.06 (5.80)	—
13. Dummy for born 1930–1939	1.12 (.11)	.98 (.10)	1.12 (.13)	1.01 (.09)	.88 (.10)	.97 (.11)	.90 (.16)	1.26 (.18)	.96 (.12)	1.04 (.11)	1.01 (.24)
14. Dummy for born 1940–1949	2.32 (.24)	1.98 (.26)	2.27 (.31)	2.22 (.16)	1.59 (.18)	1.84 (.20)	1.84 (.27)	2.72 (.42)	1.96 (.16)	2.09 (.16)	2.20 (.54)
15. R^2	.96	.96	.96	.96	.96	.97	.96	.96	.96	.96	.97

Note: See note to Table 1.3. All equations include 48 state effects. Standard errors are in parentheses.

tended school (row 4). Likewise, we include the log of real per capita income in the state at the time the cohorts in our sample entered school (row 5).[10] Regardless of whether they are included separately or jointly, each of these variables has a relatively small and statistically insignificant effect on the return to education. Moreover, the estimated effects of the three main school quality variables (pupil/ teacher ratio, term length, and relative teacher wage) are unaffected by the inclusion of these family background variables.

Teacher Characteristics

Columns 4–6 explore the role of teacher characteristics on the returns to schooling. The fraction of male teachers is included because, holding constant the level of teacher salaries, one might expect the quality of the teaching staff to vary with the fraction of male teachers. For example, assuming that female teachers were paid less than otherwise identical males during the period 1926–1966, one can view the percentage of male teachers as a proxy for lower-quality teachers. Alternatively, one can view the fraction of male teachers as an indicator of higher nonwage compensation or better working conditions within the schools, which would be likely to attract relatively more men into the teaching profession, with relative wages held constant.

The results indicate that an increase in the fraction of male teachers in the state has a substantial negative impact on students' return to education. An increase in the fraction of male teachers from 19 to 42 percent, which is the range observed across states in 1966, is associated with an 0.8-percentage-point reduction in the return to years of education above the threshold. Whether the fraction of male teachers influences the return to education because males are less effective teachers, or through some other channel, is difficult to ascertain.

Columns 5 and 6 add the mean years of education of teachers in the state to the regression equation. The estimated coefficient of mean teacher education is positive and statistically significant, whereas the estimated effect of teachers' experience is negligible. Notice that the pupil/ teacher ratio and relative teacher wage continue to be significant determinants of the return to education when these teacher quality variables are included; in fact, their estimated coefficients are hardly affected by the addition of the teacher quality variables. Furthermore, the addition of controls for the average education and experience of teachers hardly changes the estimated coefficient of the fraction of male teachers.

Educational Distribution

Estimates of the high school completion rate and the college completion rate for each state of birth and cohort group are included in the models in columns 8 and 9. These variables are added to control for biases that may arise as more schooling is acquired by a higher fraction of a given cohort. For example, suppose that more schools are built in a state, leading to a decrease in the travel time for students and a reduction in the pupil/teacher ratio. Suppose further that individuals differ in their expected returns to education and that as more schools are built, some students with lower expected returns to education stay in school longer. In this case, one might expect increases in school quality to be correlated with *lower* returns to education, reflecting a negative correlation between the average rate of return to education and the fraction of individuals with higher education. In our data there is a strong positive correlation (both in a cross section and within particular states over time) between average educational attainment and measures of education quality.[11] Therefore, if rates of return vary systematically across the population and if individuals with higher expected returns choose more schooling, there is a possible downward bias in our estimates of the effect of schooling quality on returns to education. This can be controlled in part by including measures of the fraction of individuals at higher education levels in each cohort.

Neither the high school graduation rate nor the college graduation rate has a statistically significant effect on the return to education. Moreover, the high school graduation rate has a negative coefficient, and the college graduation rate has a small, positive coefficient. These results provide no evidence that students sort themselves into different education levels on the basis of different expected returns to schooling.

We have also explored the effect of the dispersion in educational attainment in a state on the return to education. As discussed further below, improvements in school quality are associated with lower dispersion in the distribution of education. Some models of ability bias in the estimated return to schooling predict that a reduction in the dispersion in the educational distribution is associated with higher returns to education. We find little support for this hypothesis in our data. For example, the standard deviation of years of education has a small and statistically insignificant ($t = -0.59$) negative effect if it is added to the model in column 10 of Table 1.3. The inclusion of this variable hardly changes the impact of the school quality variables.

Private Schools

Our measures of school quality are based on the characteristics of the public school system in each state. Not all students attend public schools, however. During the period 1920–1960, the fraction of students enrolled in private schools grew from 7.5 percent to 13.6 percent. The fraction of private school enrollment also varies across states: in 1938, for example, the share of private enrollments ranged from less than 2 percent in many southern states to over 20 percent in New Hampshire and Rhode Island. The presence of private schools introduces two potential sources of unobserved variation in school quality. First, private schools may be more or less effective than public schools.[12] Second, private schools may have different staffing levels, teacher salaries, and term lengths than the public schools. In an effort to examine these issues, we collected information on private school enrollments and pupil/teacher ratios by state and cohort. Our information on the pupil/teacher ratio in private schools is limited to Catholic schools, but 90 percent of private-school students attended Catholic schools during our sample period.

Evidence on the effect of accounting for private school enrollment is presented in columns 9 and 10 of Table 1.4. In column 9 we include the fraction of students enrolled in all private schools as an additional explanatory variable for the rate of return to education. When pupil/teacher ratios, term length, and relative teacher salaries in the public schools are controlled for, the coefficient of the private school enrollment variable is numerically small and statistically insignificant. These results suggest that increases in private school enrollment do not by themselves affect returns to education.

The specification in column 10 is an attempt to measure the biases created by using data for the public schools to proxy pupil/teacher ratios for the state as a whole. The average pupil/teacher ratio in a state is a weighted average of ratios in the public and private systems. Hence, the measurement error in using the public school ratio as a proxy for the overall state average is the product of the fraction of enrollment in private schools and the gap between the private and public school ratios.[13] An estimate of this error component is included in the model in column 10. As predicted by a naive model of attenuation bias, the addition of this control variable raises the estimated coefficient of the pupil/teacher ratio. Furthermore, the estimated coefficient of the error component is (roughly) equal to the estimated coefficient of the pupil/teacher ratio in the public schools. Nevertheless, the relatively modest changes in the coefficients of the public school quality variables suggest that the biases introduced by measuring only the quality of public schools are small.

Up to this point we have proceeded by considering individually extensions to the basic quality variables (family background, teacher quality, educational attainment, and private schools). In column 11 we include several of the additional variables jointly. With the exception of the term length variable, the school quality variables have their expected signs and are statistically significant. In contrast, the variables measuring family background characteristics, student educational achievement, and private school attendance generally have insignificant and small effects. The data seem to accord a greater role to school quality than to other variables in determining the return to education.

Evidence for Black and White Men Born in the South

Despite the limited evidence of family background effects in the return to education, the wide variation in school quality for men from different states and cohorts presumably reflects differences in incomes and tastes for education over time and across states. To the extent that *unmeasured* differences in family incomes and tastes affect individuals' returns to education, the estimated school quality effects in Tables 1.3 and 1.4 may be overstated. A potentially better test of the effects of school quality is based on the earnings experiences of blacks. The rapid improvements in school quality that occurred in the black schools of the segregated southern states between 1920 and 1960 provide an arguably exogenous experiment for studying the effects of school quality.

In a related paper (Card and Krueger 1992b, see Chapter 2 in this volume), we have examined the effects of school quality on the returns to education for southern-born black and white men who worked in northern cities in 1960, 1970, or 1980. Our results are qualitatively and quantitatively similar to those in Tables 1.3 and 1.4. For example, the estimated coefficient of the pupil/teacher ratio in a model similar to the one in column 7 of Table 1.3 is -5.9, with a standard error of 2.39. The estimated coefficients of term length and teacher wages are also similar to those in Table 1.3. We believe that our findings for southern-born black and white men provide additional support for a causal interpretation of the school quality effects in Tables 1.3 and 1.4.

1.3.4. Adjustments for Mobility of Preschool and School-Age Children

In our analysis so far, we have implicitly assumed that an individual attends public school in his state of birth. Interstate mobility of preschool and school-age children introduces a problem similar to measurement error in the interpretation of the returns to education for individuals born in a particular state. To proceed, it is useful to concentrate on a single cohort and to assume that individuals are educated in only one state. Let γ_j represent the estimated rate of return to education for individuals *born* in state j (in a particular cohort), and let γ_i^* represent the rate of return for individuals *educated* in state i. Finally, let p_{ij} represent the probability that an individual attended school in state i, given that he was born in state j. Then

$$\gamma_j = \sum_i \gamma_i^* \cdot p_{ij}.$$

Let P represent a matrix whose i, j element is p_{ji}. Then the vector of coefficients γ is related to the vector of true returns γ^* by $\gamma = P\gamma^*$. Given estimates of γ and P, one can obtain an estimate of γ^* by $\gamma^* = P^{-1}\gamma$. Notice that if individuals are always educated in their state of birth, then P is an identity matrix and $\gamma^* = \gamma$.

We obtained an estimate of the matrix P by cross-tabulating state of birth with current state of residence for white children aged 6–12 (both male and female) in the Public-Use Sample of the 1940 census. For most states, the probability that a 6–12-year-old is living in his or her state of birth is around 90 percent, although it is lower for children born in the District of Columbia (62%). In principle, this estimate of the matrix P is appropriate only for children born between 1928 and 1934, and only for those with 1–6 years of schooling. Nonetheless, we used this transition matrix to transform the estimated rates of return for each of the three birth cohorts into estimates of the rate of return for attending school in different states. We then reestimated the regression models in Table 1.3, using the corrected rates of return as dependent variables.[14]

The mobility-adjusted results are qualitatively similar to those in Table 1.3. The correction has the effect of expanding the standard deviation of the estimated returns by 19 percent for the 1920–1929 birth cohort, 11 percent for the 1930–1939 cohort, and 8 percent for the 1940–1949 cohort. As a consequence, the magnitudes of the estimated coefficients for the school quality variables are typically 5–15 percent larger than in the uncorrected model, although the associated standard errors rise by roughly the same proportion. On balance, the results suggest that adjustments for interstate mobility have a relatively minor impact on the qualitative and quantitative conclusions in Table 1.3. This reflects the relatively low mobility rates of preschool and school-age children and the absence of a strong connection between interstate mobility and the geographic pattern of the measured quality of education.

1.3.5. Log-Linear Specification

The preceding estimates examine the relationship between school quality and the return to education for years of schooling beyond the level attained by the second percentile of the education distribution. This specification of the education variable was selected for its ability to capture the nonlinear return structure illustrated in Figures 1.1 and 1.2. Compared to a conventional log-linear specification, the linear-spline specification provides a slightly better fit to the micro data: the difference in maximized log likelihoods between the spline model and a conventional linear return to education model is 99.0 for the 1920–1929 cohort, 150.0 for the 1930–1939 cohort, and 315.1 for the 1940–1949 cohort.

Nevertheless, a log-linear specification is widely used in the literature, and it is useful to check the sensitivity of our estimates to the functional form assumptions. Consequently, we have reestimated the returns to education by state and cohort using a linear specification for education. The two sets of returns have very similar weighted means (6.42 for the spline estimates vs. 6.45 for the linear estimate and are highly correlated (the correlation coefficient across 147 observations is .997). The close correspondence between the two sets of estimated returns is understandable, given that the spline specification differs from the linear specification for only 2 percent of the sample.

Table 1.5 presents estimates of the relation between our school quality measures and the returns to education derived from a log-linear specification. Except for the choice of the dependent variable, the models are the same as in Table 1.3. The coefficient estimates in

Table 1.5 are 10–20 percent smaller than those in Table 1.3. Regardless of specification, however, the school quality variables have statistically significant and sizable effects on the return to education. These results suggest that the relationship between school quality and the return to education is not particularly sensitive to the specification used to estimate the return to education.

1.4. The Effects of School Quality on Education and Earnings

Our analysis of the relation between school quality and the return to education has the advantage of controlling for unobserved differences across cohort and state of birth groups. Any background factors (such as family income) that raise the earnings of individuals from a particular group are absorbed by the cohort-specific state of birth effects included in our first-stage equation. A disadvantage of concentrating on the *return* to education is that changes in school quality may simply widen the distribution of earnings without raising average incomes. It is even conceivable that changes in school quality alter the distribution of schooling, and the slope of the earnings-schooling relation, with no effect on the distribution of earnings.

To explore these issues, we proceed in two steps. First we analyze the influence of changes in school quality on the location and shape of the earnings-schooling relationship. This requires that we analyze the effect of school quality on the educational distribution (in particular, on the level of education attained by the second percentile of the distribution) and on the intercepts of the schooling-earnings relation. Second, we present some simple reduced-form evidence on the connection between school quality and the levels of education and earnings. In contrast to our analysis of the returns to education, the effects of school quality on the education distribution and on the levels of earnings cannot be identified in models that include unrestricted cohort-specific state of birth effects. This limitation should be kept in mind in interpreting the results.

1.4.1. Location and Shape of the Earnings–Education Relationship

Figure 1.5a illustrates the effect of a reduction in the pupil/teacher ratio by 10 students on the earnings–schooling relationship, under the

41

Table 1.5
Determinants of the Return to Education: Linear Returns (Dependent Variable: Percentage Return to Education)

Independent variable	Excluding state effects					Including 49 state effects				
	(1)	(2)	(3)	(4)	(5)	(6)	(7)	(8)	(9)	(10)
Pupil/teacher ratio (/100)	—	-3.96	—	—	-1.15	—	-8.33	—	—	-8.03
		(1.49)			(1.58)		(2.68)			(3.08)
Term length (hundreds of days)	—	—	3.74	—	1.97	—	—	1.83	—	.04
			(.62)		(.91)			(.67)		(.95)
Relative teacher wage	—	—	—	1.47	.97	—	—	—	.81	.76
				(.25)	(.32)				(.34)	(.43)
Dummy for born 1930–1939	1.17	1.07	1.03	1.16	1.06	1.18	.97	1.11	1.17	.97
	(.13)	(.13)	(.12)	(.11)	(.12)	(.07)	(.09)	(.07)	(.06)	(.09)
Dummy for born 1940–1949	2.29	2.13	2.08	2.27	2.12	2.27	1.94	2.18	2.27	1.95
	(.12)	(.13)	(.11)	(.11)	(.17)	(.06)	(.12)	(.07)	(.06)	(.12)
R^2	.73	.74	.78	.78	.79	.95	.95	.95	.95	.96

Note: See note to Table 1.3. Mean and standard deviation of the dependent variable are 6.452 and 1.100, respectively. Standard errors are in parentheses.

assumption that the educational distribution is unaffected by a reduction in class size. The parameters for the figure are obtained from column 10 of Table 1.3. This figure is a simplification of the actual impact of a reduction in class size on earnings for two reasons. First, the level of education achieved by the second percentile of the education distribution (the kink point) increases as class size declines. An auxiliary regression of the threshold level of education (the second percentile) on state effects, cohort effects, and the three quality measures indicates that a 10-student decline in the pupil/teacher ratio is associated with an increase in the kink point of 1.13 years (t = 2.08). Second, a decrease in the pupil/teacher ratio is associated with a small (albeit statistically insignificant) upward shift in the *intercepts* of the earnings–schooling relation. A regression of the state of birth-specific intercepts of the earnings–schooling relation on state of birth effects, cohort effects, and the three school quality variables yields coefficients of -0.25 (t = 0.68) for the pupil/teacher ratio (divided by 100), -0.17 (t = -1.43) for the term length variable (divided by 100), and 0.11 (t = 1.88) for the relative teacher wage. The quality variables are jointly insignificant (p-value = .31) in this model.

Figure 1.5b illustrates the effect of a 10-student reduction in the pupil/teacher ratio including these additional effects. It is clear from the figure that a decrease in the pupil/teacher ratio rotates and shifts out the earnings–schooling relationship, with a crossover point around the twelfth or thirteenth grade level. (In fact, when we narrow the sample to individuals who have exactly 12 years of schooling, we find that school quality has an insignificant effect on earnings, suggesting that the crossover point is around the twelfth grade.) At a *fixed* level of education, individuals with postsecondary education appear to benefit from improved school quality, whereas those with less than a high school education appear to earn less. However, an increase in school quality raises schooling levels, particularly in the lower tail of the education distribution. These gains in education offset the apparent losses associated with the shift in the earnings–schooling function, leaving individuals in the lower tail of the earnings distribution approximately as well off and individuals in the mid and upper portions of the earnings distribution better off.

To further study the effects of changes in school quality on individuals in the lower tail of the earnings distribution, we used a regression of log earnings on state of residence effects, age, age squared, marital status, and SMSA residence to compute earnings residuals

Figure 1.5

Effect of Reducing Pupil/Teacher Ratio by 10

a) Ignoring Effects on Intercept and Education Distribution;

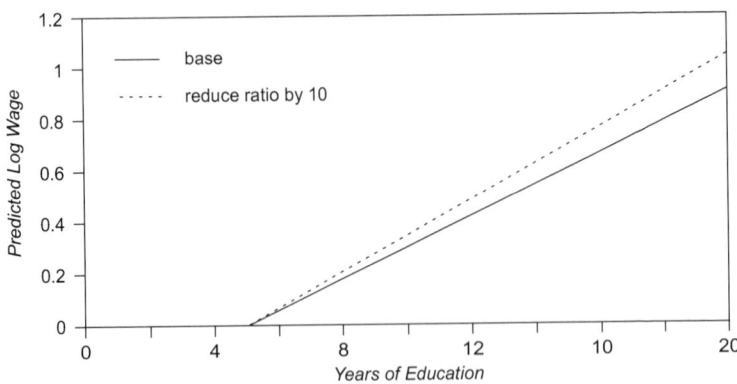

b) Including Effects on Intercept and Education Distribution

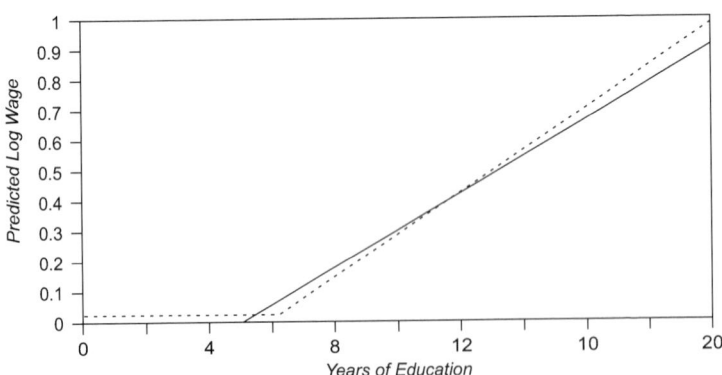

within state of birth and cohort cells. We then regressed the tenth and twenty-fifth percentiles of the adjusted earnings distributions for each cell on state of birth dummies, cohort dummies, and the school quality measures. These regressions indicated small but generally *positive* (and marginally significant) effects of higher school quality on earnings of the tenth and twenty-fifth percentiles. There is certainly no evidence of a negative effect of school quality on the lower tail of the earnings distribution.

1.4.2. Reduced-Form Estimates

To summarize the effect of school quality on mean earnings, we conclude with some simple reduced-form estimates of the effect of school quality on log earnings and education. The results are presented in Table 1.6, below. These reduced-form models include the school quality measures, state of residence and state of birth effects, and demographic variables (age, age squared, and indicators for marital status and residence in an SMSA). Notice that education is excluded from the earnings models in columns 1–6: the estimated school quality effects therefore incorporate any effects on the level of education, as well as effects on the return to each year of schooling. We emphasize that these models are estimated using a pooled sample of men from the three 10-year birth cohorts we have analyzed throughout this chapter. Unlike our earlier models, these models therefore constrain the state of birth and state of residence effects to be similar across cohorts.

The results in Table 1.6 suggest that increases in school quality are associated with increases in both mean earnings and average years of education. When the quality variables are included individually, each is a significant determinant of earnings and average education. When the three variables are included jointly, the pattern of coefficient estimates is similar to the pattern we found in Tables 1.3–1.5: the pupil/teacher ratio and the relative teacher wage remain significant, and the term length variable falls to insignificance. For reference we also report two restrictive specifications of the earnings models. The model in column 5 excludes the state of birth dummies and therefore uses both within-state and between-state variation in school characteristics to estimate the school quality effects. This exclusion, which is implicit in models reported by Rizzuto and Wachtel (1980), yields much larger school quality effects. The model in column 6 includes the state of birth effects but excludes current state of residence effects. This exclusion lowers the goodness of fit of the earnings model but has little impact on the magnitude of the school quality coefficients.

According to the estimates in columns 4 and 10, a decrease in the pupil/teacher ratio by 10 students is predicted to raise average earnings by 4.2 percent and raise average education by 0.6 years, In this sample the conventional return to education (i.e., the coefficient of education when it is added to the list of variables in the earnings model and the school quality variables are excluded) is 5.38 percent. Thus a 0.6-year increase in average education might be expected to

Table 1.6
Reduced-Form Estimates of the Effect of School Quality on Earnings: 1980 Census

	Dependent variable									
	Log weekly wage						Education			
Independent variable	(1)	(2)	(3)	(4)	(5)	(6)	(7)	(8)	(9)	(10)
Pupil/teacher ratio (/100)	-4.24	—	—	-4.15	-7.10	-4.29	-59.18	—	—	-59.71
	(.59)			(.69)	(.26)	(.69)	(3.47)			(4.00)
Term length (/1,000)	—	1.20	—	.18	.15	.30	—	15.23	—	1.16
		(.15)		(.22)	(.14)	(.23)		(.90)		(1.32)
Relative teacher wage (/100)	—	—	4.77	4.48	10.93	3.49	—	—	60.13	59.77
			(.68)	(.93)	(.47)	(.94)			(3.96)	(5.43)
50 state of residence dummies	yes	yes	yes	yes	yes	no	yes	yes	yes	yes
48 state of birth dummies	yes	yes	yes	yes	no	yes	yes	yes	yes	yes
R^2	.088	.088	.088	.088	.085	.075	.100	.100	.100	.100
p-value for F-test of quality variables	—	—	—	.0001	.0001	.0001	—	—	—	.0001

Note: Each equation also includes age and ist square, a dummy indicating current marital status, two cohort dummies, and a dummy indicating residence in an SMSA. Sample size is 1,018.477. Standard errors in parentheses.

increase earnings by 3.2 percent. The overall gain in earnings from a reduction in the pupil/teacher ratio is therefore 30 percent bigger than would be expected on the basis of the increase in average education alone. A similar calculation for the relative teacher wage shows that a 30 percent increase in teacher wages increases average education by 0.18 years and average log wages by 1.34 percent. The gain in earnings is roughly 40 percent bigger than would be expected on the basis of the increase in education alone.

We have also used the 1970 census to estimate reduced-form equations similar to the ones in Table 1.6 above for a sample of white men born in 1913–1939. The results are comparable, although the effects of the relative teacher wage variable on mean earnings for the 1970 sample are smaller and statistically insignificant (except when the state of birth effects are excluded from the model). The coefficient of the pupil/teacher variable on mean earnings is larger in 1970 than in 1980, whereas the coefficients of the quality variables on mean education are uniformly smaller. However, the 1970 sample is substantially smaller (378,000 vs. 1,018,000 in 1980) and the sampling errors are large enough that few of these differences are highly significant.

We draw two conclusions from the reduced-form relations between earnings, education, and school quality. First, increases in school quality during the past century are associated with increases in years of schooling and average wages. Second, the increases in earnings appear to reflect both a gain for the added years of education *and* an increase in the return for each existing year of education. Both conclusions should be tempered by our inability to control for unobserved cohort-specific factors that may raise the earnings of individuals from states with better schools in the reduced-form models. When these conclusions are taken together with the evidence we have assembled on the returns to education, however, we believe that there is strong support for the conclusion that increases in school quality lead to higher earnings.

1.5. Conclusions

The estimates presented in this chapter provide new evidence that the quality of schooling affects earnings. Men who are educated in states with higher-quality school systems earn higher economic returns for their years of schooling. Although the evidence is necessarily nonexperimental, we believe that our findings are consistent with a causal interpretation of the role of school quality. In the first place, our findings are based on statistical models that control for any differences across state of birth and cohort groups in the overall level of earnings. Second, we have controlled for differences in the rates of return to education earned by current residents in different regions of the country. Third, we have controlled for any permanent differences across states in the return to education earned by different cohorts of men and for differences in family background measures (education and earnings of the parents' generation) that may affect subsequent labor market performance. Finally, our reduced-form analysis confirms that increases in school quality increase the average earnings of students. Thus the effects of school quality are not simply redistributive, nor are they an artifact of changes in the distribution of schooling attainments.

Our findings underscore the paradox we noted in the Introduction: school quality appears to have an important effect on labor market performance but is widely believed to have no impact on standardized achievement tests. We note, however, that two other experimental studies of school characteristics and test scores *are* consistent with positive school quality effects. A large-scale randomized study of class sizes in Tennessee suggests that reductions in the pupil/ teacher ratio for elementary school students significantly increase test scores on reading and math exams (see Finn and Achilles 1990). Another randomized study finds that lengthening the school term by providing extra instruction during the summer has a positive effect on disadvantaged students' test scores (see Sipe, Grossman, and Milliner 1988). Although more work is needed to resolve the available evidence, we believe that success in the labor market is at least as important a yardstick for measuring the performance of the education system as success on standardized tests. At a minimum, our finding of a positive link between school quality and the economic returns to education should give pause to those who argue that investments in the public school system have no benefits for students.

Appendix A: Data Sources

1. Basic Data on School Quality

The following series were extracted from various issues of the *Biennial Survey of Education* and the *Digest of Education Statistics: (a)* the number of pupils enrolled in full-time public elementary and secondary schools; *(b)* the average number of days in the school term (full-time public elementary and secondary schools); *(c)* the average number of days attended by each enrolled student (full-time public elementary and secondary schools) (1920–1958 only); *(d)* the number of instructional staff, including supervisors and principals (full-time public elementary and secondary schools); *(e)* the percentage of teachers who are male (full-time public elementary and secondary schools); and *(f)* the average annual salary per member of the instructional staff (full-time public elementary and secondary schools).

These data were collected by state for alternating years, beginning with 1919–1920. In some cases, the figures in the most recently published *Biennial Survey* were revised in subsequent editions. We have attempted to incorporate as many of these revisions as possible. For 1960 and later we collected a variable representing the percentage of school days attended by enrolled students. This percentage was then used to construct an estimate of average days attended from the series on the length of the school term. The data from the biennial editions of the survey are allocated to the previous two years: for example, data from the 1937–1938 edition are used for both 1937 and 1938.

2. Construction of the Relative Teacher Wage

Two wage series were combined to create a relative wage index for teachers in each state. For 1920–1938, we used the wage paid to laborers on federal road construction projects. This wage is available on a regional basis (for nine census regions) in the *Statistical Abstract of the United States*. Data for 1920–1929 are taken from the 1930 edition, table 358. Data for 1930–1956 are taken from the 1957 edition, table 271. For 1940–1966, we use the average state-level wage of workers covered by the social security system, from U.S. Department of Labor Employment and Training Administration Handbook Number 394. To convert the regional construction wage rates into state-level averages, we formed the average ratio of the state social security wage to the regional construction wage in the period 1940–1944. This average ratio was then applied to the construction wage in the period 1920–1938 to obtain a state-specific average.

3. Data on Education and Experience of Teachers

1. 1940
We used the Public-Use Sample of the 1940 census to form extracts of teachers in each of the 48 (mainland) states and District of Columbia. Teachers were identified by industry (educational services) and occupation (those not elsewhere classified). We sampled only the teachers who reported either white or black race, positive earnings and weeks worked, and nonallocated age, sex, race, industry, occupation, and years of education. The extract contains 9,161 teachers.

2. 1950
We used the Public-Use Sample of the 1950 census to form extracts of teachers in each of the 48 (mainland) states and District of Columbia. (Owing to technical difficulties, our Public-Use Sample excludes one-eighth of the available sample.) Teachers were identified by industry (educational services) and occupation (teachers not elsewhere classified). We sampled only those teachers who reported either white or black race and who reported nonallocated age, sex, race, industry, occupation, and years of education. The extract contains 3,206 teachers.

3. 1960
We used the Public-Use Sample of the 1960 census to form extracts of teachers in each of the 48 (mainland) states and District of Columbia. Teachers were identified by industry (educational services) and occupation (elementary school and secondary school teachers). We sampled only those teachers who reported either white or black race and who reported nonallocated age. The extract contains 16,052 teachers.

4. Data on Family Background

1. Average Per Capita Income
We collected average personal income per capita by state for the years 1930, 1940, and 1950 from *State Personal Income: Estimates for 1929–1982, Revised Estimates* (Bureau of Economic Analysis 1984). The income data were originally derived from the National Income and

Product Accounts. The consumer price index was used to convert the data into real dollars. The state-level per capita income in 1930 was assigned to the cohort of men born in the 1920s, the state-level per capita income in 1940 was assigned to the cohort of men born in the 1930s, and the state-level per capita income in 1950 was assigned to the cohort of men born in the 1940s. These years roughly correspond to the years in which educational expenditures for each cohort would have been determined.

2. Median Education of Parents' Generation

As a measure of the education of each cohort's parents, we collected information on the median education of white persons aged 25 or older by state in 1940, 1950, and 1960. These data are reported in *Statistical Abstract of the United States* (nos. 66, 75, 85) and were originally derived from the 1940, 1950, and 1960 censuses. In 1940, the education data are reported only for native-born individuals, and in 1950 and 1960 the data pertain to native and foreign-born individuals. The median education of adults in 1940 was assigned to the 1920s cohort, the median education of adults in 1950 was assigned to the 1930s cohort, and the median education of adults in 1960 was assigned to the 1940s cohort.

5. Private Schools

State-level data on the number of students enrolled in private schools, the number of students enrolled in Catholic schools, and the number of teachers in Catholic schools were collected from the *Biennial Survey*. Unfortunately, these variables are available only on an irregular basis. Data for 1937–1938 were assigned to the cohort born in the 1920s, data for 1949-1950 were assigned to the cohort born in the 1930s, and data for 1955–1956 were assigned to the cohort born in the 1940s.

Appendix B

1. 1980 Micro Data Samples

Our samples are taken from the Public-Use A Sample of the 1980 census (a 5% sample of the population). The samples consist of men born in the 48 mainland states or the District of Columbia between 1920 and 1949 and currently living in any of the 50 states or District of Columbia. Year of birth is estimated from information on age and quarter of birth. We include only those individuals whose race is identified as "white." Individuals with imputed information on age, race, sex, education, weeks worked, or total annual earnings are excluded, as are individuals who report no weeks of work in 1979. In addition, individuals with wage or salary income in 1979 less than $101 and those with average weekly wage and salary income of less than $36 or greater than $2,500 are excluded. The final sample sizes are 279,008 for those born in 1920–1929, 299,063 for those born in 1930–1939, and 441,675 for those born in 1940–1949. These samples are used to form the first-stage estimates of the returns to education in our two-step procedure and the reduced-form estimates presented in Table 1.6.

2

School Quality and Black–White Relative Earnings: A Direct Assessment

During the 1960s and 1970s African American men made substantial progress toward earnings equality with whites. The differential in average weekly wages between black and white men narrowed from 40 percent in 1960 to 25 percent in 1980. By comparison, black–white relative wages were remarkably stable during the 1950s and 1980s.[1] Despite the singular importance of the wage gains from 1960 to 1980, economists remain divided as to their cause. Smith and Welch (1986, 1989) argue that improvements in the relative quality of black education were mainly responsible for the relative rise in black wages after 1960. Other researchers, including Freeman (1973), Vroman (1974), and Donohue and Heckman (1991), argue that federal government policies, including passage of the Civil Rights Act of 1964, were instrumental in closing the wage gap.

Nationwide trends in earnings and schooling data suggest that both hypotheses have some merit. Tabulations from the Current Population Survey show a rise in black–white relative earnings in the years immediately following passage of the Civil Rights Act.[2] This change is often cited as evidence that equal employment opportunity programs led to a closing of the earnings gap. Blacks who entered the labor market in the 1960s, however, had received substantially more and better educa-

This chapter is a revised version of: Card, D., Krueger, A. (1992). School Quality and Black-White Relative Earnings: A Direct Assessment, in: Quarterly Journal of Economics 107, 151–200, © Oxford University Press, 1992, reprinted by permission of Oxford University Press. The authors are grateful to Michael Boozer, Tom Cuniff, Dean Hyslop, and Lisa Krueger for outstanding research assistance and also thank Orley Ashenfelter, James Heckman, and Lawrence Katz for helpful comments.

tion than any previous generation of black workers. In the 1920s, for example, pupil–teacher ratios in southern black schools were 50 percent higher than those in white schools, while the average school term was 20 percent shorter. By the late 1950s conditions in black and white schools were similar in many Southern states. Because better-educated cohorts of black workers began to enter the labor force at about the time the Civil Rights Act took effect, nationwide earnings patterns cannot easily distinguish the effects of improved school quality from the impact of federal antidiscrimination policies.

Nevertheless, aggregate trends in relative school quality mask wide differences across states in the rate of convergence of black and white school quality. In this chapter we use these interstate differences to disentangle the role of school quality in the evolution of the black–white earnings gap. The key to our analysis is a set of state-specific school quality measures for the black and white schools in the eighteen segregated southern states during the period from 1915 to 1966. To our knowledge, this is the most complete series of state-level data on the quality of southern schools presently available. We combine these quality measures with state-specific estimates of the rate of return to schooling and the mean level of earnings for southern-born men in the 1960, 1970, and 1980 Censuses. We then use the combined earnings and schooling data to answer two questions. What is the effect of relative school quality on the relative returns to education earned by black and white men? What fraction of the closing of the black–white earnings gap between 1960 and 1980 is explained by changes in relative school quality?

Before turning to these questions, we present a descriptive analysis of the earnings gap between black and white men in the 1960, 1970, and 1980 Censuses. Our analysis establishes the importance of intercohort changes in determining the evolution of the black–white earnings gap. We then decompose intercohort changes in the wage gap into components attributable to earnings growth among southern-born and non-southern-born blacks. Sixty percent of the closing of the earnings gap between cohorts born in the 1920s and cohorts born in the 1940s is attributed to the closing of the black–white wage gap for southern-born workers. Among southern-born men increases in the return to education for later cohorts of blacks can explain most of the narrowing of the relative wage gap. Cross-tabulations of rates of return to education by race and region of birth show that the return to schooling for later cohorts of southern-born blacks rose relative to both southern-born whites and northern-born blacks. This pattern suggests that the rise in the return to education for southern-born blacks was driven by improvements in the quality of black schools, and not simply by an economy wide reduction in discrimination against better-educated black workers.

In Section 2.2. of this chapter we present estimates of school quality by cohort, race, and state of birth, and link these quality measures to estimated rates of return to education for southern-born workers. To control for differences in the return to education in different regions of the country, we estimate rates of return to schooling for men who were born in the south between 1910 and 1949 and who worked in a northern metropolitan area in 1960, 1970, or 1980. We find a strong correlation between measures of school quality for black and white pupils and their rates of return to schooling. Changes in relative pupil–teacher ratios, term lengths, and teachers' salaries can explain at least one half of the intercohort growth in black–white relative returns to education, and 15–25 percent of the overall convergence in black relative returns to education between 1960 and 1980.

We conclude our study with a direct assessment of the effects of school quality on the black–white wage gap. Here, we follow a simple "reduced-form" approach and regress measures of the black–white wage gap by cohort and state of birth on measures of the corresponding gap in school quality. Again, there is a positive correlation between relative school quality and black–white relative wages. Changes in school quality explain one-quarter of the decline in the black–white wage gap between earlier and later cohorts of workers, and 15–20 percent of the closing of the overall black-white wage gap for southern-born workers between 1960 and 1980.

2.1. The Evolution of Black–White Earnings: 1960–1980

Table 2.1 presents estimates of average wage rates for black and white male workers in the 1960, 1970, and 1980 decennial censuses.[3] The table gives overall averages of log weekly wages for men age 21–60 together with means for each ten-year birth cohort. The three right-hand columns contain estimated black–white wage gaps by cohort of birth and census year. Over all cohorts the mean log wage differential was -0.48 in 1960, -0.39 in 1970, and -0.29 in 1980. A similar trend is apparent in the ratio of average wage levels (in the bottom row of the table), which rose from 0.62 in 1960 to 0.67 in 1970, and 0.75 in 1980.

An analysis of the wage gaps in Table 2.1 suggests that much of the overall increase in black relative earnings between 1960 and 1980 came about through the replacement of older cohorts of workers by younger cohorts with smaller wage gaps. For example, between 1960 and 1970 the black–white wage gap for the 1910–1919 birth cohort fell only 1.8 percent, while the gaps for the 1920–1929 and 1930–1939 cohorts actually increased slightly. However, the entry of the 1940–1949 cohort together with the exit of the 1900–1909 cohort reduced the overall wage gap by close to ten percentage points.

Changes in the wage gap between 1960 and 1980 are decomposed into within-cohort and between-cohort components in Table 2.2. To understand this decomposition, write the overall wage gap between black and white workers in 1960, g_{60}, as a weighted average of the wage gaps for cohorts 1 (born 1900–1909), 2 (born 1910–1919), 3 (born 1920–1929), and 4 (born 1930–1939):

$$g_{60} = \alpha_{60}^1 \, g_{60}^1 + \alpha_{60}^2 \, g_{60}^2 + \alpha_{60}^3 \, g_{60}^3 + \alpha_{60}^4 \, g_{60}^4,$$

where α_{60}^c is the relative weight of cohort c in the labor force in 1960 (assumed to be equal for whites and blacks), and g_{60}^c is the relative wage gap for cohort c in 1960.[4] Then the change in the wage gap between 1960 and 1970 is

$$
\begin{aligned}
(1) \qquad g_{70} - g_{60} = &\; \alpha_{60}^2 \cdot (g_{70}^2 - g_{60}^2) + \alpha_{60}^3 \cdot (g_{70}^3 - g_{60}^3) \\
&+ \alpha_{60}^4 \cdot (g_{70}^4 - g_{60}^4) + \alpha_{60}^1 \cdot (g_{70}^5 - g_{60}^1) \\
&+ (\alpha_{70}^2 - \alpha_{60}^2) \cdot (g_{70}^2 - g_{70}^5) + (\alpha_{70}^3 - \alpha_{60}^3) \\
&\cdot (g_{70}^3 - g_{70}^5) + (\alpha_{70}^4 - \alpha_{60}^2) \cdot (g_{70}^2 - g_{70}^5)
\end{aligned}
$$

where g_{70}^5 refers to the wage gap for cohort 5 (born 1940–1949) in 1970. The first three terms of this decomposition represent the *within-cohort* changes in wage gaps for the three continuing cohorts. Between 1960 and 1970 these terms are trivial, yielding a net change in the overall wage gap of -0.002. Between 1970 and 1980, on the other hand, changes for two of the continuing cohorts are larger: 11 percent for the 1920–1929 cohort and 7.2 percent for the 1930–1939 cohort. These improvements were offset by an increase in the relative wage gap for the 1940–1949 cohort.

Table 2.1

Mean Log Wages and Wage Differentials by Cohort in 1960,1970 and 1980

Cohort:	1960		1970		1980		Log wage differential Black–White		
	Whites	Blacks	Whites	Blacks	Whites	Blacks	1960	1970	1980
1900–1909									
Mean log wage	4.317	4.085					-0.532		
Std error	(0.003)	(0.008)					(0.009)		
Share	0.177	0,173							
1910–1919									
Mean log wage	4.680	4.152	5.123	4.613			-0.528	-0.510	
Std error	(0.002)	(0.007)	(0.002)	(0.006)			(0.007)	(0.006)	
Share	0.254	0.250	0.199	0.180					
1920–1929									
Mean log wage	4.667	4.170	5.209	4.726	5.921	5.548	-0.498	-0.483	-0.373
Std error	(0.002)	(0.006)	(0.001)	(0.005)	(0.002)	(0.004)	(0.006)	(0.005)	(0.005)
Share	0.297	0.301	0.284	0.243	0.177	0.146			
1930–1939									
Mean log wage	4.311	3.931	5.163	4.747	5.959	5.615	-0.379	-0.416	-0.344
Std error	0.002	(0.006)	(0.001)	(0.004)	(0.002)	(0.004)	(0.007)	(0.005)	(0.004)
Share	0.272	0.276	0.242	0.259	0.190	0.189			
1940–1949									
Mean log wage			4.759	4.541	5.858	5.576		-0.218	-0.282
Std error			(0.001)	(0.004)	(0.002)	(0.003)		(0.005)	(0.003)
Share			0.311	0.318	0.281	0.279			

Table 2.1 (continued)

Mean Log Wages and Wage Differentials by Cohort in 1960, 1970, and 1980

	1960		1970		1980		Log wage differential Black − White		
Cohort:	Whites	Blacks	Whites	Blacks	Whites	Blacks	1960	1970	1980
1950–1959									
Mean log wage					5,416	5,213			-0.203
Std error					(0.001)	(0.003)			(0.003)
Share					0.353	0.385			
All age 21–60									
Mean log wage	4,564	4,085	5,041	4,652	5,732	5,439	-0.480	-0.388	-0.293
Std error	(0.001)	(0.003)	(0.001)	(0.002)	(0.001)	(0.002)	(0.003)	(0.003)	(0.002)
Mean wage	111,2	69,5	183,3	122,9	369,1	276,4			
Ratio of arithmetic Means of blacks/whites	0.624		0.671		0.749				

Notes: Based on tabulations of weekly earnings of men born in the 48 mainland states in Public-Use Extracts of the 1960,1970, and 1980 Censuses. See Appendix A for sample selection criteria. The entries in rows labeled "Share" give the relative size of the birth cohort among all men age 21–60 in the respective Census sample.

The next term in the decomposition captures the direct effect of replacing the oldest cohort (the 1900–1909 cohort in 1960, for example) with the youngest cohort. The effect is simply the weight of the oldest cohort in the base year, multiplied by the difference between the wage gap for the oldest cohort in the base year and the gap for the youngest cohort in the final year. This term contributes a 5.5 percent reduction in the average wage gap between 1960 and 1970, and a 5.8 percent reduction between 1970 and 1980.

The final three terms in the decomposition reflect the decreasing importance of older cohorts in later censuses. Between 1960 and 1970, for example, the relative weight of the 1910–1919 cohort declined by 0.063. This weight is shifted to the entering cohort: the net effect is the product of the change in weights for the cohort and the difference in wage gaps between the continuing cohort and the entering cohort. Reweighting of the continuing cohorts contributes a 3.7 point decline in the overall wage gap between 1960 and 1970, and a 2.6 percent decline in the overall gap between 1970 and 1980.

Table 2.2

Decomposition of the Change in the Black–White Relative Wage Gap: 1960–1980

	1960–1970	1970–1980
1.Reduction in relative wage gap	0.091	0.095
2.Component attributable to change in wage gap of continuing cohorts	-0.002	0.025
3.Component attributable to replacement of oldest cohort with youngest cohort	0.055	0.058
4.Component attributable to reweighting of wage gaps for continuing cohorts	0.037	0.026
5.Residual component	0.001	-0.014

Note: The data are based on differences in log wages for men age 21–60 in the 1960, 1970 and 1980 Census. Cohorts are weighted by the relative size of the cohort in the combined workforce of black and white workers.

The results in Table 2.2 confirm that virtually all of the decline in the black–white wage gap between 1960 and 1970 was due to the entry of younger and larger cohorts (with substantially smaller wage gaps) and the exit of older and smaller cohorts (with substantially higher wage gaps). Between 1970 and 1980, on the other hand, within-cohort changes among the two older cohorts of workers contributed about one-quarter of the overall decline in the wage gap. Over the twenty-year period, within-cohort changes contributed 10 percent of the overall nineteen-point decline in the black–white relative wage gap.[5]

2.1.1. The Importance of Southern-Born Workers for the Black–White Wage Gap

Any explanation for the rise in relative earnings of later cohorts of black men must focus on improvements for southern-born workers, simply because a large majority (over 80%) of blacks born between 1900 and 1960 were born in the South. The importance of changes among southern-born men for the evolution of the overall wage gap is illustrated in Table 2.3. The decomposition in this table uses the fact that the wage gap (g) for a particular cohort can be written as

$$g = \gamma^B(y_S^B - y^W) + (1 - \gamma_B) \cdot (y_N^B - y^W),$$

where γ^B represents the fraction of black workers born in the south, y^W represents the mean log wage of white workers, and y_S^B and y_N^B represent the means of log wages for blacks born inside and outside the south, respectively. If the fraction of blacks born in the south is approximately constant, then the *change* in the relative wage gap between any two cohorts, Δg, can be written as

$$(2) \qquad \Delta g = \gamma^B(\Delta y_S^B - \Delta y^W) + (1 - \gamma_B) \cdot (\Delta y_N^B - \Delta y^W)$$

where Δy^W is the intercohort change in the mean log wage for white workers, and Δy_S^B and Δy_N^B are the corresponding changes for blacks born inside and outside the south. The first of these terms measures the change in the overall wage gap attributable to the relative earnings growth of southern-born blacks, while the second measures the change attributable to the relative earnings growth of non-southern-born blacks. Intercohort changes in the regional distribution of black births add a third "residual" component to this breakdown.

The first column of Table 2.3 compares the wage gap of the 1930–1939 cohort (measured in 1970) with that of the 1920–1929 cohort (measured in 1960). The entry in row 1 shows that the black-white wage gap was 8.2 percent lower for the 1930–1939 cohort than for the 1920–1929 cohort at a similar point in their lifecycle. The entry in row 3 shows that 7.2 percentage points of this change is due to the relative earnings gains of southern-born blacks. The share of this "southern-born effect" in the total intercohort change is reported in row 8. An alternative comparison of the same two cohorts is presented in the second column of Table 2.3, using data from the 1970 Census to measure the wage gap for the 1920–1929 cohort, and data from the 1980 Census to measure the wage gap for the 1930–1939 cohort. The intercohort gap is larger in the later comparison, as is the share of the change attributable to relative earnings growth for southern-born black workers.

The relative contribution of southern-born blacks can be further decomposed by noting that

$$\Delta y^{W} = \Delta y_{S}^{W} + (1 - \gamma^{W}) \cdot (\Delta y_{N}^{W} - \Delta y_{S}^{W}),$$

where y^{W} is the fraction of whites born in the south and ΔY_{N}^{W} and ΔY_{S}^{W} represent the intercohort changes in mean log wages for northern-born and southern-born whites. Thus,

$$\gamma^{B} (\Delta y_{S}^{B} - \Delta y^{W}) = \gamma^{B}\Delta g_{S} + \gamma^{B}(1 - \gamma^{W}) \cdot (\Delta y_{S}^{W} - \Delta y_{N}^{W}),$$

where Δg_{S} is the intercohort change in the black–white wage gap among southern-born men. The overall southern-born effect reflects both the change in the wage gap among southern-born workers (weighted by γ^{B}) and the earnings growth of southern-born whites relative to northern-born whites (weighted by $\gamma^{B}(1 - \gamma^{W})$). The shares of these two components in the overall intercohort relative wage change are reported in the bottom two rows of Table 2.3. Changes in the wage gap among southern-born workers account for 60 percent of the intercohort change in black–white relative wages. Increases in the earnings of southern-born whites relative to whites born elsewhere in the United States account for an additional 8–25 percent of the intercohort change.

The third and fourth columns of Table 2.3 present similar decompositions of the change in the black–white wage gap between the 1930–1939 birth cohort and the 1940–1949 birth cohort. Again, over 70 percent of the growth in the relative earnings of black workers is attributable to the earnings gains of southern-born blacks, with most of this reflecting the narrowing of the wage gap for southern-born workers. In view of this fact, we turn next to a decomposition of changes in the black–white wage gap for southern-born men.

Consider a linear regression model that expresses the logarithm of weekly earnings (y) as a function of a vector of characteristics X

Table 2.3

Contribution of Region of Birth to Intercohort Differences in the Black–White Wage Gap

	1930 cohort – 1920 cohort		1940 cohort – 1930 cohort	
	1930 cohort in 1970–1920 cohort in 1960	1930 cohort in 1980–1920 cohort in 1970	1940 cohort in 1970–1930 cohort in 1960	1940 cohort in 1980–1930 cohort in 1970
1. Intercohort difference in wage gap	0.082	0.139	0.161	0.134
2. Fraction blacks born in south (base cohort)	0.837	0.795	0.808	0.778
Wage growth relative to whites:				
3. Southern born blacks	0.072	0.157	0.156	0.156
4. Non-southern born blacks	0.044	0.068	0.109	0.037
Intercohort change attributable to:				
5. Wage growth of southern born blacks	0.060	0.125	0.126	0.122
6. Wage growth of non-southern born blacks	0.007	0.014	0.021	0.008
7. Residual effects	0.015	0.000	0.014	0.004
Proportion of intercohort change attributable to southern-born:				
8. Total southern-born effect (row 3/row1)	0.733	0.901	0.781	0.908
-component due to narrowing of southern-born wage gap	0.633	0.641	0.602	0.604
-component due to relative wage growth of southern-born whites	0.079	0.247	0.186	0.316

Note: See equation (2) of text for decomposition. Wage gaps and changes are measured as differences in mean log wages. Black wage growth in rows 3 and 4 is measured relative to all (northern and southern-born) whites.

(education, potential experience, the square of potential experience, and indicator variables for marital status, residence in the different Census regions, and residence in an SMSA) and a person-specific error term:

$$y = X\beta + \epsilon.$$

We have estimated the coefficients β by race and cohort of birth for southern-born whites and blacks in the 1960, 1970, and 1980 Censuses. We can then write the black–white relative wage gap for a particular age group in 1960 as

$$g_{60} = X_{60}^{B}\beta_{60}^{B} - X_{60}^{W}\beta_{60}^{W},$$

where X_{60}^{B} represents the mean of the X vector for blacks in 1960 and β_{60}^{B} represents the vector of estimated regression coefficients for blacks in 1960. The intercohort change in the wage gap for this age group between 1960 and 1970 is

$$(3) \qquad g_{70} - g_{60} = (X_{70}^{B} - X_{60}^{B})\beta_{60}^{B} + (\beta_{70}^{B} - \beta_{60}^{B})X_{70}^{B}$$
$$- (X_{70}^{W} - X_{60}^{W})\beta_{60}^{W} - (\beta_{70}^{W} - \beta_{60}^{W})X_{70}^{W}.$$

This change consists of the change in the mean characteristics for blacks (multiplied by the base-period regression coefficients for blacks); the change in the regression coefficients for blacks (multiplied by the end-period mean characteristics); and two analogous terms for whites.

Table 2.4 presents the portions of each component of this decomposition attributable to education.[6] The second and third rows of the table present the effects of changes in the mean levels of schooling for blacks and whites, respectively, between the initial and ending years. The fourth row of the table sums these two components, giving the total change in the relative wage gap attributable to changes in the relative levels of education for the two groups. In most cases the sum is small or negative. There are two reasons for this. First, mean years of education rose quickly for both blacks *and* whites, implying only modest relative gains for blacks. Second, the coefficients associated with schooling are typically lower for blacks, implying a smaller wage gain, other things being equal.

By comparison, changes in the relative return to education can in principle account for *all* of the intercohort decline in the relative wage gap. The effects of changes in the returns to education for black and white workers are presented in the fifth and sixth rows of the table, respectively, and the sum of these two components is presented in row 7. In every column of the table, the effect of changes in the relative return to education is larger than the total change in the relative wage gap.[7]

These findings parallel the results presented by Smith and Welch (1989) for all black and white workers. Regardless of how the decompositions are weighted, virtually all of the intercohort changes in the black–white wage gap can be explained by increases in the relative return to education for blacks. Notice, however, that the increasing relative returns in Table 2.4 may reflect either cohort or year effects, since the comparisons are drawn across Censuses. In fact, the analysis in Section 2.3. below suggests that an important component of the increased relative return to education for blacks between 1970 and 1980 is attributable to an economywide time effect, rather than a cohort-specific effect.

Last, it is worth pointing out that increases in the return to education for southern-born blacks occurred relative to both southern-born whites and northern-born blacks. This fact is illustrated in Table 2.5, which uses data from the 1980 Census to estimate rates of return for black and white workers by race, cohort of birth, southern-born status, and region of residence.[8] The bottom rows of the table give the intercohort differences in the rates of return to education between the 1920–1929 birth cohort and the 1940–1949 birth cohort as of 1980.

Looking across the columns of the table, it is clear that rates of return to education vary by region of residence. As noted by Chiswick (1974) and Smith and Welch (1989), rates of return to education are generally higher in the south and lower in the north–central region. However, a comparison of southern-born and non-southern-born men living in the *same* region shows that southern-born men from earlier birth cohorts earned systematically lower rates of return to education. For blacks the difference in returns between southern-born and non-southern born men in the 1920–1929 cohort is two–four percentage points. For whites in the same cohort the gap is a point or less. For the 1940–1949 cohort the gap in returns between southern-born and non-southern-born blacks is only about one percentage point, while the gap for whites averages about 0.5 percentage points.

Table 2.4

Contribution of Education to Changes in the Black–White Wage Differential Among Southern-born Men

Age group	1960 –1970				1970 –1980			
	21– 30	31– 40	41– 50	51– 60	21– 30	31– 40	41– 50	51– 60
1.Actual change in wage gap	0.120	0.062	0.007	0.000	0.007	0.104	0.112	0.079
Contribution of changes in years of schooling:								
2.Change in blk. educ. * return in base year	0.101	0.083	0.054	0.025	0.096	0.121	0.087	0.066
3.Change in wht. educ. * return in base year	-0.094	-0.079	-0.071	-0.063	-0.062	-0.112	-0.086	-0.066
4.Subtotal	0.007	0.004	-0.017	-0.038	0.034	0.009	0.001	-0.009
Contribution of changes in return of schooling:								
5.Change in blk.return *educ. in final year	0.237	0.155	0.074	0.084	0.005	0.145	0.150	0.021
6.Change in wht. return * educ. in final year	-0.054	-0.083	-0.049	0.002	0.318	-0.036	0.001	0.071
7.Subtotal	0.183	0.072	0.025	0.086	0.323	0.109	0.151	0.092
8.Total change attributable to education	0.190	0.076	0.008	0.048	0.357	0.118	0.152	0.082

Note: See text for decomposition. The calculations in the first column, for example, are based on a comparison of individuals born during 1930 and 1939 in 1960 with those born during 1940 and 1949 in 1970. Returns to schooling are obtained from a linear regression of log weekly wages on schooling, experience and its square, and indicator variables for marital status, residence in an SMSA, and residence in each of four Census regions.

Thus, there were substantial increases in the return to education for later cohorts of southern-born blacks relative to both southern-born whites and non-southern-born blacks. The relative rise in the return to schooling for southern-born blacks over their northern-born counterparts suggests that the higher returns were not simply a consequence of antidiscrimination policies. Rather, we believe that the changes reflect an increase in the market value of a southern education for black workers. To explain this increase, we turn to data on the quality of schools available to southern-born men.

Table 2.5

Rates of Return to Schooling by Region of Residence and Region of Birth in 1980 (Estimated Standard Errors in Parentheses)

	Blacks				Whites			
	Region of residence:				Region of residence:			
Region of birth	North–central	South	West	North–east	North–central	South	West	North–east
1920–1929 cohort:								
Southern-born	1.97	3.81	2.86	3.09	4.09	5.30	3.27	6.67
	(0.32)	(0.21)	(0.46)	(0.36)	(0.29)	(0.15)	(0.33)	(0.53)
Non-southern-born	4.88	7.91	5.60	5.22	4.91	6.74	4.18	6.28
	(0.55)	(0.85)	(1.00)	(0.56)	(0.15)	(0.27)	(0.19)	(0.16)
1930–1939 cohort:								
Southern-born	4.24	5.75	5.36	4.45	5.14	6.69	5.40	7.62
	(0.32)	(0.19)	(0.43)	(0.35)	(0.28)	(0.14)	(0.34)	(0.64)
Non-southern-born	5.47	5.65	6.24	6.60	6.04	9.02	6.15	7.97
	(0.50)	(0.80)	(0.80)	(0.50)	(0.15)	(0.25)	(0.18)	(0.16)
1940–1949 cohort:								
Southern-born	6.09	7.69	7.65	6.41	6.42	7.99	7.35	8.39
	(0.33)	(0.18)	(0.47)	(0.38)	(0.33)	(0.15)	(0.37)	(0.57)
Non-southern-born	6.86	9.49	7.13	7.96	6.85	10.00	7.24	8.43
	(0.42)	(0.63)	(0.59)	(0.43)	(0.15)	(0.24)	(0.18)	(0.15)
Change in rate of return 1940–1949 cohort: 1920–1929 cohort:								
Southern-born	4.12	3.88	4.79	3.32	2.33	2.69	4.08	1.72
	(0.46)	(0.28)	(0.66)	(0.52)	(0.44)	(0.21)	(0.50)	(0.78)
Non-southern-born	1.98	1.58	1.53	2.74	1.94	3.26	3.06	2.15
	(0.69)	(1.06)	(1.16)	(0.71)	(0.21)	(0.36)	(0.26)	(0.22)

Notes: Entries in table are rates of return to education (times 100) from linear regressions of log weekly earnings on potential experience and ist square, indicators for residence in an SMSA and being married, regions-of-residence indicators (for three major regions), and interactions of years of completed education with four regions of residence indicators.Regressions are estimated separately for each cohort of birth and for southern or non-southern region-of-birth.

2.2. Two Kinds of Schools

We have collected state-level data by race on three aspects of school quality: the ratio of students to teachers, average term length, and average annual teacher salaries. These data pertain to grades K-12 in public schools and cover the period from 1915 to 1966.[9] Data by race in this time period are only available for seventeen southern and border states and the District of Columbia.[10] Nevertheless, the analysis in the previous section suggests that individuals born in these states, who comprise more than 80 percent of blacks born in the United States, form a critical group for understanding the narrowing of the black–white earnings gap.

Several sources were canvassed to derive the final compilation of school quality data. Most of the data from 1915 through 1920 are taken from either state reports of education or the U.S. Office of Education's *Biennial Survey of Education*. Unfortunately, these sources are incomplete, and several states lack data on term length or teacher pay before 1920. Between 1922 and 1954, most of the data are available in the *Biennial Survey of Education*.[11] Missing data were supplemented by the state education reports, whenever possible.[12]

After the *Brown v. Board of Education* decision in 1954, the federal government and most states ceased publication of schooling data by race. Despite the *Brown* decision, however, most southern states continued to operate segregated schools until well into the 1960s. The table below shows the percent of southern-born blacks (men and women) who attended all-black schools, by birth cohort and level of schooling, based on retrospective responses in two household surveys.[13] The fraction of southern-born black students attending all-black schools was remarkably stable at approximately 90 percent for cohorts born before 1949.

In light of this fact we have used data on the numbers of black and white students and teachers in each state, along with average salaries by race, to estimate relative school quality for 1955–1966.[14] These data are derived from annual reports issued by the Southern Education Reporting Service (SERS), a civil rights monitoring group set up by a board of southern newspaper editors after the *Brown* decision.[15] SERS obtained data on white and black enrollment, teacher salaries, and numbers of teachers directly from the state education agencies. Although there are some gaps in the available data, we have been able to assemble a complete series on the pupil–teacher ratio by state and race, and fairly complete series on teacher pay for states other than Missouri, Kentucky, and Tennessee.

	Birth cohort:						
	1900–1909	1910–1919	1920–1929	1930–1939	1940–1949	1950–1959	1960–1969
Survey: National Survey of Black Americans (sample size = 1,536)							
1.Grade school	93.5	98.3	95.7	96.1	93.4	77.8	47.8
2.Junior high	90.6	92.6	93.3	94.3	90.0	48.4	18.2
3.High school	93.6	92.3	90.7	88.8	85.7	29.9	11.5
4.Any school	94.2	98.9	96.7	96.6	94.6	79.2	50.7
Survey: General Social Survey (sample size = 305)							
5.High school	88.0	93.9	89.1	90.2	80.8	23.4	9.5

Figure 2.1 shows the relative ratios of the three school quality variables in the white and black schools of the south from 1915 to 1966.[16] Inspection of the relative school quality data suggests three conclusions. First, during most of the twentieth century the quality of education for black students lagged far behind that for whites. As recently as 1940 pupil–teacher ratios were 25 percent higher in black schools, the average term length was 10 percent shorter in the black schools, and average annual salaries were 45 percent lower for black teachers.

Second, there were notable gains in the relative quality of black schools during this century. The convergence in black–white school quality began well before the 1954 *Brown v. Board of Education* decision, and in fact, there is little evidence of a break in the series around the time of the desegregation order.[17] The gap in pupil–teacher ratios between black and white schools, for example, fell in almost every year of our sample period. In 1915 the average pupil–teacher ratio in southern black schools was 61, compared with 38 in white schools. By 1966 the pupil–teacher ratio was 26 for black students and 24 for white students. The difference in term lengths between black and white schools and the gap in salaries between black and white teachers were virtually eliminated by the mid-1950s.

Third, as noted by Smith (1984), the rate of improvement in the relative quality of black schools varied from decade to decade. During the first ten years of our sample period (1915–1925), black relative teacher salaries and pupil–teacher ratios showed substantial gains. Relative conditions for black pupils showed comparatively little change in the late 1920s and early 1930s. After 1932 there was a marked acceleration in the rate of convergence of teacher salaries and the length of the school term.[18]

Figure 2.1

Relative School Quality in Eighteen Segregated States, 1915–1966

a) Ratio of White-to-Black Pupils/Teacher

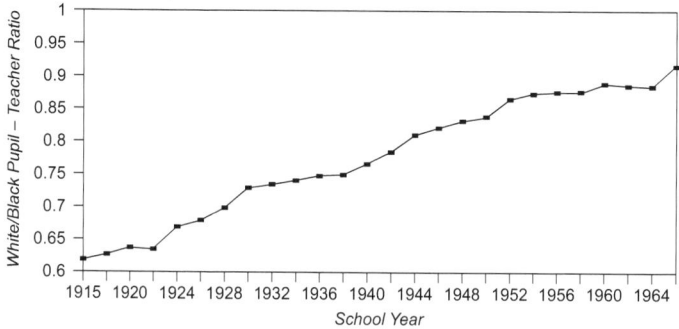

b) Ratio of White-to-Black Term Length

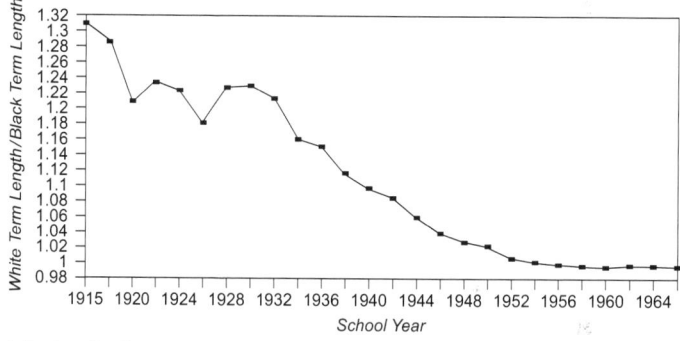

c) Ratio of White-to-Black Teacher Pay

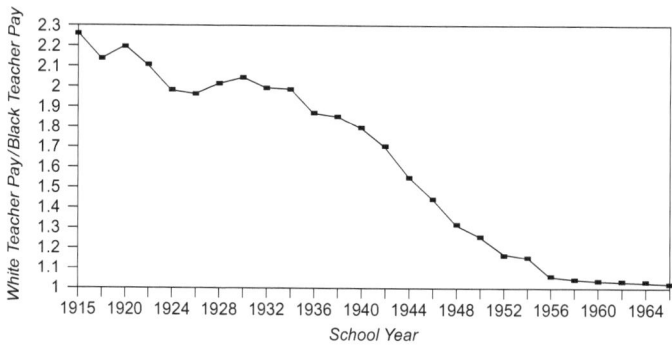

2.2.1. Interstate Differences in Relative Black–White School Quality

The aggregate data in Figure 2.1 mask wide differences across the southern states in the relative quality of black schools, and in the timing of changes in the relative quality of black education. Interstate differences in relative school quality were especially large in the early part of the twentieth century. In 1920, for example, pupil–teacher ratios in the black schools of Mississippi were twice as high as those in the white schools. In Kentucky, Missouri, West Virginia, and Washington, D.C., pupil–teacher ratios were comparable for white and black students. Similarly, black–white relative term lengths ranged from 0.55 in South Carolina to 1.0 in many border states. Perhaps most dramatically, the ratio of black to white teacher salaries ranged from one third in Mississippi and South Carolina to one in West Virginia and Washington, D.C.[19]

A key determinant of the relative quality of black schools in a state was the fraction of blacks in the population. Throughout most of our sample period black schools had more meager resources (both in absolute terms and relative to white schools) in states with a higher fraction of blacks.[20] This relationship is illustrated in Figure 2.2, below, which graphs the relative pupil–teacher ratio in the white and black schools in each state in 1920 against the fraction of blacks in the 1920 Census. Over 70 percent of the interstate variation in the relative quality of black schools is accounted for by the relative size of the black population.

States also differed in the timing of relative improvements in the quality of black schools. In the border states the NAACP's legal campaign against unequal salaries for black teachers led to rapid wage increases in the late 1930s and early 1940s.[21] Similar changes followed more than a decade later in the deep-southern states, spurred by expanding legal pressure and the hope that more equal school expenditures might forestall a Supreme Court challenge to the segregated school systems.[22]

Some indication of the differences in timing of relative improvements in black school quality is provided in Figure 2.3. This figure shows pupil–teacher ratios for the black and white schools in two groups of states: those with over 30 percent black population in the 1920 Census, and those with less.[23] Throughout most of the 1915–1966 period, the two groups of states had very similar pupil–teacher ratios in the white schools. In states with a higher concentration of blacks, however, pupil–teacher ratios for black students were uniformly higher.

Figure 2.2

White–Black Pupil–Teacher Ratio versus Percent of Blacks
in State Population

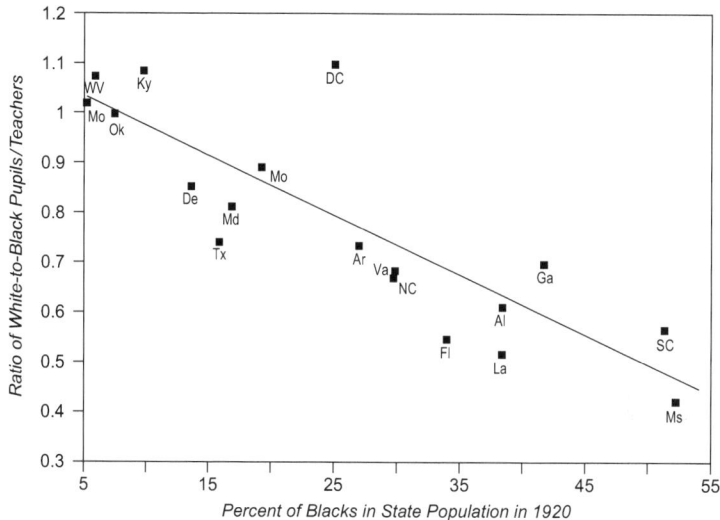

Note: The fitted OLS line is shown on the plot

Only in the late 1950s did pupil–teacher ratios in the black schools of Alabama, Mississippi, and South Carolina reach levels achieved in the white schools in the 1920s.

A particularly revealing comparison is between South Carolina and North Carolina. Data on pupil–teacher ratios for these two states are plotted in Figure 2.4.[24] Despite their geographic proximity, the Carolinas had very different policies regarding black education. Whereas North Carolina was among the most progressive of the nonborder southern states vis-à-vis black schooling; South Carolina was among the least progressive.[25]

At the beginning of our sample period, the quality of black schools in South Carolina ranked near the bottom of the entire country. On the other hand, schools for whites were actually better in South Carolina than in many southern states, including North Carolina. This pattern provides a natural comparison that is explored below, in Section 2.3.

Figure 2.3

Pupil–Teacher Ratio in Black and White Schools by Proportion of Blacks in State Population (the figures in parentheses indicate whether the proportion of blacks in the state in 1920 was more than or less than 30 percent)

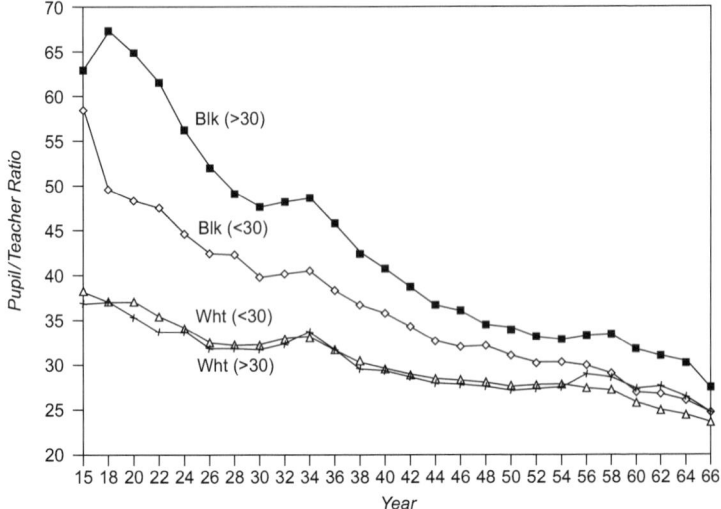

Figure 2.4

Pupil–Teacher Ratio by Race, North Carolina versus South Carolina

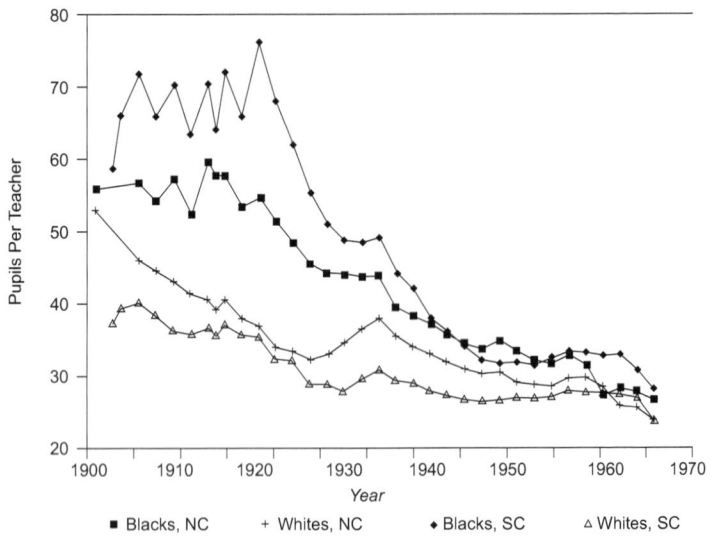

The schooling data presented so far pertain to individual school years. In the next section we examine rates of return to schooling for men born in ten-year cohorts. Consequently, we need to construct average quality measures for individuals born during a particular decade in a particular state. Our method is to assign to each individual an average of the quality variables during the time he attended school, assuming that each child began his schooling at age six and attended continuously for as many years as his completed education (up to twelve). We then take averages of the quality variables across individuals in a given cohort from a given state. This procedure abstracts from such important considerations as repeated grades and delayed age of school entry. Nevertheless, averaging the school inputs in this way tends to smooth any short-term fluctuations in the school quality variables. In fact, the average assigned to a particular cohort is a weighted average of twenty years of school quality data.[26]

School quality measures for men born in the 1910s, 1920s, 1930s, and 1940s are reported in Appendix C, at the end of the chapter. As expected, Appendix C shows considerable variation in the levels of the school quality variables across states, and in the rate at which the gap between black and white school quality was reduced. This variation provides the basis for our analysis of school quality effects in the closing of the black–white wage gap.

2.3. School Quality and the Return to Education

How much of the improved economic position of black workers can be explained by advances in relative school quality? In light of the evidence in Section 2.1. relating the earnings gains of black workers to relative increases in the rate of return to education, we provide a first answer to this question by analyzing the connection between school quality and returns to education. We estimate rates of return to education by state of birth and cohort from a simple log-linear regression that includes interactions between state of birth and years of completed education. Specifically, we estimate the following wage equation separately by race, Census year, and ten-year birth cohort:

$$(4) \qquad y_{ijs} = \rho_s E_{ijs} + X_{ijs}\beta + \alpha_j + \mu_s + \epsilon_{ijs},$$

where y_{ijs} is the logarithm of the weekly wage earned by individual i living in state j and born in state s, E_{ijs} represents years of education of individual i, ρ_s is the return to education for workers born in state s, X_{ijs} is a vector consisting of potential labor market experience and its square and a current marital status dummy, α_j is a state-of-residence effect, μ_s is a state-of-birth effect, and ϵ_{ijs} is stochastic error term.[27] The equation is estimated separately for the 1910–1919, 1920–1929, and 1930–1939 cohorts using data from the 1960 Census, for the 1910–1929, 1920–1929, 1930–1939, and 1940–1949 cohorts using data from the 1970 Census, and for the 1920–1929, 1930–1939, and 1940–1949 cohorts using data from the 1980 Census.[28] These samples yield a set of 360 estimated rates of return to education for eighteen states of birth, two race groups, and five cohorts in three Censuses.

An important feature of our analysis is that the returns to education are estimated for the subset of southern-born men living in the metropolitan areas of nine northern states (namely: Illinois, Michigan, Indiana, Wisconsin, Ohio, Pennsylvania, New York, New Jersey, California). Together, residents of metropolitan areas in these states account for 30 percent of all southern-born blacks, and 83 percent of all southern-born blacks living outside the south.[29] There are two important advantages to analyzing returns to education for southern-born workers who have moved to the north. First, we abstract from any changes over time in discrimination against better-educated black workers in the south (although we still capture any similar changes that occurred in the north). Second, as noted in Table 2.5, returns to education vary across regions – and particularly between the south and the rest of the country. By limiting the sample to individuals in northern metropolitan areas, we are able to eliminate most of this regional variation.[30]

In the second step of our analysis, we relate the percentage return to education for each cohort-race-state-year cell to the quality of education received by men born in the corresponding cohort, state, and race group. Specifically, we estimate

$$(5) \qquad \rho^c_{str} = bQ^c_{sr} + a^c_r + u_s + v_{tr},$$

where ρ^c_{str} is the estimated return to education (times 100) for individuals in race group r born in cohort c and state s, measured in year t (t = 1960, 1970, 1980), and Q^c_{sr} is a measure of average school quality for this race-cohort-state group. We include race-specific cohort effects (a^c_r) as well as state effects (u_s) and race-specific year effects (v_{tr}).[31] Differences between the cohort effects for blacks and whites measure the black-white gap in the return to education. Similarly, the difference-in-differences of the black and white cohort effects between earlier and later cohorts measures the intercohort convergence in black-white returns. A comparison of this difference-in-differences with and without the school quality variables included in the regression indicates how much of the intercohort convergence in black-white relative returns can be explained by changes in school quality.

The specification of equation (5) assumes that each worker is educated in his state of birth. Although this is not always the case, we believe that it is not a bad approximation. To check this, we used microdata from the 1940 Census to calculate the probability that five–fifteen-year-old children were living in their state of birth. The estimates show that over 90 percent of school-age children in 1940 were living in the state where they were born. We also used information from the National Survey of Black Americans to compare respondents' state of birth with the state where they grew up.[32] For blacks born between 1900 and 1949, 82 percent report they grew up in their state of birth.[33] On the basis of these results we conclude that education quality in an individual's state of birth is a reasonable indicator of true education quality.[34]

2.3.1. The Returns to Education by Race

Table 2.6 illustrates the wide variation across states in the rates of return to education for black and white men. The rates of return are pooled estimates for cohorts born in the south between 1910 and 1939 and observed living in northern metropolitan areas in 1970. The states are listed in order of the quality of black schools in the state, from worst to best, according to an index of school quality as of 1940.[35] With the exception of Delaware and the District of Columbia, the rates of return are estimated with reasonable precision. The racial gap in the return to education (in column 3) ranges from 4.5 percentage points for men born in South Carolina and Georgia, to a negative (although statistically insignificant) gap for men born in Missouri and West Virginia. Reading down column 2, the pattern of increasing returns is consistent with the notion that better schools lead to higher returns: black men born in states like Delaware, West Virginia, and Missouri earned roughly 3 percent higher earnings *per year of schooling* than those born in states with lower quality schools, such as Mississippi, Georgia, and South Carolina.

The contrast between South Carolina and North Carolina is especially interesting because, as shown in Figure 2.4, the quality of black schools was higher in North Carolina than in South Carolina in the 1915–1940 period, while the reverse was true for white schools. The estimated returns reflect these differences. Blacks from North Carolina earned much higher rates of return to schooling than those from South Carolina, while whites from South Carolina earned slightly higher returns than those from North Carolina. It should be stressed that these returns are estimated for samples of men from the two states who were working in the same set of northern labor markets.

The relationship between relative school quality and the black–white gap in the return to education is illustrated in Figure 2.5, which graphs the differences in returns to education from column 3 of Table 2.6 against the average difference in the pupil–teacher ratio for men in the 1910–1919, 1920–1929, and 1930–1939 cohorts.[36] Racial differences in school quality are highly correlated with the difference in returns to education: variation in the relative pupil–teacher ratio explains over 60 percent of interstate differences in the relative return to education for men in these cohorts.

Figure 2.5

Difference in Return vs. Difference in Pupil–Teacher Ratio

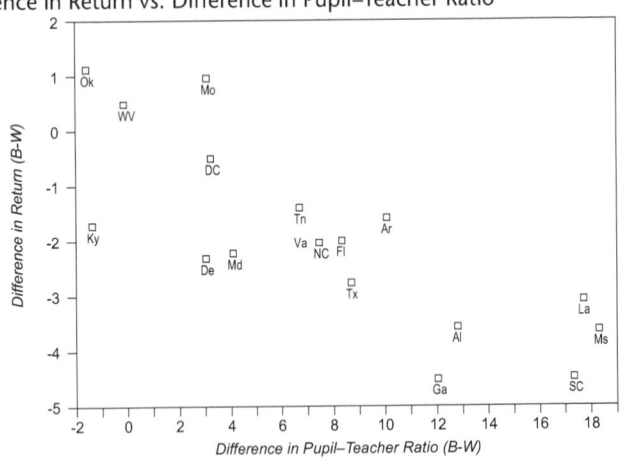

Table 2.6

Percentage Return to Education by State of Birth for Men Living in Metropolitan Areas of Nine States (standard errors in parentheses)

State of birth:	Whites (1)	Blacks (2)	Difference (1) - (2)
Louisiana	5.72	2.65	3.07
	(0.69)	(0.54)	(0.88)
Mississippi	6.44	2.80	3.64
	(0.66)	(0.38)	(0.77)
South Carolina	6.55	2.07	4.47
	(0.88)	(0.46)	(0.99)
Georgia	7.19	2.68	4.51
	(0.61)	(0.41)	(0.74)
Alabama	6.24	2.69	3.55
	(0.51)	(0.40)	(0.65)
Arkansas	5.32	3.72	1.60
	(0.41)	(0.56)	(0.70)
Texas	6.47	3.71	2.76
	(0.25)	(0.59)	(0.64)
North Carolina	6.03	4.01	2.02
	(0.55)	(0.49)	(0.74)
Virginia	6.42	4.40	2.02
	(0.46)	(0.55)	(0.72)
Florida	5.22	3.23	2.00
	(0.80)	(0.90)	(1.20)

Table 2.6 (continued)

Percentage Return to Education by State of Birth for Men Living in Metropolitan Areas of Nine States (standard errors in parentheses)

State of birth:	Whites (1)	Blacks (2)	Difference (1) - (2)
Oklahoma	5.49	6.61	-1.13
	(0.35)	(1.27)	(1.31)
Tennessee	4.55	3.16	1.39
	(0.35)	(0.61)	(0.70)
Maryland	7.33	5.11	2.22
	(0.61)	(1.18)	(1.33)
Delaware	7.96	5.64	2.31
	(1.37)	(4.12)	(4.34)
West Virginia	5.91	6.40	-0.49
	(0.35)	(1.37)	(1.41)
Kentucky	4.99	3.28	1.71
	(0.26)	(0.92)	(0.95)
Missouri	6.21	7.17	-0.96
	(0.31)	(1.24)	(1.28)
D.C.	7.19	6.71	0.49
	(1.11)	(3.09)	(3.28)

Note: Entries in colums 1 and 2 are coefficients of education (times 100) from a regression of log weekly wages on education, potential experience, and ist square, an indicator for marital status, nine state-of-residence dummies, and eighteen state-of-birth dummies. Regressions are fit separately by race for men born 1910 to 1939 and living in one of nine northern states. Data are from the 1970 status.

Differences over time in the return to education for southern-born blacks and whites living in northern cities are illustrated in the table below, which is formed from weighted averages of the cohort-and-state-specific estimated rates of return from equation (4). The relative trends shown by these estimates are similar to the trends in returns for *all* southern-born men (reported in Appendix B), although the rates of return are uniformly lower for the northern urban residents. The black–white difference in returns to education fell by 1.53 points between 1960 and 1980, from an initial gap of 3.0 percentage points in 1960 to 1.47 points in 1980.

	Average return to education (standard errors)		
	Blacks	Whites	Difference
1960 census	3.04	6.04	-3.00
	(0.20)	(0.15)	(0.25)
1970 census	3.91	6.58	-2.67
	(0.15)	(0.10)	(0.18)
1980 census	4.33	5.80	-1.47
	(0.12)	(0.08)	(0.14)

2.3.2. Estimation Results

Table 2.7 reports regression estimates of equation (5), using the set of 360 estimated rates of return to education by cohort, race, state of birth, and Census year.[37] We begin by examining the effect of the pupil–teacher ratio because, unlike the other two school quality measures, this variable is available for all states in all years. The first three columns pool together the returns to education for blacks and whites, while columns 4–7 present separate estimates by race. Columns 8 and 9 contain results using only the estimated returns for black men in 1960.

The model in the first column excludes the pupil–teacher ratio and state effects. The coefficients on the interaction terms between the black dummy and the cohort effects (rows 6–9) indicate the racial gap in the return to education for each cohort of workers, controlling for race-specific year effects. Between the 1910–1919 cohort and the 1930–1939 cohort, the black-white gap in the return to education closed by nearly 40 percent, from a 3.31 percentage point deficit per year of schooling for the 1910–1919 cohort to a 2.02 percentage point deficit for the 1930–1939 cohort. The estimated cohort effects indicate a slight widening in the gap in relative returns between the 1930–1939 and 1940–1949 cohorts, although this difference is not statistically significant.[38] Assuming ten years of education, the 0.94 point decline in the racial gap in the return to education between the 1910–1919 cohort and 1940–1949 cohort implies a 9.4 percentage point reduction in the black–white earnings gap: about one half of the decline in the earnings gap actually observed between these cohorts of southern-born workers (see Appendix B).

The coefficient of -7.45 (t = 4.2) on the pupil–teacher ratio in column 2 indicates that a higher pupil–teacher ratio is associated with a lower return to education.[39] To interpret the magnitude of this coefficient, suppose that average class size declined by ten pupils. This would lead to a 0.75 percentage point increase in the rate of return for each year of education, or a 9 percent increase in earnings for a high school graduate. Column 3 adds state effects to the model and thus identifies the effect of the pupil–teacher ratio from changes in class-size that occurred within states over time. In this specification the impact of the pupil–teacher ratio is smaller, but still sizable and statistically significant (t = 2.5).[40]

The pupil–teacher ratio also has a negative effect on the return to education in the models in columns 4–7, which are estimated separately by race. The estimated coefficient is somewhat larger for whites than blacks when the state effects are excluded (compare columns 4 and 6), whereas the opposite holds when state effects are included (columns 5 and 7). In either case, the difference between the coefficients of the pupil–teacher ratio for blacks and whites is statistically insignificant. Thus, there is no evidence against the (more precise) pooled specifications in columns 2–3.

A comparison of the estimated cohort-race interactions in columns 1 and 2 shows that the addition of the pupil–teacher ratio can explain much of the intercohort convergence in black–white returns to education. For example, when the pupil–teacher ratio is included in column 2, the unexplained change in the black–white return gap between the 1910–1919 cohort and the 1930–1939 cohort falls from 1.29 points (in column 1) to 0.59 points. Similarly, the unexplained change between the 1910–1919 and 1940–1949 cohorts falls from 0.94 points to 0.09 points. Changes in the relative pupil–teacher ratio therefore explain 54 percent of the convergence in the return to education between the 1910–1919 cohort and the 1930–1939 cohort, and over 90 percent of the convergence between the 1910–1919 and 1940–1949 cohorts.

These shares are only slightly lower when state effects are added to the model. A comparison of the race–cohort interactions in col-

Table 2.7

The Effect of the Pupil–Teacher Ratio on the Return to Education (standard errors in parentheses)

Variable	Blacks and whites 1960 – 1980			Blacks 1960 – 1980		Whites 1960 – 1980		Blacks 1960	
	(1)	(2)	(3)	(4)	(5)	(6)	(7)	(8)	(9)
1.Intercept	5.58	8.08	8.04	5.47	5.81	8.81	6.86	4.38	8.40
	(0.25)	(0.64)	(0.91)	(1.06)	(2.47)	(1.13)	(2.06)	(2.05)	(5.94)
2.Pupil–teacher ration (/ 100)	—	-7.45	-5.91	-6.38	-5.85	-9.62	-3.13	-4.15	-10.42
		(1.77)	(2.39)	(2.03)	(4.96)	(3.26)	(5.56)	(4.02)	(12.12)
3.Dummy for born 1920–1929	0.22	0.03	0.08	0.33	0.36	-0.03	0.16	0.60	0.14
	(0.26)	(0.26)	(0.25)	(0.35)	(0.50)	(0.28)	(0.29)	(0.59)	(1.11)
4.Dummy for born 1930–1939	1.57	1.17	1.27	1.92	1.98	1.05	1.42	1.71	0.75
	(0.27)	(0.28)	(0.28)	(0.45)	(0.83)	(0.33)	(0.40)	(0.92)	(2.03)
5.Dummy for born 1940–1949	3.80	3.31	3.37	3.59	3.69	3.16	3.54	—	—
	(0.29)	(0.31)	(0.32)	(0.54)	(0.99)	(0.37)	(0.46)		
6.Black * born 1910–1919	-3.31	-2.08	-2.38	—	—	—	—	—	—
	(0.41)	(0.49)	(0.53)						
7. Black * born 1920–1929	-2.73	-1.86	-2.09	—	—	—	—	—	—
	(0.37)	(0.41)	(0.42)						
8.Black * born 1930–1939	-2.02	-1.49	-1.66	—	—	—	—	—	—
	(0.42)	(0.43)	(0.42)						
9.Black * born 1940–1949	-2.37	-1.99	-2.06	—	—	—	—	—	—
	(0.49)	(0.48)	(0.47)						

Table 2.7 (continued)

The Effect of the Pupil-Teacher Ratio on the Return to Education (standard errors in parentheses)

Variable	Blacks and whites 1960 – 1980			Blacks 1960 – 1980		Whites 1960 – 1980		Blacks 1960	
	(1)	(2)	(3)	(4)	(5)	(6)	(7)	(8)	(9)
10. Dummy for 1970	-0.18 (0.23)	-0.18 (0.23)	-0.20 (0.22)	0.01 (0.31)	-0.00 (0.31)	-0.18 (0.24)	-0.20 (0.23)	—	—
11. Dummy for 1980	0.20 (0.40)	0.19 (0.39)	0.19 (0.37)	—	—	—	—	—	—
12. Black * 1970	1.12 (0.41)	1.09 (0.40)	1.12 (0.39)	—	—	—	—	—	—
13. Black * 1980	1.12 (0.41)	1.09 (0.40)	1.12 (0.39)	—	—	—	—	—	—
14. 17 state dummies	No	No	Yes	No	Yes	No	Yes	No	Yes
15. R^2	0.71	0.72	0.75	0.59	0.64	0.67	0.74	0.20	0.44

Notes: Sample sizes are 360 for columns 1–3, 180 for columns 4–7, and 54 for columns 8–9. Equations are estimated by weighted least squares, with weights equal to the inverse sampling variances of the estimated returns. The mean and standard deviation of the dependent variable in columns 1–3 are 5.663 and 3.671, respectively.

umn 3 to those in a model that includes state effects but excludes the pupil–teacher ratio (not reported in the table) indicates that changes in the pupil–teacher ratio account for 44 percent of the convergence in black–white returns between the 1910–1919 cohort and the 1930–1939 cohort, and 68 percent of the convergence between the 1910–1919 cohort and the 1940–1949 cohort.

While the estimates in Table 2.7 indicate important intercohort effects in the relative return to education, they also imply a sizable role for the year effects, particularly between 1970 and 1980. For example, the estimated year effects in columns 4 and 6 suggest that rates of return to schooling for blacks were constant between 1960 and 1970, and fell only slightly for whites. However, rates of return for blacks fell by 0.6 points between 1970 and 1980, and by 1.7 points for whites. Thus, changes in the year effects contributed a 1.1 percentage point increase in the relative return to education for blacks between 1960 and 1980. This is about 70 percent of the overall 1.53 percentage point increase in relative rates of return observed in our data – virtually all of it occurring between 1970 and 1980.

Closer examination of the returns for individual cohorts indicates that the rise in relative returns in the 1970s was concentrated among older workers. For whites born in the 1920s and 1930s, rates of return to education fell by almost two percentage points between 1970 and 1980. Yet blacks in the same cohorts experienced less than a point decline. In contrast, there was little change in relative rates of return between 1970 and 1980 for men born in the 1940s.

One explanation for this pattern is that the relative value of "skill" in the labor market fell between 1970 and 1980.[41] If, as the school quality hypothesis suggests, older blacks have acquired less human capital per year of schooling than whites or younger blacks, a general decline in the price of "skill" will lower the return to education more for whites and younger blacks than for older blacks. One way to verify this hypothesis is to allow for a different coefficient on the pupil–teacher ratio in 1980. If students who attended schools with lower pupil–teacher ratios have more human capital per year of schooling, and if the price of "skill" declined from 1970 to 1980, then the pupil–teacher ratio should have a smaller effect (in absolute magnitude) in 1980. Furthermore, allowing for a change in the effect of the pupil–teacher ratio in 1980 should reduce the magnitude of the 1980 year effect for black returns to education.

Both these predictions are correct. When an interaction of the pupil–teacher ratio and the 1980 year effect is added to the model in column 3 of Table 2.7, the pupil–teacher coefficient for 1960 and 1970 rises to -7.11 (with a standard error of 2.51), while the estimated interaction term is 4.36 (with a standard error of 2.89). These estimates suggest a substantial reduction in the market value of higher quality education between 1970 and 1980. Allowing for this effect, the 1980 year effect for black relative returns to education is 0.71: 40 percent smaller than the year effect reported in Table 2.7.

These results are consistent with the hypotheses that the market value of higher quality education fell between 1970 and 1980. We believe that further investigation of this hypothesis is warranted – perhaps using larger samples of workers from all states. In any case, it is clear that relative rates of return to education increased sharply for older black workers in the 1970s and that this increase contributed substantially to the reduction in the black–white gap in returns to education between 1970 and 1980.

2.3.3. The Effect of School Quality Before the Civil Rights Act

The results in columns 1–7 suggest that school quality, as measured by the pupil–teacher ratio, is associated with higher returns to education. Nevertheless, it is interesting to ask whether higher quality education had any return for blacks prior to enactment of the Civil Rights Act in 1964. To examine this question, we fit equation (5) using the estimated returns to education for black men in 1960.[42] The results are summarized in columns 8 and 9 of Table 2.7.

Unfortunately, the resulting estimates of the effect of the pupil–teacher ratio are imprecise, presumably because of the small sample size. The point estimates indicate that even in 1960 a higher pupil–teacher ratio was associated with a lower return to education for black workers, with about the same size of effect as in the pooled sample. However, the t-ratio for the pupil–teacher ratio is only slightly greater than one in column 8 and is slightly less than one in column 9. In view of the imprecision of these estimates, it is difficult to draw any firm conclusions regarding a structural change in the value of higher quality schooling for blacks after passage of the Civil Rights Act.

2.3.4. Additional Aspects of School Quality

Table 2.8 presents estimates of the effect of additional dimensions of school quality for the subset of states that have sufficient data to calculate the average term length and teacher wage by race.[43] Column (1) presents the same model as reported in the first column of Table 2.7, estimated on the subsample of state-year-cohort observations with complete school quality data. In this subsample the black-white gap in the return to education is somewhat larger for the two oldest cohorts of workers. This arises from having to drop early observations on several states that historically maintained relatively high-quality black schools (e.g. Missouri and Kentucky).

The remaining models in the table add the three school quality variables, individually and jointly, and with and without state effects. As is the case for the full sample, the pupil–teacher ratio has a negative and statistically significant effect on the return to education, regardless of whether state effects are included or excluded. Similarly, term length and the log of the teacher wage each have a statistically significant, positive effect on the return to education when they are included individually (columns 3–4 and 8–9). Indeed, the estimated coefficients suggest that these aspects of school quality have sizable impacts on earnings. The coefficient of 1.95 on the term length variable in column 8, for example, implies that a twenty-day increase in the school term increases a high school graduate's weekly wages by 4.7 percent. The coefficient of the log of the teacher wage in column 9 implies that a 20 percent increase in real teacher wages will lead to a 0.33 percentage point increase in the return to education, or about 4 percent higher earnings for a worker with twelve years of education.

Models that include all three quality measures are presented in columns 5 and 10. The schooling quality variables are highly collinear: the correlation between the pupil–teacher ratio and average term length is -0.91, while the correlation between the pupil–teacher ratio and the log of the average teacher wage is -0.77. As a result, the regression model has difficulty parsing out the individual contributions of the three quality indicators. Only the teacher wage is statistically significant when the three variables are included in the same equation. Nevertheless, the quality measures are highly jointly significant, and when they are included together, the state effects become statistically insignificant, suggesting that unobserved components of state-level school quality are *not* omitted from the equation.[44]

Table 2.8
The Effect of School Quality on the Return to Education (standard errors in parentheses)

Variable	Excluding state effects					Including 14 state effects				
	(1)	(2)	(3)	(4)	(5)	(6)	(7)	(8)	(9)	(10)
1. Pupil-teacher ratio (/100)	—	-8.50 (2.28)	—	—	2.36 (3.55)	—	-7.34 (3.15)	—	—	-3.27 (5.00)
2. Term length (/100)	—	—	3.21 (0.69)	—	0.44 (1.27)	—	—	1.95 (1.07)	—	-1.34 (1.77)
3. ln teacher wage	—	—	—	1.45 (0.25)	1.51 (0.45)	—	—	—	1.65 (0.56)	1.76 (0.88)
4. Dummy for born 1920-1929	0.02 (0.42)	-0.28 (0.42)	-0.32 (0.41)	-0.45 (0.41)	-0.44 (0.41)	0.06 (0.41)	-0.08 (0.41)	-0.14 (0.43)	-0.33 (0.43)	-0.28 (0.43)
5. Dummy for 1930-1939	1.19 (0.43)	0.65 (0.45)	0.63 (0.43)	0.27 (0.44)	0.30 (0.44)	1.22 (0.42)	0.88 (0.44)	0.89 (0.46)	0.33 (0.51)	0.35 (0.52)
6. Dummy for 1940-1949	3.43 (0.45)	2.79 (0.47)	2.80 (0.45)	1.97 (0.49)	2.00 (0.51)	3.39 (0.44)	2.97 (0.47)	3.30 (0.48)	1.92 (0.66)	1.89 (0.72)
7. Black * Born 1910-1919	-3.76 (0.57)	-2.23 (0.69)	-2.72 (0.59)	-2.54 (0.58)	-2.77 (0.68)	-3.67 (0.55)	-2.37 (0.78)	-3.07 (0.64)	-2.34 (0.70)	-2.09 (0.80)
8. Black * Born 1920-1929	-2.87 (0.42)	-1.81 (0.50)	-1.99 (0.44)	-1.65 (0.45)	-1.77 (0.49)	-2.72 (0.41)	-1.94 (0.52)	-2.27 (0.48)	-1.58 (0.55)	-1.48 (0.57)
9. Black * Born 1930-1939	-2.00 (0.47)	-1.33 (0.49)	-1.62 (0.46)	-1.23 (0.46)	-1.33 (0.49)	-1.83 (0.46)	-1.41 (0.49)	-1.70 (0.46)	-1.24 (0.49)	-1.11 (0.52)
10. Black * Born 1940-1949	-2.23 (0.55)	-1.76 (0.55)	-2.19 (0.53)	-1.91 (0.52)	-2.02 (0.55)	-1.99 (0.53)	-1.74 (0.53)	-2.07 (0.53)	-1.93 (0.52)	-1.76 (0.56)
11. Dummy for 1970	0.07 (0.30)	-0.07 (0.30)	-0.09 (0.29)	-0.09 (0.29)	-0.09 (0.29)	-0.10 (0.29)	-0.10 (0.29)	-0.10 (0.29)	-0.11 (0.28)	-0.09 (0.29)

Table 2.8 (continued)

The Effect of School Quality on the Return to Education (standard errors in parentheses)

Variable	Excluding state effects				Including 14 state effects					
	(1)	(2)	(3)	(4)	(5)	(6)	(7)	(8)	(9)	(10)
12. Dummy for 1980	-1.67	-1.67	-1.69	-1.69	-1.69	-1.70	-1.70	-1.70	-1.70	-1.70
	(0.30)	(0.29)	(0.29)	(0.28)	(0.28)	(0.28)	(0.28)	(0.28)	(0.28)	(0.28)
13. Black * 1970	0.05	0.04	0.05	0.05	0.05	0.06	0.05	0.06	0.05	0.05
	(0.47)	(0.45)	(0.45)	(0.44)	(0.44)	(0.44)	(0.44)	(0.44)	(0.44)	(0.44)
14. Black * 1980	1.08	1.08	1.10	1.09	1.10	1.12	1.10	1.11	1.11	1.10
	(0.47)	(0.46)	(0.45)	(0.44)	(0.44)	(0.45)	(0.44)	(0.44)	(0.44)	(0.44)
15. Prob-value for state effects	—	—	—	—	0.001	0.001	0.001	0.066	0.260	0.261
16. R^2	0.72	0.73	0.74	0.75	0.75	0.75	0.76	0.76	0.77	0.77

Notes. Sample size is 272. Equations are estimated by weighted least squares, with weights equal to the inverse sampling variances of the estimated returns. The mean and standard deviation of the dependent variable are 5.436 and 2.154, respectively.

The inclusion of the school quality variables reduces the black–white gap in the return to education for each cohort, and also accounts for a sizable share of the intercohort convergence in relative returns. Together, the three measures of school quality account for half of the convergence in relative returns that occurred between the 1910–1919 and 1940–1949 cohorts (compare rows 7 and 10 of columns 1 and 5). The addition of state effects to the model increases the explained fraction of the change in the black–white returns gap to nearly 80 percent.

We conclude that school quality, as measured by the relatively crude indicators available to us, can potentially explain 50 to 80 percent of the change in the black–white gap in the return to education between cohorts born in the 1910s and those born in the 1940s. These intercohort differences, in turn, explain about 30 percent of the total increase in the relative return to education for blacks between 1960 and 1980. The remainder is explained by year effects, which indicate a one percentage point increase in the relative return for black workers between 1970 and 1980. Preliminary evidence suggests that the increase in the relative return to education for black workers in the 1970s is partially due to a decline in the price of "skill," which is reflected in a smaller effect of the pupil–teacher ratio in 1980. In summary, school quality measures can account for 15–25 percent of the total increase in the relative return to education for southern-born black men between 1960 and 1980.

2.4. School Quality and the Black–White Wage Gap: Reduced-Form Estimates

We conclude our analysis by presenting some very simple "reduced-form" evidence on the correlation between relative school quality and black–white earnings differences within states. Specifically, we consider estimates of the effect of relative school quality on the gap in earnings between blacks and whites born in the same cohort and in the same state. We also consider the effects of relative school quality on the relative schooling attainments of black and white students.

There are several reasons to estimate the reduced-form relationship between relative school quality and relative wages. First, although the evidence in the previous section suggests that relative school quality is an important determinant of relative rates of return to education, it is nevertheless possible that changes in the return to education simply alter the within-group distribution of income, with little or no effect on overall mean earnings. Depending on the substitutability of skill groups, higher quality schools may actually *reduce* the earnings of less educated workers. Thus, it is important to check that relative quality is directly correlated with relative earnings, and not simply with relative rates of return to education.

Second, increases in school quality potentially affect not only the rates of return to a given level of education, but also the educational attainments of black and white workers. Although our analysis suggests that increases in relative years of schooling were not responsible for the closing of the black–white wage gap between 1960 and 1980, it is still true that education levels of later cohorts of black workers rose sharply. To the extent that these increases were driven by improvements in the quality of schools available to black students, they constitute an important benefit of improved school quality.

Finally, our analysis of returns to education in the previous section is limited to the subsample of southern-born workers who moved to northern urban areas. Although this sample restriction provides a convenient way to control for regional variation in the return to education, the estimates may not be representative of the effect of school quality on earnings for southern-born workers who stayed in the south. Furthermore, the quality of schools may affect the probability of out-migration. Estimates of the reduced-form relation between earnings and school quality using *all* southern-born workers capture both of these effects.

A simple summary of the relation between school quality and relative earnings is provided by fitting models of the form,

$$(6) \qquad y_{bts}^c - y_{wts}^c = \beta(Q_{bs}^c - Q_{ws}^c) + \mu^c + v_t + \in_{ts}^c,$$

where y_{bts}^c is the mean of log weekly earnings of black workers born in cohort c in state s and measured in year t (t = 1960, 1970, 1980), y_{wts}^c is the log of mean weekly wages of white workers from the same cohort and state, $Q_{bs}^c - Q_{ws}^c$ is the black–white gap in the quality of education for students in cohort c and state s, μ^c is a cohort effect, and v_t is a year effect.[45] We have fit this equation to cohort-level data on relative earnings and relative school quality for observations on eighteen states and four cohorts in three Census years. The earnings data are averages of log weekly wages for all southern-born men, while the school quality data are weighted averages of the state-level data, using the race-specific educational distribution of all workers born in each southern state as weights.[46]

Before turning to the estimates, it is worth considering the pattern of black-white relative earnings differentials across the Southern states. These differentials are displayed in Table 2.9.[47] In general, the wage gap is lower for states with higher relative quality black schools, such as Kentucky, Missouri, Tennessee, and West Virginia. Nonetheless, black relative earnings are surprisingly low for several states that maintained relatively good black schools, including Maryland, the District of Columbia, and Delaware. Thus, the correlation between relative school quality and the relative wage gap is negative (-0.32), but weaker than the correlation between school quality and the return to education. It is interesting to note that the wage gap is larger for South Carolina than for North Carolina, consistent with the pattern of relative returns to education for these two states, and with the pattern of lower quality black schools in South Carolina. The bottom row of Table 2.9 indicates that the weighted average of the state-level wage gaps fell by 9.8 log points between 1960 and 1980. In spite of the different weighting scheme used to construct the time averages in Table 2.9, the decline in the average state-level gap is extremely close to the decline in the overall wage gap for all southern-born men in these cohorts.

Table 2.9

Average Black–White Wage Gap by State-of-Birth Men Born 1910–1949
(standard errors in parentheses)

	Average black–white wage gap (* 100)		
Alabama	27.78	Missouri	22.62
	(0.58)		(1.08)
Arkansas	23.29	North Carolina	28. Nov
	(0.82)		(0.53)
Delaware	38.53	Oklahoma	27.80
	(2.67)		(1.23)
Florida	35.58	South Carolina	31.27
	(0.84)		(0.64)
Georgia	32.75	Tennessee	20.24
	(0.55)		(0.79)
Kentucky	22.63	Texas	32.31
	(1.18)		(0.57)
Louisiana	38.01	Virginia	29.30
	(0.65)		(0.63)
Maryland	33.53	West Virginia	17.73
	(0.91)		(1.52)
Mississippi	28.75	District of Columbia	34.22
	(0.65)		(1.34)
Overall wage gaps by year			
1960:	36.19	1970:	31.90	1980:	26.36
	(0.45)		(0.31)		(0.25)

Note: The data are based on differences in log wages for men age 20–59 in the 1960, 1970 and 1980 Census. Entries represent weighted averages of black–white wage gaps for cohort and Census observations.

Estimates of equation (6) are presented in Table 2.10. The models in columns 1–7 are fitted to measures of relative earnings, while in columns 8 and 9 the dependent variable is the difference in mean education for black and white men born in the same state and cohort. These models are included to assess the effect that higher quality black schools may have had in increasing the relative educational attainment of black students during our sample period.

The benchmark model in column 1 includes only cohort and year effects. The estimated cohort effects in rows 5–8 indicate the black-white earnings gap for each ten-year birth cohort, relative to the black-white wage gap for the 1910–1919 cohort. For example, the co-efficient of 0.066 in row 6 indicates that the black-white relative wages were 6.6 percentage points higher for the 1930–1939 cohort than for the 1910–1919 cohort. Between the 1910–1919 and 1940–1949 cohort, the black-white earnings gap for all southern-born men closed by 13.7 percentage points. Notice also that the year effect for 1980 is positive and significant, implying that black-white relative wages closed by some 3.7 percentage points between 1960 and 1980, holding constant cohort effects. Thus, slightly more than one third of the overall 9.8 percentage point decline in the black-white wage gap between 1960 and 1980 is attributed to year effects, while the remainder is attributed to cohort effects.

In column 2 we add the relative pupil–teacher ratio to the model. This variable has a negative and statistically significant ($t = 2.8$) coefficient, implying that the black-white wage gap is greater for states and cohorts with a larger gap between the quality of black and white schools. The addition of the relative school quality measure reduces the estimated cohort effects in column 2 relative to those in column 1. Forty percent of the decline in the black-white wage gap between the 1910–1919 and 1930–1939 cohorts is explained by the convergence in relative pupil-teacher ratios. By comparison, less than 10 percent of the decline in the wage gap between the 1930–1939 and 1940–1949 cohorts can be attributed to changes in relative school quality. Comparing the 1910–1919 and 1940–1949 cohorts, changes in the relative pupil–teacher ratio account for 25 percent of the closing of the black-white wage gap.

Columns 3 and 4 estimate the same models for the subset of observations that have complete information on the other school quality measures. Column 5 replaces the pupil–teacher gap with the gap in average school term lengths, while column 6 uses the difference

Table 2.10

The Effect of School Quality on the Black–White Gap in Wages and Education: Reduced-Form Estimates for all Southern Born Men (standard errors in parentheses)

Variable	Wage gap full sample		Wage gap subsample with complete data					Education gap full sample	
	(1)	(2)	(3)	(4)	(5)	(6)	(7)	(8)	(9)
1. Intercept	-0.388 (0.016)	-0.345 (0.022)	-0.390 (0.019)	-0.360 (0.028)	-0.373 (0.023)	-0.373 (0.026)	-0.361 (0.030)	-2.407 (0.176)	-0.727 (0.164)
2. Pupil-teacher ratio gap (/100)	—	-0.278 (0.099)	—	-0.169 (0.117)	—	—	-0.239 (0.264)	—	-0.107 (0.007)
3. Term length gap (/100)	—	—	—	—	0.056 (0.045)	—	0.017 (0.086)	—	—
4. Log teacher wage gap	—	—	—	—	—	0.020 (0.021)	-0.023 (0.041)	—	—
5. Dummy for born 1920–1929	0.013 (0.017)	-0.004 (0.018)	0.006 (0.020)	-0.006 (0.020)	0.002 (0.020)	0.004 (0.020)	-0.009 (0.024)	0.430 (0.187)	-0.205 (0.132)
6. Dummy for born 1930–1939	0.066 (0.017)	0.038 (0.020)	0.059 (0.020)	0.039 (0.024)	0.047 (0.022)	0.050 (0.022)	0.038 (0.025)	0.996 (0.186)	-0.069 (0.144)
7. Dummy for born 1940–1949	0.137 (0.018)	0.103 (0.021)	0.131 (0.021)	0.107 (0.026)	0.115 (0.024)	0.116 (0.026)	0.109 (0.027)	1.269 (0.194)	-0.056 (0.158)
8. Dummy for 1970	0.007 (0.014)	0.007 (0.014)	0.008 (0.015)	0.008 (0.015)	0.008 (0.015)	0.008 (0.015)	0.008 (0.015)	0.073 (0.154)	0.069 (0.103)
9. Dummy for 1980	0.037 (0.015)	0.038 (0.014)	0.035 (0.015)	0.035 (0.015)	0.035 (0.015)	0.035 (0.015)	0.035 (0.015)	0.242 (0.157)	0.249 (0.105)
10. R^2	0.517	0.538	0.546	0.553	0.551	0.549	0.554	0.358	0.713

Notes: Sample size is 180 for columns 1, 2, 8 and 9, and 136 for columns 3–7. The dependent variable in columns 1–7 is the difference in mean log wages between black and white men born in the same ten-year interval and state. The dependent variable in columns 8 and 9 is the difference in mean years of education between black and white men and standard deviation of the dependent variable in columns 3 and 7 are -30.338 and 8.001, respectively. The mean and standard deviation of the dependent variable of columns 8 and 9 are -1.419 and 0.801, respectively.

in the log of mean teacher wages. The quality variables are statistically insignificant in the smaller sample of data, although they all have their expected signs.[48] Interestingly, when the school quality variables are included, individually the pupil–teacher ratio tends to account for the greatest share of the decline in the black–white wage gap for different cohorts. For example, comparing the 1910-1919 and 1940-1949 cohorts, the black–white earnings gap is reduced by 18 percent when the pupil–teacher ratio gap is included, by 12 percent when the term length gap is included, and by 11 percent when the gap in log teacher pay is included. Column 6 includes all three school quality measures in the regression model. Although the variables are statistically insignificant, both individually and jointly, their inclusion reduces the cohort effects by about the same amount as the inclusion of the pupil–teacher ratio variable in Column 4.

Finally, in columns 8 and 9 we regress the gap in years of completed education between blacks and whites on the gap in pupil-teacher ratios. The cohort effects in rows 5–8 of column 8 show a sizable 1.3 year increase in relative years of education for blacks between the 1910–1919 cohort and the 1940–1949 cohort. None of the cohort effects in column 9, on the other hand, is different from zero. Thus, virtually all of the increase in relative schooling of blacks is explainable by increases in relative school quality.[49] These results suggest that improvements in school quality were an important stimulus to increased school attendance and completion among black students. Given the lower returns to education earned by black than by white men, however, these increases in relative schooling had relatively small net effects on the convergence in relative earnings of black and white workers.

In summary, the reduced-form evidence suggests that changes in relative school quality (as measured by the pupil–teacher ratio) can explain about one quarter of intercohort changes in the black–white relative wage gap between men born in the 1910s and those born in the 1940s. Since intercohort changes account for two-thirds of the increase in the overall relative wage gap between 1960 and 1980, the reduced-form estimates imply that measured school quality can account for 15–20 percent of the convergence in black–white earnings in the two decades after 1960. This is similar to the share of the overall increase in the relative return to education attributable to school quality.

2.5. Conclusions

This chapter presents direct evidence on the role of school quality in explaining the growth of black–white relative earnings between 1960 and 1980. We find a strong relationship between school quality and the economic return to additional years of schooling for black and white workers. Changes in school quality can explain from 50 to 80 percent of the relative increase in the return to education for black workers born in 1940–1949 over those born in 1910–1919. These intercohort changes, in turn, account for some 30 percent of the overall increase in the relative return to schooling for southern-born blacks between 1960 and 1980. Thus, our estimates suggest that measures of school quality can explain 15 to 25 percent of the convergence in relative rates of return to schooling for southern-born black workers between 1960 and 1980.

The remainder of the convergence in black–white relative returns to education is attributed to an economywide increase in the relative value of black education between 1970 and 1980. While returns to education for white workers fell sharply during the 1970s, returns for older cohorts of black workers were relatively stable. One explanation for this pattern is that the market price of acquired human capital (including higher quality education) fell between 1970 and 1980. We find some initial support for this hypothesis. In addition, increased demand for skilled black workers, stimulated by government legislation and judicial pressure, may have contributed to the relative rise in the return to education for black workers in the 1970s.[50] More evidence on the nature of these changes, and on the determinants of earnings for older cohorts of black workers, should be a priority for future research.

We also find a direct relationship between the relative quality of schools for black and white students from a particular state and cohort and their relative earnings later in life. Measures of school quality can explain roughly 25 percent of the convergence in black–white relative earnings between cohorts born in 1910–1919 and those born in 1940–1949, and 15–20 percent of the overall growth in black–white relative earnings between 1960 and 1980.

In our view, the evidence suggests that changes in school quality are responsible for some, but by no means all, of the narrowing of the black–white earnings gap between 1960 and 1980. Given the limited nature of the school quality information currently available, and measurement errors induced by interstate mobility of children, our estimates may well understate the role of school quality. Data on other dimensions of school quality, such as teacher education or experience, could possibly increase the explanatory power of measured school quality. Nevertheless, a significant share of the earnings gains made by black workers between 1970 and 1980 arose through increases in the relative earnings of continuing cohorts of older black workers. If the quality of education is a permanent attribute of individuals (as we have assumed), these changes cannot be explained by school quality effects.

Appendix A: Description of Census Data

Results in Tables 2.1–2.10 and Appendix B use data from the 1960, 1970, and 1980 Censuses. The 1980 Census sample is taken from the Public-Use A Sample, which is a self-weighting sample of 5 percent of the U.S. population. The 1970 Census sample is taken from two 1 percent Public-Use samples: the 1 percent State Sample (5% Form) and the 1 percent State Sample (15% Form). Thus, in 1970 we have a self-weighting 2 percent sample of the population. The 1960 Census sample is taken from the 1 percent Public-Use Sample, and is a self-weighting sample of 1 percent of the U.S. population.

To the extent possible, we constructed the extracts from each Census in a similar fashion. Year of birth is derived from information on current age and quarter of birth. The extracts only include men born in the 48 continental states whose race is identified as "white" or "black," and who worked at least one week in the previous year. In 1970 and 1980 individuals with imputed information on age, race, sex, education, weeks worked, or annual earnings are excluded from the sample. The imputation flags available in the 1960 Census are limited; our extract of the 1960 Census excludes individuals with imputed age. In each Census extract the weekly wage is calculated as the ratio of annual earnings to weeks worked in the preceding year. We exclude individuals whose real weekly wage (in 1979 dollars) is less than $35 or greater than $2,501. The 1960 and 1970 Censuses report weeks of work and annual earnings in several intervals. We converted the interval estimates of weeks worked to continuous amounts by assigning the mean of each interval, which we estimated from the 1980 Census. Interval estimates of annual earnings were converted to continuous dollars by taking the midpoint of each interval.

The samples used in Tables 2.1, 2.2, 2.3, and 2.5 use men born in all 48 states. The samples used in Table 2.4 are based on men born in the southern region (using the Census Bureau's definition of the southern region). The data underlying the estimates in Tables 2.6–2.8 consist of men born in the eighteen segregated states who resided in a metropolitan area of one of nine states (Illinois, Michigan, Indiana, Wisconsin, Ohio, Pennsylvania, New York, New Jersey, California) when the Census took place. The data in Tables 2.9 and 2.10 are based on men born in the eighteen segregated states, regardless of their residence. Table 2.6 is estimated from a sample of 9,677 blacks and 18,778 whites. The sample sizes for the first-step estimates used in Tables 2.7–2.8 and Tables 2.9–2.10 are below.

Sample size Tables 2.7–2.8			Sample size Tables 2.9–2.10		
Year	Blacks	Whites	Year	Blacks	Whites
1960	5,826	9,884	1960	19,731	75,561
1970	12,793	25,600	1970	42,683	193,182
1980	21,467	41,120	1980	67,432	329,695

Appendix B

Decomposition of Average Wages: Southern-Born Men (estimated standard errors in parentheses)

	1960		1970		1980		Black–White		
	Whites	Blacks	Whites	Blacks	Whites	Blacks	1960	1970	1980
1900–1909:									
Number	14,055	4,331							
Mn log wage	4,461	4,057					-0.404		
Std dev	0.603	0.586					(0.010)		
Mean ed	8.808	6.106					-2.702		
Beta-ed	0.057	0.020					-0.037		
Std(beta)	(0.002)	(0.004)					(0.004)		
Weight	0.170	0.182							
1910–1919:									
Number	20,136	6,171	32,811	8,288					
Mn log wage	4,534	4,119	4,972	4,568			-0.414	-0.404	
Std dev	0.567	0.561	0.604	0.578			(0.008)	(0.007)	
Mean ed	9.608	7.069	9.910	7.342			-2.540	-2.568	
Beta-ed	0.060	0.032	0.057	0.032			-0.028	-0.025	
Std(beta)	(0.002)	(0.003)	(0.001)	(0.003)			(0.003)	(0.003)	
Weight	0.243	0.260	0.186	0.198					
1920–1929:									
Number	24,813	7,025	43,456	10,376	78,749	16,460			
Mn log wage	4,539	4,125	5,079	4,672	5,832	5,507	-0.414	-0.407	-0.326
Std dev	0.511	0.533	0.565	0.554	0.595	0.601	(0.007)	(0.006)	(0.005)
Mean ed	10.397	8.356	10.787	8.773	11.233	9.432	-2.041	-2.013	-1.800
Beta-ed	0.068	0.046	0.065	0.040	0.051	0.034	-0.022	-0.025	-0.017
Std(beta)	(0.001)	(0.003)	(0.001)	(0.002)	(0.001)	(0.002)	(0.003)	(0.002)	(0.002)
Weight	0.300	0.296	0.247	0.248	0.173	0.164			

Appendix B (continued)

Decomposition of Average Wages: Southern-Born Men (estimated standard errors in parentheses)

	1960		1970		1980		Black–White		
	Whites	Blacks	Whites	Blacks	Whites	Blacks	1960	1970	1980
1930–1939:									
Number	23,705	6,210	44,811	10,822	92,427	20,823			
Mn log wage	4.208	3.888	5.045	4.693	5.874	5.580	-0.320	-0.352	-0.295
Std dev	0.549	0.544	0.510	0.532	0.557	0.577	(0.008)	(0.006)	(0.004)
Mean ed	11.027	9.453	11.553	10.155	12.117	10.948	-1.574	-1.398	-1.169
Beta-ed	0.087	0.063	0.075	0.062	0.064	0.054	(0.003)	(0.002)	(0.002)
Std(beta)	(0.002)	(0.003)	(0.001)	(0.002)	(0.001)	(0.002)	-0.025	-0.014	-0.011
Weight	0.287	0.262	0.255	0.258	0.203	0.207	(0.003)	(0.002)	(0.002)
1940–1949:									
Number			54,879	12,400	130,661	28,728			
Mn log wage			4.692	4.492	5.792	5.544		-0.200	-0.248
Std dev			0.563	0.567	0.530	0.558		(0.006)	(0.004)
Mean ed			12.107	11.074	13.033	12.119		-1.033	-0.914
Beta-ed			0.092	0.084	0.078	0.074		(0.003)	(0.002)
Std(beta)			(0.001)	(0.003)	(0.001)	(0.002)		-0.008	-0.005
Weight			0.312	0.296	0.287	0.286		(0.003)	(0.002)
1950–1959:									
Number					153,048	34,561			
Mn log wage					5.380	5.188			-0.193
Std dev					0.555	0.571			(0.003)
Mean ed					12.781	12.217			-0.563
Beta-ed					0.067	0.084			0.017
Std(beta)					(0.001)	(0.002)			(0.002)
Weight					0.336	0.344			
All									
Mean log wage	4.430	4.049	4.930	4.604	5.677	5.423	-0.380	-0.326	-0.253
	(0.002)	(0.004)	(0.001)	(0.003)	(0.001)	(0.002)	(0.004)	(0.003)	(0.002)

Notes: "Number" refers to number of workers in cohort. "Mn log wage" refers to the mean of log average weekly earnings in the cohort. "Std dev" refers to the standard deviation of log weekly earnings in the cohort. Beta-ed refers to the estimated return to education in a regression that controls for potential experience and its square, marital status, region of residence, and residence in an SMSA. Std(beta) refers to the estimated standard error of the return to education. Entries in the columns labeled "Black–White" refer to differences between means for blacks and whites in the same cohort. "Weight" refers to the ratio of the number of workers in the cohort to the total number of male workers age 21–60 in the relevant census.

Appendix C

State	Black schools			White schools			White to black ratio		
	Teacher salary	Pupils/ teachers	Term length	Teacher salary	Pupils/ teachers	Term length	Teacher salary	Pupils/ teachers	Term length
				1910–1919 birth cohort					
Alabama	617	55.5	117.8	1,482	35.4	146.9	2.40	0.64	1.25
Arkansas	721	50.4	124.1	1,278	37.8	143.8	1.77	0.75	1.16
Delaware	NA	33.2	NA	NA	29.3	NA	NA	0.88	NA
Florida	NA	45.4	NA	NA	30.4	NA	NA	0.67	NA
Georgia	597	52.9	132.0	1,520	35.8	147.4	2.55	0.68	1.12
Kentucky	NA	40.1	NA	NA	39.2	NA	NA	0.98	NA
Louisiana	848	56.8	109.8	2,046	31.1	170.6	2.41	0.55	1.55
Maryland	1,687	37.8	171.5	2,636	32.0	186.5	1.56	0.85	1.09
Mississippi	NA	55.8	NA	NA	29.7	NA	NA	0.53	NA
Missouri	NA	29.3	NA	NA	29.4	NA	NA	1.00	NA
North Carolina	837	47.8	135.4	1,575	34.4	148.2	1.88	0.72	1.09
Oklahoma	NA	36.2	NA	NA	35.9	NA	NA	0.99	NA
South Carolina	509	60.1	98.0	1,740	30.8	160.1	3.42	0.51	1.63
Tennessee	NA	45.9	NA	NA	37.8	NA	NA	0.82	NA
Texas	NA	45.3	NA	NA	31.2	NA	NA	0.69	NA
Virginia	896	43.0	145.7	1,590	31.7	165.0	1.77	0.74	1.13
West Virginia	1,759	27.7	NA	1,778	27.6	NA	1.01	1.00	NA
D.C.	NA	31.1	NA	Na	29.9	NA	NA	0.96	NA
				1920–1929 birth cohort					
Alabama	869	45.3	136.8	1,915	32.8	155.9	2.20	0.72	1.14
Arkansas	826	44.7	132.3	1,467	34.5	156.0	1.78	0.77	1.18
Delaware	3,165	31.0	182.5	3,579	27.1	183.0	1.13	0.87	1.00
Florida	1,201	35.9	159.0	2,529	29.0	169.5	2.11	0.81	1.07
Georgia	747	43.9	139.6	1,934	31.7	159.9	2.59	0.72	1.15
Kentucky	NA	32.5	NA	NA	34.5	NA	NA	1.06	NA
Louisiana	1,056	47.5	131.9	2,510	29.5	176.3	2.38	0.62	1.34
Maryland	2,975	35.4	181.0	3,709	32.2	187.6	1.25	0.91	1.04
Mississippi	630	48.5	116.2	1,729	31.3	157.3	2.74	0.65	1.35
Missouri	NA	32.0	NA	NA	27.5	NA	NA	0.86	NA
North Carolina	1,367	40.9	156.0	2,112	34.8	162.0	1.54	0.85	1.04
Oklahoma	2,032	30.6	168.9	2,324	32.5	172.5	1.14	1.06	1.02
South Carolina	749	45.3	127.3	2,105	29.0	173.1	2.81	0.64	1.36
Tennessee	NA	38.8	160.5	NA	31.6	165.2	NA	0.81	1.03
Texas	1,553	37.8	150.5	2,414	28.5	167.4	1.55	0.75	1.11
Virginia	1,297	38.7	166.0	2,257	31.9	172.6	1.74	0.82	1.04
West Virginia	2,550	27.7	173.2	2,539	27.2	172.1	1.00	0.98	0.99
D.C.	5,284	33.8	177.7	5,263	30.0	177.5	1.00	0.89	1.00

Appendix C (continued)

State	Black schools			White schools			White to black ratio		
	Teacher salary	Pupils/ teachers	Term length	Teacher salary	Pupils/ teachers	Term length	Teacher salary	Pupils/ teachers	Term length
				1930–1939 birth cohort					
Alabama	1,880	36.3	165.6	2,710	29.8	169.6	1.44	0.82	1.02
Arkansas	1,452	38.4	155.4	2,156	30.6	168.3	1.48	0.80	1.08
Delaware	3,927	27.5	181.8	4,214	23.9	181.5	1.07	0.87	1.00
Florida	2,582	29.0	173.7	3,622	25.6	176.0	1.40	0.88	1.01
Georgia	1,594	35.2	169.0	2,604	27.9	175.5	1.63	0.79	1.04
Kentucky	NA	26.8	172.9	NA	29.9	164.6	NA	1.12	0.95
Louisiana	2,184	37.2	162.8	3,594	26.6	178.8	1.65	0.72	1.10
Maryland	4,160	32.8	185.1	4,501	29.8	184.7	1.08	0.91	1.00
Mississippi	852	41.8	136.7	2,244	29.3	168.1	2.63	0.70	1.23
Missouri	NA	31.7	189.4	NA	26.8	179.8	NA	0.85	0.95
North Carolina	2,886	34.7	175.7	3,085	30.7	176.0	1.07	0.88	1.00
Oklahoma	3,225	24.6	175.9	3,220	27.0	176.2	1.00	1.10	1.00
South Carolina	1,628	34.1	162.3	2,718	27.1	177.7	1.67	0.79	1.09
Tennessee	NA	33.8	172.1	NA	29.1	169.8	NA	0.86	0.99
Texas	2,776	30.0	168.8	3,419	26.7	174.3	1.23	0.89	1.03
Virginia	2,505	32.9	179.2	2,934	28.2	179.6	1.17	0.86	1.00
West Virginia	3,198	26.3	174.3	3,223	27.3	173.7	1.01	1.04	1.00
D.C.	5,304	31.2	176.0	5,367	26.6	176.0	1.01	0.85	1.00
				1940–1949 birth cohort					
Alabama	3,809	31.4	175.8	3,959	28.7	175.7	1.04	0.91	1.00
Arkansas	2,929	34.5	172.6	3,262	28.1	173.4	1.11	0.81	1.00
Delaware	5,705	24.0	181.1	5,782	21.8	180.0	1.01	0.91	0.99
Florida	5,038	27.8	180.0	5,298	27.6	180.0	1.05	0.99	1.00
Georgia	3,720	31.7	179.4	4,012	28.0	179.7	1.08	0.88	1.00
Kentucky	NA	26.0	174.1	NA	27.5	172.2	NA	1.06	0.99
Louisiana	4,524	32.2	178.3	5,027	26.0	179.4	1.11	0.81	1.01
Maryland	5,779	27.4	181.8	5,828	26.3	181.6	1.01	0.96	1.00
Mississippi	2,261	38.4	163.9	3,286	27.2	170.1	1.45	0.71	1.04
Missouri	NA	28.3	185.7	NA	26.4	181.7	NA	0.93	0.98
North Carolina	4,427	31.3	180.0	4,377	28.7	180.0	0.99	0.92	1.00
Oklahoma	4,729	24.7	175.2	4,655	25.7	176.3	0.98	1.04	1.01
South Carolina	3,380	32.6	178.3	3,784	27.5	179.9	1.12	0.84	1.01
Tennessee	NA	30.4	176.6	NA	28.1	175.8	NA	0.92	1.00
Texas	4,774	26.6	174.5	5,010	25.8	174.6	1.05	0.97	1.00
Virginia	4,160	28.8	180.1	4,192	26.1	180.1	1.01	0.91	1.00
West Virginia	4,113	25.9	174.0	4,133	26.9	173.9	1.00	1.04	1.00
D.C.	6,572	28.3	177.8	6,720	27.1	178.5	1.02	0.96	1.00

Notes: Entries are weighted averages of school quality variables for men born in each state. Weights are based on distributions of educational attainment from samples of workingmen in the 1970 Census. NA means not available.

3

School Resources and Student Outcomes: An Overview of the Literature and New Evidence from North and South Carolina

Thirty years after the publication of the Coleman report (Coleman et al. 1966) marks a fitting time to reassess the connection between school resources and student achievement. Coleman's original study and much of the subsequent literature it spawned are widely interpreted as showing that higher levels of school resources, such as lower class sizes, have no effect on student test scores. For example, Hanushek's (1986) influential survey of the literature concluded: "There appears to be no strong or systematic relationship between school expenditures and student performance."

The conclusion that schooling inputs like class size and teacher pay have no impact on student achievement has come under renewed scrutiny for two main reasons. First, several meta-analyses – quantitative summaries of the estimates in the literature – suggest that greater resources do in fact lead to higher test scores. The authors of these studies argue that the literature contains too many positive estimates of the effect of resources on test scores to have occurred by chance, if resources truly do not matter (Glass and Smith 1978; McGiverin, Gilman and Tillitski 1989; Hedges and Stock 1983). Observe, for example, that Hanushek (1996a) counts more than twice as many

This chapter is a revised version of: Card, D., Krueger, A. (1996). School Resources and Student Outcomes: An Overview of the Literature and New Evidence from North and South Carolina, in: Journal of Economic Perspectives 10, 31–50. The study was funded in part by a grant from the National Institute of Child Health and Development. The authors thank Francine Blau, Brad De Long, and Timothy Taylor for comments and suggestions on earlier drafts.

positive than negative estimates of the effect of expenditures per pupil on student achievement, among the 141 "studies" that report their signs. If each estimate had a 50–50 chance of being positive or negative, the odds of observing so many positive estimates by chance would be less than one in a million.[1] Low power of the individual estimates may explain why the preponderance of studies find statistically insignificant effects, while the combined literature points in the opposite direction. Meta-analysis also provides methods for accounting for the magnitude of estimated effects in the literature, as well as their signs. Hedges, Laine, and Greenwald (1994) conduct a meta-analysis of the studies surveyed by Hanushek (1986) and conclude that "the data are more consistent with a pattern that includes at least some positive relation between dollars spent on education and output, than with a pattern of no effects or negative effects."

Second, and more germane to this chapter, is a body of literature that shifts attention away from test scores and focuses instead on how school resources affect students' educational attainment and earnings. Studying the impact of school resources on long-term outcomes like educational attainment and earnings is critical because test scores are an imperfect measure of the value of school outputs. For example, Murnane, Willett, and Levy (1995) find that adding a standardized mathematics test score to a wage equation for male workers increases the explanatory power of the model by only about 2 percentage points. Heckman (1995) concludes, "neither g [a measure of generalized intelligence] nor AFQT [the Armed Forces Qualifying Test] explains all that much of the variance in log wages." In contrast to the literature on test scores, a number of studies have found a positive and statistically significant association between educational resources and students' educational attainment and earnings.

Researchers face a number of obstacles in studying the connection between school resources and economic outcomes. One difficulty is the need to wait until students finish school and join the labor market. Consequently, researchers must have access to data sets that report *both* the current earnings and completed education of adults *and* information on the resources available in the schools they attended. Furthermore, since differences in the structure of the labor market may affect the reward to skills, and thus the measured impact of school resources, evaluations of the economic returns to school resources may require nontrivial identification assumptions, or complex econometric modelling, or both. Another problem is that compared to test score outcomes, the variance in earnings is large, making it more difficult to detect modest effects of school quality

Omitted variables, such as parental background or state-level political variables, may bias the measured effect of school resources. (Of course, a parallel problem arises in nonexperimental studies of the effect of school resources on test scores.) Since the children of wealthier parents often attend schools with smaller class sizes and better-paid teachers, and since family background is thought to exert an independent effect on children's economic outcomes, there may be a spurious positive association between school resources and measured outcomes, even if school resources have no effect per se. On the other hand, students with weaker backgrounds may be assigned to remedial classes with higher resources per student, inducing a spurious negative correlation between school resources and student outcomes.

A study of economic outcomes requires a theoretical framework that incorporates the diverse interactions between family background, school inputs, educational attainment, and earnings. We therefore begin this chapter by outlining the key implications of such a model. This framework is then used to interpret estimates of the effect of school resources on educational attainment and earnings. Our reading of the empirical literature is that school resources tend to be positively associated with earnings and educational attainment, but that the relationship is not always robust to specific features of the data set or empirical specification.

A difficult problem for most studies in the literature, including our own, is the presence of omitted variables that may be correlated with school quality. A potentially confounding problem is that many studies rely on aggregated (that is, school district or state-level) school quality data rather than school- or classroom-level data. One way to overcome these problems is to follow students who were exposed to dramatically different educational resources for reasons having little to do with their own ability or their parents' wealth. The vastly different treatment of black and white students during the segregation era provides such a setting. One of the most dramatic "natural experiments" involving school resources is furnished by North Carolina and South Carolina. Early in the twentieth century, the level of resources devoted to black students was much lower in South Carolina than it was in North Carolina. Because resources were diverted from black schools to white schools, the reverse was true for whites: school resources were greater for white students in South Carolina than they were in North Carolina. By mid-century, school resources had converged to roughly similar levels for blacks and whites in the Carolinas. The wide disparities in school quality for black and white students in North and South Carolina in the early part of the century were caused by different, and arguably exogenous, factors than those that generate variability in school resources in most data sets today. Did these differences in school resources lead to corresponding differences in educational attainment and earnings? Did the economic outcomes for succeeding cohorts converge as school resources converged? Based on our analysis of 1960, 1970, and 1980 census micro data, the answers to these two questions seem to be "yes" and "yes."

3.1. Theoretical Framework

A useful framework for interpreting much of the literature on schooling, earnings, and school quality can be summarized by four theoretical propositions.[2]

Proposition 1: Earnings rise with educational attainment. If two individuals are otherwise identical, the person with more education tends to earn more. This proposition is based on one of the most firmly established empirical regularities in economics. A positive association between earnings and education holds across individuals even if one controls for other factors, such as IQ, family background, and work experience (Griliches 1977). It also holds across identical twins with different levels of education and between groups who obtained different levels of schooling because of compulsory schooling laws or because they grew up near a college (Angrist and Krueger 1991; Kane and Rouse 1993; Harmon and Walker 1995; Ashenfelter and Krueger 1994; Card 1995). Although some of the observed correlation between earnings and education may be due to omitted variables – for example, those with more education may end up with higher earnings because of unobserved ability or family background factors – our reading of the literature is that this component is relatively small, on the order of 10–15 percent of the total effect. Further, random measurement errors in self-reported schooling may bias downward the observed slope between earnings and education by a similar magnitude.

Figure 3.1
Hypothetical Relationship

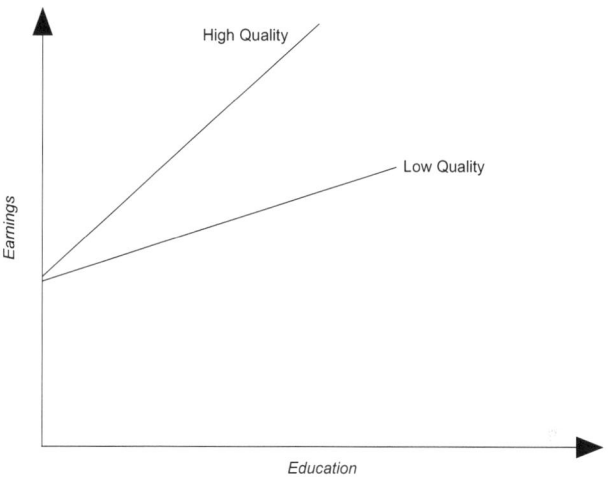

Proposition 2: The marginal payoff to additional schooling is higher for those who attend higher quality schools. This proposition is almost tautological: one would expect students who have access to higher quality schools to benefit more per year of schooling than students who have access to lower quality schools.[3] Figure 3.1, which shows the earnings-education profile rotating counterclockwise from the Y-intercept for those who attend higher quality schools, illustrates the notion that higher quality schooling increases the slope of the earnings–schooling relationship. Note, however, that it is an open question whether measured school resources (such as the pupil–teacher ratio) are related to the more abstract concept of "school quality."

Proposition 3: If the monetary payoff to an additional year of schooling rises, some students will attend school longer. The observed relationship between school quality and earnings that emerges from a complete model of schooling and earnings is more complicated than that depicted in Figure 3.1 for several reasons. As school quality increases, some students will attend school longer. This response may arise because students react to the economic incentives created by a higher payoff to schooling, or because school is more pleasant if quality is higher. In either event, a wide class of economic models predicts that improved school quality benefits some students by inducing them to stay in school longer, and this increase in educational attainment leads to higher pay.

Figure 3.2
Observed Relationship

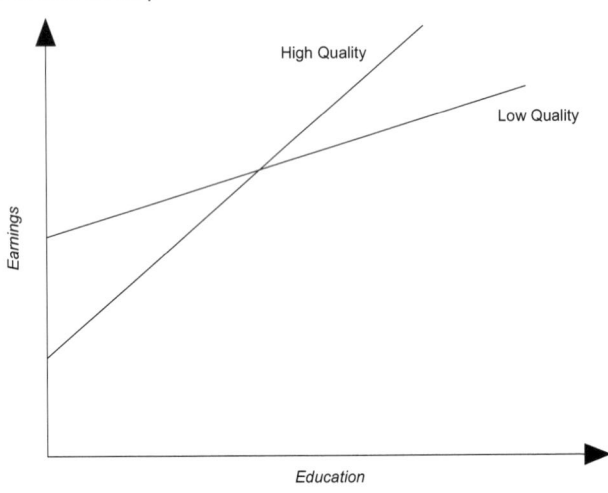

Proposition 4: A portion of the observed association between earnings and education is due to unobserved factors that are jointly correlated with both variables. In other words, those who select higher education tend to have greater earnings ability, irrespective of their education. Moreover, students who attend school longer in response to improved school quality (the implication from Proposition 3) will tend to be drawn disproportionately from the pool of more able students at lower grade levels. An interesting implication of this proposition is that the *observed* earnings–education profile will not rotate around the Y-intercept at a zero level of education as in Figure 3.1, but at a higher level of education, as illustrated in Figure 3.2. To understand why, consider what happens to the group of workers with the lowest level of education. If school quality improves, the more able workers of this group will attend school longer, lowering the average earnings ability of those who remain at a low level of education, and thus lowering the Y-intercept in Figure 3.2. As school quality improves, the shrinking group of students with a low level of education will increasingly consist of less able individuals, who will appear to earn less, on average.

Omitted factors such as family background or student ability complicate the observed relationship between earnings and measured school quality in other ways as well. Suppose, for example, that students from wealthier families tend to stay in school longer and that these students would tend to earn more later on because of their family connections, regardless of their higher education. In addition, suppose that wealthier families demand smaller class sizes, even though class size has no effect on actual school "quality" (that is, suppose there is no causal effect of school spending on education or earnings). In this case, the data will show a positive association between school spending and both educational attainment and earnings, although both correlations are spurious, and merely reflect the failure to account for the independent effect of family wealth.

Nevertheless, the presence of omitted family background effects will not necessarily bias the correlation between measured school quality and the *slope* of the earnings-schooling relationship. To understand why, continue to suppose that children from wealthier family backgrounds in a given school or school district tend to have higher education and higher earnings, so that part of the measured payoff to each additional year of schooling reflects omitted-variables bias. Under reasonable conditions, the magnitude of this bias will be similar for students from high-quality and low-quality school systems. Thus, comparing across school systems, the measured return to each additional year of schooling would be biased upward by a similar amount. In this case, *differences* in the slopes of the earnings-schooling relationship across higher and lower quality school systems will reflect true differences in the quality of schooling.

3.2. Empirical Findings

For a detailed survey of the empirical literature on the link between school quality and economic outcomes, the interested reader might begin with Betts (1996) and Card and Krueger (1996a). Here, we concentrate on summarizing the effect of two particular educational inputs–expenditures per pupil and the pupil–teacher ratio on educational attainment and earnings. We emphasize the pupil–teacher ratio because differences in class size account for close to one-half of the variation in expenditure per pupil across school districts, and because changes in class size are the object of many educational reform proposals.

The theoretical framework outlined above suggests two empirical strategies. In one approach, the structural earnings–schooling relationship illustrated in Figure 3.2 can be estimated, along with the effect of school quality, as measured by expenditures per pupil or the pupil–teacher ratio, on educational attainment. Alternatively, one can estimate the reduced form relationship between earnings and school resources; that is, a regression of earnings on measures of school quality like expenditures per pupil or the pupil–teacher ratio, without holding educational attainment constant.

The earliest wave of studies on school resources and economic outcomes, conducted in the late 1960s and 1970s, followed a third approach: researchers simply added measures of school quality to a standard human capital wage equation. Such models typically used educational attainment, work experience, parental education, urban residence, and, in some cases, IQ as explanatory variables. Earnings were based on individual observations. When a variable representing school quality was added, it was usually measured by average expenditures per pupil at the state or district level. All of these studies found that spending per student was positively associated with students' subsequent earnings, and most of the estimates were statistically significant at conventional levels.[4] The estimated elasticities from this literature fall in a fairly tight range: a 10 percent increase in school spending leads to about a 1 to 2 percent increase in subsequent earnings.

These specifications imply that the earnings–education profile has a fixed slope and that differences in school quality make this relationship shift up and down in a parallel fashion, as opposed to a tilting of the profile shown in Figure 3.1. A potentially undesirable feature of this specification is that it implies that more school resources raise (or lower) earnings by the same amount, regardless of the length of time that students are exposed to the greater resources in school. Additionally, because the studies hold educational attainment constant, the possibility that improved school quality might lead to higher wages by encouraging students to attend school longer is missed.

A second wave of studies allowed for school resources to have a differential effect on the slope *and* intercept of the earnings–education relationship. For example, Akin and Garfinkel (1980) estimate several wage regressions using micro data from the Panel Study on Income Dynamics (PSID). The dependent variable in their specification is the log of the wage rate (averaged over 5 years), and the key explanatory variables of interest are state expenditures per student (in the decade in which the workers would have attended school), expenditures per student times years of education, and years of education. Their results indicate that greater spending per student is associated with higher earnings, but contrary to the prediction in Figure 3.2, the effect comes about from an upward shift in the Y-intercept rather than a steepening of the education gradient. Link, Radledge and Lewis (1980) replicate the Akin and Garfinkel model with the PSID as well as with the National Longitudinal Survey (NLS) of Young Men and generally find similar results.[5] Interestingly, both studies also find that if school resources are constrained to only affect the earnings-education slope, the earnings profile rotates as in Figure 3.1. Altonji and Dunn (1996) use within-family differences in school resources to estimate this type of model with data from the NLS. By looking within families, they adjust for differences in omitted family background factors. Their findings imply that a 10 percent increase in spending per student is associated with a 1.3 percent increase in earnings. Interestingly, they find the estimated effect of school resources is greater, not smaller, when family background characteristics are held constant.

A potential problem with these second-wave studies is that the reward to skills may vary systematically across geographic areas with varying levels of school resources, and workers tend to stay in the area where they grew up. For example, in the southern United States, the return to education historically has been relatively high, while wages and school spending per student were relatively low. This pattern could make it appear that higher school spending depresses the return to education, when the truth is that the south has invested less in education, keeping its return relatively high, and north–south migration has been insufficient to reduce the differential. Thus, the second-wave estimates may confound labor market effects and school resource effects

A third wave of estimates attempts to overcome problems caused by differential labor market structures across regions.[6] The conceptual experiment underlying these estimates is straightforward. Consider the workers observed in a particular labor market, say Chicago. Some workers in Chicago were educated in states with higher quality school systems and others were educated in states with lower quality schools. Among those working in Chicago, we would expect the earnings–education gradient to be steeper for workers who were educated in states with higher quality schools. A weakness of this strategy is that there may be something "unusual" about those who moved from one area to another that confounds the effect of school resources.

In Card and Krueger (1992a, see Chapter 2 in this volume), we find that, in a given set of labor markets, the earnings–education slope does tend to increase for students who were educated in states with fewer pupils per teacher, higher average teacher pay, or a longer school year. In other words, the payoff to each additional year of education is greater for workers who come from areas with more resource-intensive schools, looking within a fixed labor market. This finding is strongest when cohorts from given states are compared over time, which removes any effect of permanent state effects (such as unchanging state-level political variables). Identification of school-resource effects in these fixed-effects models comes from comparing successive cohorts of individuals from states like Alabama, which raised their school spending relative to other states like New York. Further analysis indicates that the earnings-intercept tends to decline as resources increase. In short, the earnings relationship appears to pivot around a mid-level of education, as illustrated in Figure 3.2. We found that the crossover point in Figure 3.2 occurs around the high school graduate level. Our analysis makes use of the large samples afforded by the 1980 census.

Heckman, Layne-Farrar, and Todd (1996) extend this analysis using the 1970, 1980, and 1990 censuses. When they estimate virtually the same models as ours, they find similar effects of school resources in 1980, and they find somewhat larger effects in 1970 and 1990. The finding of larger effects of school resources in 1970 and 1990 is perhaps not surprising, since the payoff to education in general was at a relatively low level in 1980. Heckman, Layne-Farrar, and Todd also find that the intercept of the earnings–education relationship declines as school resources increase.

Heckman, Layne-Farrar, and Todd (1996) expand our basic econometric specification in several important directions. When they include regional aggregate supply and demand variables, the general pattern of results holds up. But when they allow for differential school resource effects by level of education, they find that school resources have little effect on earnings for workers who have not attended school beyond high school. The only education group for which resources are significantly related to earnings are those with a college education or higher. As school resources are measured at the secondary and elementary school level, this result may seem perplexing. One interpretation, however, is that higher school quality induces the most promising students to go further in school at each grade level, so the sample at each level of education becomes more select as school resources change.[7] Nonetheless, the effects of selective educational attainment are just conjecture at this stage, and the interpretation of the earnings–quality relationship *conditional* on education is still an open question. The reduced form models, which do not condition on education, provide one way of sidestepping this issue.

Another assumption that Heckman, Layne-Farrar, and Todd (1996) relax is the restriction that school quality has the same effect on the earnings-education slope in all regions. Regional differences in supply and demand conditions may alter the payoff to skills, and hence school quality, across regions. A related issue that they address is non-random migration. Workers may selectively sort across regions based on their comparative earnings advantage. (As noted earlier, the identification of school resource effects in Chapter 2 relies on the fact that migrants from states with different levels of school quality end up working in a common labor market.) As a partial control for selective migration, Heckman, Layne-Farrar, and Todd control for the distance between the workers' region of origin and destination. These extensions weaken the effect of school resources and suggest that the return to higher school quality, as measured by the pupil–teacher ratio, varies across regions.[8]

The finding that school quality raises wages is not found in every data set. For example, using data from the National Longitudinal Survey of Youth (NLSY), Betts (1995) finds a statistically insignificant effect of school resources (measured by the high school's teacher–pupil ratio, teacher salary, and so on) on the earnings of young workers – on either the slope or the intercept in Figure 3.2. These data have important limitations for this purpose, however. The standard errors of the estimates from the NLSY are large, making it difficult to rule out small positive effects with a reasonable degree of confidence.[9] In addition, the sample has an average age of just 23, which means that many of the individuals have not yet finished school or settled into their careers, so wage effects for those with higher levels of schooling may be difficult to find. Nonetheless, Betts and others have interpreted his findings as evidence that school resources do not matter when the resources are measured at the school level, as opposed to the state or district level. We return to this point below.

Recall that school resources may also influence educational attainment. A majority of the studies of which we are aware have found positive and statistically significant effects of smaller class size on educational attainment. Some of these studies use micro data on individual's educational outcomes and school resources, while others use state- or district-level data. For example, Sander (1993) relates high school graduation rates to the pupil–teacher ratio across 154 Illinois school districts and for a subsample of 86 school districts in which there is only one high school in the district. In both cases, he finds that a 10 percent decrease in the pupil–teacher ratio is associated with about a 1.5 percentage point increase in the graduation rate. Heckman, Layne-Farrar, and Todd (1996) likewise find that a reduction in a state's pupil-teacher ratio tends to reduce the fraction of high school dropouts from that state and to raise the fraction of individuals who graduate from high school and (especially) college.

An advantage of the reduced form estimation approach – which entails a regression of earnings on school quality measures without controlling for educational attainment – is that it incorporates all the possible effects of school resources: on educational attainment, on the earnings–education profile, and on the intercept of the earnings-schooling relationship. In Chapter 2, we estimate a reduced form regression of (log) weekly wages on the state's pupil–teacher ratio, the worker's age and marital status, and dummy variables for residence in a metropolitan area, the state where the worker lives, and (in some models) the state where the worker was born. These models are relatively parsimonious, and so they are particularly susceptible to confounding effects from omitted variables. Nevertheless, the reduced form models have the advantage of making less restrictive identifying assumptions, and they are probably the most comparable specifications estimated across papers in the literature. Our reduced form estimates (based on the 1980 census) imply that a 10 percent reduction in the average pupil–teacher ratio is associated with a 1.1 percent increase in weekly earnings. Betts's (1995) estimates, which are based on NLSY earnings data and high school-level schooling data, imply that a 10 percent reduction in the average teacher–pupil ratio leads to a 0.4 percent increase in earnings.[10] Using the High School and Beyond Survey, Grogger's (1996) reduced form estimates imply that a 10 percent increase in mean spending per student leads to a 0.7 percent increase in wages.

To summarize, much of the literature finds evidence of a positive and statistically significant relationship between school resources and earnings. By our count, some two-thirds of the two dozen studies on the impact of school spending or class size on earnings have found a statistically significant, positive effect of school resources

(Card and Krueger 1996a). Positive effects of class size on educational attainment are also typically found in the literature.

But we do not wish to paint an overly optimistic picture. Several important studies find statistically insignificant effects of varying school resources. Heckman, Layne-Farrar, and Todd (1996) have shown that the effect of school resources measured in Card and Krueger (1992a, Chapter 2 in this volume) break down when some of the identifying assumptions (like linear education) are relaxed. Moreover, there are always questions in observational studies as to whether relevant variables have been left out. Because wealthier families tend to invest more in their children at home, and to live in communities with better endowed schools, omitted family background may be a particular problem.

Betts (1996) and Hanushek (1996a) note that biases created by omitted variables are possibly larger in studies that measure school resources at a more aggregative level, like the state or school district level. Hanushek, Rivkin, and Taylor (1996) argue that state political variables are a particular problem for aggregate studies. Although this is possible, the fact that the models reported in Card and Krueger (1992a) and Heckman, Layne-Farrar, and Todd (1996) that include state-fixed effects tend to show *larger* effects of school quality, rather than smaller, suggests to us that omitted state-level variables may lead to the opposite bias. In any event, the argument that omitted variables are a bigger problem for studies that use aggregate school quality data would be stronger if such omitted variables could be identified, and if their inclusion in the regression models was shown to attenuate the effect of aggregate school resource measures.

A related problem concerns the endogeneity of school resources within schools (or within school districts). Children who perform poorly may be assigned to smaller classes, for example. With individual-level resource data, this may lead to downward-biased estimates of the effects of school resources. On the other hand, highly motivated children may be attracted to magnet schools with higher resources per pupil, leading to upward-biased estimates. In either case, the use of aggregated school quality measures will tend to lessen the biases of endogenous school resources within schools or districts. Finally, measurement error in school resources should be a cause for concern. Even the best micro data sets tend to have school resource data for one year, providing only a snapshot of the student's educational career, while district- or state-level resource data are more likely to "average out" year-to-year fluctuations in resources. Aggregated data reduce or eliminate random measurement errors that make it difficult to detect school resource effects using micro-level school quality data.

Ideally, these sources of bias could be eliminated by a randomized experiment, in which students are assigned to classes with different pupil–teacher ratios (or differences in other resources) and then followed over time. We are aware of only one large-scale randomized experiment involving class sizes, which pertained to elementary students in Tennessee (Mosteller 1995). This experiment showed a positive effect of lower class size on test scores at the lowest grades. We know of no randomized experiment that has been used to evaluate economic outcomes of schooling. In the absence of a true random experiment, it may be useful to consider the evidence generated by "natural experiments" – situations in which large differences in school resources were provided to seemingly similar individuals for arbitrary reasons. One interesting example of such a situation is the experience of black and white students in North and South Carolina, to which we now turn.

3.3. A Comparison of North and South Carolina

Racially segregated schooling led to profound differences in the level of school resources available to black and white children in different areas of the United States in the first half of this century. A striking comparison is provided by two neighboring states: North Carolina and South Carolina. Figure 3.3 displays the pupil–teacher ratio in black and white schools in the two states over the past century.[11] Although the Carolinas are similar in some respects, they differed dramatically in terms of the school resources they provided for black and white children. Whereas North Carolina was among the most progressive of the nonborder Southern states vis-à-vis black schooling, South Carolina was among the least progressive (Harlan 1958). For white students, the pattern was reversed: schools were better funded in South Carolina than in North Carolina throughout the first half of the century. In 1916, for example, black schools had 72 students per teacher in South Carolina and 47 in North Carolina, while white schools had 41 students per teacher in North Carolina and 37 in South Carolina. The school term was also much shorter for blacks in South Carolina than in North Carolina, while the opposite pattern held for whites. In both states, the pupil–teacher ratios in black and white schools converged to almost the same level by the late 1960s.[12]

What caused the great disparities in school resources for black and white students in North and South Carolina? Researchers from Bond (1934) to Margo (1990) have observed that in areas where blacks were more numerous, a greater share of school resources were diverted from the black schools to white schools, raising the resources in white schools and depressing them in black schools. An exclusionary political system enabled this discriminatory practice to persist until the 1960s (Boozer, Krueger, and Wolkon 1992). Viewed in this light, the Carolina's varying experiences largely came about by historical accident. South Carolina had a much higher proportion of blacks in its population than did North Carolina (58% of South Carolinians were black in 1900 versus 33% of North Carolinians), in part because of historical differences in slave populations driven by different cropping patterns (Fogel and Engerman 1974). In South Carolina, cotton was the most important crop, whereas in North Carolina, tobacco was more important.

Figure 3.3

Pupil–Teacher Ratio by Race: North Carolina and South Carolina

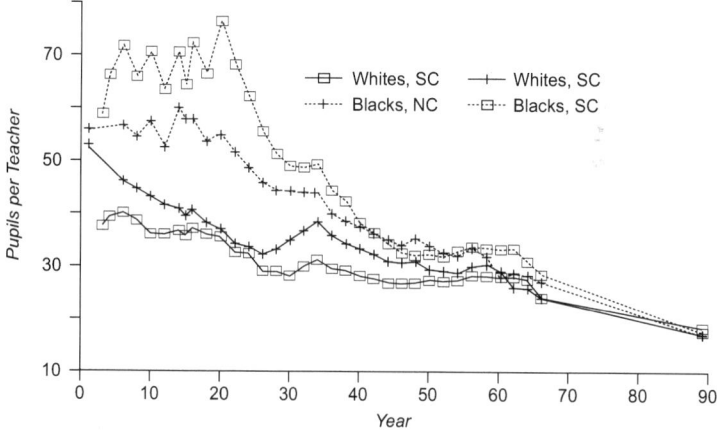

The experiences of North and South Carolina provide a potentially useful laboratory for evaluating the effect of school resources. A very different set of forces led to differences in school resources for students in these two states than the factors that determine resource decisions in a typical school district today. If omitted variables plague aggregate studies of earnings, we would not expect to find earnings and educational attainment mirroring racial differences in school resources in South and North Carolina over time, unless these omitted state variables somehow changed along with the allocation of school resources. It is therefore valuable to check whether the convergence in school resources for whites and blacks from North and South Carolina led to a parallel convergence in the relative levels of educational attainment and earnings for individuals from the two states.

Figure 3.4

Average Education Levels by Cohort: Men Born in North Carolina and Men Born in South Carolina

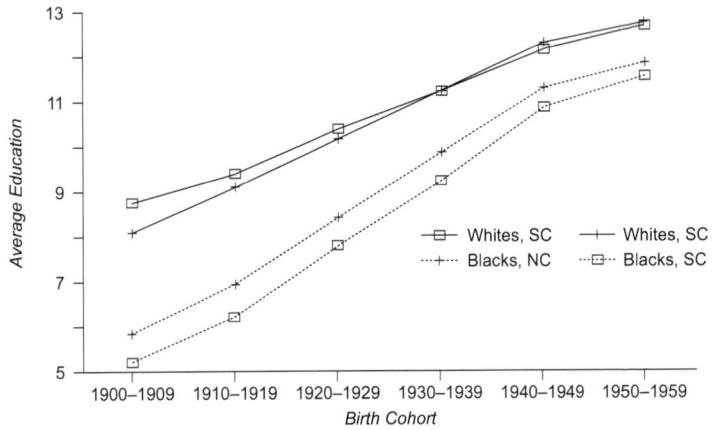

We used micro data from the 1960, 1970, and 1980 censuses to examine trends in education and earnings for succeeding generations of men born in the Carolinas between 1900 and 1959. We restrict the sample to men because labor force participation rates were much lower for women. For convenience, we group together men from 10-year birth cohorts. (The details of the sample and statistical analysis are described in more depth in the Appendix.) Figure 3.4 shows trends in average educational attainment by race for each cohort of North and South Carolinians. The corresponding differences in average education by race and cohort are presented in columns 2 and 5 of Table 3.1. Examination of the data in the figure and table suggests that trends in relative education between the two states roughly mirror the trends in relative school resources by race. For the 1900–1909 birth cohort, blacks in North Carolina had about 14 fewer pupils per teacher than blacks in South Carolina. This gap was associated with 0.65 more years of education, on average, for blacks born in North Carolina. For whites in the same cohort, the situation was reversed. Whites in South Carolina had about 4 fewer pupils per teacher, and this gap was associated with a 0.67 year education gap in favor of South Carolina-born whites. For both blacks and whites, the education gaps narrowed over succeeding generations, as the resource gaps closed between the states.

Table 3.1

Differences in Pupil–Teacher Ratio, Education and Earnings Between Men Born in North and South Carolina By Race and Birth Cohort

	Mean for North Carolina minus mean for South Carolina					
	Blacks			Whites		
	P/T ratio	Education	Log earnings	P/T ratio	Education	Log earnings
Birth cohort	(1)	(2)	(3)	(4)	(5)	(6)
1900–1909	-13.6	0.65	0.06	3.9	-0.67	-0.08
		(0.10)	(0.02)		(0.08)	(0.02)
1910–1919	-9.7	0.73	-0.02	4.0	-0.29	-0.03
		(0.07)	(0.02)		(0.05)	(0.01)
1920–1929	-4.2	0.62	0.01	6.0	-0.25	-0.04
		(0.06)	(0.01)		(0.05)	(0.01)
1930–1939	0.5	0.64	0.01	3.9	0.03	-0.02
		(0.07)	(0.02)		(0.05)	(0.01)
1940–1949	-1.7	0.43	0.01	1.1	0.14	-0.03
		(0.08)	(0.02)		(0.06)	(0.01)
1950–1959	-1.1	0.30	0.02	-0.5	0.07	-0.02
		(0.12)	(0.03)		(0.09)	(0.02)
Difference between cohorts						
1940–1949	11.9	-0.22	-0.05	-2.8	0.81	0.05
1900–1909		(0.13)	(0.03)		(0.10)	(0.02)
1950–1959	12.5	-0.35	-0.04	-4.4	0.74	0.05
1900–1909		(0.16)	(0.04)		(0.12)	(0.02)

Notes: Standard errors in parentheses. Reported coefficients are the mean for North Carolina minus the mean for South Carolina. P/T ratio refers to the average pupil-teacher ratio in the state for a representative member for each race/birth cohort, assuming ten years of education. Education refers to mean years of completed education for all men in the respective race/birth cohort group. Earnings refer to mean log earnings for those with positive earnings, adjusting for state/region of residence, residence in an SMSA, year of observation, and age at census. See Appendix for details.

Source: Based on authors' tabulations of school system data and tabulations of 1960, 1970 and 1980 census data. See Appendix for data sources.

Trends for earnings point in the same direction, but are noisier. Columns 3 and 6 of Table 3.1 report regression-adjusted mean earnings gaps by race for cohorts of men from North and South Carolina. The main motivation for the regression adjustment is to compensate for differences in earnings associated with working in different regions of the country and in a metropolitan as opposed to nonmetropolitan area (see the Appendix for further details).[13] In essence, the estimated wage differentials are standardized so as to compare individuals who work in the same job market.

Looking at black men in the 1900–1909 birth cohort, those from North Carolina enjoyed a 6 percent wage advantage over their counterparts from South Carolina. In contrast, white men in this cohort from South Carolina enjoyed an 8 percent wage advantage over their counterparts from North Carolina. In both cases, the wage gaps vanished over succeeding generations. The pattern of the North Carolina-South Carolina wage differentials by race and cohort are consistent with the view that meager school resources put black men from South Carolina at competitive disadvantage, while generous resources gave white men from South Carolina a leg up in the job market. One troubling finding for this interpretation, however, is that the cross-state wage gaps seemed to close very quickly for blacks, whereas the school quality gap was more persistent. Given the sampling variability of the estimates, however, the cohort-specific wage gaps should be viewed cautiously.

How consistent are the data in Table 3.1 with the earlier literature on earnings and school quality? To answer this question, recall that the reduced form estimates in the literature suggest that a 10 percent reduction in class size would be associated with an increase in earnings of 0.4 to 1.1 percent. Thus, the roughly 12-student narrowing of the gap in the average pupil–teacher ratio between North and South Carolina for blacks born in the 1940s relative to those born in the 1900s (a 28% reduction) might have been expected to raise earnings by 1–3 percent.[14] The actual narrowing in the earnings gap was about 5 percent (with a standard error of 3%) – roughly consistent with the earlier literature. The patterns for whites are somewhat harder to explain, since the relative change in school quality is more modest. Based on earlier estimates, the three-student reduction in the pupil-teacher ratio gap between North and South Carolina whites born in the 1940s relative to those born in the 1900s might have been expected to raise earnings by 0.4–1.1 percent, while the actual earnings convergence was also 5 percent (with a standard error of 2%). One possible explanation for the larger than expected wage differences is that other aspects of school resources, such as the length of the school year, differed substantially between North and South Carolina early in the century as well, and then converged.

We conclude that the magnitude of the observed earnings convergence for black men in the two states is roughly consistent with the earlier literature, while the magnitude of convergence for white men is, if anything, greater than expected. However, despite the strong intuitive appeal of the North Carolina–South Carolina comparison on a priori grounds, and the availability of over 130,000 wage observations from the 1960, 1970, and 1980 censuses, it is evident that the power of the data to yield precise estimates of cross-state earnings differentials by race and cohort is limited. There is a general lesson here. Because earnings are so variable, and school resource effects are at best modest, small data sets are unlikely to find significant effects of school resources.

South Carolina and North Carolina represent just one possible comparison. What about the other segregated states? In Card and Krueger (1992b), we use data from all 18 segregated states to relate the level of school resources in the black and white schools to subsequent earnings of individuals educated in those states. To control for differential labor market effects, in much of our analysis we focused on workers who attended school in the south but later were observed working in a common set of northern labor markets. This technique has the advantage of controlling for labor market differences that may be correlated with school quality differences: for example, states that discriminated in terms of school resources may be more likely to allow discrimination in terms of labor market conditions. The results indicated that the payoff to each year of education was greater for individuals (of either racial group) who were from states that devoted more resources to education. Furthermore, reduced form models indicate that the level of earnings and educational attainment were positively associated with school resources. Thus, the comparison of North and South Carolina is not an isolated example.

3.4. Conclusions

Does the literature on school resources, earnings, and educational attainment prove beyond a reasonable doubt that resources matter? We do not believe that the evidence justifies so strong a conclusion. The available evidence is not unambiguous or ubiquitous, and it suffers from all the standard criticisms of drawing causal inferences from observational data.

To some extent, interpreting the literature depends on the strength of one's prior expectations. If one starts from the position that school resources do not make a difference, then one can point to the bulk of the evidence on the lack of a statistically significant connection between school resources and test scores, and a handful of studies on economic outcomes, to support that view. On the other hand, if one starts from the view that resources do make a difference, then the available evidence on school quality and economic outcomes may be interpreted as generally supportive. Perhaps the strongest evidence that resources matter comes from an analysis of the vast differences in resources for blacks and whites who attended schools in the segregated states. We suspect that further research focusing on particular episodes of large changes in school quality – such as our "case study" of North and South Carolina – might be valuable.

Thirty years after the Coleman report, it is unfortunate and frustrating that more is not known about schooling. While most of the literature on test scores points to little, if any, effect of school resources, some observational studies and one actual experiment have found a connection. Decisions about educational resources and reform have to be made in an environment of much uncertainty.

Appendix: Description of Data Used in the North and South Carolina Comparison

The estimates in Figure 3.4 and Table 3.1 are based on samples drawn from the Public Use Samples of the U.S. Census. Specifically, the sample is drawn from the 1960 1 percent public use sample, the 1970 1 percent sample (15% form) and the 1970 1 percent sample (5% form), and the 5 percent sample of the 1980 census. In principle, the census provides self-weighting samples of the population. Thus, the sample contains 1 percent of the population in 1960, 2 percent in 1970, and 5 percent in 1980. We assigned sample weights so that the sample each census year received equal weight (that is, observations from 1960 were assigned a weight of 1.0, observations from 1970 were assigned a weight of 0.5, and observations from 1980 were assigned a weight of 0.2). Our extract consists of white and black men born in North Carolina or South Carolina between 1900 and 1959, who were age 25 to 65 at the time the census was conducted. These restrictions yielded a sample of 168,353 observations. Education is measured as the highest year of schooling completed. Figure 3.4 simply reports average education level by 10-year-of-birth cohort, race and state of birth.

Further restrictions were placed on the sample for the analysis of annual earnings in Table 3.1. First, wage and salary income was converted to 1995 dollars using the CPI-U. The sample was then restricted to men with annual wage and salary income of at least $500, and weekly wage and salary income between $30 and $2,500. Restricting the sample to those with nonzero wage and salary earnings reduced the sample by 19 percent, and restricting the range of the annual and weekly wage reduced the sample by an additional 2 percent. The final sample used for the analysis of earnings thus has 132,989 observations (40,837 blacks and 92,152 whites).

The estimates reported in Table 3.1 were derived from regressions of log annual earnings on 10-year birth cohort dummies and their interactions with a born-in-North-Carolina dummy, a 1970-year dummy, a 1980-year dummy, nine region of residence dummies interacted with three Census-year dummies, dummies indicating residence in North Carolina and South Carolina, a dummy variable indicating whether the worker lives in a standard metropolitan statistical area (SMSA) interacted with census year and a cubic in current age. Separate weighted regressions were estimated for blacks and whites. The coefficient on the cohort dummies interacted with the born-in-North-Carolina dummy are reported in Table 3.1. Subject to the log approximation, these coefficients can be interpreted as the proportionate difference in earnings between workers from North and South Carolina who live in the same region, for each cohort and race.

4

Experimental Estimates of Education Production Functions

The large literature on the effect of school resources on student achievement generally finds ambiguous, conflicting, and weak results. Even quantitative summaries of the literature tend to reach conflicting conclusions. For example, based on the fact that most estimates of the effect of school inputs on student achievement are statistically insignificant, Hanushek (1986) concludes, "There appears to be no strong or systematic relationship between school expenditures and student performance." By contrast, Hedges, Laine, and Greenwald (1994) conduct a meta-analysis of (a subset of) the studies enumerated by Hanushek and conclude, "the data are more consistent with a pattern that includes at least some positive relation between dollars spent on education and output, than with a pattern of no effects or negative effects."

Much of the uncertainty in the literature derives from the fact that the appropriate specification–including the functional form, level

This chapter is a revised version of: Krueger, A. (1999). Experimental Estimates of Education Production Functions, in: Quarterly Journal of Economics 114, 497–532, Oxford University Press, 1999, reprinted by permission of Oxford University Press. The author thanks Helen Bain, a founder and principal director of Project STAR, for providing him with the data used in this study, Jayne Zaharias, DeWayne Fulton, and Van Cain for answering several questions regarding the data, and Jessica Baraka, Aaron Saiger, and Diane Whitmore for providing outstanding research assistance. The STAR data have been collected and maintained by the Center of Excellence for Research in Basic Skills at Tennessee State University. The STAR data are available from www.telalink.net/~heros Helpful comments on the research were provided by Charles Achilles, Jessica Baraka, Ronald Ehrenberg, William Evans, Jeremy Finn, John Folger, Victor Fuchs, Joseph Hotz, Lawrence Katz, Cecilia Rouse, James P. Smith, two referees, and seminar participants at the Milken Institute, Massachusetts Institute of Technology, National Bureau of Economic Research, Princeton University, Vanderbilt University, University of California at Los Angeles, the Kennedy School (Harvard University), the London School of Economics, Stockholm University, the Econometric Society, World Bank, and Society of Labor Economists. Financial support was provided by the National Institute of Childhood Health and Development.

of aggregation, relevant control variables, and identification – of the "education production function" is uncertain.[1] Some specifications do consistently yield significant effects, however. Notably, estimates that use cross-state variation in school resources typically find positive effects of school resources, whereas studies that use within-state data are more likely to find insignificant or wrong-signed estimates (see Hanushek 1996b).[2] Many of these specification issues arise because of the possibility of omitted variables, either at the student, class, school, or state level. Moreover, functional form issues are driven in part by concern for omitted variables, as researchers often specify education production functions in terms of test-score changes to difference out omitted characteristics that might be correlated with school resources (although such differencing could introduce greater problems if the omitted characteristics affect the trajectory of student performance). A classical experiment, in which students are randomly assigned to classes with different resources, would help overcome many of these specification issues and provide guidance for observational studies.

This chapter provides an econometric analysis of the only large-scale randomized experiment on class size ever conducted in the United States, the Tennessee Student/Teacher Achievement Ratio experiment, known as Project STAR. Project STAR was a longitudinal study in which kindergarten students *and* their teachers were randomly assigned to one of three groups beginning in the 1985–1986 school year: small classes (13–17 students per teacher), regular-size classes (22–25 students), and regular/aide classes (22–25 students) which also included a full-time teacher's aide. After their initial assignment, the design called for students to remain in the same class type for four years. Some 6,000–7,000 students were involved in the project each year. Over all four years, the sample included 11,600 students from 80 schools. Each school was required to have at least one of each class-size type, and random assignment took place *within* schools. The students were given a battery of standardized tests at the end of each school year. In a review article Mosteller (1995) described Project STAR as "a controlled experiment which is one of the most important educational investigations ever carried out and illustrates the kind and magnitude of research needed in the field of education to strengthen schools."

The STAR data have been examined extensively by an internal team of researchers. This analysis has found that students in small classes tended to perform better than students in larger classes, while students in classes with a teacher aide typically did not perform differently than students in regular-size classes without an aide (see Folger and Breda 1989; Finn and Achilles 1990; and Word et al. 1990). Past research primarily consists of comparisons being made of means between the assignment groups, and analysis of variance at the class level. In this research, little attention has been paid to potential threats to the validity of the experiment or to the longitudinal structure of the data.

As in any experiment, there were deviations from the ideal experimental design in the actual implementation of Project STAR. First, students in regular-size classes were randomly assigned again between classes with and without full-time aides at the beginning of first grade, while students in small classes continued on in small classes, often with the same set of classmates.[3] Re-randomization was done to placate the the parents of children in regular classes who complained about their children's initial assignment. Because analysis of data for kindergartners did not indicate a significant effect of a teacher aide on achievement in regular-size classes, it was felt that this procedure would create few problems. But if the constancy of the use of children's classmates influences their achievement, then the experimental comparison after kindergarten is compromised by the re-randomization.

A second limitation of the experiment is that approximately 10 percent of students switched between small and regular classes between grades, primarily this was because of behavioral problems or parental complaints. These nonrandom transitions could also compromise the experimental results. Furthermore, because some students and their families naturally relocate during the school year, actual class size varied more than intended in small classes (11 to 20) and in regular classes (15 to 30). Finally, as in most longitudinal studies of schooling, sample attrition was common – half of students who were present in kindergarten were missing in at least one subsequent year. And some students may have nonrandomly switched to another public school or enrolled in private school upon learning their class-type assignments. These limitations of the experiment have not been adequately addressed in previous work.

This chapter has three related goals. First, to probe the sensitivity of the experimental estimates to flaws in the experimental design. Second, to use the experiment to identify an appropriate specification of the education production function to estimate with nonexperimental data. Third, to use the experimental results to interpret estimates from the literature based on observational data. The conclusion makes a rough attempt to compare the benefits and costs of reducing class size from 22 to 15 students.

4.1. Background on Project STAR and Data
4.1.1. Design and Implementation

Project STAR was funded by the Tennessee legislature, at a total cost of approximately $12 million over four years.[4] The Tennessee legislature required that the study include students in inner-city, suburban, urban, and rural schools. The research was designed and carried out by a team of researchers at Tennessee State University, Memphis State University, the University of Tennessee, and Vanderbilt University. To be eligible to participate in the experiment, a public school was required to sign up for four years and be large enough to accommodate at least three classes per grade, so within each school students could be assigned to a small class (13–17), regular class (22–25 students), or regular plus a full-time aide class.[5] The statewide pupil–teacher ratio in kindergarten in 1985–1986 was 22.3, so students assigned to regular classes fared about as well as the average student in the state (Word et al. 1990). Schools with more than 67 students per grade had more than three classes. One limitation of the comparison between regular and regular/aide classes is that in grades 1–3 each regular class had the services of a part-time aide 25–33 percent of the time on average, so the variability in aide services was restricted.[6]

The cohort of students who entered kindergarten in the 1985–1986 school year participated in the experiment through third grade. Any student who entered a participating school in a relevant grade was added to the experiment, and participating students who repeated a grade, skipped a grade, or left the school exited the sample. Entering students were randomly assigned to one of the three types of classes (small, regular, or regular/aide) in the summer before they began kindergarten.[7] Students were typically notified of their initial class assignment very close to the beginning of the school year. Students in regular classes and in regular/aide classes were randomly reassigned between these two types of classes at the end of kindergarten, while students initially in small classes continued on in small classes. Notice, however, that results from the kindergarten year are uncontaminated by this feature of the experiment.

Because kindergarten attendance was not mandatory in Tennessee at the time of the study, many new students entered the program in first grade. Additionally, students were added to the sample over time because they repeated a grade or because their families moved to a school zone that included a participating school. In all, some 2,200 new students entered the project in first grade and were randomly assigned to the three types of classes. Another 1,600 and 1,200 new students entered the experiment in the second and third grades, respectively. Newly entering students were randomly assigned to class types, although the uneven availability of slots in small and regular classes often led to an unbalanced allocation of new students across class types.

A total of 11,600 children were involved in the experiment over all four years. After third grade, the experiment ended, and all of the students were assigned to regular-size classes. Although data have been collected on students through ninth grade, the present study only has access to data covering grades kindergarden to third grade. Data were collected on students each fall and spring during the experiment. Class type is based on the class attended in the fall. All students who attended a STAR class in either the fall or spring are included in the database.

Unfortunately, the STAR data set does not contain the students' original class type assignments resulting from the randomization procedure; only the class types that students actually were enrolled in each year are available. It is possible that some students had been switched from their randomly assigned class to another class before the school year started or early in the fall. To determine the frequency of such switches, we obtained and (double-) entered data on the initial random assignments from the actual enrollment sheets that had been compiled in the summer prior to the start of kindergarten for 1,581 students from 18 participating STAR schools.[8] It turns out that only 0.3 percent of students in the experiment were *not* enrolled in the class type to which they had been randomly assigned in kindergarten. Moreover, only one student in this sample who had been assigned a regular or regular/aide class enrolled in a small class. Consequently, in the analysis below, we will refer to the class type in which students are enrolled during the first year they enter the experiment as their initial random assignment.

A limitation of the experiment is that baseline test score information on the students is not available, so one cannot examine whether the treatment and control groups "looked similar" on this measure before the experiment began. Nonetheless, if the students were successfully randomly assigned between class types, one would expect those assigned to small- and regular-size classes to look similar along other measurable dimensions at base line. Tables 4.1 and 4.2 provide some evidence on the differences among students assigned to the three class types.

Table 4.1 disaggregates the data into waves, based upon the grade during which the students entered the program, because this was the first time the students were randomly assigned to a class type. The sample consists of all students who were enrolled in a STAR class when the fall or spring data were collected. Sample means by class type for several variables are presented. As one would expect, students assigned to small classes had fewer students in their class than those in regular classes, on average. There are small differences in the fraction of students on free lunch, in the racial mix, and in the average age of students in classes of different size, although some of these differences are statistically significant (see rows 1–4).[9] Because random assignment was only valid within schools, these differences suggest the importance of controlling for school effects as is done in Table 4.2.

Table 4.2 presents p-values for joint F-tests of the differences among small, regular, and regular/aide classes for the variables presented in Table 4.1. Unlike results reported in Table 4.1, these p-values are conditional on school effects. None of the three background variables displays a statistically significant association with class-type assignment at the 10 percent level, which suggests that random assignment produced relatively similar groups in each class size, on average. As an overall test of random assignment, I regressed a dummy variable indicating assignment to a small class on the three background measures in rows 1–3 and school dummies. For each wave, the student characteristics had no more than a chance association with class-type assignment. Furthermore, if the same regression model is estimated for a sample that pools all four entering waves of students together, the three student characteristics are still insignificantly related to assignment to a small class (p-value = .58). Within schools, there is no apparent evidence that initial assignment to class types was correlated with student characteristics.

Experimental Estimates of Education Production Functions

Table 4.1

Comparison of Mean Characteristics of Treatments and Controls: Unadjusted Data

Variable	Small	Regular	Regular/Aide[b]	Joint P-Value[a]
A. Students who entered STAR in kindergarten				
1. Free lunch[c]	0.47	0.48	0.50	0.09
2. White/Asian	0.68	0.67	0.66	0.26
3. Age in 1985	5.44	5.43	5.42	0.32
4. Attrition rate[d]	0.49	0.52	0.53	0.02
5. Class size in kindergarten	15.10	22.40	22.80	0.00
6. Percentile score in kindergarten	54.70	49.90	50.00	0.00
B. Students who entered STAR in first grade				
1. Free lunch	0.59	0.62	0.61	0.52
2. White/Asian	0.62	0.56	0.64	0.00
3. Age in 1985	5.78	5.86	5.88	0.03
4. Attrition rate	0.53	0.51	0.47	0.07
5. Class size in first grade	15.90	22.70	23.50	0.00
6. Percentile score in first grade	49.20	42.60	47.70	0.00
C. Students who entered STAR in second grade				
1. Free lunch	0.66	0.63	0.66	0.60
2. White/Asian	0.53	0.54	0.44	0.00
3. Age in 1985	5.94	6.00	6.03	0.66
4. Attrition rate	0.37	0.34	0.35	0.58
5. Class size in second grade	15.50	23.70	23.60	0.01
6. Percentile score in second grade	46.40	45.30	41.70	0.01
D. Students who entered STAR in third grade				
1. Free lunch	0.60	0.64	0.69	0.04
2. White/Asian	0.66	0.57	0.55	0.00
3. Age in 1985	5.95	5.92	5.99	0.39
4. Attrition rate	NA	NA	NA	NA
5. Class size in third grade	16.00	24.10	24.40	0.01
6. Percentile score in third grade	47.60	44.20	41.30	0.01

[a] P-value is for F-test of equality of all three groups.

[b] Sample size in panel A ranges from 6,299 to 6,324, in panel B ranges from 2,240 to 2,314, in panel C ranges from 1,585 to 1,679, and in panel D ranges from 1,202 to 1,283.

[c] Free lunch pertains to the fraction receiving a free lunch in the first year they are observed in the sample (i.e., in kindergarten for panel A; in first grade in panel B; etc.). Percentile score pertains to the average percentile score on the three Stanford Achievement Tests the students took in the first year they are observed in the sample.

[d] Attrition rate is the fraction that ever exits the sample prior to completing third grade, even if they return to the sample in a subsequent year. Attrition rate is unavailable in third grade.

Table 4.2

P-Values for Tests of Within-School Differences Among Small, Regular and Regular/Aide Classes

Variable	Grade entered STAR program			
	K	1	2	3
1. Free lunch	.46	.29	.58	.18
2. White/Asian	.66	.28	.15	.21
3. Age	.38	.12	.48	.40
4. Attrition rate	.01	.07	.58	NA
5. Actual class size	.00	.00	.00	.00
6. Percentile score	.00	.00	.46	.00

Notes: Each p-value is for an F-test of the null hypothesis that assignment to a small, regular, or regular/aide class has no effect on the outcome variable in that grade, conditional on school of attendance. All rows except 4 pertain to the first grade in which the student entered the STAR program. The attrition rate in row 4 measures whether the student ever left the sample after initially being observed.

To check whether teacher assignment was independent of observed teacher characteristics, I regressed each of three teacher characteristics (experience, race, or education) on dummies indicating the class type the teachers were assigned to and school dummies, and then performed an F-test of the hypothesis that the class-type dummies jointly had no effect. These regressions were calculated for each of the four grade levels, so there was a total of twelve regressions. In each case, the p-value for the class-type dummies exceeded .05.[10] These results are as one would expect with random assignment of teachers to the different class types.

There was a high rate of attrition from the project. Only half the students who entered the project in kindergarten were present for all grades kindergarten to third grade. For the kindergarten cohort, students in small classes were three–four percentage points more likely to stay in the sample than those in regular-size classes. This pattern was reversed among those who entered in first grade, however. Attrition could occur for several reasons, including students moving to another school, students repeating a grade, and students being advanced a grade. Although I lack data on retention rates for the early grades, Word et al. (1990) report that over the four years of the project, 19.8 percent of students in small classes were retained, while 27.4 percent of students in regular classes were retained. This is consistent with the lower attrition rate of students in small classes. Some of the analysis that follows makes a crude attempt to adjust for possible nonrandom attrition.

It is virtually impossible to prescribe the exact number of students in a class: families move in and out of a school district during the course of a year; students become sick; and varying numbers of students are enrolled in schools. As a result, in some cases actual class size deviated from the intended ranges. Table 4.3 reports the frequency distribution of class size for first graders, by assignment to small, regular, or regular/aide classes. Although students assigned to small classes clearly were more likely to attend classes with fewer students, there was considerable variability in class size within each class-type assignment, and some overlap between the distributions.

Table 4.3

Distribution of Children Across Actual Class Sizes by Random Assignment Group in First Grade

Actual class size in first grade	Assignment group in first grade		
	Small	Regular	Aide
12	24	0	0
13	182	0	0
14	252	0	0
15	465	0	0
16	256	16	0
17	561	17	0
18	108	36	0
19	57	76	57
20	20	200	120
21	0	378	378
22	0	594	329
23	0	437	460
24	0	384	264
25	0	175	225
26	0	130	234
27	0	54	108
28	0	28	56
29	0	29	58
30	0	30	30
Average class size	15,7	22,7	23,4

Note: Actual class was determined by counting the number of students in the data set with the same class identification.

It is also virtually impossible to prevent some students from switching between class types over time. Table 4.4 shows a transition matrix between class types for students who continued from K–1, 1–2, and 2–3 grades. If students remained in their same class type over time, all the off-diagonal elements would be zero. The re-randomization of students in regular classes in first grade is apparent in panel A. But in second and third grades, when students were supposed to remain in their same type of class, 9–11 percent of students switched class-size types. Students were moved between class types because of behavioral problems or, in some cases, parental complaints. Obviously, if the movement between class types was associated with student characteristics (e.g. students with stronger academic backgrounds more likely to move into small classes), these transitions would bias a simple comparison of outcomes across class types.

Table 4.4

Transitions Between Class-Size in Adjacent Grades Number of Students in Each Type of Class

A. Kindergarten to first grade				
	First grade			
Kindergarten	Small	Regular	Reg/aide	All
Small	1292	60	48	1400
Regular	126	737	663	1526
Aide	122	761	706	1589
All	1540	1558	1417	4515

B. First grade to second grade				
	Second grade			
First grade	Small	Regular	Reg/aide	All
Small	1435	23	24	1482
Regular	152	1498	202	1852
Aide	40	115	1560	1715
All	1627	1636	1786	5049

C. Second grade to third grade				
	Third grade			
Second grade	Small	Regular	Reg/aide	All
Small	1564	37	35	1636
Regular	167	1485	152	1804
Aide	40	76	1857	1973
All	1771	1598	2044	5413

To address this potential problem, and the variability of class size for a given type of assignment, in some of the analysis that follows initial random assignment is used as an instrumental variable for actual class size.

4.1.2. Data and Standardized Tests

Students were tested at the end of March or beginning of April of each year. The tests consisted of the Stanford Achievement Test (SAT), which measured achievement in reading, word recognition, and math in grades K–3, and the Tennessee Basic Skills First (BSF) test, which measured achievement in reading and math in grades 1–3. The tests were tailored to each grade level. Because there are no natural units for the test results, I scaled the test scores into percentile ranks. Specifically, in each grade level the regular and regular/aide students were pooled together, and students were assigned percentile scores based on their raw test scores, ranging from 0 (lowest score) to 100 (highest score). A separate percentile distribution was generated for each subject test (e.g. Math-SAT, Reading-SAT, Word-SAT, etc.). For each test I then determined where in the distribution of the regular-class students every student in the small classes would fall, and the students in the small classes were assigned these percentile scores. Finally, to summarize overall achievement, the *average* of the three SAT percentile rankings was calculated.[11] If the performance of students in the small classes was distributed in the same way as performance of students in the regular classes, the average percentile score for students in the small classes would be 50.

An examination of the correlations among the tests indicates that the strongest correlations typically are between tests of the same subject matter; for example, in second grade the SAT and BSF reading tests have a correlation of .80. Tests of the same subjects tend to have a higher correlation from one grade to the next than do tests of different subjects. The SAT and BSF tests are also highly correlated with each other: the correlation between the average SAT percentile and the average BSF percentile is .79 in first grade and .85 in second grade. For most of the subsequent analysis, the SAT exam is the primary focus of study because this test has been used on a national level for a long period of time. The main findings are similar for the BSF test, however.

The average of the three SAT exams by class type is presented in the last row of Table 4.1. Figure 4.1 displays the kernel density of the average test score distributions for students in small and regular classes at each grade level.[12] In all grades, the average student in small classes performed better on this summary test measure than did those in regular or regular/aide classes. There does not seem to be a very strong or consistent effect of the teacher aide, however. The rest of the chapter probes the robustness of these findings.

Figure 4.1

Distribution of Test Percentile Scores by Class Size and Grade

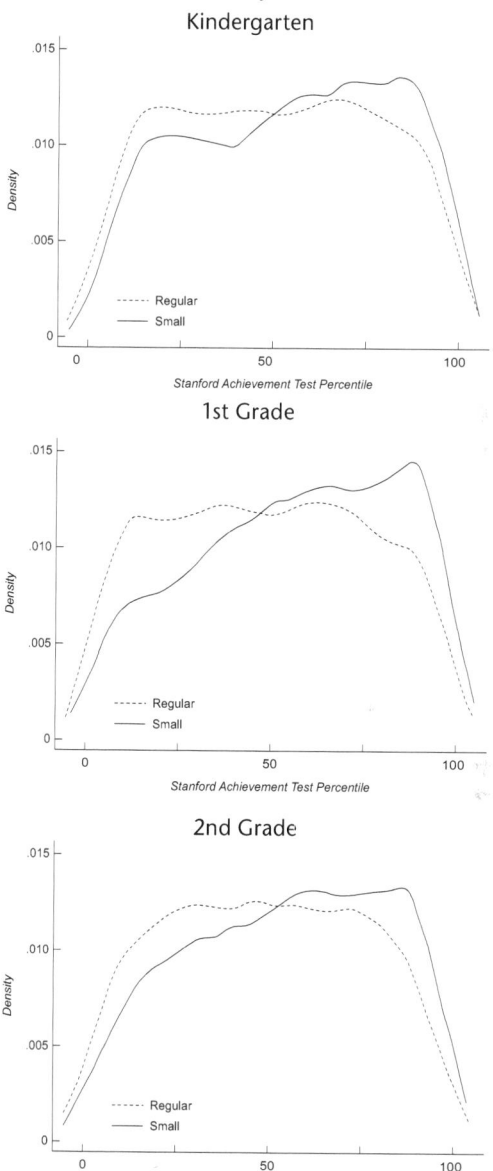

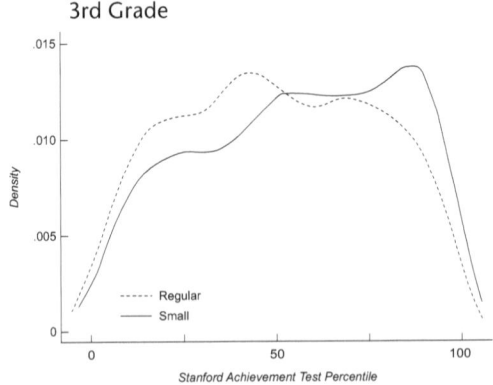

3rd Grade

Observe also that the average test score of students in all class types tends to be lower for those who entered the experiment in higher grades. This pattern is likely to reflect the fact that kindergarten was optional and higher-achieving students were more likely to attend kindergarten, as well as the tendency of lower-achieving students to be retained and disproportionately added to the sample at higher grade levels. Because of this feature of the data, I control for the grade in which the student entered Project STAR in some of the analysis below.

The Appendix presents means for several variables that are available in the data set.

4.2. Statistical Models

To see the advantage of a randomized experiment in estimating the effect of school resources on student achievement, consider the following general model:

$$(1) \qquad\qquad Y_{ij} = aS_{ij} + bF_{ij} + \epsilon_{ij}$$

where Y_{ij} is the achievement level of student i in school j, S_{ij}, is a vector of school characteristics, F_{ij} is a vector representing the family background of the student, and ϵ_{ij} is a stochastic error component. In principle, S_{ij}, and F_{ij} include information cumulated over the student's life; for example, classroom size and teacher qualifications for each year the student attended school. The entire history of family background variables and school resources may contribute to students' achievement in any given year. In addition, children's unobserved inherent ability may contribute to their achievement. In any actual application we will generally lack data on some relevant school, family, or student characteristics. These omitted variables will then appear in the error term. If the omitted variables are correlated with the included variables, then the estimated parameters will be biased.

If a school characteristic such as class size is determined by random assignment, however, it will be independent of the omitted variables. Thus, with random assignment, a simple comparison of mean achievement between children in small and large classes provides an unbiased estimate of the effect of class size on achievement.

We begin analyzing the STAR data by estimating the following regression equation for students in each grade level:

$$(2) \qquad Y_{ics} = \beta_0 + \beta_1 SMALL_{cs} + \beta_2 REG/A_{cs} + \beta_3 X_{ics} + \alpha_s + \epsilon_{ics},$$

Where Y_{ics} is the average percentile score on the SAT test of student i in class c at school s, $SMALL_{cs}$ is a dummy variable indicating whether the student was assigned to a small class that year, REG/A_{cs} is a dummy variable indicating whether the student was assigned to a regular-size class with an aide that year, and X_{ics} is a vector of observed student and teacher covariates (e.g. gender). The independence between class-size assignment and other variables is only valid within schools, because randomization was done within schools. Consequently, a separate dummy variable is included for each school to absorb the school effects, α_s.

The equation is estimated by ordinary least squares (OLS). In calculating the standard errors, however, the error term ϵ_{ics} is modeled in a components-of-variance framework. Specifically, ϵ_{ics} is assumed to consist of two components: $\epsilon_{ics} = \mu_{cs} + \epsilon'_{ics}$, where μ_{cs} is a class-specific random component that is common to all members of the same class, and ϵ'_{ics} is an idiosyncratic error term. The class-specific component μ_{cs} may exist because of unobserved teacher characteristics, or because some students may exert a common influence over others in the class.

Because several students were reassigned to different classes after their initial random assignment, in part based on their performance, equation (1) was also estimated using dummies indicating students' *initial* assignment the first year they entered the program, rather than their actual assignment each year. Models including initial assignment are labeled "reduced-form" models, because one can think of initial assignment as an excluded variable that is correlated with actual class size. The initial assignment and actual assignment variables are identical in kindergarten, so the OLS and reduced-form estimates are identical for kindergarten students.

Regression results are presented in Table 4.5.[13] Columns 1–4 use actual assignment, and columns 5–8 use initial class assignment. Columns 1 and 5 omit the school dummies. As earlier analyses of the data have found, students in small classes tend to perform better than those in regular and regular/aide classes. Here, the gap in average performance is about 5 percentile points in kindergarten, 8.6 points in first grade, and 5–6 points in second and third grade. Columns 2 and 6 add unrestricted school dummies to the model. In three of four grades, including the school dummies leads to a slight increase in the effect of being assigned to a small class.

If class size were truly randomly assigned, including additional exogenous variables would not significantly alter the coefficient on the class-size dummies. In fact, including covariates seems to have a very modest effect on the class-size coefficients conditional on school effects. The student characteristics in columns 3 and 5 add considerable explanatory power. White and Asian students tend to score eight percentile points higher than black students in kindergarten, and this gap is about six points in third grade.[14] Students on free lunch score thirteen percentile points less than those not on free lunch, and girls score three-four points higher than boys in each grade level.

The teacher characteristics have notably weak explanatory power. Teacher education – as proxied by a dummy indicating whether the teacher has a master's degree – does not have a systematic effect. Hardly any of the teachers are male, so the gender results are not very meaningful. Teacher experience has a small, positive effect. Experimentation with a quadratic in experience indicated that the experience profile tends to peak at about twenty years of experience, and students in classes where the teacher has twenty years of experience tend to score about three percentile points higher than those in classes where the teacher has zero experience, all else being equal. As a whole, however, consistent with much of the previous literature, the STAR data suggest that measured teacher characteristics explain relatively little of student achievement on standardized tests.

Estimates of the effect of being in a small class which use initial assignment (columns 5–8) are only slightly smaller than the estimates which use the actual class assignment (columns 1–4), and are always statistically significant. This finding suggests that possible nonrandom movement of students between small and regular classes was not a major limitation of the experiment.

To summarize these results, based on column 4 it appears that students in small classes score about five–seven percentage points higher than those assigned to regular-size classes. Students assigned to a regular/aide class perform slightly better (one or two percentile points, on average) than students assigned to a regular class without a full-time aide, but the gap is only statistically significant in one grade level. Thus, it is possible that a teacher aide has only a trivial effect on student achievement, or that the availability of part-time aides in regular classes confounds the true effect of an aide.

Is the impact of attending a small class big or small? Unfortunately, it is unclear how percentile scores on these tests map into tangible outcomes. Nevertheless, a couple of comparisons are informative. First, relative to the standard deviation (S.D.) of the average percentile score, the effect sizes are .20 in kindergarten, .28 in first grade, .22 in second grade, and .19 in third grade (based on the model in column 4). Second, one could compare the estimated class-size effects with the effects of other student characteristics. For example, in kindergarten the impact of being assigned to a small class is about 64 percent as large as the white–black test score gap, and in third grade it is 82 percent as large. By both metrics, the magnitudes are sizable.

4.2.1. Effects of Attrition

Table 4.6 provides some simple evidence on the impact of sample attrition. As is common in longitudinal studies of education, attrition was very high from Project STAR classes. If the students originally assigned to regular classes who left the sample had higher test scores, on average, than students assigned to small classes who also left the sample, then the small class effects will be biased upwards. One reason why this pattern of attrition might occur is that high-income parents of children in larger classes might have been more likely to subsequently enroll their children in private schools over time than similar parents of children in small classes. At heart, adjusting for possible nonrandom attrition is a matter of imputing test scores for

Experimental Estimates of Education Production Functions

Table 4.5

OLS and Reduced-Form Estimates of Effect of Class-Size Assignment on Average Percentile of Stanford Achievement Test

Explanatory variable	OLS: actual class size				Reduced form: initial class size			
	(1)	(2)	(3)	(4)	(5)	(6)	(7)	(8)
				A. Kindergarten				
Small class	4.82	5.37	5.36	5.37	4.82	5.37	5.36	5.37
	(2.19)	(1.26)	(1.21)	(1.19)	(2.19)	(1.25)	(1.21)	(1.19)
Regular/aide class	0.12	0.29	0.53	0.31	0.12	0.29	0.53	0.31
	(2.23)	(1.13)	(1.09)	(1.07)	(2.23)	(1.13)	(1.09)	(1.07)
White/Asian (1 = yes)	–	–	8.35	8.44	–	–	8.35	8.44
			(1.35)	(1.36)			(1.35)	(1.36)
Girl (1 = yes)	–	–	4.48	4.39	–	–	4.48	4.39
			(.63)	(.63)			(.63)	(.63)
Free lunch (1 = yes)	–	–	-13.15	-13.07	–	–	-13.15	-13.07
			(.77)	(.77)			(.77)	(.77)
White teacher	–	–	–	-0.57	–	–	–	-0.57
				(2.10)				(2.10)
Teacher experience	–	–	–	0.26	–	–	–	0.26
				(.10)				(.10)
Master's degree	–	–	–	-0.51	–	–	–	-0.51
				(1.06)				(1.06)
School fixed effects	No	Yes	Yes	Yes	No	Yes	Yes	Yes
R^2	0.01	0.25	0.31	0.31	0.01	0.25	0.31	0.31
				B. First grade				
Small class	8.57	8.43	7.91	7.4	7.54	7.17	6.79	6.37
	(1.97)	(1.21)	(1.17)	(1.18)	(1.76)	(1.14)	(1.10)	(1.11)
Regular/aide class	3.44	2.22	2.23	1.78	1.92	1.69	1.64	1.48
	(2.05)	(1.00)	(0.98)	(0.98)	(1.12)	(0.80)	(0.76)	(0.76)
White/Asian (1 = yes)	–	–	6.97	6.97	–	–	6.86	6.85
			(1.18)	(1.19)			(1.18)	(1.18)
Girl (1 = yes)	–	–	3.8	3.85	–	–	3.76	3.82
			(.56)	(.56)			(.56)	(.56)
Free lunch (1 = yes)	–	–	-13.49	-13.61	–	–	-13.65	-13.77
			(.87)	(.87)			(.88)	(.87)
White teacher	–	–	–	-4.28	–	–	–	-4.4
				(1.96)				(1.97)
Male teacher	–	–	–	11.82	–	–	–	13.06
				(3.33)				(3.38)
Teacher experience	–	–	–	0.05	–	–	–	0.06
				(0.06)				(.06)
Master's degree	–	–	–	0.48	–	–	–	0.63
				(1.07)				(1.09)
School fixed effects	No	Yes	Yes	Yes	No	Yes	Yes	Yes
R^2	0.02	0.24	0.3	0.3	0.01	0.23	0.29	0.3

Table 4.5 (continued)

OLS and Reduced-Form Estimates of Effect of Class-Size Assignment on Average Percentile of Stanford Achievement Test

Explanatory variable	OLS: actual class size				Reduced form: initial class size			
	(1)	(2)	(3)	(4)	(5)	(6)	(7)	(8)
				C. Second grade				
Small class	5.93	6.33	5.83	5.79	5.31	5.52	5.27	5.26
	(1.97)	(1.29)	(1.23)	(1.23)	(1.70)	(1.16)	(1.10)	(1.10)
Regular/aide class	1.97	1.88	1.64	1.58	0.47	1.44	1.16	1.18
	(2.05)	(1.10)	(1.07)	(1.06)	(1.23)	(0.87)	(0.81)	(0.81)
White/Asian (1 = yes)	–	–	6.35	6.36			6.27	6.29
			(1.20)	(1.19)			(1.21)	(1.20)
Girl (1 = yes)	–	–	3.48	3.45	–	–	3.48	3.44
			(.60)	(.60)			(.60)	(.60)
Free lunch (1 = yes)	–	–	-13.61	-13.61	–	–	-13.75	13.77
			(.72)	(.72)			(.73)	(.73)
White teacher	–	–	–	0.39	–	–	–	0.43
				(1.75)				(1.76)
Male teacher	–	–	–	1.32	–	–	–	0.82
				(3.96)				(4.23)
Teacher experience	–	–	–	0.1	–	–	–	0.1
				(.06)				(.07)
Master's degree	–	–	–	-1.06	–	–	–	-1.16
				(1.06)				(1.05)
School fixed effects	No	Yes	Yes	Yes	No	Yes	Yes	Yes
R^2	0.01	0.22	0.28	0.28	0.01	0.21	0.28	0.28
				D. Third grade				
Small class	5.32	5.58	5.01	5	5.51	5.42	5.3	5.24
	(1.91)	(1.22)	(1.19)	(1.19)	(1.46)	(1.08)	(1.03)	(1.04)
Regular/aide class	-0.22	-0.16	-0.33	-0.75	-0.3	0.12	0.13	-0.1
	(1.95)	(1.12)	(1.11)	(1.07)	(1.17)	(0.85)	(0.81)	(0.78)
White/Asian (1 = yes)	–	–	6.12	6.11	–	–	5.97	5.96
			(1.45)	(1.44)			(1.44)	(1.43)
Girl (1 = yes)	–	–	4.16	4.16	–	–	4.17	4.18
			(.66)	(.65)			(.66)	(.66)
Free lunch (1 = yes)	–	–	-13.02	-12.96	–	–	-13.21	13.16
			(.81)	(.81)			(.82)	(.81)
White teacher	–	–	–	0.64	–	–	–	0.19
				(1.75)				(1.75)
Male teacher	–	–	–	-7.42	–	–	–	-6.83
				(2.80)				(2.76)
Teacher experience	–	–	–	0.04	–	–	–	0.03
				(.06)				(.06)
Master's degree	–	–	–	1.1	–	–	–	0.88
				(1.15)				(1.15)
School fixed effects	No	Yes	Yes	Yes	No	Yes	Yes	Yes
R^2	0.01	0.17	0.22	0.23	0.01	0.16	0.22	0.22

Notes: All models include constants. Robust standard errors that allow for correlated residuals among students in the same class are in parentheses. Sample size is 5,861 for kindergarten, 6,452 for first grade, 5,950 for second grade, and 6,109 for third grade.

Table 4.6

Exploration of Effect of Attrition Dependent Variable: Average Percentile Score on SAT

Grade	Actual test data		Actual and imputed test data	
	Coefficient on small class dum.	Sample size	Coefficient on small class dum.	Sample size
K	5,32	5,900	5,32	5,900
	(.76)		(.76)	
1	6,95	6,632	6,3	8,328
	(.74)		(.68)	
2	5,59	6,282	5,64	9,773
	(.76)		(.65)	
3	5,58	6,339	5,49	10,919
	(.79)		(.79)	

Notes: Estimates of reduced-form models are presented. Each regression includes the following explanatory variables: a dummy variable indicating initial assignment to a small class; a dummy variable indicating initial assignment to a regular/aide class, unrestricted school effects; a dummy variable for student gender; and a dummy variable for student race. The reported coefficient on small class dummy is relative to regular classes. Standard errors are in parentheses.

students who exited the sample. With longitudinal data, this can be done crudely by assigning the student's most recent test percentile to that student in years when the student was absent from the sample.[15]

The sample used in the first panel of Table 4.6 includes the largest number of students with nonmissing data available each grade. These results correspond to the model estimated in column 7 of Table 4.5, except the free lunch variable is omitted because it changes over time. For simplicity, only the coefficient on the dummy variable indicating initial assignment to a small class is reported in the table. The sample used in the second panel is larger than the sample in column 1 because it includes the column 1 sample plus any student who entered the program in an earlier grade and exited the sample by the current grade, assigning imputed test percentiles to students who exited the sample. To be included in the sample, it is necessary to have test data in at least some year. (Because kindergarten students could not have previously exited the sample, the sample size is the same in the first row.) The estimates using imputed test percentiles for missing observations are qualitatively quite similar to the estimates using the subsample of observations who were present in each particular grade.[16] Thus, nonrandom attrition does not appear to bias the estimated class size effects in Table 4.5.

The sample used in column 2 of Table 4.6 excludes students who were listed on the enrollment logs for kindergarten but withdrew from school prior to the start of school. For example, if a parent chose to withdraw a child from a STAR public school and enroll him or her in a private school immediately upon learning that the child was assigned to a regular-size class, the student is excluded from the sample. This type of behavior appears to have been rare (based on our inspection of notes on a sampling of enrollment sheets), but 12 percent of students who were listed on the enrollment logs and assigned to a class prior to the start of school were not actually enrolled in the school the following fall. These students moved to another school zone, enrolled in private school, or were withdrawn from kindergarten over the summer for some other reason. Using data for eighteen of the participating schools for which we were able to obtain initial kindergarten enrollment sheets, we calculate that 10.4 percent of students who were listed on the enrollment sheets and assigned to small kindergarten classes were missing from our sample by the start of kindergarten; the corresponding figures for regular/aide and regular classes are 12.2 percent and 14.3 percent, respectively. The differential withdrawal rate between the regular and small classes is statistically significant ($t = 1.86$), while the difference between the regular/aide and small class is not ($t = 0.86$). These findings suggest that 2 to 4 percent of students may have been withdrawn from the STAR schools because they were not assigned to a small class.

An upper bound estimate of the impact on test scores of the higher kindergarten withdrawal rate for students in regular and regular/aide classes can be calculated. Suppose that the 2–4 percent extra students who withdrew from regular and regular aide classes all would have scored in the one-hundredth percentile of the SAT exams. With this intentionally extreme assumption, the average score of students in the regular and regular/aide classes would only have increased by one-two percentile points if the extra students had not withdrawn from kindergarten. At the opposite extreme, if the higher withdrawal rate is due to the lowest achieving students leaving regular-size classes, the regular-size class students would have scored one-two points lower, on average, if they had remained. The actual impact is probably even smaller, however, because the extra withdrawals probably would have scored closer to the average student if they remained in the STAR schools. But even the upper and lower bounds estimates suggest that the higher withdrawal rate from regular-size classes does not have much impact on the results.

4.2.2. Two-Stage Least Squares (2SLS) Models

As noted, students in the Project STAR experiment who were assigned to small classes had varying numbers of students in their classes because of student mobility and enrollment differences across schools. Similarly, students in the regular-size classes had variable class sizes. A more appropriate model of achievement would take actual class size into account. A natural model for this situation is a triangular model of student achievement in which the actual number of students in the class is included on the right-hand side, and initial assignment to a class type is used as an instrumental variable for actual class size. Specifically, we estimate the following model by 2SLS:

(3) $$CS_{ics} = \pi_0 + \pi_1 S_{ios} + \pi_2 R_{ios} + \pi_3 X_{ics} + \delta_s + \tau_{ics}$$

(4) $$Y_{ics} = \beta_0 + \beta_1 CS_{ics} + \beta_2 X_{ics} + \alpha_s + \epsilon_{ics},$$

where CS_{ics} is the actual number of students in the class, S_{ios} is a dummy variable indicating assignment to a small class the first year the student is observed in the experiment, R_{ios} is a dummy variable indicating assignment to a regular class the first year the student is observed in the experiment, and all other variables are defined as before. Again, the error term (ϵ_{ics}) is treated as consisting of a common class effect and an idiosyncratic individual effect, and the standard errors are adjusted for correlation in the residuals among students in the same class.[17]

Table 4.7

OLS And 2SLS Estimates of Effect of Class Size on Achievement Dependent Variable: Average Percentile Score on Sat

Grade	OLS	2SLS	Sample size
	(1)	(2)	(3)
K	-.62	-.71	5,861
	(.14)	(.14)	
1	-.85	-.88	6,452
	(.13)	(.16)	
2	-.59	-.67	5,950
	(.12)	(.14)	
3	-.61	-.81	6,109
	(.13)	(.15)	

Notes: The coefficient on the actual number of students in each class is reported. All models also control for school effects; student's race, gender, and free lunch status; teacher race, experience, and education. Robust standard errors that allow for correlated errors among students in the same class are reported in parentheses.

In this setup, only variation in class size due to *initial* assignment to a regular or small class is used to provide variation in actual class size in the test score equation. Due to the random assignment of initial class type, one would expect that this excluded instrumental variable is uncorrelated with ϵ_{ics} as required for 2SLS to be consistent.[18] If attending a small class has a beneficial effect on students' test scores, β_1 would be negative.

Table 4.7 presents OLS and 2SLS estimates of equation (4). The 2SLS estimates tend to be a little larger in absolute value, especially in third grade. According to the 2SLS estimates, a reduction of ten students is associated with a seven-to-nine point increase in the average percentile ranking of students, depending on the grade. There is no obvious trend over grade levels in the effect of class size in these data.

Table 4.8

2SLS Estimates of Effect of Class Size on Achievement, by Entry Grade and Current Grade Dependent Variable: Average Score on Stanford Achievement Test

Current grade	Entering grade			
	K	1	2	3
K	-,71			
	(.15)			
1	-0,89	-,49		
	(.17)	(.23)		
2	-,49	-,70	-,24	
	(.16)	(.29)	(.21)	
3	-,66	-1,21	-,71	-,66
	(.17)	(.34)	(.28)	(.28)

Notes: The coefficient on the actual number of students in each class is reported. All models also control for school effects; student's race, gender, and free lunch status; teacher race, experience, and education. Robust standard errors that allow for correlation of residuals among students in the same class are reported in parentheses. Sample size in column 1 begins at 5,901 and ends at 3,124; sample size in column 2 begins at 2,190 and ends at 1,110; sample size in column 3 begins at 1,492 and ends at 1,010; sample size in column 4 is 1,110.

Table 4.8 presents additional 2SLS estimates of the effect of actual class size on achievement, disaggregating the sample by the grade the student entered Project STAR and current grade. The model and identification strategy are the same as in Table 4.7, column 2. The results indicate that for each cohort of students, those attending smaller classes tend to score higher on the standardized test by the end of the *first* year they entered the experiment. If assignment to small or regular classes was somehow nonrandom, then the initial assignment would have to have been skewed in the direction of producing higher test scores in the small classes for each wave of students who entered the program – an unlikely event. Interestingly, for the wave of students who entered in kindergarten, the beneficial effect of attending a small class does not appear to increase as students spend more time in their class assignment. For students entering the experiment in first or second grade, however, the test score gap between those in small- and regular-size classes grows as students progress to higher grades. The effect of time spent in a small class is explored further by pooling students in all grades together below.

4.2.3. Models with Pooled Data

To explore the cumulative effects of having been in a small or regular class, several models were estimated with the data pooled over students and grades. The general model was of the form,

$$(5) \qquad Y_{ig} = \beta_0 + \beta_1 S_{io} + \beta_2 REG/A_{io} + \beta_3 N^S_{ig} + \beta_4 N^A_{ig} + \beta_5 X_{ig}$$

$$+ \alpha_g + \alpha_f + \alpha_s + \epsilon_{ig},$$

where g indicates grade level (K, 1, 2, or 3) and i indicates students, Y_{ig} is the test score, S_{io} and REG/A_{io} are dummy variables indicating a student's class type in the first year he or she participated in the program, N^S_{ig} and N^A_{ig} are the cumulative number of years (including the current grade) the student has spent in a small or regular/aide class, X_{ig} is a vector of student, teacher, and class characteristics, α_g is a set of three current grade dummies, α_f is a set of three dummies indicating the first year the student entered the STAR sample, and α_s is a set of school fixed effects. Estimation is done by OLS, and robust standard errors that allow for a random individual component in the error term are reported.

Results including various sets of explanatory variables are reported in Table 4.9. Estimates shown in column 1 exclude student, teacher, and classmate characteristics. In column 2, regressors for measured student and teacher characteristics are included. Both of these models indicate that achievement of students in small classes jumps up by about four percentile points the first year a student attends a small class $(\beta_1 + \beta_3)$, and increases by about one percentile point for each additional year the student spends in a small class thereafter. Both the initial effect of being in a small class and the cumulative effect are statistically significant in these models.

Column 3 adds four variables reflecting the composition of a student's classmates. Students in small classes were more likely to remain with their classmates in first grade because students in regular classes were randomly reassigned between regular classes with and without full-time aides. Two variables are included to control for the impact of the constancy of one's classmates. First, the fraction of each, student's classmates who were in that student's class the preceding year is included. If a student is new to the school in a particular grade, this variable will have a value of 0; and if a student attends a class that consists only of students who were in that student's class the preceding year, the variable will have a value of 1. As a second measure of the environment in the class, we take the average of this variable over all the other students in the class. This variable might influence achievement because the extent to which other students in a class know each other could influence one's adjustment to the class.

Table 4.9

Estimates of Pooled Models Dependent Variable: Average Percentile Ranking on SAT Test Coefficient Estimates with Robust Standard Errors in Parentheses

Variable	(1)	(2)	(3)
Initial class small (1 = yes)	2.87	3.16	2.99
	(.83)	(.80)	(.80)
Initial class regular/aide (1 = yes)	0.29	0.49	0.58
	(.69)	(.67)	(.67)
Cumulative years in small class	1.19	1.05	0.65
	(.39)	(.38)	(.39)
Cumulative years in regular/aide class	0.37	0.25	0.14
	(.39)	(.37)	(.37)
Fraction of classmates in class previous year	–	–	0.6
			(1.03)
Average fraction of classmates together previous year	–	–	-0.46
			(1.52)
Fraction of classmates on free lunch	–	–	-2.73
			(1.62)
Fraction of classmates who attended kindergarten	–	–	6.85
			(1.67)
Student and teacher characteristics	No	Yes	Yes
3 current grade dummies; 3 dummies indicating first grade appeared in sample; school effects	Yes	Yes	Yes
R^2	0.18	0.23	0.23
Sample size	25,249	24,350	24,349

Notes: Student and teacher characteristics are as follows: student race, gender, and free lunch status; and teacher race, gender, experience, and master's degree or higher status. OLS estimates are reported, with robust standard errors that adjust for a possible correlation of residuals for the same student over time in parentheses.

In addition to these two "class constancy" variables, the regression includes the fraction of students in a class who receive free lunch and the fraction of students in the class who were present in the experiment during kindergarten. Because students on free lunch score lower on standardized tests than other students, a higher proportion of classmates on free lunch in a class may lower overall performance. The fraction of a class that attended kindergarten could affect achievement because kindergarten attendance is likely to make the class more socialized for school, which should enable the teacher to convey more material. Due to the random assignment of students, these variables should be uncorrelated with any omitted variables within schools.

Including these four variables hardly changes the initial jump in test scores associated with attending a small class (see column 3), although the cumulative effect of time spent in a small class is reduced by one-third when they are included, and is only on the margin of statistical significance ($t = 1.66$). Also notice that attendance in classes with a higher proportion of classmates who attended kindergarten has a large, positive effect on a student's own achievement. A two-standard-deviation change in the fraction of one's classmates who attended kindergarten is associated with about a three-percentile-point change in test scores. Test scores are not significantly related to the variables measuring the constancy of one's classmates. However, these variables are set to zero in kindergarten as all kindergarten students are new to the class. If the model in column 3 is estimated using the subsample from first grade on, students who are new to classes that include many students who were together the previous grade tend to score significantly lower on the SAT exam ($t = -3.2$). Thus, if a student is new to a class, he or she does better if most of the other students are new to the class as well. A higher fraction of classmates on free lunch has a negative, marginally statistically significant effect on achievement in this sample.

The pooled models in Table 4.9 allow for a one-time, discrete improvement in test scores from attending a small class, and for a constant increase for each additional year the student spends in a small class. One could estimate a more general model. Most obviously, the initial effect of being in a small class could vary by grade level (i.e., interact grade dummies and *SMALL*), and the linear effect of cumulative years in a small class could be generalized by including a set of unrestricted dummies indicating the number of past years spent in a small class. In results not presented here, such a less restrictive model was estimated. The estimates in Table 4.9 are nested in this model, so they can be tested against it. An F-test rejects the parsimonious specification in Table 4.9 at the .01 level. However, inspection of the coefficients suggests that the main reason for the rejection is that the initial effect of being in a small class is smaller in grades 2 and 3 than in kindergarten and first grade; the linear trend appears to be a plausible representation of the cumulative effect of time spent in a small class. Despite this rejection, the parsimonious model is a convenient way to summarize the dynamic effects of attending a small class in the early grades.

The relationship between the pooled model and the "value added" specification, which Hanushek and Taylor (1990) suggest is superior to other specifications of the education production function, should be emphasized. The value-added model only identifies the cumulative effect of time spent in a small class; the initial effect is differenced out. This can be seen by taking the first-difference of equation (5). If the estimates in Table 4.9 had indicated that there was no effect of the initial year spent in a small class, the value-added specification would capture the only parameter of interest. But the pooled estimates and the results in Table 4.8 indicate that perhaps the most important benefit of attending a small class occurs the first year a student is placed in a small class. This benefit is missed in the value-added specification.

This point is illustrated by estimating the following value-added specification by OLS:

$$(6) \quad Y_{ics,g} - Y_{ics,g-1} + \beta_0 + \beta_1 SMALL_{ics,g} + \beta_2 X_{ics,g} + \alpha_g + \alpha_s + \epsilon_{ics,g},$$

where the dependent variable is the change in students' percentile test scores between the end of grade g and $g-1$, and $SMALL_{ics,g}$ is class size during grade g. The coefficient β_1 essentially corresponds to the coefficient on cumulative time spent in a small class in equation (5). When this specification is estimated, the estimate of β_1 is 1.2, with a t-ratio of 3.1.[19] This value-added effect is of similar magnitude to the coefficient on the cumulative years in a small class variable in the models in Table 4.9. Thus, although the estimated value-added specification indicates that students gain from attending small classes, the benefit is less than the full effect that accounts for the discrete gain that occurs the first year students are in a small class.

Prais (1996) and Hanushek (1998) interpret the STAR experiment as providing evidence that smaller classes did not improve performance because previously published cross-sectional results do not show the achievement test gap between students in small and regular classes expanding significantly over time. For example, Hanushek (1998) writes: "If smaller classes were valuable in each grade, the achievement gap would widen. It does not. In fact, the gap remains essentially unchanged through the sixth grade.... The inescapable conclusion is that the smaller classes at best matter in kindergarten." This conclusion strikes me as questionable for two reasons. First, the mix of students compared at various grade levels in the results cited by Hanushek changes over time; half of the students exit or enter the sample after kindergarten. When the same students are tracked over time, the value-added and pooled specifications show students in small classes gaining about one percentile rank per year relative to students in regular classes. Second, students appear to benefit particularly from attending a small class the first year they attend one, whether that is in kindergarten, first, second, or third grade (see Table 4.8). The discrete jump in scores occurring the first year students attend a small class, combined with the entry of new waves of students over time, can distort the simple cross-sectional comparison of gains for the changing mix of students.

4.2.4. Heterogeneous Treatment Effects

The effect of being in a small class may vary for students with different backgrounds. Table 4.10 presents OLS estimates of the pooled model (equation (5)) for several subsamples of students. The pooled model was selected to summarize the class-size effects over all grade levels, although a less restrictive model would fit the data better.

Smaller classes tend to have a larger initial effect, but a smaller cumulative effect, for boys as compared with girls. Students on free lunch and black students tend to have both a larger initial effect and larger cumulative effect than those not on free lunch and white students. Finally, inner-city students tend to have a more beneficial effect of attending a small class in the first year they attend one than students from other areas, and a sharper gain over time from remaining in a small class.[20] Word et al. (1990) similarly found that smaller classes had a more beneficial effect for black students, students on free lunch, and inner-city students, but did not examine whether these differences were due to the initial effect or cumulative effect of time spent in a small class. In general, the pattern of effects reported in Table 4.10 suggests that the lower achieving students benefit the most from attending smaller classes.

Summers and Wolfe (1977) also find that attending a small class is more beneficial for low achieving students than for high achieving students.

Table 10

Separate Estimates for Select Samples Dependent Variable: Average Percentile Ranking on SAT Test (Coefficient estimates with robust standard errors in parentheses)

	Boys	Girls
Small	4.18	1.28
	(1.11)	(1.13)
Cumulative years in small class	.60	.92
	(.56)	(.54)
Sample size	12,576	11,773

	Free lunch	Not on free lunch
Small	3.14	2.85
	(1.10)	(1.12)
Cumulative years in small class	.94	.55
	(.59)	(.51)
Sample size	12,064	12,285

	Black	White
Small	3.84	2.58
	(1.29)	(1.02)
Cumulative years in small class	1.04	.66
	(.68)	(.48)
Sample size	8,150	16,069

	Inner city	Metropolitan	Towns	Rural
Small	3.74	2.92	3.09	2.58
	(1.68)	(1.55)	(2.83)	(1.23)
Cumulative years in small class	1.71	.57	-1.35	1.03
	(.90)	(.83)	(1.50)	(.56)
Sample size	5,154	5,906	1,872	11,417

Note: Model and covariates are the same as column 3 of Table 4.9.

The effect of attending a small class can also be estimated for each of the 80 schools in Project STAR. To estimate school-level small-class effects, I pooled the data for students across grades, and for each school regressed the percentile score on dummies indicating attendance in small and regular/aide classes, current grade dummies, and dummies indicating the grade the student entered project STAR. A parsimonious model was estimated for simplicity and to preserve degrees of freedom. A kernel density for the coefficients on the small-class dummy is shown in Figure 4.2. Two-thirds of the school-specific small-class effects are positive, while one-third are negative. Furthermore, 2.5 percent of the 80 coefficients had t-ratios less than -2, while 30 percent had t-ratios exceeding +2. The mean coefficient estimate is 4.6. The standard deviation of the coefficients (after adjusting for sampling variability) 7.5 percentage points.[21] Thus, some schools are more adept at translating smaller classes into student achievement than are other schools.

Figure 4.2

Kernel Density of School-Level Small-Class Effects

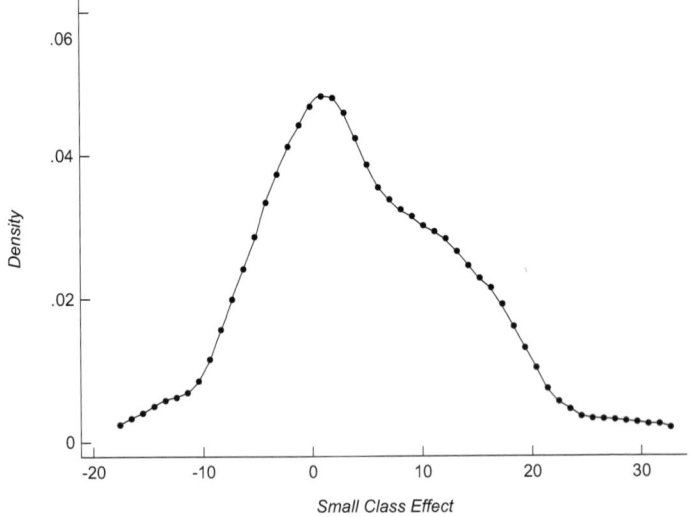

4.2.5. Hawthorne and John Henry Effects

It has been suggested by some that the effectiveness of small classes found in the STAR experiment may have resulted from "Hawthorne effects," in which teachers in small classes responded to the fact that they were part of an experiment, rather than a true causal effect of small classes themselves.[22] Others have suggested that the effect sizes might actually be larger than measured by the STAR experiment because teachers in regular classes provided greater than normal effort to demonstrate that they could overcome the bad luck of being assigned more students: a "John Henry" effect. Either set of responses could limit the external validity of the results of the STAR experiment.

As a partial check on these potential "reactive" effects, I examined the relationship between class size and student achievement *just* among students assigned to regular-size classes. Recall that there is considerable variability in class size even in the regular-size classes (see Table 4.3).[23] Obviously, Hawthorne and John Henry effects do not apply to a sample in which all teachers were randomly assigned to the control group. On the other hand, variability in class size is likely to be due primarily to idiosyncratic factors in this sample, such as integer effects in assigning classes and student mobility during the school year. Moreover, there is limited variability in class sizes within schools because many schools had only one regular-size class per grade.

To estimate the effect of class size on achievement for the control sample, I pooled the sample of students in regular-size classes across all grade levels, and regressed the average SAT test score on the number of students in the class, grade level dummies, and student and teacher characteristics.[24] The coefficient on class size in this regression is -.55, with a t-ratio of -4.3. If school dummies are added to this model, the coefficient on class size falls to -.39, but remains statistically significant ($t = -3.1$). Based on these estimates, an eight-student reduction in class size is associated with a three-to-four-percentile increase in test scores, which is insignificantly different from estimates derived from the experimental variations in class size. These regression results do not provide much evidence of either Hawthorne or John Henry effects. And given that much of the variability in class size in the control group may be due to measurement errors (e.g. students moving in and out of class during the school year), it is noteworthy that these regressions find any evidence of class-size effects.

4.2.6. Separate Subject Test Results for SAT and BSF

Table 4.11 presents estimates of the pooled data model corresponding to column 3 of Table 4.9 for each of the main subsections of the SAT test, as well as for the subsections of the BSF test and the average of the math and reading percentile scores on the BSF test. These results indicate relatively minor differences in the initial and cumulative effects of attending a small class on the math, reading and word recognition tests. Furthermore, the BSF test shows the same basic pattern as the SAT test – a discrete increase in performance for attending a small class, with a small (statistically insignificant) increase thereafter. On the whole, little seems to have been lost by focusing on the average of the SAT tests as the mainstay of the analysis.

Table 4.11

Estimates of Pooled Data Model by Subject Test Dependent Variable: Percentile Score on SAT or BSF Test (Coefficient estimates with robust standard errors in parentheses)

	Stanford Achievement Test			Basic skills First		
	Math	Reading	Word	Math	Reading	Avg.
Small	2.83	3.52	2.97	1.09	3.04	2.02
	(.88)	(.88)	(.87)	(1.05)	(1.08)	(.96)
Cumulative years in small	.45	.43	.80	1.23	.41	.83
class	(.42)	(.43)	(.42)	(.44)	(.46)	(.41)
Sample size	23,794	23,461	23,630	18,174	18,010	18,250

Note: Model and covariates are the same as in column 3 of Table 4.9.

4.3. Conclusions

One well-designed experiment should trump a phalanx of poorly controlled, imprecise observational studies based on uncertain statistical specifications. The implementation of the STAR experiment was not flawless, but my re-analysis suggests that the flaws in the experiment did not jeopardize its main results. Adjustments for school effects, attrition, re-randomization after kindergarten, nonrandom transitions, and variability in actual class size do not overturn the main findings of Finn and Achilles (1990), Folger and Breda (1989), and Word et al. (1990): students in small classes scored higher on standardized tests than students in regular-size classes. The results also indicate that the provision of a full-time teacher aide has only a modest effect on student achievement, although this effect may be attenuated because of the frequent availability of part-time aides in regular classes.

Interestingly, at least for the early grades, my analysis suggests that the main benefit of attending a small class seems to arise by the end of the initial year a student attends a small class. After the first year, additional time spent in a small class has a positive but smaller effect on test scores. One possible explanation for this pattern is that attending a small class in the lower grades may confer a one-time, "school socialization effect" which permanently raises the level of student achievement without greatly affecting the trajectory.

Because much of the previous literature estimates class-size effects using a "value-added" specification that uses student test score gains as the dependent variable and current class size as the main explanatory variable, much of the past research may miss the main benefit of smaller classes. More research is needed to develop an appropriate model of student learning. But for now, one should be concerned that the value-added specification may miss much of the value that is added from attending a smaller class. Moreover, studies that identify class-size effects by comparing differences in the *level* of test scores between students who were subject to different class sizes for exogenous reasons, such as Angrist and Lavy's (1999) clever use of Maimonides' law, may stand a better chance of uncovering the total effect of class size than estimates based on the value-added specification.

No single study, even an experimental one, could be definitive. The STAR results suggest that the magnitude of the achievement gains from attending smaller classes varies across schools and student characteristics. It is possible (though probably unlikely) that Tennessee has a much higher concentration of students or schools that benefit from smaller classes than other states. It is also possible that reducing class size does not have a beneficial effect for students after the third grade. Obviously, more experimentation would help resolve these issues. It would also be helpful to compare the STAR findings with the rest of the literature. Before concluding that the weight of the literature suggests that attending a small class does not matter for the average student, it would be useful to know how many of the studies enumerated in Hanushek's (1986, 1996b) surveys have sufficient power to reject either the level effect (for level specifications) or cumulative effect (for value-added specifications) of attending a small class that is implied by the Project STAR data.

Experiments of the scale and quality of Project STAR are disappointingly rare in the education field. When these experiments are conducted, they should be analyzed and followed up to the fullest extent possible. The students who participated in Project STAR were returned to regular classes after third grade, and have been followed up through the ninth grade. Nye et al. (1994) find that students who were placed in small classes have lasting achievement gains through at least the seventh grade, although it is difficult to compare the magnitude of the benefits with those at earlier grades because of changes in the tests that were administered. The students studied in Project

STAR are currently in high school. To learn more about the long-term benefits of attending smaller classes, it would be useful to continue studying the academic – and just as importantly, nonacademic – outcomes of the STAR participants as they enter early adulthood.

In the meantime, we can perform the following rough benefit- cost analysis to gauge the likely order of magnitudes of the economic effects of reducing class size in the early grades. The STAR experiment reduced class size by seven or eight students, or about by one-third. Folger and Parker (1990) estimate that the cost of reducing class size in Tennessee (including capital costs) would be proportional to the total annual educational expenditures per student. In 1995–1996 total expenditures per enrolled public school student in the United States were $6,459 (National Center for Educational Statistics 1996), so reducing class size by one-third would increase costs per student by about $2,151 per year. We discount all benefits and costs to the present. Using a 3 percent real discount rate, the present value of the additional costs of reducing class size by one-third for the wave of entering kindergarten students for four years would be approximately $7,400.

The economic benefits of the STAR experiment are much more difficult to assess than the costs. The Table 4.5 results suggest that test scores for students in small classes rose by about 0.22 standard deviations. I am not aware of any study that links achievement on the Stanford Achievement Test to later economic outcomes. Furthermore, it is possible that the cognitive gains from attending smaller classes will dissipate or grow by the time the STAR students enter the labor market. As a rough assumption, suppose that the 0.22 S.D. gain persists. How does this translate into economic benefits? Estimates based on the High School and Beyond sample in Murnane, Willet, and Levy (1995) indicate that male high school seniors who score 0.22 S.D.'s higher on the basic math achievement test in 1980 earned 1.7 percent higher earnings six years later. The comparable figure for females was 2.4 percent. Average earnings for workers age 18 and older in the United States in 1996 were $34,705 for men and $20,570 for women (U.S. Census Bureau 1996). If we assume that real earnings will be unchanged in the future and that Murnane, Willet, and Levy's estimates can be applied to the STAR experiment, then the present value of the earnings gain from raising test scores .22 S.D.'s is $9,603 for men and $7,851 for women, assuming that students enter the workforce at age 20 and retire at age 65, and using a real discount rate of 3 percent.

Many assumptions underlying this cost–benefit calculation could turn out to be wrong, including the following: real earnings may grow or shrink; the effect of test scores on future earnings may be different than assumed; class size may influence other economic outcomes, such as crime and dependency; the cost of reducing class size may be different than assumed. There is no substitute for directly measuring the economic outcomes that may be affected by reducing class size. Nonetheless, these calculations suggest that the benefit of reducing class size in terms of future earnings is in the same ballpark as the costs.

Appendix

Summary Statistics (Means with Standard Deviations in Parentheses)

Variable	K	1	Grade 2	3	All
Class size	20.3	21.0	21.1	21.3	20.9
	(4.0)	(4.0)	(4.1)	(4.4)	(4.1)
Percentile score avg. SAT	51.4	51.5	51.2	51.0	51.3
	(26.7)	(26.9)	(26.5)	(27.0)	(26.8)
Percentile score avg. BSF	NA	51.8	51.6	51.4	51.6
		(26.1)	(26.2)	(26.1)	(26.1)
Free lunch	.48	.52	.51	.50	.51
White	.67	.67	.65	.66	.66
Girl	.49	.48	.48	.48	.47
Age[a]	5.43	6.58	7.67	8.70	7.12
	(0.35)	(0.49)	(0.56)	(0.59)	(1.31)
Exited sample[b]	.29	.26	.21	NA	.43
Retained	NA	NA	NA	.04	NA
Percent of teachers[c] with MA+ degree	.35	.35	.37	.44	.38
Percent of teachers who are White	.83	.82	.79	.79	.81
Percent of teachers who are male	.00	.00	.01	.03	.01
No. of schools	79	76	75	75	80
No. of students	6,323	6,828	6,839	6,801	11,599
No. of small classes	127	124	133	140	524
No. of reg. classes	99	115	100	89	403
No. of reg/aide classes	99	100	107	107	413

[a] Age as of September of the school year they are observed.
[b] The fraction that exited the sample in the next year, for K–2; for All it is the fraction that ever exited the sample.
[c] Teacher characteristics are weighted by the number of students in each teacher's class.

III

Minimum Wages and Employment Demand

Introduction

Models of employment demand at the firm and market level are critical to economists' understanding of such diverse phenomena as international trade, technological change, immigration, and income support programs. Conventional demand models – formulated on the assumption that employers take wages as given – predict that higher wages lead to a reduction in employment demand. The trade-off between wages and employment imposes a fundamental constraint on policy makers and trade unions interested in raising wages, subsidizing the creation of new jobs, or imposing other interventions on the labor market.

While the nature of the employment demand relationship is extremely important, research has been hindered by the fact that in most situations wages and employment are *jointly* determined. Normally, one cannot interpret a series of observations on employment and wages as movements *along* the demand curve, as employment and wages are jointly determined by supply and demand. A clear exception is the minimum wage. As explained in introductory economics textbooks, the imposition of a binding minimum wage is predicted to cause a fall in employment that depends on the underlying elasticity of demand.

Chapters 7, 8, and 9 explore the effects of minimum wages on the demand for relatively low-wage workers. Our interest in this issue was sparked during the late 1980s, when several states responded to the decade long freeze in the nominal value of the Federal minimum wage by adopting their own state-specific minimum wages. This set the stage for an extremely simple approach to measuring the effect of minimum wages. In this so-called "natural experiments" approach, employers in states with an increase in the minimum wage are treated like participants in a randomized experiment who are assigned to the treatment group. Employers in other states with no change in the minimum wage are treated like participants in the control group. Under certain assumptions, comparisons between the two groups before and after the rise in the minimum wage reveal the behavioral response of the "treated" firms to the higher minimum wage. Our friend and colleague Richard A. Lester had used a similar approach in the 1940s to study the effect of the (then new) Federal minimum wage. But by the 1970s, the accepted methodology for evaluating the employment effects of the minimum wage was based on year-to-year comparisons of national employment rates of low-wage workers (mainly teenagers).

Chapter 7 (written by David Card) represents a twist on the simple natural experiments approach. In 1989, Congress passed an amendment to the Federal minimum wage law that raised the national minimum wage by 27 percent. At that time, 15 states and the District of Columbia had minimum wages above the prevailing Federal rate. Thus, when the new national minimum took effect, it had a much bigger impact in some states (where the state minimum wage had not been raised) than in others (where it had). Simple comparisons of state-specific changes in wages and employment between 1989 and 1990 showed that teenage wages rose faster in states where the "bite" of the new Federal minimum was larger. But, surprisingly, there was no indication of a corresponding loss in teenage employment.

Intrigued by these findings, when the State of New Jersey voted in 1992 to raise its minimum wage by nearly 20 percent above the then-prevailing Federal rate, we decided to conduct a longitudinal survey of fast food restaurants in New Jersey and nearby regions of Pennsylvania. The first wave of the survey was conducted in February and March of 1992 – just a month before the New Jersey increase took effect. At the time, we were not sure the minimum wage would actually increase as the state legislature changed parties and attempted to repeal the minimum wage increase. As it turned out, the effort to repeal the increase fell a few votes shy of succeeding. Consequently, we contacted the same restaurants in November and December of 1992, about 8 months after the increase, to survey them again.

Chapter 8 presents an analysis of the results from this survey. Consistent with the findings from state-wide comparisons in Chapter 7, our analysis of the impacts of the New Jersey minimum wage showed no negative employment effects of the increase. Importantly, we obtained similar results when we conducted a "between-state" analysis, focusing on the difference in employment growth at restaurants in New Jersey and Pennsylvania, and a "within-state" analysis, building on the fact that some restaurants in New Jersey were already paying wages at or above the new minimum wage *before* the increase. We also documented other interesting features – like wide variation in starting wages within relatively narrow geographic areas, and the widespread use of recruiting bonuses – that suggested to us that the key assumptions of the conventional employment demand model are incorrect. Instead, we concluded that evidence from the fast food sector favors a more general model with some employer discretion in wage setting.

Our findings on the impact of the New Jersey minimum wage increase were challenged almost immediately. Some commentators argued that our survey was unrepresentative, or that the employment measures derived from our survey led to misleading inferences about the effect of the minimum wage. To address these criticisms, we obtained access to confidential establishment-level employment data reported to the Bureau of Labor Statistics for a large set of fast food restaurants in New Jersey and contiguous counties of Pennsylvania. These data are based in Unemployment Insurance payroll tax records, and presumably have little or no measurement error. Moreover, the samples included *all* restaurants in the relevant geographic area for a set of restaurant chains, eliminating concerns over non-representative sampling.

Chapter 9 presents the findings from our analysis of this new sample. As in our original survey, we found that employment growth in the fast food industry was, if anything, slightly stronger in New Jersey than in nearby counties of Pennsylvania in the period immediately after the rise in the New Jersey minimum wage. We also re-analyzed the results from a sample constructed by critics of our original analysis, and compared the patterns of employment growth in their sample and ours. Taking the available evidence as a whole, we believe that the rise in the New Jersey minimum wage had little or no effect on employment in the fast food sector of the state, and certainly no important negative effect.

The final chapter in this section (written by David Card) shifts the focus of attention from the effect of minimum wages to the effect of union-negotiated contract provisions on employment demand. North American union contracts are typically 2 or 3 years long. During the high-inflation era of the 1970s, many contracts ended with a real wage that differed substantially from the level anticipated at the signing date of the contract. The empirical analysis studies the effect of contract wages on end-of-contract employment, using unexpected price shocks experienced over the life of each contract as an exogenous source of variation in the level of real wages. In this setting, the predictions of the conventional employment demand model are verified: employment is significantly negatively related to the level of real wages. The contrast to the findings of our studies of minimum wages is interesting. Unlike minimum wage employers, who often report unfilled vacancies, most unionized employers have queues of applicants willing to start work. Arguably, then, the key assumption of the conventional demand model – that the employer takes wages as given – is more appropriate in the union contract setting than in the low-wage labor markets that are most affected by minimum wage legislation.

5

Using Regional Variation in Wages to Measure the Effects of the Federal Minimum Wage

One of the traditional criticisms of a federal minimum wage policy is that it imposes a higher relative wage floor in regions with lower average wages (see Stigler 1946, pp.360–61). An appropriate minimum wage for New Jersey, for example, may have devastating labor market consequences in Mississippi.[1] From an evaluation perspective, however, a uniform minimum wage is an under-appreciated asset. A rise in the federal minimum wage will typically affect a larger fraction of workers in some states than in others. This variation provides a simple natural experiment for measuring the effect of legislated wage floors, with a "treatment effect" that varies across states depending on the fraction of workers initially earning less than the new minimum.

This chapter examines the experiences following the April 1990 rise in the federal minimum wage to evaluate the effects of minimum wages on the teenage labor market. In 1989, one-quarter of all 16–19-year-olds earned between $3.35 per hour (the existing federal minimum rate) and $3.80 per hour (the new minimum). Across states, however, this fraction varied from under 10% in New England and California to over 50% in many southern states. Much of this variation is attributable to the presence of state-specific wage floors above the federal rate. In the late 1980s many states responded to the decade-long freeze in the federal minimum wage by raising their own

This chapter is a revised version of: Card, D. (1992). Using Regional Variation in Wages to Measure the Effects of the Federal Minimum Wage, in: Industrial and Labor Relations Review 46, 22–37, © Cornell University, 1992. The author thanks Christopher Burns for research assistance and Charles Brown, Gary Fields, Larry Katz, and Alan Krueger for their comments.

minimum rates above $3.35 per hour. These state-specific wage floors created remarkable geographic dispersion in teenage wage rates, setting the stage for the empirical analysis reported here.

5.1. Minimum Wage Statutes in 1989–1990

The federal minimum wage increased to $3.35 per hour in January 1981 and remained frozen throughout the 1980s. By the close of the decade, cumulative inflation had eroded the purchasing power of the minimum wage to its lowest level since January 1950.[2] The decline in the real value of the federal minimum wage prompted state legislatures and wage boards to respond with state-specific minimum rates above the federal standard. The first of these higher minimums arose in the New England states – Maine ($3.45 effective January 1985), Massachusetts and Rhode Island (both $3.55 effective July 1986), New Hampshire ($3.45 effective January 1987), and Connecticut ($3.75 effective October 1987). By 1989 a total of 16 states and the District of Columbia had wage floors above $3.35.[3]

Political pressure for an increase in the federal minimum wage culminated in March 1989 with passage of a House resolution to raise the minimum to $4.55 over three years. A similar bill passed the Senate but was vetoed by the President. A bill providing for smaller wage increases and a liberalized youth subminimum was introduced in November 1989 and passed into law with Presidential support. This bill raised the minimum wage in two steps – to $3.80 on April 1, 1990, and to $4.25 on April 1, 1991 – and set a training minimum equal to 85 percent of the regular minimum wage for employees aged 16–19.

Other provisions of the federal minimum wage were modified only slightly by the April 1990 law. The tip credit, which allows employees to credit a portion of their tips toward the minimum, was raised from 40 percent to 45 percent. Consequently, the federal minimum wage for tipped employees rose from $2.01 to $2.09 per hour. Exemptions for smaller businesses were also expanded and simplified. Previously, retail and service enterprises with an annual sales volume of less than $250,000 were exempt from coverage. This threshold was raised to $500,000 and extended to all industries.[4]

5.2. The Effect on Teenagers: An Overview

Because teenagers are typically at the bottom of the earnings distribution, and because a large fraction of low-paid workers are teenagers, the minimum wage literature has concentrated on the youth labor market (see the chapters of the Minimum Wage Study Commission (1981) and the review article by Brown, Gilroy, and Kohen (1982)). Simple models of the teenage labor market predict varying responses to the rise in the federal minimum wage, depending on the fraction of workers initially earning below the new rate. (See Welch 1976 for a thorough overview.) Examination of the interstate patterns of wage and employment growth for teenagers between 1989 and 1990 provides a credible test of the proposition that changes in teenage labor market outcomes reflect changes in the minimum wage, rather than other factors that coincided with the law.[5]

Table 5.1 presents some descriptive information on teenagers taken from the monthly files of the Current Population Survey (CPS) in 1989 and 1990. Each month, individuals in the two "outgoing rotation groups" of the survey are asked to provide supplementary information on earnings and hours on their main job (if they have one). The data in Table 5.1 and throughout this chapter are based on the responses for this quarter sample of the CPS. To facilitate a comparison of the periods before and after the rise in the minimum wage, the samples include only the April–December surveys of each year.

The first and sixth columns of Table 5.1 present data for all teenagers, and the remaining columns pertain to employed teenagers and those with hourly wages in specified intervals.[6] The U.S. teenage population includes a high fraction of nonwhites (20%) and Hispanics (10%); the respective proportions of the working population are lower. Employed teenagers also tend to be older and have more years of completed education than nonworking teenagers. A majority of teenagers (56.5%) report that they are "attending or enrolled in high school, college, or university." A slightly lower fraction (48%) report that their main activity during the survey week was "in school." These fractions must be interpreted carefully, since school attendance rates vary over the year. During 1989 the average fraction of teenagers enrolled in school varied from 77 percent in April to 14 percent in July and August.

The CPS collects hourly wage information for individuals who are paid by the hour (93% of teenagers) and usual weekly earnings for

Table 5.1

Characteristics of Teenagers and Teenage Workers, 1989 and 1990

| | | April–December 1989 | | | | | April–December 1990 | | | |
| | | | Workers with wage | | | | | Workers with wage | | |
Description	All	All workers	<$3.35	$3.35–3.79	≥$3.80	All	All workers	<$3.35	$3.35–3.79	≥$3.80
1. Percent of all	—	49.0	3.5	11.9	31.1	—	46.4	2.6	3.4	38.2
2. Percent of workers	—	100.0	7.1	24.4	63.6	—	100.0	5.6	7.4	82.3
3. Female (%)	49.7	48.3	61.0	53.4	45.6	49.7	48.3	62.1	51.7	47.8
4. Nonwhite (%)	19.0	11.9	10.7	15.1	10.8	19.7	11.8	8.3	17.5	11.4
5. Hispanic (%)	9.9	8.1	5.5	6.9	8.8	10.4	8.7	7.9	5.9	9.2
6. Educ < 12(%)	62.8	53.0	65.2	68.1	45.8	64.4	53.1	68.6	73.4	49.9
7. Age 16–17 (%)	48.2	38.9	52.4	54.3	31.6	48.0	37.6	50.1	54.2	35.0
8. Enrolled in school	56.6	45.6	51.3	55.8	41.2	57.4	46.3	48.3	61.3	45.3
9. Hours/week	—	26.6	22.0	22.5	28.8	—	26.4	22.8	20.1	27.1
10. Avg. wage ($/hr.)	—	4.61	2.46	3.49	5.28	—	4.84	2.46	3.54	5.12
Including tips and commissions:										
11. Av. wage ($/hr.)	—	4.77	3.06	3.61	5.41	—	4.99	3.04	3.67	5.24
12. Weekly wage (%/week)	—	134.3	69.5	82.2	161.0	—	137.8	70.7	79.7	147.2
13. Percent reporting tips > 0	—	11.0	24.5	12.2	9.8	—	11.5	28.2	13.3	10.9
Industry distribution										
14. Agriculture	—	4.2	6.0	2.2	3.4	—	4.4	8.9	2.5	3.3
15. Retail trade	—	50.1	49.5	68.4	45.2	—	50.0	48.0	63.5	50.1
16. Service	—	26.2	35.8	22.6	25.9	—	27.0	37.9	27.2	26.1
17. Sample size	18,511	9,205	674	2,326	5,735	18,549	8,625	499	653	7,049

Note: Data are taken from 1989 and 1990 monthly Current Population Survey files (outgoing rotation groups for April–December for each year). "All workers" include unpaid and self-employed workers. Workers in specified wage ranges exclude self-employed workers and those with allocated allocated hourly or weekly earnings. The wage measure in row 10 is based on straight-time wages of hourly rated workers. Wage in row 11 includes pro-rated tips and comissions for hourly rated workers.

other workers. The wage measure presented in row 10 of Table 5.1 and used to define the columns of the table is the reported wage for hourly rated workers and the ratio of usual weekly earnings to usual weekly hours for other workers. By this "straight-time" wage measure, teenage workers earned an average of $4.61 per hour in 1989, compared to an average of $10.10 for all workers in the United States. Seven percent of teenagers earned less than the federal minimum wage of $3.35 per hour, 24 percent earned from $3.35 to $4.24 per hour, and 64 percent earned $3.80 per hour or more. Another 5 percent either were self-employed, worked without pay, or failed to report earnings information.[7]

One difficulty with the wage measure in row 10 of Table 5.1 is that some workers who report being paid by the hour also receive tips or commissions. This practice is especially widespread in retail trade, where over one-half of the teenagers are employed (see row 15 of the table). For hourly rated workers the CPS also collects usual weekly earnings *including* regular tips and commissions. This information can be used to construct an estimate of average weekly tips and an alternative measure of hourly wages. The average level of wages including pro-rated tips (in row 11 of Table 5.1) is 3 percent higher than the average based on straight-time earnings, reflecting the addition of tips and commissions for just over 10 percent of teenage workers.[8]

The characteristics of teenagers with "straight-time" earnings less than the minimum wage are presented in the third column of Table 5.1. There are various explanations for subminimum pay, including noncoverage (for tipped employees in retail trade and full-time students under the student subminimum),[9] employer noncompliance, and measurement error. Examination of the wage distribution of teenagers earning less than $3.35 shows a substantial spike (21% of workers) near the tipped minimum of $2.01 per hour, suggesting that many subminimum-wage workers are exempt from the $3.35 standard. This is further confirmed by the higher incidence of tip income among subminimum wage teenagers: 25 percent of subminimum wage earners report strictly positive tip income, versus 11 percent overall. When hourly wages are calculated including tip income, 19 percent of workers with straight-time pay less than $3.35 have effective wages above the minimum wage. Even including usual tip income, however, a substantial number of teenagers reported subminimum wages in 1989.

Employer noncompliance may partly explain this finding. Compared with other teenagers, subminimum wage workers are more likely to work in agriculture and household services, where noncompliance may be higher. Another factor is the relatively high fraction of subminimum wage workers who report being paid by the week or month, rather than by the hour (25%, versus 7% of all working teenagers). Some salaried workers are legally exempt from the minimum wage, and others may have over-reported their usual weekly hours, leading to a downward bias in their imputed hourly wage.

The next column of Table 5.1 presents the characteristics of teenagers reporting hourly wages of $3.35 to $3.79 in 1989. For simplicity, I refer to this group as "affected workers," since a rise in the minimum wage is most likely to affect employees of complying firms in the covered sector who previously earned less than the new rate. Affected teenagers are more likely to be enrolled in school than those with either higher or lower wages, and they are also more likely to be employed in retail trade. Some 40 percent of affected workers report an hourly wage *exactly* equal to the 1989 minimum wage. Their wage distribution shows additional spikes at $3.50 and $3.75, with an average of $3.49 per hour.

The five right-hand columns of Table 5.1 present corresponding information for 1990. Teenagers as a whole reported slightly higher enrollment rates during April–December of 1990 than in the same months of 1989. The teenage employment rate, on the other hand, fell by 2.5 percentage points.[10] For comparison, the annual average teenage employment rates for 1989 and 1990 (published by the Bureau of Labor Statistics) were 47.5 percent and 45.4 percent. Thus, the employment data for April to December reflect a slightly larger downturn than the annual averages.

The teenage wage distribution also shifted between 1989 and 1990, with a sharp reduction in the fraction of workers earning $3.35–$3.79 per hour (from 24.4% to 7.4%) and a mean increase of 5 percent. A comparison of the 1989 and 1990 distributions shows the elimination of the previous spike at $3.35 per hour and the emergence of a new spike at $3.80. Interestingly, there was only a slight reduction in the fraction of teenagers reporting wages (exclusive of tips) that were under $3.35.

Although these patterns are suggestive of the effect of the new minimum wage law, even stronger evidence of its impact is provided in Figure 5.1, which shows quarterly averages of the fractions of teenagers earning less than $3.35, exactly $3.35, and $3.36–$3.79 per hour from 1989-I to 1990-IV. The figure indicates an abrupt drop in the fraction earning less than $3.80 per hour in the second quarter of 1990 (that is, after April 1). Most of this drop reflects a reduction in the fraction earning $3.35–$3.79, with little evidence of an effect on the fraction earning less than $3.35. The effect of the minimum wage law was mainly concentrated on workers who previously earned at least the old minimum wage but less than the new rate.

Two other aspects of Figure 5.1 also deserve comment. First, there is only a slight dip in the fraction earning less than $3.80 per hour in the first quarter of 1990, even though the new minimum wage was signed into law in November 1989. Most employers evidently waited until the effective date of the law to increase the wages of their teenage employees. Second, the fraction of workers earning exactly $3.35 shows a continuing decline after 1990-II, suggesting some lag in the adjustment of wages (or in the reporting process).

Before turning to a regional analysis of the effects of the increased federal minimum wage, it is worthwhile to analyze the aggregate change in teenage employment between 1989 and 1990. Much of the existing literature has used the correlation between minimum wages and aggregate teenage employment to infer the effect of the law. As noted in Table 5.1, teenage employment fell between 1989 and 1990. Part of this decline is clearly attributable to the 1990 recession, which began in midyear. The youth labor market is highly cyclical, and the onset of a recession would be expected to lower teenage employment by several percentage points. This historical relationship is illustrated in Figure 5.2, which graphs annual average teenage employment rates for 1975–1990 along with the predicted rates from a linear regression on a trend and the overall employment-population ratio.[11] The prediction equation tracks the actual teenage employment rate up to 1989 remarkably well; the 1990 rate, however, was about 0.6% lower than expected. Although it may be tempting to attribute this discrepancy to the effect of the increased minimum wage, it should be noted that the real minimum wage was relatively high in 1976, 1979, and 1981, and then trended down throughout the late 1980s with little apparent effect on employment.[12]

Figure 5.1

Share of Teenagers Earning Less Than $3.80 per Hour, 1989–1990

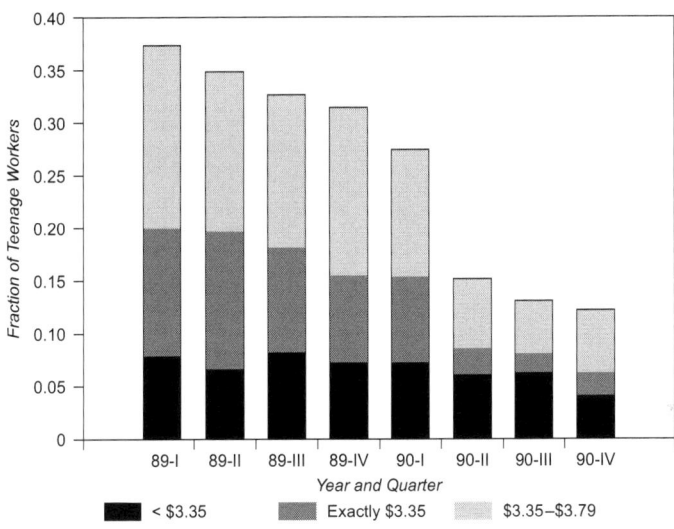

Figure 5.2

Actual and Predicted Teenage Employment–Population Rate, 1975–1990

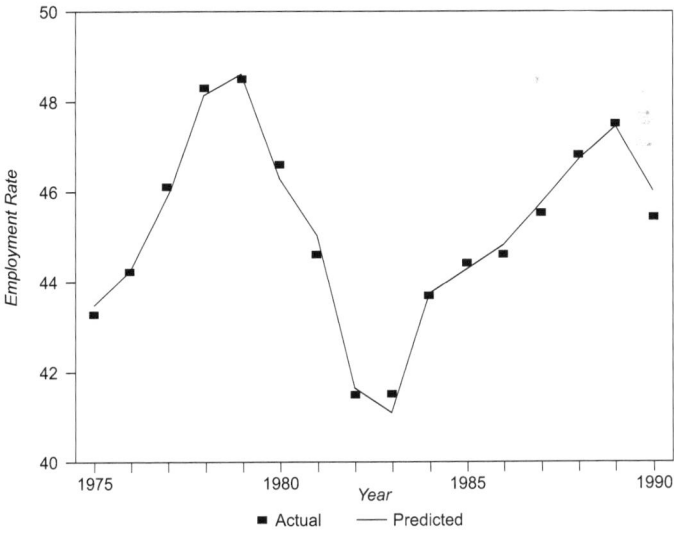

5.3. A Grouped Analysis

The nationwide data in Table 5.1 and Figure 5.1 conceal consider-able interstate variation in the distribution of teenage wages prior to the rise in the federal minimum wage. This wide variation suggests two complementary approaches to analyzing the effect of the 1990 increase in the minimum wage. The first is to aggregate states into groups with similar fractions of affected workers in 1989. This ap-proach generates relatively large sample sizes in each group, permit-ting a quarterly analysis along the lines of Figure 5.1. A second ap-proach is to use all the states and pool the months before and after April 1990 for each state. I first present the grouped analysis, then turn to a state-by-state analysis.

Figure 5.3 plots the fraction of workers earning $3.35–$3.79 by quarter for three groups of states: states with under 20 percent of teen-age workers earning $3.35 – $3.79 in 1989 ("high-wage states"); states with over 40 percent of teenage workers earning $3.35 – $3.79 in 1989 ("low-wage states"); and all other states ("medium-wage states"). The high-wage group contains 16 states, most of which had passed state-specific minimum wages above $3.35 per hour (all of New England, New York, New Jersey, Minnesota, Delaware, Maryland, District of Columbia, Nevada, Washington, California, Alaska, and Hawaii). The low-wage group contains 11 southern and mountain states (West Virginia, South Carolina, Kentucky, Tennessee, Mississippi, Arkan-sas, Louisiana, Oklahoma, Montana, Wyoming, New Mexico) plus North Dakota and South Dakota. The medium-wage group includes the remaining 22 states.

As expected, the impact of the 1990 minimum wage law is concen-trated among the low- and medium-wage states. Both state groups show a sharp decline in the fraction of teenagers earning $3.35–$3.79 per hour after April 1, 1990. By the end of 1990, the fractions of teenagers earning $3.35 to $3.79 per hour were remarkably similar across states.

Table 5.2 presents quarterly averages of teenage wages and employ-ment rates by state group, along with their sampling errors and the differences in the outcomes between corresponding quarters of 1989 and 1990. Assuming that underlying labor market trends were the same in the three groups of states, one way to estimate the effect of the federal minimum wage is to compare outcomes in 1990 to out-comes for the same quarter in 1989, and then to compare these differ-ences across the three groups of states. To facilitate this comparison, the bottom row of the table gives the average differences between the second, third, and fourth quarters of 1989 and 1990.

Looking first at earnings, the high-wage states show an average 4 percent wage gain between 1989 and 1990, with no evidence of an accelerated trend after 1990-I (that is, after the increase in the minimum wage). Average wages in the low- and medium-wage states, on the other hand, show a noticeable upsurge in 1990-II. Comparing the last three quarters of 1989 and 1990 across the three groups, the data in Table 5.2 suggest that the rise in the federal minimum wage increased average teenage wages by 2 percent in the medium-wage states and by 6 percent in the low-wage states.

Figure 5.3

Fraction of Teenage Workers Earning $3.35–$3.79 per Hour: Three Groups of States, 1989–1900

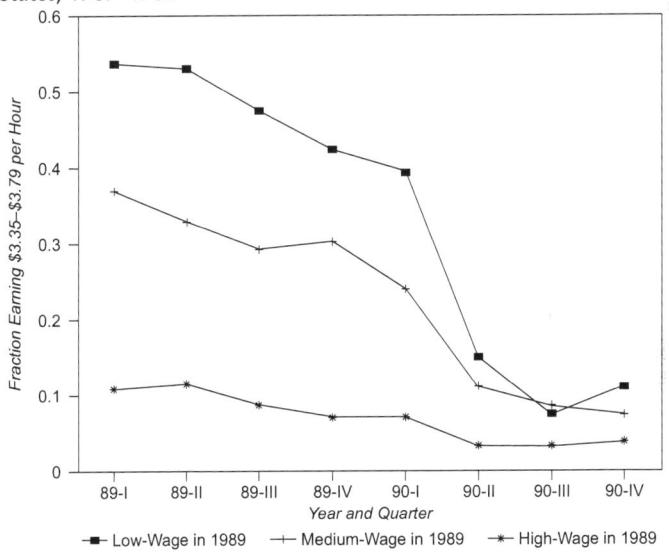

As a benchmark, it is useful to compare these estimated effects to the wage gains implied by a naive model in which the only effect of the minimum wage is to raise the earnings of affected workers up to the new minimum. Such a model will tend to understate the wage gains if there are significant disemployment effects of the rise in the minimum wage, or if the increase in the minimum wage "spills over" to higher-wage workers.[13] In low-wage states the fraction of affected workers fell from over 50 percent in 1989 to 10 percent in 1990-IV. Ignoring any disemployment or spillover effects, the predicted effect of the increased federal minimum on average wages in the low-wage states is then 0.40 times the average percentage increase for a wage earner who moves from the affected wage range to the new minimum wage. As shown in Table 5.1, the average wage of affected workers was $3.49 per hour. An increase to $3.80 is therefore equivalent to a 9 percent wage increase. Thus, if the only effect of the minimum wage is to increase the earnings of workers in the $3.35–3.79 range up to $3.80, the predicted wage impact in the low-wage states in 3.6 percent. A similar calculation for the medium-wage states implies a 2.1 percent wage impact. These benchmarks provide a close approximation to the observed wage gain in the medium-wage states but significantly under-predict the wage gain in low-wage states.

Table 5.2

Mean Log Wages and Employment Rated in Three Groups of States (standard errors in parentheses)

State group	Mean log wages			Employment rates		
	Low-wage	Medium-wage	High-wage	Low/-wage	Medium-wage	High-wage
1989						
I	1.33	1.41	1.56	33.9	44.4	44.3
	(0.01)	(0.01)	(0.01)	(1.4)	(0.9)	(1.1)
II	1.33	1.42	1.58	37.9	50.8	45.4
	(0.01)	(0.01)	(0.01)	(1.5)	(0.9)	(1.2)
III	1.35	1.43	1.61	45.4	55.7	52.0
	(0.01)	(0.01)	(0.01)	(1.5)	(0.9)	(1.1)
IV	1.37	1.44	1.58	41.7	47.5	46.6
	(0.02)	(0.01)	(0.01)	(1.5)	(0.9)	(1.1)
1990						
I	1.38	1.44	1.61	37.8	45.5	42.0
	(0.02)	(0.01)	(0.01)	(1.5)	(0.9)	(1.1)
II	1.45	1.48	1.62	44.1	50.0	45.8
	(0.01)	(0.01)	(0.01)	(1.5)	(0.9)	(1.1)
III	1.43	1.48	1.66	42.6	50.8	49.0
	(0.02)	(0.01)	(0.01)	(1.5)	(0.9)	(1.1)
IV	1.47	1.50	1.61	34.7	45.1	41.0
	(0.02)	(0.01)	(0.01)	(1.4)	(0.9)	(1.1)
Change from 1989 to same quarter of 1990						
I	0.05	0.03	0.05	3.9	1.1	-2.3
	(0.02)	(0.01)	(0.01)	(2.0)	(1.3)	(1.5)
II	0.12	0.06	0.04	6.2	-0.8	0.4
	(0.02)	(0.01)	(0.01)	(2.1)	(1.3)	(1.6)
III	0.08	0.05	0.05	-2.8	-4.9	-3.0
	(0.02)	(0.01)	(0.01)	(2.1)	(1.3)	(1.5)
IV	0.10	0.06	0.03	-7.0	-2.4	-5.6
	(0.02)	(0.01)	(0.02)	(2.1)	(1.3)	(1.5)
Average for II, III, IV	0.10	0.06	0.04	-1.2	-2.7	-2.7
	(0.01)	(0.01)	(0.01)	(1.2)	(0.8)	(0.9)

Note: The low-wage group includes states with more than 40% of teens earning $3.35–$3.79 per hour in 1989; the high-wage group includes states with less than 20% of teens earning $3.35–$3.79 per hour in 1989; and the medium-wage group includes all other states.

The right-hand columns of Table 5.2 present teenage employment-population rates by state group and quarter. One obvious aspect of these data is the seasonal pattern of employment, which shows a peak in the third quarter and a trough in the first. It is also interesting to note that teenage employment *increased* in all three groups of states between 1990-I and 1990-II, although employment rates were uniformly lower in 1990 than in 1989. The quarterly differences in the lower panel indicate that teenage employment fell by more in the high-wage states than in the low-wage states. Averaged over the last three quarters of each year, teenage employment growth was 1.5 percent higher in the low-wage states than in the high-wage states (standard error = 1.5%), with no difference between the medium-wage and high-wage states.

Ignoring other sources of relative teenage employment growth, the data in Table 5.2 suggest that the rise in the federal minimum wage *increased* teenage employment in the low-wage states, with no measurable effect in the medium-wage states. The effect in low-wage states is the opposite of the prediction from conventional models of the teenage labor market. One explanation for this finding is interstate variation in the timing and severity of the 1990 downturn. In fact, there is some evidence of a stronger downturn in the initially high-wage states and a more moderate recession in the low-wage states. Between the last three quarters of 1989 and 1990 the employment-population ratio for all workers grew by 0.45 percentage points in the low-wage states, fell by 0.01 points in the medium-wage states, and fell by 0.23 points in the high-wage states. These differences can potentially explain at least some of the differences in teenage employment growth among the three state groups.

To investigate this question more formally, I fit a regression model to the quarterly teenage employment rates in the three state groups, including group-specific intercepts, quarterly dummies, the overall employment rate for the state-group and quarter, and group-specific dummies measuring the change in teenage employment after 1990-II (that is, after the increase in the minimum wage).[14] The estimated employment effects in the post-increase period are -2.5 percent for the low-wage states, -2.7 percent for the medium-wage states, and -2.6 percent for the high- wage states. These estimates suggest that differences in the strength of the aggregate labor market can potentially explain almost all of the intergroup variation in teenage employment growth between the last three quarters of 1989 and 1990. Accounting for aggregate factors, however, there is no indication of an adverse employment effect in the low-wage states, where the increase in the federal minimum wage raised teenage wages by 6 percent.

5.4. An Analysis by State

An alternative to the grouping strategy used in Table 5.2 and Figure 5.3 is to treat each state as a separate observation, and to correlate changes in employment, wages, and other outcomes with the fraction of affected workers in the state. Owing to the relatively small numbers of observations for many states, I have not analyzed quarterly data by state. Rather, I have aggregated data for the last three quarters of 1989 and 1990 for each state. Comparisons between 1989 and 1990 allow a "pre/post" comparison of the effect of the increase in the federal minimum wage on April 1, 1990. The data for the two years are drawn from the same months and therefore are unaffected by any systematic seasonal effects.

Figure 5.4

Change in Mean Log Wage of Teenage Workes vs. Percent Earning $3.35–$3.79 per Hour in 1989

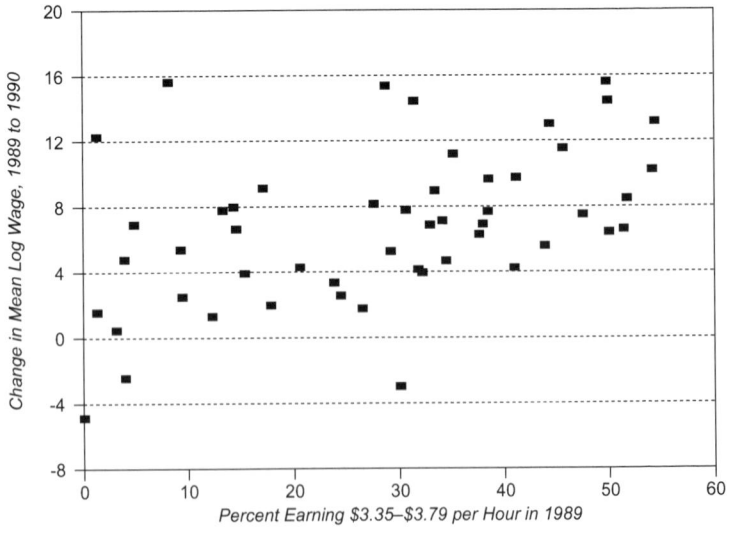

Figure 5.4 illustrates the interstate correlation between the fraction of teenagers earning $3.35–$3.79 per hour in 1989 and the increase in mean log wages between 1989 and 1990. The estimated regression model corresponding to the figure is presented in the first column of Table 5.3.[15] The estimated slope is 0.15, somewhat higher than the benchmark effect (.088) predicted by assuming that the rise in the minimum wage simply raised the wages of those in the affected wage range to $3.80 per hour. As suggested by the figure, the estimated regression coefficient is fairly precise: variation in the fraction of affected workers in 1989 explains a respectable 30 percent of the interstate variation in wage growth between 1989 and 1990.

Columns 2 and 3 of Table 5.3 introduce two alternative "macro-level" labor market indicators into the wage change equation. These are the change in the overall employment-population rate in the state between 1989 and 1990, and the corresponding change in the overall unemployment rate. Both variables are based on state-level averages published in the Bureau of Labor Statistics' "Geographic Profiles of Employment and Unemployment." Changes in overall employment or unemployment rates help to control for any state-specific labor demand shocks that may be correlated with the fraction of affected workers. As it happens, neither of these variables is very highly correlated with the growth rate of teenage wages, and their inclusion hardly affects the model.

Figure 5.5 plots state-level observations on the change in the teenage employment population rate between 1989 and 1990 against the fraction of affected wage earners in 1989. Unlike the corresponding plot for wage changes, this figure suggests no strong relation between the fraction of affected wage earners and the change in employment rates. The estimated regression models in columns 4–6 of Table 5.3 confirm this visual impression. Whether or not overall labor market indicators are included as additional controls, the fraction of affected teenagers in 1989 has virtually no effect on the change in employment rates.[16]

Table 5.3

Estimated Regression Equations for State-Average Changes in Wages and Employment Rates of Teenagers, 1989–1990 (estimated errors in parentheses)

Explanatory Variable	Equations for change in mean log wage			Equations for change in teen employment-population ratio					
	(1)	(2)	(3)	(4)	(5)	(6)	(7)	(8)	(9)
1. Fraction of affected teens	0.15 (0.03)	0.14 (0.04)	0.15 (0.04)	0.02 (0.03)	-0.01 (0.03)	0.02 (0.04)	–	–	–
2. Change in overall Emp./pop. ratio	–	0.46 (0.60)	–	–	1.24 (0.60)	–	–	1.27 (0.66)	–
3. Change in overall unemployment rate	–	–	-024 (0.92)	–	–	-0.16 (0.95)	–	–	-0.13 (0.98)
4. Change in mean log Teenage wage*	–	–	–	–	–	–	0.12 (0.22)	-0.06 (0.24)	0.10 (0.30)
5. R^2	0.30	0.31	0.30	0.01	0.09	0.01	0.01	0.09	0.01

Note: Estimated on a sample of 51 state observations. Regressions are weighted by average CPS extract sizes for teenage workers in each state. All regressions include an unrestricted constant. The mean and standard deviation of the dependent variable in columns 1–3 are 0.0571 and 0.0417; the mean and standard deviation of the dependent variable in columns 4–9 are -0.0225 and 0.0361.

* In columns 7–9, the change in mean log is instrumented by the fraction of teenage workers earning $3.35–3.79 in 1989.

Figure 5.5

Change in Teenage Employment Rates vs. Percent Earning $3.35–$3.79 per Hour in 1989

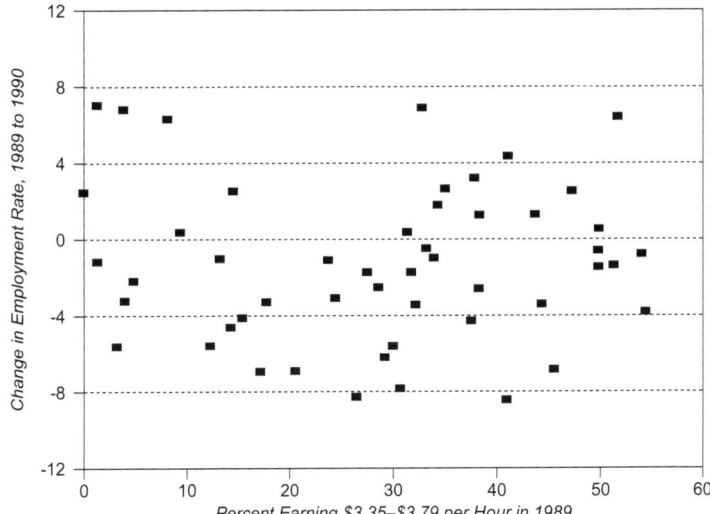

The estimated wage change models in columns 1–3 and the estimated employment change models in columns 4–6 can be interpreted as "reduced-form" equations from a very simple structural model that explains the wage increase between 1989 and 1990 in state i (ΔW_i) as a function of the fraction of teenagers in the affected wage range in the state in 1989 ($F89_i$) and other variables (X_1), and the employment change in state i (ΔE_i) as a movement *along* the teenage employment demand function:

$$(1) \qquad \Delta W_i = a + bF89_i + cX_i + e_i$$

$$(2) \qquad \Delta E_i = \alpha + \beta\Delta W_i + \gamma X_i + \epsilon_i.$$

Here the coefficient β is a conventional labor demand elasticity, and e_i and ϵ_i, are residual components of wage growth and employment demand. The reduced-form employment change equation is

$$(3) \qquad \Delta E_i = \alpha + b\beta F89_i + (\gamma + c\beta) X_i + \beta e_i + \epsilon_i.$$

Comparison of (1) and (3) shows that the elasticity of demand for teenage labor can be obtained by taking the ratio of the "Fraction Affected" coefficient in the employment growth equation to the corresponding coefficient in the wage growth equation. Alternatively, the same numerical estimate of the demand elasticity can be recovered by estimating the employment change equation (2) by two-stage least squares, using the fraction of teenagers in the affected wage range as an instrumental variable for the change in teenage wages. Such estimates are presented in columns 7–9 of Table 5.3.

The implied employment demand elasticities are uniformly small. When the overall employment-population ratio is included as a control variable (column 8), the estimated elasticity is negative but close to 0. Without controlling for overall labor market conditions (column 7) or using the overall unemployment rate as a control (column 9), the estimated elasticity is positive but close to 0. As suggested by the grouped analysis in Table 5.2, there is no evidence of a significant disemployment effect of the federal minimum wage.

The analysis in Table 5.3 can be extended in several directions. One extension is to model the dynamic structure of employment growth. Another is to consider more general measures of the impact of the federal minimum wage on state-specific wage changes. Both issues are addressed by the estimates in Table 5.4.

The first 4 columns of Table 5.4 report reduced-form employment growth regressions that include lagged values of the dependent variable.[17] For simplicity, I have only reported models that include the overall employment–population ratio; models that include the aggregate unemployment rate as an alternative control variable yield similar conclusions. The estimates in column 1 suggest that the lagged employment growth exerts a significant negative effect on current growth. This pattern is consistent with an underlying second-order autoregressive model of teenage employment at the state level.[18] In column 2, I include the lagged value of the overall employment change. Controlling for the contemporaneous aggregate employment change and the lagged dependent variable, this variable has a small and statistically insignificant coefficient. In both specifications the coefficient of the fraction of affected teenage wage earners (in row 1) is small and insignificantly different from 0.

One potential difficulty with the estimated models in columns 1 and 2 is the presence of measurement error in the lagged dependent variable. Random sampling errors in the state-specific teenage employment rate will tend to create a negative bias in the estimated coefficient of the lagged teenage employment growth rate. To check for

Table 5.4

Estimated Regression Equations for State-Average Changes in the Employment Rate of Teenagers, 1989–1990 (estimated standard errors in parentheses)

Explanatory variable	Reduced-form employment equations				Structural employment demand equations[b]				
	OLS (1)	OLS (2)	IV[a] (3)	OLS (4)	(5)	(6)	(7)	(8)	(9)
1. Fraction of affected teens	0.02 (0.04)	0.02 (0.04)	0.02 (0.06)	-0.00 (0.04)	—	—	—	—	—
2. Change in overall emp./pop. ratio	1.05 (0.58)	1.05 (0.59)	1.04 (0.65)	0.81 (0.62)	0.96 (0.65)	0.82 (0.67)	0.92 (0.64)	0.94 (0.64)	1.10 (0.62)
3. Lagged change in teen emp/pop. rate	-0.41 (0.18)	-0.41 (0.20)	-0.44 (0.63)	-0.44 (0.19)	-0.44 (0.20)	-0.44 (0.21)	-0.45 (0.20)	-0.45 (0.20)	-0.40 (0.20)
4. Lagged change in overall emp/pop.	—	-0.03 (0.64)	—	—	—	—	—	—	—
5. Change in regional Emp/pop. rate	—	—	—	1.61 (1.49)	—	1.63 (1.60)	—	—	—
6. Change in mean log teenage wage*	—	—	—	—	0.16 (0.28)	-0.02 (0.36)	0.19 (0.27)	0.18 (0.27)	0.06 (0.23)
7. R^2	0.18	0.18	0.11	0.20	0.18	0.19	0.18	0.18	0.17

Notes: See note to Table 5.3. In all columns the dependent variable is the change in the state-average teenage employment rate from 1989 to 1990 (April–December only).

[a] In column 3 the lagged change in the teenage employment–population ratio is instrumented by the lagged change in the overall employment-population ratio.

[b] The change in mean log teenage wage is endogenous. In column 5 and 6 the instrument is the change in mean log teenage wage in 1989; in column 7 the instrument is the fraction of teenager in the state earning $3.35–$3.79 per hour in 1989; in column 8 the instruments are the fractions earning exactly $3.35 and $3.35–$3.79 per hour in 1989; and in column 9 the intruments are the fractions earning less than $3.35 per hour and $3.35–$3.79 per hour in 1989.

the magnitude of this bias, column 3 presents a model in which the lagged dependent variable is instrumented by the lagged change in the overall employment–population ratio. The results of this exercise suggest the bias is small enough to be safely ignored.

Although labor demand shocks affecting teenage employment in a state are likely to be captured by the overall employment rate in the state, it is possible that other regional shocks may also play a role. To test this hypothesis, in column 4 of Table 5.4 I present a model that includes the change in the overall employment rate for nine different regions of the country. The addition of this variable lowers the coefficient on the state-specific employment rate, although the regional employment change is not itself statistically significant. The coefficient of the fraction of affected wage earners also falls slightly (to -0.003).

Columns 5–9 of Table 5.4 present instrumental variables estimates of the state-specific teenage employment demand equation, allowing for an effect of the lagged dependent variable. These models differ by the choice of variable(s) used as instruments for the change in teenage wages. Following the specifications of Table 3, columns 5 and 6 present models that use the fraction of teenagers earning $3.35–3.79 per hour in 1989 to instrument the wage change. In columns 7–9, I use three alternative measures of the wage impact of the federal minimum. The model in column 7 uses the fraction of teenagers earning exactly $3.35 per hour in 1989. The model in column 8 uses both the fraction of teenagers at the old minimum wage and the fraction in the affected wage range. Finally, the model in column 9 uses the fraction of teenagers earning less than $3.35 and the fraction earning $3.35–3.79 per hour in 1989. Regardless of specification, the models suggest negligible wage elasticities, although the estimated standard errors are large enough that one cannot rule out a small negative employment demand elasticity.

The results in Table 5.3 and 5.4 suggest that interstate differences in teenage employment growth between 1989 and 1990 were unrelated to the state-specific wage impact of the federal minimum wage increase. Another closely monitored outcome for teenagers is the fraction enrolled in school. A standard hypothesis in the literature is that increases in the minimum wage will increase school enrollment. (See, for example, Ehrenberg and Marcus 1980.) This prediction, however, is based on the assumption that increases in the minimum wage reduce teenage employment opportunities. In light of the results in

Tables 5.3 and 5.4, it is interesting to correlate interstate changes in enrollment with differences in the wage effect of the federal minimum wage.

To abstract from the seasonal pattern of school enrollment, I used CPS data for September–December of 1989 and 1990 to construct state-specific estimates of the change in the fraction of teenagers enrolled in school (either full- or part-time). In the United States as a whole, the fraction of teenagers enrolled in school during September–December rose from 73.7 percent in 1989 to 74.6 percent in 1990. Across states, changes in enrollment are negatively correlated with changes in employment rates (the correlation is -0.19, with a probability value of 0.18). I then fit a simple regression model for the change in enrollment as a function of the change in the overall employment rate in the state and the fraction of teenagers in the affected wage range in 1989. The coefficient of the overall employment change variable is -0.46 (with a standard error of 0.77), suggesting that enrollment growth was faster (although not significantly so) in states that experienced bigger employment reductions between 1989 and 1990. The coefficient of the fraction affected variable is -0.003 (with a standard error of 0.05), implying that changes in enrollment were essentially unrelated to the potential wage impact of the rise in the federal minimum wage. As with the employment results, there is no evidence of a connection between teenage school enrollment and the minimum wage.

5.5. Conclusions

I have used the experiences generated by the April 1990 rise in the federal minimum wage to measure the effects of the minimum wage on teenagers. The imposition of a national wage standard sets up a very useful natural experiment in which the "treatment effect" in any particular state depends on the fraction of workers initially earning less than the new minimum. By the end of the 1980s, interstate dispersion in teenage wages was remarkable. Many states had already passed state-specific minimum wages above the new federal standard. The fraction of teenagers potentially affected by the rise in the minimum wage ranged from under 5 percent in some New England and West Coast states to over 50 percent in some southern states.

The 1990 law raised the minimum wage by 13 percent. Estimates in the previous literature (Brown, Gilroy, and Kohen 1982) suggest that this increase would lower aggregate teenage employment by 1 to 4 percentage points. More important, however, these employment losses should have been concentrated in low-wage states, providing a test of the hypothesis that the changes are attributable to the minimum wage.

Comparisons of grouped and individual state data confirm that the rise in the minimum wage raised average teenage wages. The wage gains were as big as or slightly bigger than the increases predicted by assuming that individuals earning less than the new minimum rate had their wages "topped up" to the new standard. On the other hand, there is no evidence that the rise in the minimum wage significantly lowered teenage employment rates or altered school enrollment patterns. These findings, although at odds with conventional predictions, are consistent with the earlier "case study" literature (Lester 1960) and with the findings of two other studies using a similar methodology: my study of the 1988 California minimum wage law, and Katz and Krueger's study of the effects of the recent federal minimum wage increases on the fast-food industry in Texas (both in this issue).

6

Minimum Wages and Employment: A Case Study of the Fast-Food Industry in New Jersey and Pennsylvania

How do employers in a low-wage labor market respond to an increase in the minimum wage? The prediction from conventional economic theory is unambiguous: a rise in the minimum wage leads perfectly competitive employers to cut employment (Stigler 1946). Although studies in the 1970s based on aggregate teenage employment rates usually confirmed this prediction,[1] earlier studies based on comparisons of employment at affected and unaffected establishments often did not (e.g. Lester 1960, 1964). Several studies that rely on a similar comparative methodology have failed to detect a negative employment effect of higher minimum wages. Analyses of the 1990–1991 increases in the federal minimum wage (see Chapter 5; Katz and Krueger 1992) and of an earlier increase in the minimum wage in California (Card 1992b) find no adverse employment impact. A study of minimum-wage floors in Britain (Machin and Manning 1994) reaches a similar conclusion.

This chapter presents new evidence on the effect of minimum wages on establishment-level employment outcomes. We analyze the experiences of 410 fast-food restaurants in New Jersey and Pennsylva-

This chapter is a revised version of: Card, D., Krueger, A. (1994). Minimum Wages and Employment: A Case Study of the Fast Food Industry in New Jersey and Pennsylvania, in: American Economic Review 84, 772–793. The authors are grateful to the Institute for Research on Poverty, University of Wisconsin, for partial financial support. The authors thank Orley Ashenfelter, Charles Brown, Richard Lester, Gary Solon, two anonymous referees, and seminar participants at Princeton, Michigan State, Texas A&M, University of Michigan, University of Pennsylvania, University of Chicago, and the NBER for comments and suggestions. We also acknowledge the expert research assistance of Susan Belden, Chris Burris, Geraldine Harris, and Jonathan Orszag.

nia following the increase in New Jersey's minimum wage from $4.25 to $5.05 per hour. Comparisons of employment, wages, and prices at stores in New Jersey and Pennsylvania before and after the rise offer a simple method for evaluating the effects of the minimum wage. Comparisons within New Jersey between initially high-wage stores (those paying more than the new minimum rate prior to its effective date) and other stores provide an alternative estimate of the impact of the new law.

In addition to the simplicity of our empirical methodology, several other features of the New Jersey law and our data set are also significant. First, the rise in the minimum wage occurred during a recession. The increase had been legislated two years earlier when the state economy was relatively healthy. By the time of the actual increase, the unemployment rate in New Jersey had risen substantially and last-minute political action almost succeeded in reducing the minimum-wage increase. It is unlikely that the effects of the higher minimum wage were obscured by a rising tide of general economic conditions.

Second, New Jersey is a relatively small state with an economy that is closely linked to nearby states. We believe that a control group of fast-food stores in eastern Pennsylvania forms a natural basis for comparison with the experiences of restaurants in New Jersey. Wage variation across stores in New Jersey, however, allows us to compare the experiences of high-wage and low-wage stores within New Jersey and to test the validity of the Pennsylvania control group. Moreover, since seasonal patterns of employment are similar in New Jersey and eastern Pennsylvania, as well as across high- and low-wage stores within New Jersey, our comparative methodology effectively "differences out" any seasonal employment effects.

Third, we successfully followed nearly 100 percent of stores from a first wave of interviews conducted just before the rise in the minimum wage (in February and March 1992) to a second wave conducted 7–8 months after (in November and December 1992). We have complete information on store closings and take account of employment changes at the closed stores in our analyses. We therefore measure the overall effect of the minimum wage on average employment, and not simply its effect on surviving establishments.

Our analysis of employment trends at stores that were open for business before the increase in the minimum wage ignores any potential effect of minimum wages on the rate of new store openings. To assess the likely magnitude of this effect we relate state-specific growth rates in the number of McDonald's fast-food outlets between 1986 and 1991 to measures of the relative minimum wage in each state.

6.1. The New Jersey Law

A bill signed into law in November 1989 raised the federal minimum wage from $3.35 per hour to $3.80 effective April 1, 1990, with a further increase to $4.25 per hour on April 1, 1991. In early 1990 the New Jersey legislature went one step further, enacting parallel increases in the state minimum wage for 1990 and 1991 and an increase to $5.05 per hour effective April 1, 1992. The scheduled 1992 increase gave New Jersey the highest state minimum wage in the country and was strongly opposed by business leaders in the state (see Bureau of National Affairs, Daily Labor Report, May 5, 1990).

In the two years between passage of the $5.05 minimum wage and its effective date, New Jersey's economy slipped into recession. Concerned with the potentially adverse impact of a higher minimum wage, the state legislature voted in March 1992 to phase in the 80-cent increase over two years. The vote fell just short of the margin required to override a gubernatorial veto, and the Governor allowed the $5.05 rate to go into effect on April 1 before vetoing the two-step legislation. Faced with the prospect of having to roll back wages for minimum-wage earners, the legislature dropped the issue. Despite a strong last-minute challenge, the $5.05 minimum rate took effect as originally planned.

6.2. Sample Design and Evaluation

Early in 1992 we decided to evaluate the impending increase in the New Jersey minimum wage by surveying fast-food restaurants in New Jersey and eastern Pennsylvania.[2] Our choice of the fast-food industry was driven by several factors. First, fast-food stores are a leading employer of low-wage workers: in 1987, franchised restaurants employed 25 percent of all workers in the restaurant industry (see U.S. Department of Commerce 1990, table 13). Second, fast-food restaurants comply with minimum-wage regulations and would be expected to raise wages in response to a rise in the minimum wage. Third, the job

183

requirements and products of fast-food restaurants are relatively homogeneous, making it easier to obtain reliable measures of employment, wages, and product prices. The absence of tips greatly simplifies the measurement of wages in the industry. Fourth, it is relatively easy to construct a sample frame of franchised restaurants. Finally, past experience (Katz and Krueger 1992) suggested that fast-food restaurants have high response rates to telephone surveys.[3]

Table 6.1

Sample Design and Response Rated

	All	Stores in:	
		NJ	PA
Wave 1, February 15 – March 4, 1992:			
Number of stores in sample frame:[a]	473	365	109
Number of refusals:	63	33	30
Number interviewed:	410	331	79
Response rate (percentage):	86.7	90.9	72.5
Wave 2, November 5 – December 31, 1992:			
Number of stores in sample frame:	410	331	79
Number closed:	6	5	1
Number under rennovation:	2	2	0
Number temporarily closed:[b]	2	2	0
Number of refusals:	1	1	0
Number interviewed:[c]	399	321	78

[a] Stores with working phone numbers only; 29 stores in original sample frame had disconnected phone numbers.

[b] Includes one store closed because of highway construction and one store closed because of a fire.

[c] Includes 371 phone interviews and 28 personal interviews of stores that refused an initial request for a phone interview.

Based on these considerations we constructed a sample frame of fast-food restaurants in New Jersey and eastern Pennsylvania from the Burger King, KFC, Wendy's, and Roy Rogers chains.[4] The first wave of the survey was conducted by telephone in late February and early March 1992, a little over a month before the scheduled increase in New Jersey's minimum wage. The survey included questions on employment, starting wages, prices, and other store characteristics.[5]

Table 6.1 shows that 473 stores in our sample frame had working telephone numbers when we tried to reach them in February-March 1992. Restaurants were called as many as nine times to elicit a response. We obtained completed interviews (with some item nonresponse) from 410 of the restaurants, for an overall response rate of 87 percent. The response rate was higher in New Jersey (91%) than in Pennsylvania (72.5%) because our interviewer made fewer call-backs to nonrespondents in Pennsylvania.[6] In the analysis below we investigate possible biases associated with the degree of difficulty in obtaining the first-wave interview.

The second wave of the survey was conducted in November and December 1992, about eight months after the minimum-wage increase. Only the 410 stores that responded in the first wave were contacted in the second round of interviews. We successfully interviewed 371 (90%) of these stores by phone in November 1992. Because of a concern that nonresponding restaurants might have closed, we hired an interviewer to drive to each of the 39 nonrespondents and determine whether the store was still open, and to conduct a personal interview if possible. The interviewer discovered that six restaurants were permanently closed, two were temporarily closed (one because of a fire, one because of road construction), and two were under renovation.[7] Of the 29 stores open for business, all but one granted a request for a personal interview. As a result, we have second-wave interview data for 99.8 percent of the restaurants that responded in the first wave of the survey, and information on closure status for 100 percent of the sample.

Table 6.2 presents the means for several key variables in our data set, averaged over the subset of nonmissing responses for each variable. In constructing the means, employment in wave 2 is set to 0 for the permanently closed stores but is treated as missing for the temporarily closed stores. (Full-time-equivalent (FTE) employment was calculated as the number of full-time workers (including managers) plus 0.5 times the number of part-time workers.)[8] Means are presented separately for stores in New Jersey and Pennsylvania, along with t statistics for the null hypothesis that the means are equal in the two states.

Rows 1a–e show the distribution of stores by chain and ownership status (company-owned versus franchisee-owned). The Burger King, Roy Rogers, and Wendy's stores in our sample have similar average food prices, store hours, and employment levels. The KFC stores are smaller and are open for fewer hours. They also offer a more expensive main course than stores in the other chains (chicken vs. hamburgers).

Minimum Wages and Employment: A Case Study

Table 6.2

Means of Key Variables

Variable	Stores in:		t^a
	NJ	PA	
1. Distribution of store types (%):			
a. Burger King	41.1	44.3	-0.5
b. KFC	20.5	15.2	1.2
c. Roy Rogers	24.8	21.5	0.6
d. Wendy's	13.6	19.0	-1.1
e. Company-owned	34.1	35.4	-0.2
2. Means in wave 1:			
a. FTE employment	20.4	23.3	-2.0
	(0.51)	(1.35)	
b. Percentage full-time employees	32.8	35.0	-0.7
	(1.3)	(2.7)	
c. Starting wage	4.61	4.63	-0.4
	(0.02)	(0.04)	
d. Wage = $4.25 (%)	30.5	32.9	-0.4
	(2.5)	(5.3)	
e. Price of full meal	3.35	3.04	4.0
	(0.04)	(0.07)	
f. Hours open (weekday)	14.4	14.5	-0.3
	(0.2)	(0.3)	
g. Recruiting bonus	23.6	29.1	-1.0
	(2.3)	(5.1)	
3. Means in wave 2:			
a. FTE employment	21.0	21.2	-0.2
	(0.52)	(0.94)	
b. Percentage full-time employees	35.9	30.4	1.8
	(1.4)	(2.8)	
c. Starting wage	5.08	4.62	10.8
	(0.01)	(0.04)	
d. Wage = $4.25 (%)	0.0	25.3	-
		(4.9)	
e. Wage = $5.05 (%)	85.2	1.3	36.1
	(2.0)	(1.3)	
e. Price of full meal	3.41	3.03	5.0
	(0.04)	(0.07)	
f. Hours open (weekday)	14.4	14.7	-0.8
	(0.2)	(0.3)	
g. Recruiting bonus	20.3	23.4	-0.6
	(2.3)	(4.9)	

Notes: See text for definitions. Standard errors are given in parentheses.
[a] Test of equality of means in New Jersey and Pennsylvania.

In wave 1, average employment was 23.3 full-time equivalent workers per store in Pennsylvania, compared with an average of 20.4 in New Jersey. Starting wages were very similar among stores in the two states, although the average price of a "full meal" (medium soda, small fries, and an entree) was significantly higher in New Jersey. There were no significant cross-state differences in average hours of operation, the fraction of full-time workers, or the prevalence of bonus programs to recruit new workers.[9]

The average starting wage at fast-food restaurants in New Jersey increased by 10 percent following the rise in the minimum wage. Further insight into this change is provided in Figure 6.1, which shows the distributions of starting wages in the two states before and after the rise. In wave 1, the distributions in New Jersey and Pennsylvania were very similar. By wave 2 virtually all restaurants in New Jersey that had been paying less than $5.05 per hour reported a starting wage equal to the new rate. Interestingly, the minimum-wage increase had no apparent "spillover" on higher-wage restaurants in the state: the mean percentage wage change for these stores was -3.1 percent.

Despite the increase in wages, full-time-equivalent employment *increased* in New Jersey relative to Pennsylvania. Whereas New Jersey stores were initially smaller, employment gains in New Jersey coupled with losses in Pennsylvania led to a small and statistically insignificant interstate difference in wave 2. Only two other variables show a relative change between waves 1 and 2: the fraction of full-time employees and the price of a meal. Both variables increased in New Jersey relative to Pennsylvania.

We can assess the reliability of our survey questionnaire by comparing the responses of 11 stores that were inadvertently interviewed twice in the first wave of the survey.[10] Assuming that measurement errors in the two interviews are independent of each other and independent of the true variable, the correlation between responses gives an estimate of the "reliability ratio" (the ratio of the variance of the signal to the combined variance of the signal and noise). The estimated reliability ratios are fairly high, ranging from 0.70 for full-time equivalent employment to 0.98 for the price of a meal.[11]

We have also checked whether stores with missing data for any key variables are different from restaurants with complete responses. We find that stores with missing data on employment, wages, or prices are similar in other respects to stores with complete data. There is a significant size differential associated with the likelihood of the store closing after wave 1. The six stores that closed were smaller than other stores (with an average employment of only 12.4 full-time-equivalent employees in wave 1).[12]

Figure 6.1

Distribution of Starting Wage Rates

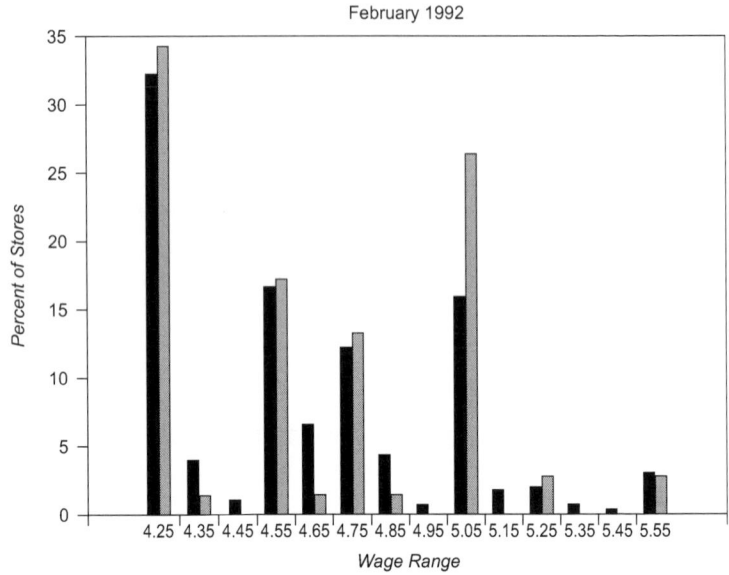

February 1992

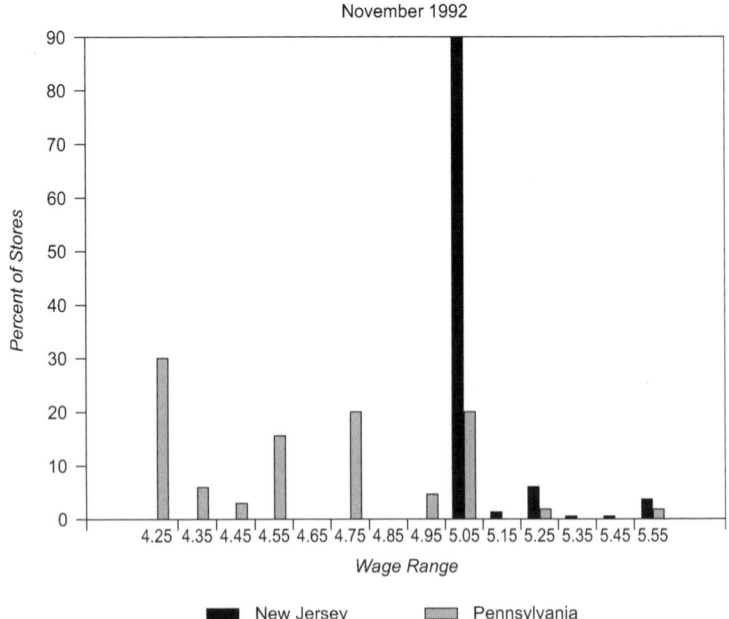

November 1992

New Jersey   Pennsylvania

6.3. Employment Effects of the Minimum-Wage Increase
6.3.1. Differences in Differences

Table 6.3 summarizes the levels and changes in average employment per store in our survey. We present data by state in columns 1 and 2, and for stores in New Jersey classified by whether the starting wage in wave 1 was exactly $4.25 per hour (column 4) between $4.26 and $4.99 per hour (column 5) or $5.00 or more per hour (column 6), We also show the differences in average employment between New Jersey and Pennsylvania stores (column 3) and between stores in the various wage ranges in New Jersey (columns 7–8).

Row 3 of the table presents the changes in average employment between waves 1 and 2. These entries are simply the differences between the averages for the two waves (i.e., row 2 minus row 1). An alternative estimate of the change is presented in row 4: here we have computed the change in employment over the subsample of stores that reported valid employment data in both waves. We refer to this group of stores as the balanced subsample. Finally, row 5 presents the average change in employment in the balanced subsample, treating wave-2 employment at the four temporarily closed stores as zero, rather than as missing.

As noted in Table 6.2, New Jersey stores were initially smaller than their Pennsylvania counterparts but grew relative to Pennsylvania stores after the rise in the minimum wage. The relative gain (the "difference in differences" of the changes in employment) is 2.76 FTE employees (or 135), with a t statistic of 2.03. Inspection of the averages in rows 4 and 5 shows that the relative change between New Jersey and Pennsylvania stores is virtually identical when the analysis is restricted to the balanced subsample, and it is only slightly smaller when wave-2 employment at the temporarily closed stores is treated as zero.

Within New Jersey, employment expanded at the low-wage stores (those paying $4.25 per hour in wave 1) and contracted at the high-wage stores (those paying $5.00 or more per hour). Indeed, the average change in employment at the high-wage stores (-2.16 FTE employees) is almost identical to the change among Pennsylvania stores (-2.28 FTE employees). Since high-wage stores in New Jersey should have been largely unaffected by the new minimum wage, this comparison provides a specification test of the validity of the Pennsylvania control group. The test is clearly passed. Regardless of whether the affected stores are compared to stores in Pennsylvania or high-wage

Table 6.3
Average Employment per Store Before and After the Rise in New Jersey(NJ) Minimum Wage

Variable	Stores by state			Stores in NJ[a]			Differences within NJ[b]	
	PA	NJ	Difference NJ-PA	Wage - $4.25	Wage - $4.26–$4.99	Wage ≥ $5.00	Low – high	Midrange – high
	(1)	(2)	(3)	(4)	(5)	(6)	(7)	(8)
1. FTE employment before, all available observations	23.33 (1.35)	20.44 (0.51)	-2.89 (1.44)	19.56 (0.77)	20.08 (0.84)	22.25 (1.14)	-2.69 (1.37)	-2.17 (1.41)
2. FTE employment after, all available observations	21.17 (0.94)	21.03 (0.52)	-0.14 (1.07)	20.88 (1.01)	20.96 (0.76)	20.21 (1.03)	0.67 (1.44)	0.75 (1.27)
3. Change in mean FTE employment	-2.16 (1.25)	0.59 (0.54)	2.76 (1.36)	1.32 (0.95)	0.87 (0.84)	-2.04 (1.14)	3.36 (1.48)	2.91 (1.41)
4. Change in mean FTE employment, balanced sample of stores[c]	-2.28 (1.25)	0.47 (0.48)	2.75 (1.34)	1.21 (0.82)	0.71 (0.69)	-2.16 (1.01)	3.36 (1.30)	2.87 (1.22)
5. Change in mean FTE employment setting FTE as temporarily closed stores to 0[d]	-2.28 (1.25)	0.23 (0.49)	2.51 (1.35)	0.90 (0.87)	0.49 (0.69)	-2.39 (1.02)	3.29 (1.34)	2.88 (1.23)

Notes: Standard errors are shown in parentheses. The sample consists of all stores with available data on employment. FTE (full-time-equivalent) employment counts each part-time worker as half a full-time worker. Employment at six closed stores is set to zero. Employment at four temporarily closed stores is treated as missing.

[a] Stores in New Jersey were classified by whether starting wage in wave 1 equals $4.25 per hour (N = 101), is between $4.26 and $4.99 per hour (N = 140), or is $5.00 per hour or higher (N = 73).

[b] Difference in employment between low-wage ($4.25 per hour) and high-wage (≥ $5.00 per hour) stores; and difference in employment between midrange ($4.26–$4.99 per hour) and high-wage stores.

[c] Subset of stores with available employment data in wave 1 and wave 2.

[d] In this row only, wave 2 employment at four temporarily closed stores is set to 0. Employment changes are based on the subset of stores with available employment data in wave 1 and wave 2.

stores in New Jersey, the estimated employment effect of the minimum wage is similar.

The results in Table 6.3 suggest that employment contracted between February and November of 1992 at fast-food stores that were unaffected by the rise in the minimum wage (stores in Pennsylvania and stores in New Jersey paying $5.00 per hour or more in wave 1). We suspect that the reason for this contraction was the continued worsening of the economies of the middle-Atlantic states during 1992.[13] Unemployment rates in New Jersey, Pennsylvania, and New York all trended upward between 1991 and 1993, with a larger increase in New Jersey than Pennsylvania during 1992. Since sales of franchised fast-food restaurants are pro-cyclical, the rise in unemployment would be expected to lower fast-food employment in the absence of other factors.[14]

6.3.2. Regression-Adjusted Models

The comparisons in Table 6.3 make no allowance for other sources of variation in employment growth, such as differences across chains. These are incorporated in the estimates in Table 6.4. The entries in this table are regression coefficients from models of the form:

(1a)
$$\Delta E_i = a + bX_i + cNJ_i + \epsilon_i$$

or

(1b)
$$\Delta E_i = a' + b'X_i + c'\text{GAP}_i + \epsilon'_i$$

where ΔE_i is the change in employment from wave 1 to wave 2 at store i, X_i is a set of characteristics of store i, and NJ_i is a dummy variable that equals 1 for stores in New Jersey. GAP_i is an alternative measure of the impact of the minimum wage at store i based on the initial wage at that store (W_{1i}):

GAP_i = 0 for stores in Pennsylvania
$\quad\quad\quad$ = 0 for stores in New Jersey with $W_{1i} \geq \$5.05$
$\quad\quad\quad$ = $(5.05 - W_{1i}) / W_{1i}$ for other stores in New Jersey.

GAP_i is the proportional increase in wages at store i necessary to meet the new minimum rate. Variation in GAP_i reflects both the New Jersey-Pennsylvania contrast and differences within New Jersey based

191

on reported starting wages in wave 1. Indeed, the value of GAP_i is a strong predictor of the actual proportional wage change between waves 1 and 2 ($R^2 = 0.75$), and conditional on GAP_i there is no difference in wage behavior between stores in New Jersey and Pennsylvania.[15]

The estimate in column 1 of Table 6.4 is directly comparable to the simple difference-in-differences of employment changes in column 4, row 4 of Table 6.3. The discrepancy between the two estimates is due to the restricted sample in Table 6.4. In Table 6.4 and the remaining tables in this section we restrict our analysis to the set of stores with available employment *and* wage data in both waves of the survey. This restriction results in a slightly smaller estimate of the relative increase in employment in New Jersey.

Table 6.4

Reduced Form Models for Change in Employment

	Model				
Independent variable	(1)	(2)	(3)	(4)	(5)
1. New Jersey dummy	2.33	2.30	–	–	–
	(1.19)	(1.20)			
2. Initial wage gap[a]	–	–	15.65	14.92	11.91
			(6.08)	(6.21)	(7.39)
3. Controls for chain and ownership[b]	no	yes	no	yes	yes
4. Controls for region[c]	no	no	no	no	yes
5. Standard error of regression	8.79	8.78	8.76	8.76	8.75
6. Probability value for controls[d]	–	0.34	–	0.44	0.40

Notes: Standard errors are given in parentheses. The sample consists of 357 stores with available data on employment and starting wages in waves 1 and 2. The dependent variable in all models is change in FTE employment. The mean and standard deviation of the dependent variable are -0.237 and 8.825, respectively. All models include an unrestricted constant (not reported).

[a] Proportional increase in starting wage necessary to raise starting wage to new minimum rate. For stores in Pennsylvania the wage gap is 0.

[b] Three dummy variables for chain type and whether or not the store is company-owned are included.

[c] Dummy variables for two regions of New Jersey and two regions of eastern Pennsylvania are included.

[d] Probability value of joint F-test for exclusion of all control variables.

The model in column 2 introduces a set of four control variables: dummies for three of the chains and another dummy for company-owned stores. As shown by the probability values in row 6, these covariates add little to the model and have no effect on the size of the estimated New Jersey dummy.

The specifications in columns 3–5 use the GAP variable to measure the effect of the minimum wage. This variable gives a slightly better fit than the simple New Jersey dummy, although its implications for the New Jersey-Pennsylvania comparison are similar. The mean value of GAP_i among New Jersey stores is 0.11. Thus the estimate in column 3 implies a 1.72 increase in FTE employment in New Jersey relative to Pennsylvania.

Since GAP_i varies within New Jersey, it is possible to add both GAP_i and NJ_i to the employment model. The estimated coefficient of the New Jersey dummy then provides a test of the Pennsylvania control group. When we estimate these models, the coefficient of the New Jersey dummy is insignificant (with t ratios of 0.3–0.7), implying that inferences about the effect of the minimum wage are similar whether the comparison is made across states or across stores in New Jersey with higher and lower initial wages.

An even stronger test is provided in column 5, where we have added dummies representing three regions of New Jersey (North, Central, and South) and two regions of eastern Pennsylvania (Allentown-Easton and the northern suburbs of Philadelphia). These dummies control for any region-specific demand shocks and identify the effect of the minimum wage by comparing employment changes at higher- and lower-wage stores within the same region of New Jersey. The probability value in row 6 shows no evidence of regional components in employment growth. The addition of the region dummies attenuates the GAP coefficient and raises its standard error, however, making it no longer possible to reject the of the minimum wage. One explanation for this attenuation is the presence of measurement error in the starting wage. Even if employment growth has no regional component, the addition of region dummies will lead to some attenuation of the estimated GAP coefficient if some of the true variation in GAP is explained by region. Indeed, calculations based on the estimated reliability of the GAP variable (from the set of 11 double interviews) suggest that the fall in the estimated GAP coefficient from column 4 to column 5 is just equal to the expected change attributable to measurement error.[16]

We have also estimated the models in Table 6.4, using as a dependent variable the proportional change in employment at each store.[17] The estimated coefficients of the New Jersey dummy and the GAP variable are uniformly positive in these models but insignificantly different from 0 at conventional levels. The implied employment effects of the minimum wage are also smaller when the dependent variable is expressed in proportional terms. For example, the GAP coefficient in column 3 of Table 6.4 implies that the increase in minimum wages raised employment at New Jersey stores that were initially paying $4.25 per hour by 14 percent. The estimated GAP coefficient from a corresponding proportional model implies an effect of only 7 percent. The difference is attributable to heterogeneity in the effect of the minimum wage at larger and smaller stores. Weighted versions of the proportional-change models (using initial employment as a weight) give rise to wage elasticities similar to the elasticities implied by the estimates in Table 6.4 (see below).

6.3.3. Specification Tests

The results in Tables 6.3 and 6.4 seem to contradict the standard prediction that a rise in the minimum wage will reduce employment. Table 6.5 presents some alternative specifications that probe the robustness of this conclusion. For completeness, we report estimates of models for the change in employment (columns 1 and 2) and estimates of models for the proportional change in employment (columns 3 and 4).[18] The first row of the table reproduces the "base specification" from columns 2 and 4 of Table 6.4. (Note that these models include chain dummies and a dummy for company-owned stores). Row 2 presents an alternative set of estimates when we set wave-2 employment at the temporarily closed stores to 0 (expanding our sample size by 4). This change has a small attenuating effect on the coefficient of the New Jersey dummy (since all four stores are in New Jersey) but less effect on the GAP coefficient (since the size of GAP is uncorrelated with the probability of a temporary closure within New Jersey).

Rows 3–5 present estimation results using alternative measures of full-time-equivalent employment. In row 3, employment is redefined to exclude management employees. This change has no effect relative to the base specification. In rows 4 and 5, we include managers in FTE employment but reweight part-time workers as either 40 percent or 60 percent of full-time workers (instead of 50%).[19] These changes have little effect on the models for the level of employment but yield slightly smaller point estimates in the proportional-employment-change models.

In row 6 we present estimates obtained from a subsample that excludes 35 stores in towns along the New Jersey shore. The exclusion of these stores, which may have a different seasonal pattern than other stores in our sample, leads to slightly larger minimum-wage effects. A similar finding emerges in row 7 when we add a set of dummy variables that indicate the week of the wave-2 interview.[20]

As noted earlier, we made an extra effort to obtain responses from New Jersey stores in the first wave of our survey. The fraction of stores called three or more times to obtain an interview was higher in New Jersey than in Pennsylvania. To check the sensitivity of our results to this sampling feature, we reestimated our models on a subsample that excludes any stores that were called back more than twice. The results, in row 8, are very similar to the base specification.

Row 9 presents weighted estimation results for the proportional-employment-change models, using as weights the initial levels of employment in each store. Since the proportional change in average employment is an employment-weighted average of the proportional changes at each store, a weighted version of the proportional-change model should give rise to elasticities that are similar to the implied elasticities arising from the levels models. Consistent with this expectation, the weighted estimates are larger than the unweighted estimates, and significantly different from 0 at conventional levels. The weighted estimate of the New Jersey dummy (0.13) implies a 13 percent relative increase in New Jersey employment – the same proportional employment effect implied by the simple difference-in-differences in Table 6.3. Similarly, the weighted estimate of the GAP coefficient in the proportional-change model (0.81) is close to the implied elasticity of employment with respect to wages from the basic levels specification in row 1, column 5.[21] These findings suggest that the proportional effect of the rise in the minimum wage was concentrated among larger stores.

One explanation for our finding that a rise in the minimum wage has a positive employment effect is that unobserved demand shocks within New Jersey outweighed the negative employment effect of the minimum wage. To address this possibility, rows 10 and 11 present estimation results based on subsamples of stores in two narrowly defined areas: towns around Newark (row 10) and towns around Camden (row 11). In each case the sample area is identified by the first three digits of the store's zip code.[22] Within both areas the change in employment is positively correlated with the GAP variable, although in neither case is the effect statistically significant.

Table 6.5

Specification Tests of Reduced-Form Employment Models

Specification	Change in employment		Proportional change in employment	
	NJ dummy (1)	Gap measure (2)	NJ dummy (3)	Gap measure (4)
1. Base specification	2.30	14.92	0.05	0.34
	(1.19)	(6.21)	(0.05)	(0.26)
2. Treat four temporarily closed stores as permanently closed[a]	2.20	14.42	0.04	0.34
	(1.21)	(6.31)	(0.05)	(0.27)
3. Exclude managers in employment count[b]	2.34	14.69	0.05	0.28
	(1.17)	(6.05)	(0.07)	(0.34
4. Weight part-time as 0.4 x full-time[c]	2.34	15.23	0.06	0.30
	(1.20)	(6.23)	(0.06)	(0.33)
5. Weight part-time as 0.6 x full-time[d]	2.27	14.60	0.04	0.17
	(1.21)	(6.26)	(0.06)	(0.29)
6. Exclude stores in NJ shore area[e]	2.58	16.88	0.06	0.42
	(1.19)	(6.36)	(0.05)	(0.27)
7. Add controls for wave-2 interview date[f]	2.27	15.76	0.05	0.40
	(1.20)	(6.24)	(0.05)	(0.26)
8. Exclude stores called more than twice in wave 1[g]	2.41	14.08	0.05	0.31
	(1.28)	(7.11)	(0.05)	(0.29)
9. Weight by initial employment[h]	–	–	0.13	0.81
			(0.05)	(0.26)
10 Stores in towns around Newark[i]	–	33.75	–	0.90
		(16.75)		(0.74)
11 Stores in towns around Camden[j]	–	10.91	–	0.21
		(14.09)		(0.70)
12 Pennsylvania stores only[k]	–	-0.30	–	-0.33
		(22.00)		(0.74)

Notes: Standard errors are given in parentheses. Entries represent estimated coefficient of New Jersey dummy (columns 1 and 3) or initial wage gap (columns 2 and 4) in regression models for the change in employment or the percentage change in employment. All models also include chain dummies and an indicator for company-owned stores.

[a] Wave 2 employment at four temporarily closed stores is set to 0 (rather than missing).

[b] Full-time equivalent employment excludes managers and assistant managers.

[c] Full-time equivalent employment equals number of managers, assistant managers, and full-time nonmanagement workers, plus 0.4 times the number of part-time nonmanagement workers.

[d] Full-time equivalent employment equals number of managers, assistant managers, and full-time nonmanagement workers, plus 0.6 times the number of part-time nonmanagement workers.

[e] Sample excludes 35 stores located in towns along the New Jersey shore.

[f] Models include three dummy variables indentifying week of wave 2 interview in November–December 1992.

[g] Sample excludes 70 stores (69 in New Jersey) that were contacted three or more times before obtaining the wave 1 interview.

[h] Regression model is estimated by weighted least squares, using employment in wave 1 as a weight. "Subsample of 51 stores in towns around Newark."

[i] Subsample of 51 stores in towns around Newark.

[j] Subsample of 54 stores in town around Camden.

[k] Subsample of Pennsylvania stores only. Wage gap is defined as percentage increase in starting wage necessary to raise starting wage to $5.05.

To the extent that fast-food product market conditions are constant within local areas, these results suggest that our findings are not driven by unobserved demand shocks. Our analysis of price changes (reported below) also supports this conclusion.

A final specification check is presented in row 12 of Table 6.5. In this row we exclude stores in New Jersey and (incorrectly) define the GAP variable for Pennsylvania stores as the proportional increase in wages necessary to raise the wage to $5.05 per hour. In principle the size of the wage gap for stores in Pennsylvania should have no systematic relation with employment growth. In practice, this is the case. There is no indication that the wage gap is spuriously related to employment growth.

We have also investigated whether the first-differenced specification used in our employment models is appropriate. A first-differenced model implies that the level of employment in period t is related to the lagged level of employment with a coefficient of 1. If short-run employment fluctuations are smoothed, however, the true coefficient of lagged employment may be less than 1. Imposing the assumption of a unit coefficient may then lead to biases. To test the first-differenced specification we reestimated models for the change in employment including wave 1 employment as an additional explanatory variable. To over-come any mechanical correlation between base-period employment and the change in employment (attributable to measurement error) we instrumented wave 1 employment with the number of cash registers in the store in wave 1 and the number of registers in the store that were open at 11:00 A.M. In all of the specifications the coefficient of wave 1 employment is close to zero. For example, in a specification including the GAP variable and ownership and chain dummies, the coefficient of wave 1 employment is 0.04, with a standard error of 0.24. We conclude that the first-differenced specification is appropriate.

6.3.4. Full-Time and Part-Time Substitution

Our analysis so far has concentrated on full-time-equivalent employment and ignored possible changes in the distribution of full- and part-time workers. An increase in the minimum wage could lead to an increase in full-time employment relative to part-time employment for at least two reasons. First, in a conventional model one would expect a minimum-wage increase to induce employers to substitute

Table 6.6

Effects of Minimum-Wage Increase on Other Outcomes

Outcome measure	Mean change in outcome			Regression of change in outcome variable on:		
	NJ (1)	PA (2)	NJ-PA (3)	NJ dummy (4)	Wage gap[a] (5)	Wage gap[b] (6)
Store characteristics:						
1. Fraction full-time workers[c] (%)	2.64 (1.71)	-4.65 (3.80)	7.29 (4.17)	7.30 (3.96)	33.64 (20.95)	20.28 (24.34)
2. Number of hours open per weekday	-0.00 (0.06)	0.11 (0.08)	-0.11 (0.10)	-0.11 (0.12)	-0.24 (0.65)	0.04 (0.76)
3. Number of cash registers	-0.04 (0.04)	0.13 (0.10)	-0.17 (0.11)	-0.18 (0.10)	-0.31 (0.53)	0.29 (0.62)
4. Number of cash registers open at 11:00	-0.03 (0.05)	-0.20 (0.08)	0.17 (0.10)	0.17 (0.12)	0.15 (0.62)	-0.47 (0.74)
Employee meal program:						
5. Low-price meal program (%)	-4.67 (2.65)	-1.28 (3.86)	-3.39 (4.68)	-2.01 (5.63)	-30.31 (29.80)	-33.15 (35.04)
6. Free meal program (%)	8.41 (2.17)	6.41 (3.33)	2.00 (3.97)	0.49 (4.50)	29.90 (23.75)	36.91 (27.90)
7. Combination of low-price and free meals	-4.04 (1.98)	-5.13 (3.11)	1.09 (3.69)	1.20 (4.32)	-11.87 (22.87)	-19.19 (26.81)
Wage profile:						
8. Time to first raise (weeks)	3.77 (0.89)	1.26 (1.97)	2.51 (2.16)	2.21 (2.03)	4.02 (10.81)	-5.10 (12.74)
9. Usual amount of first raise (cents)	-0.01 (0.01)	-0.02 (0.02)	0.01 (0.02)	0.01 (0.02)	0.03 (0.11)	0.03 (0.11)
10. Slope of wage profile (% per week)	-0.10 (0.04)	-0.11 (0.09)	0.01 (0.10)	0.01 (0.30)	-0.09 (0.56)	-0.08 (0.57)

Notes: Entries in columns 1 and 2 represent mean changes in the outcome variable indicated by the row heading for stores with available data on the outcome in waves 1 and 2. Entries in columns 4–5 represent estimated regression coefficients of indicated variable (NJ dummy or initial wage gap) in models for the change in the outcome variable. Regression models include chain dummies and an indicator for company-owned stores.

[a] The wage gap is the proportional increase in starting wage necessary to raise the wage to the new minimum rate. For stores in Pennsylvania, the wage gap is zero.

[b] Models in column 6 include dummies for two regions of New Jersey and two regions of eastern Pennsylvania.

[c] Fraction of part-time employees in total full-time-equivalent employment.

skilled workers and capital for minimum-wage workers. Full-time workers in fast-food restaurants are typically older and may well possess higher skills than part-time workers. Thus, a conventional model predicts that stores may respond to an increase in the minimum wage by increasing the proportion of full-time workers. Nevertheless, 81 percent of restaurants paid full-time and part-time workers exactly the same starting wage in wave 1 of our survey.[23] This suggests either that full-time workers have the same skills as part-time workers or that equity concerns lead restaurants to pay equal wages for unequally productive workers. If full-time workers are more productive (but equally paid), there may be a second reason for stores to substitute full-time workers for part-time workers; namely, a minimum-wage increase enables the industry to attract more full-time workers, and stores would naturally want to hire a greater proportion of full-time workers if they are more productive.

Row 1 of Table 6.6 presents the mean changes in the proportion of full-time workers in New Jersey and Pennsylvania between waves 1 and 2 of our survey, and coefficient estimates from regressions of the change in the proportion of full-time workers on the wage-gap variable, chain dummies, a company-ownership dummy, and region dummies (in column 6). The results are ambiguous. The fraction of full-time workers increased in New Jersey relative to Pennsylvania by 7.3 percent (t ratio = 1.84), but regressions on the wage-gap variable show no significant shift in the fraction of full-time workers.[24]

6.3.5. Other Employment-Related Measures

Rows 2–4 of Table 6.6 present results for other outcome variables that we expect to be related to the level of restaurant employment. In particular, we examine whether the rise in the minimum wage is associated with a change in the number of hours a restaurant is open on a weekday, the number of cash registers in the restaurant, and the number of cash registers typically in operation in the restaurant at 11:00 A.M. Consistent with our employment results, none of these variables shows a statistically significant decline in New Jersey relative to Pennsylvania. Similarly, regressions including the gap variable provide no evidence that the minimum-wage increase led to a systematic change in any of these variables (see columns 5 and 6).

6.4. Nonwage Offsets

One explanation of our finding that a rise in the minimum wage does not lower employment is that restaurants can offset the effect of the minimum wage by reducing nonwage compensation. For example, if workers value fringe benefits and wages equally, employers can simply reduce the level of fringe benefits by the amount of the minimum-wage increase, leaving their employment costs unchanged. The main fringe benefits for fast-food employees are free and reduced-price meals. In the first wave of our survey about 19 percent of fast-food restaurants offered workers free meals, 72 percent offered reduced-price meals, and 9 percent offered a combination of both free and reduced-price meals. Low-price meals are an obvious fringe benefit to cut if the minimum-wage increase forces restaurants to pay higher wages.

Rows 5 and 6 of Table 6.6 present estimates of the effect of the minimum-wage increase on the incidence of free meals and reduced-price meals. The proportion of restaurants offering reduced-price meals fell in both New Jersey and Pennsylvania after the minimum wage increased, with a somewhat greater decline in New Jersey. Contrary to an offset story, however, the reduction in reduced-price meal programs was accompanied by an increase in the fraction of stores offering free meals. Relative to stores in Pennsylvania, New Jersey employers actually shifted toward more generous fringe benefits (i.e. free meals rather than reduced-price meals). However, the relative shift is not statistically significant.

We continue to find a statistically insignificant effect of the minimum-wage increase on the likelihood of receiving free or reduced-price meals in columns 5 and 6, where we report coefficient estimates of the GAP variable from regression models for the change in the incidence of these programs. The results provide no evidence that employers offset the minimum-wage increase by reducing free or reduced-price meals.

Another possibility is that employers responded to the increase in the minimum wage by reducing on-the-job training and flattening the tenure-wage profile (see Mincer and Leighton 1981). Indeed, one manager told our interviewer in wave 1 that her workers were forgoing ordinary scheduled raises because the minimum wage was about to rise, and this would provide a raise for all her workers. To determine whether this phenomenon occurred more generally, we analyzed store managers' responses to questions on the amount of time before a normal wage increase and the usual amount of such raises. In rows 8 and 9 we report the average changes between waves 1 and 2 for these two variables, as well as regression coefficients from models that include the wage-gap variable.[25] Although the average time to the first pay raise increased by 2.5 weeks in New Jersey relative to Pennsylvania, the increase is not statistically significant. Furthermore, there is only a trivial difference in the relative change in the amount of the first pay increment between New Jersey and Pennsylvania stores.

Finally, we examined a related variable: the "slope" of the wage profile, which we measure by the ratio of the typical first raise to the amount of time until the first raise is given. As shown in row 10, the slope of the wage profile flattened in both New Jersey and Pennsylvania, with no significant relative difference between states. The change in the slope is also uncorrelated with the GAP variable. In summary, we can find no indication that New Jersey employers changed either their fringe benefits or their wage profiles to offset the rise in the minimum wage.[26]

6.5. Price Effects of the Minimum-Wage Increase

A final issue we examine is the effect of the minimum wage on the prices of meals at fast-food restaurants. A competitive model of the fast-food industry implies that an increase in the minimum wage will lead to an increase in product prices. If we assume constant returns to scale in the industry, the increase in price should be proportional to the share of minimum-wage labor in total factor cost. The average restaurant in New Jersey initially paid about half its workers less than the new minimum wage. If wages rose by roughly 15 percent for these workers, and if labor's share of total costs is 30 percent, we would expect prices to rise by about 2.2 percent (= 0.15 x 0.5 x 0.3) due to the minimum-wage rise.[27]

In each wave of our survey we asked managers for the prices of three standard items: a medium soda, a small order of french fries, and a main course. The main course was a basic hamburger at Burger King, Roy Rogers, and Wendy's restaurants, and two pieces of chicken at KFC stores. We define "full meal" price as the after-tax price of a medium soda, a small order of french fries, and a main course.

Table 6.7 presents reduced-form estimates of the effect of the minimum-wage increase on prices. The dependent variable in these models is the change in the logarithm of the price of a full meal at each store. The key independent variable is either a dummy indicating whether the store is located in New Jersey or the proportional wage increase required to meet the minimum wage (the GAP variable defined above).

The estimated New Jersey dummy in column 1 shows that after-tax meal prices rose 3.2 percent faster in New Jersey than in Pennsylvania between February and November 1992.[28] The effect is slightly larger controlling for chain and company-ownership (see column 2). Since the New Jersey sales tax rate fell by 1 percentage point between the waves of our survey, these estimates suggest that pretax prices rose 4 percent faster as a result of the minimum-wage increase in New Jersey – slightly more than the increase needed to pass through the cost increase caused by the minimum-wage hike.

Table 6.7

Reduced Form Models for Change in the Price of a Full Meal

Independent variable	Dependent variable: change in the log price of a full meal				
	(1)	(2)	(3)	(4)	(5)
1. New Jersey dummy	0.033	0.037	–	–	–
	(0.014)	(0.014)			
2. Initial wage gap[a]	–	–	0.077	0.146	0.063
			(0.075)	(0.074)	(0.089)
3. Controls for chain and ownership[b]	no	yes	no	yes	yes
4. Controls for region[c]	no	no	no	no	yes
5. Standard error of regression	0.101	0.097	0.302	0.098	0.097

Notes: Standard errors are given in parentheses. Entries are estimated regression coefficients for models fit to the change in the log price of a full meal (entree, medium soda, small fries). The sample contains 315 stores with valid data on prices, wages, and employment for waves 1 and 2. The mean and standard deviation of the dependent variable are 0.0173 and 0.1017, respectively.

[a] Proportional increase in starting wage necessary to raise the wage to the new minimum-wage rate. For stores in Pennsylvania the wage gap is 0.

[b] Three dummy variables for chain type and whether or not the store is company-owned are included.

[c] Dummy variables for two regions of New Jersey and two regions of eastern Pennsylvania are included.

The pattern of price changes *within* New Jersey is less consistent with a simple "pass-through" view of minimum-wage cost increases. In fact, meal prices rose at approximately the same rate at stores in New Jersey with differing levels of initial wages. Inspection of the estimated GAP coefficients in column 5 of Table 6.7 confirms that within regions of New Jersey, the GAP variable is statistically insignificant.

In sum, these results provide mixed evidence that higher minimum wages result in higher fast-food prices. The strongest evidence emerges from a comparison of New Jersey and Pennsylvania stores. The magnitude of the price increase is consistent with predictions from a conventional model of a competitive industry. On the other hand, we find no evidence that prices rose faster among stores in New Jersey that were most affected by the rise in the minimum wage.

One potential explanation for the latter finding is that stores in New Jersey compete in the same product market. As a result, restaurants that are most affected by the minimum wage are unable to increase their product prices faster than their competitors. In contrast, stores in New Jersey and Pennsylvania are in separate product markets, enabling prices to rise in New Jersey relative to Pennsylvania when overall costs rise in New Jersey. Note that this explanation seems to rule out the possibility that store-specific demand shocks can account for the anomalous rise in employment at stores in New Jersey with lower initial wages.

6.6. Store Openings

An important potential effect of higher minimum wages is to discourage the opening of new businesses. Although our sample design allows us to estimate the effect of the minimum wage on *existing* restaurants in New Jersey, we cannot address the effect of the higher minimum wage on potential entrants.[29] To assess the likely size of such an effect, we used national restaurant directories for the McDonald's restaurant chain to compare the numbers of operating restaurants and the numbers of newly opened restaurants in different states over the 1986–1991 period. Many states raised their minimum wages during this period. In addition, the federal minimum wage increased in the early 1990's from $3.35 to $4.25, with differing effects in different states depending on the level of wages in the state. These policies create an opportunity to measure the impact of minimum-wage laws on store opening rates across states.

The results of our analysis are presented in Table 6.8. We regressed the growth rate in the number of McDonald's stores in each state on two alternative measures of the minimum wage in the state and a set of other control variables (population growth and the change in the state unemployment rate). The first minimum-wage measure is the fraction of workers in the state's retail trade industry in 1986 whose

Table 6.8

Estimated Effect of Minimum Wages in Numbers of McDonald's Restaurants, 1986-1991

Independent variable	Dependent variable: proportional increase in number of stores				Dependent variable: (number of newly opened stores)/(number in 1986)			
	(1)	(2)	(3)	(4)	(5)	(6)	(7)	(8)
Minimum-wage variable:								
1. Fraction of retail workers in affected wage range 1986[a]	0.033	—	0.13	—	0.37	—	0.16	—
	(0.20)		(0.19)		(0.22)		(0.21)	
2. (State minimum wage in 1991)/(average retail wage in 1986)[b]	—	0.38	—	0.47	—	0.47	—	0.56
		(0.22)		(0.22)		(0.23)		(0.24)
Other control variables:								
3. Proportional growth in population, 1986–1991	—	—	0.88	1.03	—	—	0.86	1.04
			(0.23)	(0.23)			(0.25)	(0.25)
4. Change in unemployment rates, 1986–1991	—	—	-1.78	-1.40	—	—	-1.85	1.40
			(0.62)	(0.61)			(0.68)	(0.65)
5. Standard error of regression	0.083	0.083	0.071	0.068	0.088	0.088	0.077	0.073

Notes: Standard errors are shown in parentheses. The sample contains 51 state-level observations (including the District of Columbia) on the number of McDonald's restaurants open in 1986 and 1991. The dependent variable in columns 1–4 is the proportional increase in the number of restaurants open. The mean and standard deviation are 0.246 and 0.085, respectively. The dependent variable in columns 5–8 is the ratio of the number of new stores opened between 1986 and 1991 to the number open in 1986. The mean and standard deviation are 0.293 and 0.091, respectively. All regressions are weighted by the state population in 1986.

[a] Fraction of all workers in retail trade in the state in 1986 earning an hourly wage between $3.35 per hour and the "effective" state minimum wage in 1990 (i.e., the maximum of the federal minimum wage in 1990 ($3.80) and the state minimum wage as of April 1, 1990).

[b] Maximum of state and federal minimum wage as of April 1, 1990, divided by the average hourly wage of workers in retail trade in the state in 1986.

wages fell between the existing federal minimum wage in 1986 ($3.35 per hour) and the effective minimum wage in the state in April 1990 (the maximum of the federal minimum wage and the state minimum wages as of April 1990).[30] The second is the ratio of the state's effective minimum wage in 1990 to the average hourly wage of retail trade workers in the state in 1986. Both of these measures are designed to gauge the degree of upward wage pressure exerted by state or federal minimum-wage changes between 1986 and 1990.

The results provide no evidence that higher minimum-wage rates (relative to the retail-trade wages in a state) exert a negative effect on either the net number of restaurants or the rate of new openings. To the contrary, all the estimates show positive effects of higher minimum wages on the number of operating or newly opened stores, although many of the point estimates are insignificantly different from zero. While this evidence is limited, we conclude that the effects of minimum wages on fast-food store opening rates are probably small.

6.7. Broader Evidence on Employment Changes in New Jersey

Our establishment-level analysis suggests that the rise in the minimum wage in New Jersey may have increased employment in the fast-food industry. Is this just an anomaly associated with our particular sample, or a phenomenon unique to the fast-food industry? Data from the monthly Current Population Survey (CPS) allow us to compare state-wide employment trends in New Jersey and the surrounding states, providing a check on the interpretation of our findings. Using monthly CPS files for 1991 and 1992, we computed employment-population rates for teenagers and adults (age 25 and older) for New Jersey, Pennsylvania, New York, and the entire United States. Since the New Jersey minimum wage rose on April 1, 1992, we computed the employment rates for April–December of both 1991 and 1992. The relative changes in employment in New Jersey and the surrounding states then give an indication of the effect of the new law.

A comparison of changes in adult employment rates show that the New Jersey labor market fared slightly worse over the 1991–1992 period than either the U.S. labor market as a whole or labor markets in Pennsylvania or New York (see Card and Krueger 1993, table 9).[31] Among teenagers, however, the situation was reversed. In New Jersey, teenage employment rates fell by 0.7 percent from 1991 to 1992. In New York, Pennsylvania, and the United States as a whole, teenage employment rates dropped faster. Relative to teenagers in Pennsylvania, for example, the teenage employment rate in New Jersey rose by 2.0 percentage points. While this point estimate is consistent with our findings for the fast-food industry, the standard error is too large (3.2%) to allow any confident assessment.

6.8. Interpretation

As in the earlier study by Katz and Krueger (1992), our empirical findings on the effects of the New Jersey minimum wage are inconsistent with the predictions of a conventional competitive model of the fast-food industry. Our employment results are consistent with several alternative models, although none of these models can also explain the apparent rise in fast-food prices in New Jersey. In this section we briefly summarize the predictions of the standard model and some simple alternatives, and we highlight the difficulties posed by our findings.

6.8.1. Standard Competitive Model

A standard competitive model predicts that establishment-level employment will fall if the wage is exogenously raised. For an entire industry, total employment is predicted to fall, and product price is predicted to rise in response to an increase in a binding minimum wage. Estimates from the time-series literature on minimum-wage effects can be used to get a rough idea of the elasticity of low-wage employment to the minimum wage. The surveys by Brown, Gilroy, and Kohen (1982, 1983) conclude that a 10 percent increase in the coverage-adjusted minimum wage will reduce teenage employment rates by 1–3 percent. Since this effect is for all teenagers, and not just those employed in low-wage industries, it is surely a lower bound on the magnitude of the effect for fast-food workers. The 18 percent increase in the New Jersey minimum wage is therefore predicted to reduce employment at fast-food stores by 0.4–1.0 employees per store. Our empirical results clearly reject the upper range of these estimates, although we cannot reject a small negative effect in some of our specifications.

A possible defense of the competitive model is that unobserved demand shocks affected certain stores in New Jersey – specifically, those stores that were initially paying wages less than $5.00 per hour. However, such localized demand shocks should also affect product prices. (In fact, in a competitive model, product demand shocks work through a rise in prices.) Although lower-wage stores in New Jersey had relative employment gains, they did not have relative price increases. Furthermore, our analysis of employment changes in two major suburban areas (around Newark and Camden) reveals that, even within local areas, employment rose faster at the stores that had to increase wages the most because of the new minimum wage.

6.8.2. Alternative Models

An alternative to the conventional competitive model is one in which firms are price-takers in the product market but have some degree of market power in the labor market. If fast-food stores face an upward-sloping labor-supply schedule, a rise in the minimum wage can potentially increase employment at affected firms and in the industry as a whole.[32]

This same basic insight emerges from an equilibrium search model in which firms post wages and employees search among posted offers (see Dale T. Mortensen 1988). Kenneth Burdett and Mortensen (1989) derive the equilibrium wage distribution for a noncooperative wage-search/wage-posting model and show that the imposition of a binding minimum wage can increase both wages and employment relative to the initial equilibrium. Furthermore, their model predicts that the minimum wage will increase employment the most at firms that initially paid the lowest wages.

Although monopsonistic and job-search models provide a potential explanation for the observed employment effects of the New Jersey minimum wage, they cannot explain the observed price effects. In these models, industry prices should have fallen in New Jersey relative to Pennsylvania, and at low-wage stores in New Jersey relative to high-wage stores in New Jersey. Neither prediction is confirmed: indeed, prices rose faster in New Jersey than in Pennsylvania, although at about the same rate at high- and low-wage stores in New Jersey. Another puzzle for equilibrium search models is the absence of wage increases at firms that were initially paying $5.05 or more per hour.

The strict link between the employment and price effects of a rise in the minimum wage may be broken if fast-food stores can vary the quality of service (e.g. the length of the queue at peak hours, or the cleanliness of stores). Another possibility is that stores altered the *relative* prices of their various menu items. Comparisons of price changes for the three items in our survey show slight declines (-1.5%) in the price of french fries and soda in New Jersey relative to Pennsylvania, coupled with a relative increase (8%) in entree prices. These limited data suggest a possible role for relative price changes within the fast-food industry following the rise in the minimum wage.

One way to test a monopsony model is to identify stores that were initially "supply-constrained" in the labor market and test for employment gains at these stores relative to other stores. A potential indicator of market power is the use of recruitment bonuses. As we noted in Table 6.2, about 25 percent of stores in wave 1 were offering cash bonuses to employees who helped find a new worker. We compared employment changes at New Jersey stores that were offering recruitment bonuses in wave 1, and also interacted the GAP variable with a dummy for recruitment bonuses in several employment-change models. We do not find faster (or slower) employment growth at the New Jersey stores that were initially using recruitment bonuses, or any evidence that the GAP variable had a larger effect for stores that were using bonuses.

6.9. Conclusions

Contrary to the central prediction of the textbook model of the minimum wage, but consistent with a number of other studies based on cross-sectional time-series comparisons of affected and unaffected markets or employers, we find no evidence that the rise in New Jersey's minimum wage reduced employment at fast-food restaurants in the state. Regardless of whether we compare stores in New Jersey that were affected by the $5.05 minimum to stores in eastern Pennsylvania (where the minimum wage was constant at $4.25 per hour) or to stores in New Jersey that were initially paying $5.00 per hour or more (and were largely unaffected by the new law), we find that the increase in the minimum wage increased employment. We present a wide variety of alternative specifications to probe the robustness of this conclusion. None of the alternatives shows a negative employment effect. We also check our findings for the fast-food industry by comparing changes in teenage employment rates in New Jersey,

Pennsylvania, and New York in the year following the increase in the minimum wage. Again, these results point toward a relative *increase* in employment of low-wage workers in New Jersey. We also find no evidence that minimum-wage increases negatively affect the number of McDonald's outlets opened in a state.

Finally, we find that prices of fast-food meals increased in New Jersey relative to Pennsylvania, suggesting that much of the burden of the minimum-wage rise was passed on to consumers. Within New Jersey, however, we find *no* evidence that prices increased more in stores that were most affected by the minimum-wage rise. Taken as a whole, these findings are difficult to explain with the standard competitive model or with models in which employers face supply constraints (e.g. monopsony or equilibrium search models).

7

A Re-Analysis of the Effect of the New Jersey Minimum Wage with Representative Payroll Data

Replication and re-analysis are important endeavors in economies, especially when new findings run counter to conventional wisdom. In their Comment on our 1994 American Economic Review article (see Chapter 6), David Neumark and William Wascher (2000) challenge our conclusion that the April 1992 increase in the New Jersey minimum wage led to no loss of employment in the fast-food industry. Using data drawn from payroll records for a set of restaurants initially assembled by Richard Berman of the Employment Policies Institute (EPI) and later supplemented by their own data-collection efforts, Neumark and Wascher (hereafter, NW) conclude that "... the New Jersey minimum-wage increase led to a relative decline in fast-food employment in New Jersey" compared to Pennsylvania.[1] They attribute the discrepancies between their findings and ours to problems in our fast-food restaurant data set. Specifically, they argue that our use of employment data derived from telephone surveys, rather than from payroll records, led us to draw faulty inferences about the effect of the New Jersey minimum wage.

This chapter is a revised version of: Card, D., Krueger, A. (2000). Minimum Wages and Employment: A Case Study of the Fast-Food Industry in New Jersey and Pennsylvania: Reply, in: American Economic Review 90(5), 1397–1420. The analysis in Sections 7.1., 7.2., and 7.3.2., of this chapter is based on confidential Bureau of Labor Statistics (BLS) ES-202 data. The authors thank the BLS staff for assistance with these data. All opinions and analysis in this chapter reflect the views of the authors and not the U.S. government. The authors also thank seminar participants at Princeton University, the National Bureau of Economic Research, the University of Pennsylvania, the University of California-Berkeley, the Kennedy School (Harvard University), and Larry Katz and John Kennan for helpful comments, and the Princeton University Industrial Relations Section for research support.

In this chapter we attempt to reconcile the contrasting findings by analyzing administrative employment data from a new representative sample of fast-food employers in the states of New Jersey and Pennsylvania, and by re-analyzing NW's data. Most importantly, we use the Bureau of Labor Statistics's (BLS's) employer-reported ES-202 data file to examine employment growth of fast-food restaurants in a set of major chains in New Jersey and nearby counties of Pennsylvania.[2] We draw two samples from the ES-202 files: a longitudinal file that tracks a fixed sample of establishments between the years 1992 and 1993, and a series of repeated cross-sections from the end of 1991 through 1997. Because the BLS data are derived from unemployment-insurance (UI) payroll-tax records, the employment measures are free of the kinds of survey errors that NW allege affected our earlier results. In addition, because the ES-202 data include information for all covered employers in a fixed group of restaurant chains, there is no reason for us to doubt the representativeness of the BLS sample.

A comparison of fast-food employment growth in New Jersey and Pennsylvania over the period of our original study confirms the key findings in our 1994 paper, and calls into question the representativeness of the sample assembled by Berman, Neumark, and Wascher. Consistent with our original sample, the BLS fast-food data set indicates slightly faster employment growth in New Jersey than in the Pennsylvania border counties over the time period that we initially examined, although in most specifications the differential is small and statistically insignificant. We also use the BLS data to examine longer-run effects of the New Jersey minimum-wage increase, and to study the effect of the 1996 increase in the federal minimum wage, which was binding in Pennsylvania but not in New Jersey, where the state minimum wage afready exceeded the new federal standard. Our analysis of this new policy intervention provides further evidence that modest changes in the minimum wage have little systematic effect on employment.

In light of these results we go on to reexamine the Berman-Neumark-Wascher (BNW) sample and evaluate the contention that the rise in the New Jersey minimum wage caused employment to fall in the state's fast-food industry. Our re-analysis leads to four main conclusions. First, the pattern of employment growth in the BNW sample of fast-food restaurants across chains and geographic areas within New Jersey is remarkably consistent with our original survey data. In both data sets employment grew faster in areas of New Jersey where wages were forced up more by the 1992 minimum-wage increase. The differences between the BNW sample and ours are attributable to differences in the BNW sample of Pennsylvania restaurants, which unlike the more comprehensive BLS sample, and our original sample, shows a rise in fast-food employment in the state. Second, the differential employment trend in the BNW Pennsylvania sample is driven by data for restaurants from one single Burger King franchisee alone who provided all the Pennsylvania data in the original Berman sample.

Third, the employment trends measured in the BNW sample are significantly different for restaurants that reported their payroll data on a weekly, biweekly, or monthly basis. Establishments that reported on a biweekly basis had faster growth than those that reported on a monthly or weekly basis. We suspect that the different reporting bases matter because the BNW employment measure is based on payroll hours (rather than actual numbers of employees) and because weekly, biweekly, and monthly averages of payroll hours were differentially affected by seasonal factors, including the Thanksgiving holiday and a major winter storm in December 1992. Regardless of the explanation, a higher fraction of Pennsylvania restaurants reported their data in biweekly intervals, leading to a faster measured employment growth in that state. Once the employment changes are adjusted for the reporting bases, the BNW sample shows virtually identical growth in New Jersey and eastern Pennsylvania. Finally, a re-analysis of publicly available BLS data on employment trends in the two states shows no effect of the minimum wage on employment in the eating and drinking industry.

Based on all the evidence now available, including the BLS ES-202 sample, our earlier sample, publicly available BLS data, and the BNW sample, we conclude that the increase in the New Jersey minimum wage in April 1992 had little or no systematic effect on total fast-food employment in the state, although there may have been individual restaurants where employment rose or fell in response to the higher minimum wage.

7.1. Analysis of Representative BLS Fast-Food Restaurant Sample

7.1.1. Description of BLS ES-202 Data

On April 1, 1992, the New Jersey state minimum wage increased from $4.25 to $5.05 per hour, while the minimum wage in Pennsylvania remained at $4.25. To examine the effect of the New Jersey mini-mum-wage increase using representative payroll data, we applied to the BLS for permission to analyze their ES-202 data. The ES-202 da-tabase consists of employment records reported quarterly by employ-ers to their state employment security agencies for unemployment-insurance tax purposes. The first question on the New Jersey UI tax form requests the "Number of covered workers employed during the pay period which includes the 12th day of each month."[3] The BLS maintains these data as part of the Covered Employment and Wages Program. We analyze two types of samples from the ES-202 file: a lon-gitudinal file and a series of repeated cross sections.

The longitudinal sample consists of restaurants belonging to a set of the largest fast-food chains.[4] Restaurants in the sampled chains em-ployed 13 percent of all employees in the eating and drinking industry in New Jersey and eastern Pennsylvania in 1992. There is considerable overlap between the restaurants in the BLS sample and those in our orig-inal sample.[5] Our sample of fast-food restaurants from the ES-202 data was drawn as follows. We first selected all records for all establishments in the eating and drinking industry (SIC 5812) in New Jersey and eastern Pennsylvania in the first quarter of 1991, first quarter of 1994, and fourth quarter of 1996. Then restaurants in the sampled chains were identified from this universe by separately searching for the chains' names, or vari-ants of their names, in the legal name, trade name, and unit description fields of the ES-202 file. If the name of an included chain was mentioned in any of these text fields the record was then visually examined to en-sure that it belonged in the sample of included restaurant. In addition, records for all eating and drinking establishments from these quarters were visually inspected to identify any fast-food restaurants in the rel-evant chains that were missed by the computerized name search. If a restaurant in one of the relevant fast-food chains was discovered that was not identified by the initial name search, the computerized name-search algorithm was amended to include that restaurant.

The original Card-Krueger (CK) sample contained data on restau-rants in 7 counties of Pennsylvania (Bucks, Chester, Lackawanna,

Lehigh, Luzerrie, Montgomery, and Northampton). Because this is a somewhat idiosyncratic group – with some counties located right on the New Jersey border and with others located off the border – we decided to expand the sample to include 7 additional counties: Berks, Carbon, Delaware, Monroe, Philadelphia, Pike, and Wayne. In the results that follow, we present estimates for both our original 7 counties and for the larger set of 14 counties. The map in Figure 7.1, below, indicates the location of the restaurants in our initial survey, the original 7 counties in Pennsylvania, and the additional 7 counties in Pennsylvania.

Once restaurants in the relevant chains and counties were identified, we merged quarterly records for these restaurants for the period from the first quarter of 1992 to the fourth quarter of 1994 to create a longitudinal file.[6] To mirror the CK sample, only establishments with nonzero employment in February or March of 1992 – these being the months covered by wave 1 of our survey – were included in the longitudinal analysis file. The final longitudinal sample contains 687 establishments. A total of 16 (2.3%) of these establishments had zero or missing employment in November or December of 1992, which were the months covered by wave 2 of our original survey. These establishments had either closed or could not be tracked because their reporting information changed. In 1992, less than 1 percent of establishments had imputed employment data (that is, cases where the state filled in an estimate of employment because the establishment failed to report it).

A potential limitation of the BLS longitudinal sample for the present paper should be noted. The ES-202 data pertain to "reporting units" that may be either single establishment units or multiestablishment units. The BLS encouraged employers to report their data at the county level or below in the early 1990s. Some employers were in the process of switching to a county-level reporting basis during our sample period. Consequently, some restaurants that remained open were difficult to track because they changed their reporting identifiers. Fortunately, most of the restaurants that were in this situation could be tracked by searching addresses and other characteristics of the stores. All of the restaurants that were not linked to subsequent months' data were assumed closed and assigned zero employment for these for months, even though some of these restaurants may not have closed. This is probably a more common occurrence for the New Jersey than for Pennsylvania: 0.4 percent of Pennsylvania restaurants had zero or missing employment at the end of 1992, as compared to 3.4 percent of the New Jersey restaurants. In our original survey, 1.3 percent of the Pennsylvania restaurants and 2.7 percent of the New Jersey restaurants were temporarily or permanently closed at the end of 1992.[7]

Figure 7.1

Areas of New Jersey and Pennsylvania Covered by Original Survey and BLS Data

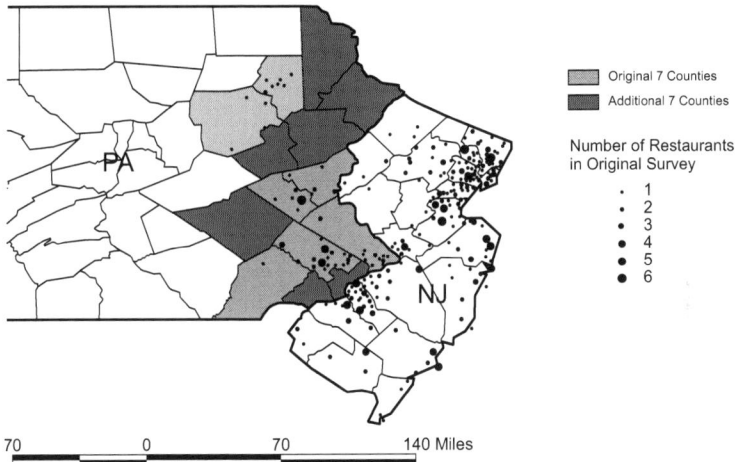

Also note that because firms are allowed to report on more than one unit in a county in the BLS data, some of the records reflect an aggregation of data for multiple establishments. We address both of these issues in the analysis set out below. Importantly, however, these problems do not affect the repeated cross-sectional files that we also analyze.

To draw the repeated cross-sectional file, the final name-search algorithm described above was applied each quarter between 1991:Q4 and 1997:Q3. Again, data were selected for the same chains in New Jersey and the 14 counties in eastern Pennsylvania. Every month's data from the sampled quarters was selected. The cross-sectional sample probably provides the cleanest estimates of the effect of the minimum-wage increase because it incorporates births as well as deaths of restaurants, and because possible problems caused by changes in reporting units over time are minimized.

7.1.2. Summary Statistics and Differences-in-Differences

Table 7.1 reports basic employment summary statistics for New Jersey and for the Pennsylvania counties, before and after the April

1992 increase in New Jersey's minimum wage. Panel A is based on the longitudinal BLS sample of fast-food restaurants. In the first row, the "before" period pertains to *average* employment in February and March of 1992, and the "after" pertains to *average* employment in November and December of 1992.[8] The second row reports employment figures for February and November, which were the most common survey months in our original telephone survey. The third row shows data for the 12-month interval from March 1992 to March 1993. Finally, for comparison, panel B of Table 7.1 reports the corresponding employment statistics calculated from the CK survey. Note that for comparability with BLS data, we have calculated total employment for restaurants in our original survey by adding together the number of full-time, part-time, and managerial workers.[9]

Several conclusions are apparent from the means in Table 7.1. First, the BLS data indicate a slight rise in employment in New Jersey's fast-food restaurants over the period we studied, and a slight decline in employment in Pennsylvania's restaurants over the same period. Our telephone survey data indicate a net gain in New Jersey relative to Pennsylvania of 2.4 workers per restaurant, whereas the BLS data in row 2 indicate a smaller net gain of 1.1 workers between February and November of 1992. Second, between March 1992 and March 1993, the BLS data indicate that both New Jersey and Pennsylvania experienced a decline in average employment, with the decline being larger in Pennsylvania. Third, the average employment level in the BLS data is somewhat greater than the average level in our data, probably because some of the observations in the BLS data pertain to multiple establishments. Fourth, our data and the BLS data both suggest that average restaurant size was initially larger in Pennsylvania than in New Jersey. By contrast, the BNW data set indicates that "full-time equivalent employment" was initially greater in New Jersey than in Pennsylvania (see Section 7.3. below). Finally, the BLS data indicate that the results for the 7 Pennsylvania counties that we used in our initial sample and the wider set of 14 counties are generally similar.

Neumark and Wascher (2000) and others have emphasized the fact that the dispersion in full-time employment changes in our data set is greater than the dispersion in changes in total hours worked in the BNW data. Interestingly, the BLS payroll data display roughly the same standard deviation of employment changes as was found in our original sample. For example, in New Jersey the standard deviation of the change in employment across reporting units between Febru-

Table 7.1

Descriptive Statistics for Fast-Food Restaurants Drawn from BLS ES-202 Data and Card-Krueger Survey

	Means with standard deviations in parentheses:								
	New Jersey			7 Pennsylvania counties			14 Pennsylvannia counties		
	Before	After	Change	Before	After	Change	Before	After	Change
A. BLS ES-202 data Febuary–March 1992 to November–December 1992	37.2	37.6	0.41	42.5	42.4	-0.12	44.8	44.3	-0.53
	(19.9)	(21.0)	(9.82)	(23.2)	(23.5)	(10.94)	(53.7)	(59.9)	(12.32)
Febuary 1992 to November 1992	37.2	37.8	0.57	42.7	42.2	-0.54	44.9	44.4	-0.58
	(19.9)	(20.9)	(10.12)	(23.8)	(23.2)	(12.82)	(53.6)	(60.4)	(13.83)
March 1992 to March 1993	37.2	34.8	-2.48	42.3	37.5	-4.80	44.7	40.7	-4.0
	(20.1)	(20.0)	(13.99)	(22.8)	(18.6)	(22.74)	(54.5)	(54.5)	(18.1)
B. Card-Krueger survey data Febuary 1992 to November 1992	29.8	30.0	0.19	33.1	30.9	-2.23	NA	NA	NA
	(12.5)	(13.0)	(9.82)	(14.7)	(10.6)	(11.98)	NA	NA	NA

Notes: Sample sizes for the first two rows are 437 for New Jersey, 127 for Pennsylvania 14 counties, and 250 for Pennsylvania 7 counties; sample sizes for third row are 436, 127, and 250, respectively; sample sizes for the last row are 309 for New Jersey and 75 for Pennsylvania. The 7 Pennsylvania counties used in the middle columns are the same counties used in Chapter 6; these 7 counties are a subset of the 14 counties in the last three columns (see text). The unit of observation for the BLS data is the "reporting unit," which in some cases includes multiple establishments. The unit of observation in the Card-Krueger data is the individual restaurant.

ary and November of 1992 was 10.12 in the BLS data, which slightly exceeds the standard deviation calculated from our survey data (9.82) over approximately the same months. One problem with this comparison is that some of the BLS reporting units combine two or more restaurants that may have been broken out over time, whereas the unit of observation in our original survey was the individual restaurant. To address this issue, we restricted the BLS sample to reporting units that initially had fewer than 40 employees: these smaller reporting units are almost certainly individual restaurants. The standard deviation of employment changes for this truncated BLS sample is 9.0 for New Jersey and 6.8 for Pennsylvania; these figures compare to 8.0 and 8.8, respectively, if we truncate our survey data in the same way.

More generally, the criticism that our telephone survey was flawed because of the substantial dispersion in measured employment growth in our sample strikes us as off the mark for three reasons. First, reporting errors in employment data collected from a telephone survey are not terribly surprising. Dispersion in our data is not out of line with measures based on other establishment-level employment surveys (e.g. Davis, Haltiwanger, and Schuh 1996).[10] Second, employment changes are the *dependent variable* in our analysis. As long as the measurement error process is the same for restaurants in New Jersey and Pennsylvania, estimates of the difference in employment growth based on our data will be unbiased. We know of no reason to suspect that the New Jersey and Pennsylvania managers who responded to our survey would misreport employment data in a systematically different way. Moreover, all of our telephone interviews were conducted by a single professional interviewer. Third, any comparison of the standard deviation of full-time equivalent employment changes is potentially sensitive to the way data on hours, or combinations of part-time and full-time employees, are scaled. For example, in their analysis NW convert weekly payroll hours data into a measure of employment by dividing by 35, but a smaller divisor would obviously lead to larger dispersion of employment in their data. The standard deviation of *proportionate* changes in employment is invariant to scaling and is fairly similar in all three data sets: 0.29 in the BLS data, 0.35 in BNW's data, and 0.39 in our earlier survey data.[11]

7.1.3. Regression-Adjusted Models

Panels A and B of Table 7.2 present basic regression estimates using the BLS ES-202 longitudinal sample of fast-food restaurants. The models presented in this table essentially parallel the main specifications in Card and Krueger (1994, see Chapter 6 in this volume). The dependent variable in the first two columns is the change in the number of employees, while the dependent variable in the last two columns is the proportionate change in the number of employees. Following Card and Krueger (1994), the denominator of the proportionate change is the average of first- and second-period employment. Employment changes are measured between February–March 1992 and November–December 1992. Columns 1 and 3 include as the only regressor a dummy variable indicating whether the restaurant is located in New Jersey or eastern Pennsylvania. These estimates correspond to the difference-in-differences estimates that can be derived from row 1 of Table 7.1. The models in columns 2 and 4 add a set of additional control variables: dummy variables for the identity of the restaurant chain, and a dummy variable indicating whether the reporting unit was a subunit of a multiumt employer.[12]

The regression results in panel A of Table 7.2, which are based on the employment changes for restaurants in the same geographic region surveyed in our earlier work, indicate small, positive coefficients on the New Jersey dummy variable.[13] Each of the estimates is individually statistically insignificant, however. We interpret these estimates as indicating that New Jersey's employment growth in the fast-food industry over this period was essentially the same as it was for the same set of restaurant chains in the 7 Pennsylvania counties.

In panel B, regression results are presented using the wider set of 14 Pennsylvania counties as the comparison group. These results also indicate somewhat faster employment growth in New Jersey following the increase in the state's minimum wage. Only in the proportionate change specifications without covariates, however, is the difference in growth rates between New Jersey and Pennsylvania restaurants close to being statistically significant.

Table 7.2

Basic Regression Results; BLS ES-202 Fast-Food Data and Card-Krueger Survey Data

Explanatory variables	Dependent variable:			
	Change in levels		Proportionate change	
	(1)	(2)	(3)	(4)
A. All of New Jersey and 7 Pennsylvania Counties, BLS Data				
New Jersey indicator	0.536	0.225	0.007	0.009
	(1.017)	(1.029)	(0.029)	(0.029)
Chain dummies and subunit dummy variable	No	Yes	No	Yes
Standard error of regression	10.09	9.99	0.286	0.281
R^2	0.001	0.029	0.000	0.046
B. All of New Jersey and 14 Pennsylvania Counties, BLS Data				
New Jersey indicator	0.946	0.272	0.045	0.032
	(0.856)	(0.859)	(0.024)	(0.024)
Chain dummies and subunit dummy variable	No	Yes	No	Yes
Standard error of regression	10.80	10.63	0.303	0.294
R^2	0.002	0.042	0.005	0.071
C. Original Card-Krueger Survey Data				
New Jersey indicator	2.411	2.488	0.029	0.030
	(1.323)	(1.323)	(0.050)	(0.049)
Chain dummies and subunit dummy variable	No	Yes	No	Yes
Standard error of regression	10.28	10.25	0.385	0.382
R^2	0.009	0.025	0.001	0.024

Notes: Each regression also includes a constant. Sample size is 564 for panel A, 687 for panel B, and 384 for panel C. Subunit dummy variable equals one if the reporting unit is a subunit of a multiunit employer. For comparability with the BLS data, employment in the CK sample is measured by the total number of full- and part-time employees. Standard errors are in parentheses.

For comparison, panel C contains the corresponding estimates from our original sample. These estimates differ (slightly) from those reported in our original paper because we now measure employment as the unweighted sum of full-time workers, part-time workers, and managerial workers to be comparable to the BLS data. The estimates based on our sample are qualitatively similar to those based on the BLS data, with positive coefficients on the New Jersey dummy variable. In addition, in both data sets the inclusion of additional explanatory variables does not add very much to the explanatory power of the model.

7.1.4. Specification Tests

The BLS data analyzed in Tables 7.1 and 7.2 suggest that the New Jersey minimum-wage increase had either no effect, or a small positive effect, on fast-food industry employment in New Jersey vis-à-vis eastern Pennsylvania. To probe this finding further, in Table 7.3 we examine a variety of other specifications and samples. Panel A of the table presents results using our original 7 Pennsylvania counties, and panel B uses the wider set of 14 counties. In all of the models, we include a full set of chain dummy variables and the subunit dummy variable. Results are reported for both the change in employment specification (column 1) and the proportionate employment growth specification (column 2).

Table 7.3

Sensitivity of New Jersey Employment Growth Differential to Specification Changes; BLS ES-202 Fast-Food Restaurant Sample

Specification and sample	Change in levels (1)	Proportionate change (2)	Sample size
A. New Jersey and 7 Pennsylvania counties			
1. Basic specification	0.225	0.009	564
	(1.029)	(0.029)	
2. Excluding closed stores	0.909	0.031	549
	(0.950)	(0.024)	
3. Excluding closed stores unless imputation code = 9	0.640	0.022	553
	(0.973)	(0.025)	
4. Drop large outlier	0.251	0.009	563
	(0.970)	(0.028)	
5. Proportionate change with initial employment in base	–	-0.001	564
		(0.032)	
6. Excluding New Jersey shore	0.032	0.008	480
	(1.092)	(0.030)	
7. March 1992 to March 1993 employment change	2.345	0.007	563
	(1.678)	(0.035)	
8. February 1992 to November 1992 employment change	1.05	0.013	564
	(1.10)	(0.032)	
B. New Jersey and 14 Pennsylvania counties			
1. Basic specification	0.272	0.032	687
	(1.029)	(0.024)	
2. Excluding closed stores	0.639	0.055	671
	(0.776)	(0.021)	
3. Excluding closed stores unless imputation code = 9	0.338	0.044	675
	(0.787)	(0.021)	
4. Drop large outlier	0.72	0.032	685
		(0.023)	
5. Proportionate change with initial employment in base	–	0.020	687
		(0.024)	
6. Excluding New Jersey shore	0.069	0.030	603
	(0.924)	(0.025)	
7. March 1992 to March 1993 employment change	1.196	0.009	686
	(1.258)	(0.027)	
8. February 1992 to November 1992 employment change	0.624	0.027	687
	(0.927)	(0.024)	

Notes: The table reports the coefficient (with standard error in parentheses) for the New Jersey dummy variable from a regression of the change in employment (column 1) or proportionate change in employment (column 2) on a New Jersey dummy variable, chain dummy variables, a dummy variable indicating whether the restaurant is reported as a subunit of a multiestablishment employer, and a constant.

For reference, the first row replicates the basic specifications from Table 7.2. Rows 2 and 3 examine the sensitivity of our results to alternative choices for handling stores with missing employment data in November–December 1992. In the base specification these stores are assigned 0 employment in the second period, which is equivalent to assuming that they all closed. Recall that some of these stores may have actually remained open but changed reporting identifiers. In row 2, we delete from the sample all stores with missing employment data in the second period; this is equivalent to assuming that all of these stores remained open but were randomly missing employment data. Finally, in row 3, we use the imputation codes in the ES-202 database to attempt to distinguish between closed stores (with an imputation code of 9) and those that had missing data for other reasons. In particular, we add back to the sample any restaurant with missing employment data (or those with 0 reported employment) if they were assigned an imputation code indicating a closure. In our opinion, this is the most appropriate sample for measuring the effect of the minimum wage on the set of stores that were in business just before the rise in the minimum. A comparison of the results in rows 2 and 3 with the base specifications indicates that eliminating stores with missing or zero second-period employment, or including such stores only if the imputation code indicated the store was closed, tends to increase the coefficient on the New Jersey dummy variable.

Two of the observations in the sample had employment increases about twice the mean wave 1 size; the next largest increase was less than the mean size.[14] These large employment changes may have occurred because one franchisee acquired another outlet, or for other reasons. To probe the impact of these two outliers, they are dropped from the sample in row 4. The estimates are not very much affected by these observations, however.

In our original paper we calculated the proportionate change in employment with average employment over the two periods in the denominator. (This procedure is widely used by analysts of micro-level establishment data, e.g. Davis, Haltiwanger, and Schuh 1996) This specification was selected because we thought it would reduce the impact of measurement error in the employment data. We have used that specification in Tables 7.2 and 7.3 of this chapter. The specification in row 5 of Table 7.3, however, measures the proportionate change in employment with the first-period employment in the denominator. With this specification, New Jersey's employment growth is slightly lower than that in the 7-county Pennsylvania sample, although employment growth in New Jersey continues to be greater than in Pennsylvania when the 14-county sample is used.

In row 6 we eliminate from the sample restaurants that are located in counties on the New Jersey shore. These counties may have different seasonal demand patterns than the rest of the sample. The results are not very different in this truncated sample, however. Another way to hold seasonal effects constant is to compare year-over-year employment changes. In row 8 we measure employment changes from March 1992 to March 1993. This 12-month change has the added advantage of allowing New Jersey employers more time to adjust to the higher minimum wage. The relative change in the level of employment in New Jersey is notably larger when March-to-March changes are used.

Finally, in row 8 we measure employment changes from February 1992 to November 1992. As mentioned, these are the months when the preponderance of data in our survey was collected. It is probably not surprising that these results are quite similar to the base specification estimates, which use the average February–March 1992 and average November–December 1992 employment data.

On the whole, we interpret the BLS longitudinal data as indicating that fast-food industry employment growth in New Jersey was about the same, or slightly stronger, than that in Pennsylvania following the increase in New Jersey's minimum wage. It is nonetheless possible to choose samples and/or specifications in which employment growth was slightly weaker in New Jersey than in Pennsylvania. This is what one would expect if the true difference in employment growth was very close to zero. In none of our specifications or subsamples do we find any indication of significantly weaker employment growth in New Jersey than in eastern Pennsylvania.

7.2. Repeated Cross Sections from the BLS ES-202 Data

As described above, we also used the quarterly BLS ES-202 data to draw repeated cross sections of fast-food restaurants for the period from 1991 to 1997. We used these cross-sectional samples to calculate total employment for New Jersey, for the 7 counties of Pennsylvania used in our original study, and for the broader set of 14 eastern Pennsylvania counties in each month. Figure 7.2 summarizes the time-series patterns of aggregate employment from these files. For each of the three geographic regions, the figure shows aggregate monthly employment in the fast-food industry relative to their respective February 1992 levels.

Figure 7.2

Employment in New Jersey and Pennsylvania Fast-Food-Restaurants, October 1991 to September 1997

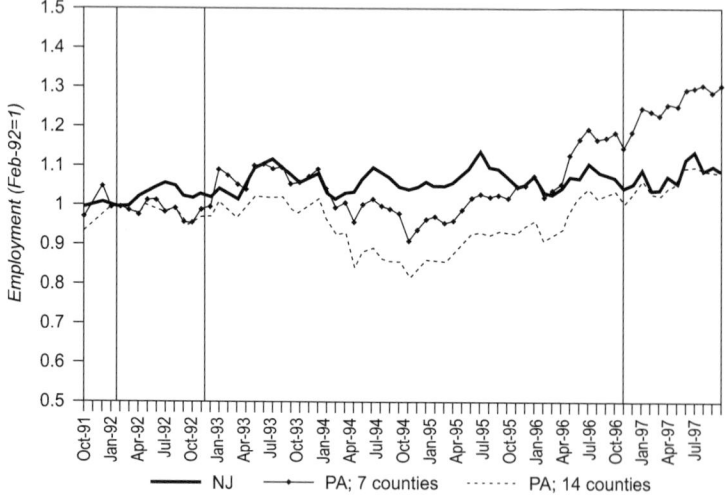

Note: Vertical lines indicate dates of original Card–Krueger survey and the October 1996 federal minimum-wage increase.
Source: Authors' calculations based on BLS ES-202 data.

The figure reveals a pattern that is consistent with the longitudinal estimates. In particular, between February and November of 1992 – the main months our survey was conducted – fast-food employment grew by 3 percent in New Jersey, while it fell by 1 percent in the 7 Pennsylvania counties and fell by 3 percent in the 14 Pennsylvania counties. Although it is possible to find some pairs of months surrounding the minimum-wage increase over which employment growth in Pennsylvania exceeded that in New Jersey, on whole the figure provides little evidence that Pennsylvania's employment growth exceeded New Jersey's in the few years following the minimum-wage increase.

7.2.1. The Effect of the 1996 Federal Minimum-Wage Increase

On October 1, 1996, the federal minimum wage increased from $4.25 per hour to $4.75 per hour. This increase was binding in Pennsylvania, but not in New Jersey, where the state's $5.05 minimum wage already exceeded the new federal standard. Consequently, the same comparison can be conducted in reverse, with New Jersey now serving as a "control group" for Pennsylvania's experience. This reverse comparison is particularly useful because any long-run economic trends that might have biased employment growth in favor of New Jersey during the previous minimum-wage hike will now have the opposite effect on our inference of the effect of the minimum wage.

The results in Figure 7.2 clearly indicate greater employment growth in Pennsylvania than in New Jersey following the 1996 minimum-wage increase. Between September 1996 and September 1997, for example, employment grew by 10 percent in the 7 Pennsylvania counties and 2 percent in New Jersey. In the 14-county Pennsylvania sample employment grew by 6 percent. It is possible that the superior growth in Pennsylvania relative to New Jersey reflects a delayed reaction to the 1992 increase in New Jersey's minimum wage, although we doubt that employment would take so long to adjust in this high-turnover industry. We also doubt that Pennsylvania's strong employment growth was caused by the 1996 increase in the federal minimum wage, but there is certainly no evidence in these data to suggest that the hike in the federal minimum wage caused Pennsylvania restaurants to lower their employment relative to what it otherwise would have been in the absence of the minimum-wage increase.

To more formally test the relationship between relative employment trends and the minimum wage using the data in Figure 7.2, we estimated a regression in which the dependent variable was the difference in log employment between New Jersey and Pennsylvania each month, and the independent variables were the log of the minimum wage in New Jersey relative to that in Pennsylvania and a linear time trend. For the 7-county sample, this regression yielded a positive coefficient with a t-ratio of 5.2 on the minimum wage. Although we would not necessarily interpret this evidence as suggesting that a higher minimum wage causes employment to rise, we see little evidence in these data that the relative value of the minimum wage reduced relative employment in the fast-food industry during the 1990s.

7.3. A Re-Analysis of the Berman-Neumark Wascher (BNW) Data Set

7.3.1. Genesis of the BNW Sample

The conclusion we draw from the BLS data and our original survey data is qualitatively different from the conclusion NW draw from the data they collected in conjunction with Berman and the EPI. This discrepancy led us to re-analyze the BNW data, devoting particular attention to the possible nonrepresentativeness of the sample.[15] Problems in the BNW sample may have arisen because a scientific sampling method was not used in the initial EPI data-collection effort, and because the data were collected three years after the minimum-wage increase, rather than before and after the increase, as in our original survey.

A fuller account of the origins of the BNW sample is provided in our earlier paper (Card and Krueger 1998). In brief, an initial sample of restaurants from two of the four chains included in our original study was assembled by EPI in late 1994 and early 1995. According to Neumark and Wascher (2000, appendix A), this initial sample of restaurants was drawn partly by using informal industry contracts, and partly from a survey of franchisees in the Chain Operators Guide. We refer to this initial sample of 71 observations, augmented with data for one New Jersey store that closed during 1992, as the "original Berman sample." Following the release of early reports using these data by Berman (1995) and Neumark and Wascher (1995), data collection continued. Neumark and Wascher (1995) reported that "to avoid conflicts of interest we subsequently took over the data collection effort from EPI, so that the remaining data came from the franchisees or corporations directly to us."[16] During the period from March to August 1995 they added information for 18 additional restaurants owned by franchisees who had already supplied some data to EPI, as well as information from 7 additional franchisees and one chain. We refer to this sample of 154 restaurants as the Neumark-Wascher (NW) sample. Data for 9 other restaurants were supplied by EPI after NW took over data collection (see Neurnark and Wascher 1995, footnote 9). We include these 9 restaurants in the pooled BNW sample, but exclude them from the original Berman subsample and from the NW subsample.[17]

Although NW attempted to draw a complete sample of restaurants not included in the original Berman sample, they successfully col-

Table 7.4

Descriptive Statistics for Levels and Changes in Employment by State, BNW Data

	Means with standard deviations in parentheses:						Difference-in-differences New Jersey– Pennsylvania (standard error)
	New Jersey			Pennsylvania			
	Before	After	Change	Before	After	Change	
Total payroll hours/35							
1. Pooled BNW sample	17.5	17.5	-0.1	15.1	15.9	0.8	-0.85
	(5.5)	(5.9)	(3.4)	(4.0)	(5.9)	(3.5)	(0.49)
2. NW subsample	17.7	16.7.	-1.0	13.4	12.4	-1.0	-0.05
	(6.1)	(6.3)	(3.3)	(3.8)	(4.9)	(3.5)	(0.61)
3. Original Berman subsample	17.1	19.3	2.1	16.9	20.4	3.4	-1.28
	(3.5)	(4.3)	(2.7)	(3.4)	(4.3)	(2.1)	(0.63)
Nonmanagement employment:							
4. Pooled BNW sample	24.8	28.4	3.6	29.0	31.3	2.2	1.39
	(6.0)	(6.8)	(3.0)	(5.5.)	(6.8)	(4.7)	(1.20)

Notes: See text for description of employment variables and samples. Sample sizes are as follows. Row 1: New Jersey 163; Pennsylvania 72. Row 2: New Jersey 114; Pennsylvania 40. Row 3: New Jersey 49; Pennsylvania 23. Row 4: New Jersey 19; Pennsylvania 33.

lected data for only a fraction of fast-food restaurants in New Jersey and eastern Pennsylvania beloning to the four chains in our original study.[18] We can obtain a lower bound estimate of the number of restaurants in this universe from the number of working telephone listings we found in January 1992 in the process of constructing our original sample. In New Jersey, where the geographic boundaries of the sample frame are unambiguous, we found 364 valid phone numbers, whereas the BNW sample contains 163 restaurants (see Card and Krueger 1995, table A.2.1). In eastern Pennsylvania, we found 109 working phone numbers in the 7 counties we surveyed, whereas the BNW sample contains 72 restaurants in 19 counties.[19] These comparisons suggest that the BNW sample includes fewer than one-half of the potential universe of restaurants. If the BNW sample were *random* this would not be a problem. As explained below, however, several features of the sample suggest otherwise. In particular, the Pennsylvania restaurants in the original Berman sample appear to differ from other restaurants in the data set, and also exhibit employment trends that differ from those in the more comprehensive BLS data set described above. Conclusions about the relative employment trends in New Jersey and Pennsylvania are very sensitive to how the data for this small subset of restaurants are treated.

7.3.2. Basic Results

Table 7.4 shows the basic patterns of fast-food employment in the pooled BNW sample and in various subsamples. The first three rows of the table report data on NW's main employment measure, which is based on average payroll hours reported for each restaurant in February and November of 1992. Franchise owners reported their data in different time intervals – weekly, biweekly, or monthly – for up to three "payroll periods" before and after the rise in the minimum wage. NW converted the data (for the maximum number of payroll periods available for each franchisee) into average weekly payroll hours divided by 35. As shown in row 1 of Table 7.4, this measure of full-time employment for the pooled BNW sample shows that stores were initially smaller in Pennsylvania than New Jersey (contrary to the pattern in the BLS ES-202 data), and that during 1992 stores in Pennsylvania expanded while stores in New Jersey contracted slightly (also contrary to the pattern in the BLS ES-202 data). The "difference-in-differences" of employment growth is shown in the right-most column of the table, and indicates that relative employment fell by 0.85 full-time equivalents in New Jersey from the period just before the rise in the minimum wage to the period 6 months later.

In rows 2 and 3 we compare these relative trends for restaurants in the original Berman sample and in NW's later sample. The difference in relative employment growth in the pooled sample is driven by data from the original Berman sample, which shows positive employment growth in both states, but especially strong growth in Pennsylvania. All 23 Pennsylvania restaurants in the original Berman sample belong to a single Burger King franchisee. Thus, any conclusion about the growth of average payroll hours in the fast-food industry in New Jersey relative to Pennsylvania hinges on the experiences of this one restaurant operator.

The final row of Table 7.4 reports relative trends in an alternative measure of employment available for a subset of restaurants in the pooled BNW sample – the total number of non-management employees. In contrast to the pattern for total payroll hours, nonmanagement employment rose *faster* in New Jersey than Pennsylvania.[20] Taken at face value, these findings suggest that the rise in the New Jersey minimum wage was associated with an increase in employment and a small decline in hours per worker.[21] Unfortunately, although one-half of restaurants in the original Berman sample supplied nonmanagement employment data, only 10 percent of restaurants in the NW subsample reported it. Thus, the BNW sample available for studying relative trends in employment versus hours is very limited.

7.3.3. Regression-Adjusted Models

The simple comparisons of relative employment growth in Table 7.4 make no allowances for other sources of variation in employment growth. The effects of controlling for some of these alternative factors are illustrated in Table 7.5. Each column of the table corresponds to a different regression model fit to the changes in employment observed for restaurants in the pooled BNW sample.

Column 1 presents a model with only a New Jersey dummy: the estimated coefficient corresponds to the simple difference-of-differences reported in row 1 of Table 7.4. Column 2 reports a model with only an indicator for observations in the NW subsample. This variable is highly significant (t-ratio over 8) and negative, implying that restaurants in the NW subsample had systematically slower employment growth than those in the original Berman sample. The model in column 3 explores the effect of chain and company-ownership controls. These are jointly significant and show considerable differences in average growth rates across chains, with slower growth among Roy Rogers and KFC restaurants than Wendy's or Burger King outlets.

Table 7.5

Estimated Regression Models for Change in Average Payroll Hours/35, BNW Data

	Specification						
	(1)	(2)	(3)	(4)	(5)	(6)	(7)
New Jersey	-0.85	–	–	–	-0.36	-0.66	-0.09
	(0.49)				(0.44)	(0.41)	(0.42)
NW subsample (1 = yes)	–	-3.49			-3.44	–	–
		(0.42)			(0.43)		
Chain dummies:							
Roy Rogers	–	–	-3.46	–	–	-3.14	-1.98
			(0.81)			(0.85)	(0.89)
Wendy's	–	–	-0.85	–	–	-0.71	1.35
			(0.67)			(0.67)	(0.70)
KFC	–	–	-6.51	–	–	-6.30	6.56
			(0.90)			(0.90)	(0.89)
Company-owned	–		-0.89	–	–	-1.31	-0.72
			(0.76)			(0.81)	(0.95)
Payroll data type:							
Biweekly	–	–	–	1.73	–	–	1.65
				(0.52)			(0.52)
Monthly	–	–	–	-2.60	–	–	-1.06
				(0.48)			(0.89)
R^2	0.01	0.23	0.41	0.30	0.23	0.10	0.45
Standard error of regression	3.47	3.07	2.70	2.95	3.08	3.32	2.62

Notes: Standard errors are in parentheses. Sample consists of 235 stores. Dependent variable in all models is the change in average weekly payroll hours divided by 35 between wave 1 and wave 2.

Finally, the model in column 4 includes indicators for whether the restaurant's employment data were derived from biweekly or monthly intervals (with weekly data the omitted category). These variables are also highly significant, and suggest that the reporting basis of the payroll data has a strong effect on measured employment trends. Relative to restaurants that provided weekly data (25% of the sample), restaurants that provided biweekly data experienced faster hours growth between the two waves of the survey, while restaurants that provided monthly data had slower hours growth.

An important lesson from columns 1–4 of Table 7.5 is that a wide variety of factors affect measured employment growth in the BNW sample. Many of these factors are also highly correlated with the New Jersey dummy. For example, a disproportionately high fraction of New Jersey stores in the pooled sample were obtained by NW. Since the NW subsample has slower growth overall, this correlation might be expected to influence the estimate of relative employment trends in New Jersey. Additionally, the Pennsylvania sample contains none of the slow-growing KFC outlets. Thus, it may be important to control for these other factors when attempting to measure the relative trend in New Jersey employment growth.

The models in columns 5–7 include the indicator for New Jersey outlets and various subsets of the other covariates. Notice that the addition of any subset of controls lowers the magnitude of the New Jersey coefficient by 20–90 percent, and also improves the precision of the estimated coefficient by 10–15 percent. None of the estimated New Jersey coefficients are statistically significant at conventional levels once the other controls are included in the model. Simply controlling for an intercept shift between restaurants in the NW subsample and the balance of the pooled data set reduces the size of the estimated New Jersey coefficient by over 50 percent.

The addition of controls indicating the time interval over which the hours data were reported has a particularly strong impact on scaled hours, and on any inference about the effect of the minimum-wage increase in these data. Even controlling for chain and owner-ship characteristics, the biweekly payroll indicator is highly statistically significant (t = 3.19). In Card and Krueger (1997, appendix) we present results suggesting that the differences in employment growth across reporting intervals are not driven by specific functional form assumptions or outliers. We are unsure of the reasons for the highly significant differences in measured growth rates between restaurants that reported data over different payroll intervals, but we suspect this pattern reflects differential seasonal factors that systematically led to the misscaling of hours in some pay periods. For example, many restaurants are closed on Thanksgiving. The Thanksgiving holiday probably was more likely to have been covered by monthly payroll intervals than weekly or biweekly ones, which would spuriously affect the growth of hours worked. Unfortunately, Neumark and Wascher did not collect data on the number of days stores were actually open during their pay periods, or on the dates which were spanned by the pay periods covered by the data they collected.[22] Consequently, no adjustment to work hours can be made to allow for whether stores were closed during holidays. Another factor that may have affected changes in payroll hours for restaurants that reported on weekly versus biweekly or monthly intervals was a massive winter storm on

December 10–13, 1992, which caused two million power outages and widespread flooding, and forced many establishments in the Northeast to shut down for several days (see *Electric Utility Week*, December 21, 1992). Some pay intervals in the BNW sample may have been more likely to include the storm than others, leading to spurious movements iii payroll hours.[23]

Absent information on whether restaurants were closed because of Thanksgiving or the December 10–13 storm for some part of their pay period, the best way to control for these extraneous factors is to add controls for the pay period to the regression model for scaled hours changes. The results in column 7 of Table 7.5 show that the addition of controls for the payroll reporting interval has a large effect on the estimated New Jersey relative employment effect, because a much lower fraction of New Jersey restaurants supplied biweekly data. Once these differences are taken into account, the employment growth differential between New Jersey and Pennsylvania all but disappears, even in the pooled BNW sample.

7.3.4. Alternative Specifications and Samples

An important conclusion that emerges from Tables 7.4 and is that the measured effects of the New Jersey minimum wage differ between restaurants in the original Berman sample and those in the subsequent NW sample. Table 7.6 reports the estimated coefficient on the New Jersey dummy from a variety of alternative models fit to the pooled BNW sample, the NW subsample, and the original Berman sample. Each row of the table corresponds to a different model specification or alternative measure of the dependent variable; each column refers to one of the three indicated samples. For example, the first row reports the estimated New Jersey effect from models that include no other controls: these correspond to the differences-in-differences reported in Table 7.4.

Row 2 of the table illustrates the influence of the data from the single Burger King franchisee that supplied the Pennsylvania observations in the original Berman sample. When the restaurants owned by this franchisee are excluded, the estimated New Jersey effect in the pooled BNW sample becomes positive.[24] Without this owner's data it is impossible to estimate the New Jersey effect in the original Berman sample. In the NW sample, however, the exclusion has a negligible effect.

Row 3 of Table 7.6 shows the estimated New Jersey coefficients from specifications that control for chain and company ownership. The results in row 4 control for the type of payroll data supplied to BNW (biweekly, weekly or monthly). As noted, once controls for the payroll period are included, the New Jersey effect falls to essentially zero in the pooled sample. In the original Berman sample, the New Jersey effect becomes positive when controls are added for the payroll period.

Table 7.6

Estimated Relative Employment Effects in New Jersey for Alternative Samples and Specifications, BNW Data

	Pooled BNW sampe	Neumark-Wascher sample	Original Berman sample
A. Change in average payroll hours/35			
1. No controls	-0.85	-0.05	-1.28
	(0.49)	(0.61)	(0.63)
2. Exclude first Pennsylvania franchisee, no controls	0.37	-0.11	-
	(0.56)	(0.62)	
3. Controls for chain and ownership	-0.66	0.27	-0.95
	(0.41)	(0.53)	(0.64)
4. Controls for chain, ownership and payroll period	-0.09	0.22	0.58
	(0.42)	(0.54)	(0.72)
B. Change in payroll hours/35 using first pay period per restaurant			
5. No controls	-0.55	0.18	0.85
	(0.50)	(0.63)	(0.67)
6. Controls for chain, ownership, and payroll period	0.07	-0.15	0.96
	(0.43)	(0.52)	(0.78)
C. Proportional change in average payroll hours/35			
7. No controls	-0.06	-0.00	-0.09
	(0.05)	(0.07)	(0.07)
8. Controls for chain and ownership	-0.05	-0.03	-0.04
	(0.05)	(0.07)	(0.07)
9. Controls for chain, ownership, and payroll period	-0.01	-0.03	-0.08
	(0.05)	(0.07)	(0.08)

Notes: Pooled BNW sample has 235 observations; NW sample has 154 observations; original Berman sample has 71 observations. In row 2, data for 26 restaurants owned by one franchisee are excluded. In this row only, pooled BNW sample has 209 observations; and NW sample has 151 observations. Dependent variable in panel A is the change in average payroll hours between the first and second waves, divided by 35. Dependent variable in panel B is the change in payroll hours for the first payroll period reported by each store between the first and second waves, divided by 35. Dependent variable in panel C is the change in average payroll hours between the first and second waves, divided by average payroll hours in the first and second waves. Standard errors are in parentheses.

In most of their analysis NW utilize an employment measure based on the average scaled hours data taken over varying numbers of payroll periods across restaurants in their sample. (Data are recorded for

233

up to three payroll periods per restaurant in each wave.) To check the sensitivity of the results to this choice, we constructed a measure using only the first payroll period for restaurants that reported more than one period. In principle, one would expect this alternative measure to show the same patterns as the averaged data. As illustrated in panel B (rows 5 and 6) of Table 7.6, the use of the alternative employment measure leads to results that are uniformly less supportive of a conclusion of a negative employment effect in New Jersey. Even in the original Berman sample the use of the simpler hours measure leads to a 33 percent reduction in the New Jersey coefficient, and yields an estimate that is insignificantly different from zero.

Finally, panel C of Table 7.6 reports estimates from models that use the proportional change in average payroll hours at each restaurant – rather than the change in the level of average hours – as the dependent variable. The latter specifications are more appropriate if employment responses to external factors (such as a rise in the minimum wage) are roughly proportional to the scale of each restaurant. Inspection of these results suggests that the signs of the New Jersey effects are generally the same as in the corresponding models for the levels of employment, although the coefficients in the proportional change models are relatively less precise.

Our conclusion from the estimates in Table 7.6 is that most (but not all) of the alternatives show a negative relative employment trend in New Jersey, although the magnitudes of the estimated effects are generally much smaller than the naive difference-in-differences estimate from the pooled BNW sample. The estimated New Jersey effect is most negative in the original Berman sample. In the NW sample or in the pooled sample that excludes data for the Pennsylvania franchisee who supplied Berman's data, the relative employment effects are small in magnitude and uniformly statistically insignificant (t-ratios of 0.7 or less). These patterns highlight the crucial role of the original Berman data in drawing inferences from the BNW sample. Without these data (or more precisely, without the observations from the single Burger King franchisee who provided the initial Pennsylvania data) the BNW sample provides little indication that the rise in the New Jersey minimum wage lowered fast-food employment. Even with these data, once controls are included for the payroll reporting periods, the differences between New Jersey and Pennsylvania are uniformly small and statistically insignificant.

7.3.5. Consistency of the BNW Sample with the Card-Krueger and BLS Samples

Neumark and Wascher (2000) argue that there is "severe measurement error" in our original survey data and argue at length that our dependent variable has a higher standard deviation than theirs. In Card and Krueger (1995, pp. 71–72) we noted that our survey data contained some measurement errors, and tried to assess the extent of the errors by using reinterview methods. Since measured employment changes are used as the *dependent* variable in our analysis, however, the presence of measurement error does not in any way affect the validity of our estimates or our calculated standard errors, provided that the mean and variance of the measurement errors in observed employment changes are the same in New Jersey and Pennsylvania. Neumark and Wascher's concern about bias due to measurement error in our dependent variable is only relevant if the variable either contains no signal, or if the means of the errors are systematically different in the two states. To check the validity of our original data it is useful to compare employment trends in the two data sets at the substate level. The public-use versions of both data sets include only the first three digits of the zip code of each restaurant, rather than full addresses. This limitation necessitates comparisons of employment trends by restaurant chain and "three-digit zip-code area."[25] We also compare the BNW data to the BLS data at the chain-by-zip-code level, which points up further problems in the BNW sample.

A useful summary of the degree of consistency between the two samples is provided by a bivariate regression of the average employment changes (by chain and zip-code area) from one sample on the corresponding changes from the other. In particular, if the employment changes in the BNW sample are taken to be the "true" change for the cell, then one would expect an intercept of 0 and a slope coefficient of 1 from a regression of the observed employment changes in our data on the changes for the same zip-code area and chain in the BNW data.[26] This prediction has to be modified slightly if the employment changes in the BNW sample are "true" but scaled differently than in our survey. In particular, if the ratio of the mean employment level in our survey to the mean employment level in the BNW sample is k, then the expected slope coefficient is k.

Table 7.7 presents estimation results from regressing employment growth rates by chain and zip-code area from our fast-food sample on the corresponding data from the BNW sample. Although 98 chain-by-zip-code cells are available in our data set, only 48 cells are present in the pooled BNW sample. Column 1 shows results for these cells, while columns 2 and 3 present results separately for chain-by-zip-code areas in New Jersey and Pennsylvania. The data underlying the analysis are also plotted in Figure 7.3.

Figure 7.3

Graph of CK Data vs. BNW Data at the Three-Digit Zip-Code-by-Chain Level

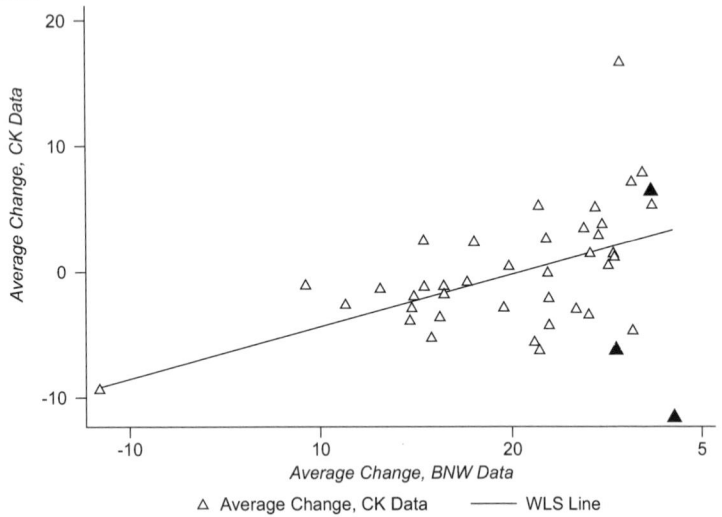

Notes: Shaded triangles indicate Berman/EPI Pennsylvania sample. The line shown on the graph is the WLS regression fit using the subsample collected by NW. Weights are the number of restaurants in the cell based on CK data.

Inspection of Figure 7.3 and the regression results in Table 7.7 suggests that there is a reasonably high degree of consistency between the two data sets: the correlation coefficient is 0.47. The two largest negative outliers are in zip codes containing a high proportion of restaurants from EPI's Pennsylvania sample. In light of this finding, and the concerns raised in Table 7.6 about the influence of the data from the franchisee who supplied these data, we show a parallel set of models in panel B of Table 7.7 that excludes this owner's data from the average changes in the BNW sample.

Table 7.7

Comparisons of Employment Growth by Chain and Zip-Code Area,
Card-Krueger Data vs. Berman-Neumark-Wascher Data

	New Jersey and Pennsylvania	New Jersey only	Pennsylvania only
A. Using combined BNW sample			
Intercept	-0.32	0.41	-3.91
	(0.56)	(0.50)	(1.77)
Change in employment in BNW sample	0.78	0.90	0.65
	(0.22)	(0.19)	(0.68)
R^2	0.22	0.38	0.09
Standard error	8.97	7.35	10.76
p-value: intercept = 0, slope = 1	0.47	0.65	0.07
Number of observations (chain X zip-code cells)	48	37	11
B. Using combined BNW sample excluding data from one franchisee			
Intercept	-0.26	0.36	-3.52
	(0.54)	(0.51)	(1.67)
Change in employment in BNW sample	0.87	0.91	0.93
	(0.21)	(0.20)	(0.73)
R^2	0.28	0.39	0.17
Standard error	8.56	7.40	10.27
p-value: intercept = 0, slope = 1	0.71	0.72	0.14
Number of observations (chain X zip-code cells)	46	36	10

Notes: Dependent variable in all models is the mean change in full-time employment for fast-food restaurants of a specific chain in a specific three-digit zip-code area, taken from the Card–Krueger data set. Independent variable is the mean change in payroll hours divided by 35 for fast-food restaurants (in the same chain and zip-code area) taken from the BNW data set. In panel B, restaurants in the BNW sample obtained from the franchisee who provided Berman's Pennsylvania data are deleted prior to forming average employment changes by chain and zip-code area. All models are fit by weighted least squares using as a weight the number of observations in the chain-by-zip-code cell in the Card–Krueger data set. Standard errors are in parentheses.

Looking first at the top panel of the table, the regression coefficient relating the employment changes in the two data sets is 0.78. An *F*-test for the joint hypothesis that this coefficient is 1 and that the intercept of the regression is 0 has a probability value of 0.47. Comparisons of the separate results for New Jersey and Pennsylvania suggest that within New Jersey the two data sets are in closer agreement. Across the relatively small number of Pennsylvania cells the samples are less consistent, although we can only marginally reject the hypothesis of a zero intercept and unit slope. Because we used the same survey methods and interviewer to collect data from New Jersey and Pennsylvania, there is no reason to suspect different measurement error properties in the two states in our sample. A comparison of the results in the bottom panel of the table shows that the exclusion of data from the franchisee who provided EPI' s Pennsylvania sample *improves* the consistency of the two data sets, particularly in Pennsylvania. While not decisive, this comparison suggests that the key differences between the BNW sample and our sample are driven by the data from the single franchisee who supplied the Pennsylvania data for the Berman sample.

To further explore the representativeness of the BNW data, the BLS ES-202 data and the BNW data were both aggregated up to the three-digit zip-code-by-chain level for common zip codes and chains. Specifically, we calculated average employment changes for establishments in each of these cells in the BLS data and in BNW' s data, and then linked the two cell-level data sets together. Because the BNW sample does not contain all of the restaurants in each cell, the sets of restaurants covered in the two data sets are not identical.[27] Nonetheless, if the two samples are representative, the cell averages should move together. The resulting cell-level data set was used to estimate a set of regressions of the employment change in BNW' s data on the employment change in the BLS data. If the BNW sample is unbiased, no other variable should predict employment growth in that data set, conditional on true employment growth.

Column 1 of Table 7.8 reports coefficients from a bivariate regression in which the cell-average employment change calculated from the BNW data set is the dependent variable and the cell-average employment change calculated from the BLS ES-202 data set is the explanatory variable. There is a positive relationship between the two measures of employment changes. Because the BNW employment variable is scaled hours, not the number of workers employed, one would not expect the slope coefficient from this regression to equal 1. In colunm 2, we add a variable to the regression model that measures the proportion of restaurants in each cell of BNW's data set that was collected by EPI. Lastly, in column 3 we interact this variable with a dummy variable indicating whether the cell is in New Jersey or Pennsylvania.

Table 7.8

Comparisons of Employment Growth by Chain and Zip-Code Area, Berman-Neumark-Wascher Data vs. Bureau Of Labor Statistics ES-202 Data (dependent variable: average change in employment, BNW data)

	1	2	3
Average change in employment,	0.17	0.10	0.09
BLS data	(0.05)	(0.05)	(0.05)
Fraction of sample collected by	-	3.46	-
EPI		(0.70)	
Fraction of sample collected by	-	-	4.33
EPI X Pennsylvania			(1.19)
Fraction of sample collected by	-	-	3.22
EPI X New Jersey			(0.75)
	0.04	-0.95	-0.96
Constant	(0.34)	(0.34)	(0.34)
R^2	0.19	0.49	0.50

Notes: Weighted least-squares estimates are presented. Weights are equal to the number of BNW observations in the cell. Cells are composed of the three-digit zip-code-by-chain areas. Standard errors are in parentheses.

The results in column 2 of Table 7.8 indicate that the proportion of observations in BNW's cells that were collected by EPI has a positive effect on employment growth, conditional on actual employment growth for the cell as measured by the BLS data. This finding suggests that the subsample of observations collected by EPI are not representative of the experience of the cell. Moreover, the larger coefficient on the Pennsylvania interaction in column 3 suggests that the problem of nonrepresentativeness in the original Berman data is particularly acute for the Pennsylvania restaurants. Together with the other evidence in Tables 7.4–7.6, this finding leads us to question the representativeness of the EPI's sample, and of the pooled BNW sample.

Neumark and Wascher (2000) argue that, "The only legitimate objection to the validity of the combined sample is that some observations added by the EPI were not drawn from the Chain Operators Guide, but rather were for franchisees identified informally." This assertion is incorrect, however, if personal contacts were used to collect data from some restaurants listed in the Chain Operators Guide and not others. Moreover, Neumark and Wascher's separate analysis of restaurants listed and not listed in the Chain Operators Guide does not address this concern. All of the restaurants in their sample could have been listed in the Chain Operators Guide, and the sample would still be nonrepresentative if personal contacts were selectively used to encourage a subset of restaurants to respond, or if a nonrandom sample of restaurants agreed to participate because they knew the purpose of the survey.

7.3.6. Patterns of Employment Changes Within New Jersey

The main inference we draw from Table 7.7 (above) is that the employment changes in the BNW and Card–Krueger data sets are reasonably highly correlated, especially within New Jersey. Larger discrepancies arise between the relatively small subsamples of Pennsylvania restaurants. A comparison of the BLS and BNW data sets also suggests that the Pennsylvania data that were collected by EPI and provided to Neumark and Wascher skew their results. The consistency of the New Jersey samples is worth emphasizing since, in our original paper, we found that comparisons of employment growth *within* New Jersey (in other words, between restaurants that were initially paying higher and lower wages, and were therefore differentially affected by the minimum-wage hike) led to the same conclusion about the effect of the minimum wage as comparisons between New Jersey and Pennsylvania.

To further check this conclusion we merged the average starting wage from the first wave of our original fast-food survey for each of the chain-by-zip-code areas in New Jersey with average employment data for the same chain-by-zip-code cell from the BNW sample. We then compared employment growth rates from the BNW sample in low-wage and high-wage cells, defined as below and above the median starting wage in February–March 1992. The results are summarized graphically in Figure 7.4. As in our original paper, employment growth within New Jersey was *faster* in chain-by-zip-code cells that had to increase wages more as a consequence of the rise in the minimum wage.

We also merged the average proportional gap between the wave 1 starting wage and the new minimum wage from our original survey to the corresponding chain-by-zip-code averages of employment growth from the BNW sample.[28] We then regressed the average changes in employment (ΔE) on the average gap measure (GAP) for the 37 overlapping cells in New Jersey. The estimated regression equation, with standard errors in parentheses, is:

$$(1) \qquad \Delta E = -2.00 + 17.98 \text{ GAP} \qquad R^2 = 0.09.$$
$$ (1.11) \quad (9.75)$$

Figure 7.4

Average FTE Employment in Low- and High-Wage Areas of New Jersey, Before and After 1992 Minimum Wage Increase

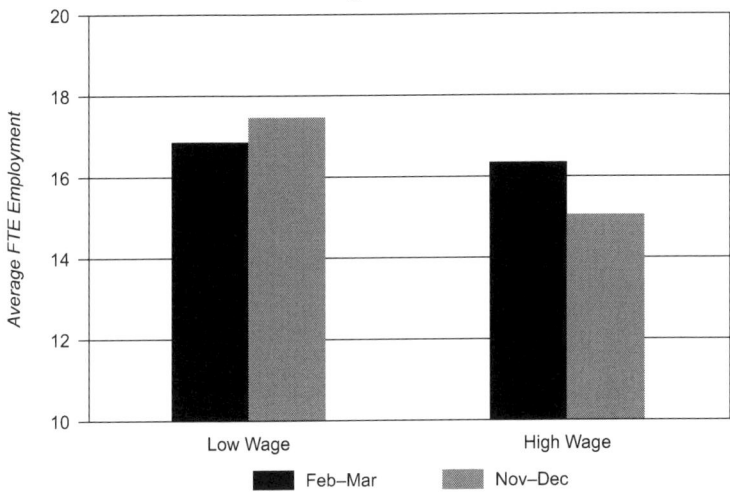

Notes: Average FTE employment is calculated from BNW data set. Restaurants were aggregated to the chain-by-zip-code level, and divided into low-wage and high-wage areas based on whether the average starting wage for restaurants in the cell in the CK data set was above or below the median starting wage in February–March 1992.

The coefficient on the GAP variable in BNW's data is similar in magnitude to the estimate we obtain if we use the New Jersey micro data from our survey to estimate the corresponding micro-level regression (13.1 with a standard error of 6.6). Furthermore, if we estimate another cell-level model with BNW's employment data and add dummy variables indicating the restaurant chain, we obtain:

$$(2) \qquad \Delta E = 0.77 + 12.00 \, GAP + \text{Chain Dummies} \qquad R^2 = 0.09.$$
$$ (0.78) \quad (5.76)$$

In this model, the coefficient on the *GAP* variable is slightly smaller than in the bivariate regression, but it has a higher *t*-ratio. The positive estimated coefficients on the *GAP* variable indicate that employment rose faster at New Jersey restaurants located in areas that were required to raise their entry wage the most when the minimum wage increased. The pattern of employment growth rates within BNW's sample of New Jersey restaurants supports our original finding that

241

the rise in the minimum wage had no adverse effect on employment growth at lower-wage relative to higher-wage restaurants in the state.

Neumark and Wascher (2000) also performed a cell-level analysis using a wage-gap variable. However, they only selectively replicate our original analysis. Neumark and Wascher (2000) describe the analysis of the wage-gap variable in our 1994 paper as follows: "This experiment continues to identify minimum-wage effects off of the difference in employment growth between New Jersey and Pennsylvania, but adds information on the extent to which the minimum-wage increase would have raised starting wages in New Jersey." This description is incomplete because it ignores the estimates in column 5 of Table 6.4 in Chapter 6, which included dummy variables for broad regions in Pennsylvania and New Jersey. In these estimates, identification of the wage-gap variable arises entirely from differences within New Jersey.[29] Indeed, this was a major motivation for our analysis of the wage-gap variable. Unfortunately, Neumark and Wascher only report results that exclude the region controls in their table 5. They do report in their text, however, that when they restrict their sample just to cells within New Jersey, they find that restaurants in areas that were required to raise their wages the most by the New Jersey minimum-wage increase also tended to have faster employment growth. These results from within New Jersey confirm an essential finding of our original paper.

7.3.7. Other Evidence for the Eating and Drinking Industry

In the final section of their Comment, Neumark, and Wascher present an analysis of aggregate-level data for the entire eating and drinking industry, taken from two publicly available sources: the BLS-790 program and the ES-202 program. The former are only available on a statewide basis, while the latter are available by county, permitting a comparison between New Jersey and the 7 counties of Pennsylvania included in our original survey. Neumark and Wascher summarize their findings from these data as providing "... complementary evidence that [the] minimum wage reduces employment in the restaurant industry."

Columns 1 and 4 of Table 7.9 reproduce two key regression models from their table 10, which suggest a negative impact of the minimum wage on employment. The specifications are fit to state-specific changes in employment between February/March and November/

Table 7.9

Estimates of Minimum-Wage Effects on Employment Growth in the Eating and Drinking Industry from February/March to November/December

| | BLS 790 data, New Jersey and Pennsylvania | | | ES-202 data, New Jersey and 7 counties of Pennsylvania | |
	NW	Revised data	Revised data and correctly dated unemployment	NW	Correctly dated unemployment
	(1)	(2)	(3)	(4)	(5)
Minimum-wage change	-0.15	-0.11	-0.03	-0.11	-0.01
	(0.10)	(0.10)	(0.08)	(0.10)	(0.07)
New Jersey	-0.05	-0.38	-0.41	0.25	0.21
	(0.95)	(0.95)	(0.80)	(0.96)	(0.72)
Change in unemployment	-0.32	-0.39	-1.47	-0.49	-1.84
	(0.47)	(0.46)	(0.44)	(0.46)	(0.39)
R^2	0.15	0.13	0.38	0.14	0.51

Notes: Standard errors are in parentheses. Models are estimated using changes in employment in SIC 58 (eating and drinking) between February/March and November/December of 1982–1996. Dependent variable in columns 1–3 is the percentage change in statewide employment in SIC 58 from the BLS 790 program. Dependent variable in columns 4–5 is the percentage change in employment from the ES202 program; New Jersey data are statewide and Pennsylvania data are for 7 counties only. Columns 1 and 4 are taken from Neumark and Wascher (2000, table 10). Models in columns 2–3 use revised BLS 790 data for 1995 and 1996. Sample size is 30 observations.

[a] In columns 1, 2, and 4 the change in unemployment represents the change in the annual average unemployment rate. In columns 3 and 5 the change in unemployment represents the difference between the average of the seasonally adjusted rates in February and March and the average of the seasonally adjusted rates in the following November and December.

December of each year from 1982 to 1996, and include as explanatory variables the percentage change in the effective minimum wage in the state, an indicator for observations from New Jersey, and the change in the annual unemployment rate from the preceding calendar year to the calendar year in which the data are observed.

As the other results in the table make clear, however, the estimated impacts of the minimum wage are extremely sensitive to minor changes in the data or control variables used by Neumark and Wascher. In column 2 we report estimates that simply replace NW's data for 1995 and 1996 with the revised BLS-790 employment data.[30] The effect of the minimum wage is smaller and statistically insignificant ($t = -1.1$) when the revised data are used. Notice also that the minimum-wage effects estimated from the BLS-790 and ES-202 data are similar when the revised data are used (compare columns 2 and 4).[31] This similarity might be expected since the BLS-790 data are benchmarked to the ES-202 data. In column 3 we report estimates from a model that controls for changes in unemployment over the same period as the dependent variable (i.e., from February/March to November/December). The use of chronologically aligned unemployment data leads to a very noticeable improvement in the fit of the model, and to a larger and more significant coefficient on the unemployment rate. More importantly, it also leads to a much smaller estimated minimum-wage effect. As shown in column 5, the effect is about the same on estimates derived from the ES-202 data. Controlling for properly aligned changes in the unemployment rate, the estimated effect of the minimum wage is negligible.[32]

We have investigated a number of other extensions to the findings in Table 7.9. For example, adding two more years of data from the BLS-790 series (albeit based on preliminary data for 1998) leads to coefficient estimates that are similar to those reported in column 3. Similarly, adding an additional year of ES-202 data has little effect on the results in column 5. We also considered an alternative estimation method that regresses the difference in employment growth rates between New Jersey and Pennsylvania on the differences in the changes in minimum wages and unemployment between the states. This specification is perhaps most comparable to the "difference-in-differences" specification used in our original paper. These results are very consistent with the estimates in columns 3 and 5: for example, the coefficient of the relative minimum-wage variable in models for the BLS-790 employment data is 0.003 (standard error 0.11) without controlling for relative unemployment, and 0.02 (standard error 0.12) controlling for relative changes in unemployment.

Based on the findings in Table 7.9, and these further analyses, we conclude that changes in the minimum wage in New Jersey and Pennsylvania over the 1980s and 1990s probably had little systematic effect on employment in the eating and drinking sectors of the two states. Thus, contrary to the impression conveyed by Neumark and Wascher's analysis based on the unrevised employment data and an incorrectly aligned aggregate unemployment variable, the aggregated BLS data are quite consistent with our findings from the fast-food sector in Section 7.1., and with our original survey results.

7.4. Conclusions

After analyzing BNW's data, our original survey data, publicly available BLS data, and most importantly, the BLS ES-202 fast-food establishment data, we reach the following conclusion: *The increase in New Jersey's minimum wage probably had no effect on total employment in New Jersey's fast-food industry, and possibly had a small positive effect.* We have previously written that, because of frictions in the labor market, a minimum-wage increase can be expected to cause some firms to reduce employment and others to raise employment, with these two effects potentially cancelling out if the rise in the minimum wage is modest (Card and Krueger 1995, especially pp. 13–14). If this view is correct, then it would not be surprising to find some specifications and data definitions that yield a negative impact of the minimum wage on employment. But we doubt that a representative survey of fast-food restaurants in New Jersey and eastern Pennsylvania would show a significant adverse impact of the minimum wage on total employment.

The only data set that indicates a significant decline in employment in New Jersey relative to Pennsylvania is the small set of restaurants collected by EPI. Results of this data set stand in contrast to our survey data, to the BLS's payroll data, and to the supplemental data collected by Neumark and Wascher. The difference between the New Jersey–Pennsylvania comparison in our original survey and BNW's data cannot be reconciled by inherent differences between a telephone survey and administrative payroll records because the BLS ES-202 data are based on administrative payroll records. Instead, we suspect the common denominator is that representative samples show statistically insignificant and small differences in employment growth between New Jersey and eastern Pennsylvania, while the nonrepresentative sample informally collected for Berman produces anomalous results.

An alternative interpretation of the full spectrum of results is that the New Jersey minimum-wage increase did not reduce total employment, but it did slightly reduce the average number of hours worked per employee. Neumark and Wascher (1995) reject this interpretation. Although we are less quick to rule out this possibility, we are skeptical about any conclusion concerning average hours worked per employee that relies so heavily on the informally collected Berman/EPI sample, and the exclusion of controls for the length of the reporting interval. Moreover, within New Jersey the BNW data indicate that hours grew more at restaurants in the lowest wage areas of the state, where the minimum-wage increase was more likely to be a binding constraint. This finding runs counter to the view that total hours declined in response to the New Jersey minimum-wage increase.

8

Unexpected Inflation, Real Wages, and Employment Determination in Union Contracts

What role do nominal wage contracts play in the determination of employment and the characteristics of the business cycle? An influential series of papers by Stanley Fischer (1977), Edmund S. Phelps and John B. Taylor (1977), and John B. Taylor (1980) argued that fixed wage contracts create a link between employment and aggregate demand. Subsequent models of macro fluctuations stress other channels for the transmission and persistence of aggregate shocks. Real business cycle models (for example, Kydland and Prescott 1982) assume that supply and demand in the labor market are equilibrated at Walrasian levels and ignore the institutional structure of wage determination. Models in the Keynesian tradition, on the other hand, have shifted attention from nominal wage rigidities to real wage rigidities (for example, Blanchard and Summers 1986) or nominal price rigidities (for example, Mankiw 1985; Blanchard and Kiyotaki 1987).

This shift in interest reflects dissatisfaction with both the theoretical underpinnings and empirical performance of nominal contracting models. On the one hand, there are as yet no convincing theoretical explanations for the existence of nominally fixed contracts. Many of the models developed over the past decade predict constant real wages or constant real earnings.[1] On the other hand, the evidence in sup-

This chapter is a revised version of: Card, D. (1990). Unexpected Inflation, Real Wages, and Employment Determination in Union Contracts, in: American Economic Review 80, 669–688. The author is grateful to Robert Hall, Robert King, and two referees for their comments on earlier drafts. Thomas Lemieux and Sara Turner provided expert assistance in data preparation.

port of nominal contracting models is also weak. The simplest of these models asserts that aggregate demand shocks lead to real wage changes that induce movements along a downward-sloping demand schedule. Although unanticipated price increases are apparently correlated with real economic activity (see the review by Gray and Spencer 1990), the absence of a clear negative correlation between aggregate employment and real wages (Geary and Kennan 1982) poses a serious challenge to models of nominal wage rigidity.

This chapter presents new evidence on the consequences of nominal contracting provisions for employment determination in the unionized sector of Canadian manufacturing. The analysis, based on data for 1,300 indexed and non-indexed contracts written between 1966 and 1982, suggests that nominal contracting provisions play an important role in the link between aggregate demand and employment. As predicted by the simple models of Gray (1976) and Fischer (1977), I find that real wage changes induced by aggregate price surprises lead to systematic employment responses in the opposite direction. Unexpected real wage changes also affect subsequent wage determination: the empirical results suggest that roughly one-third of such changes carry over to the following contract. Unanticipated price increases therefore generate short-run employment responses and persistent wage changes among firms in the union sector.

Two features of the empirical analysis distinguish these results from earlier attempts to measure the effects of nominal wage rigidities. First, the analysis is based on individual contract data rather than aggregate or industry-level data.[2] Since union contracts differ in their negotiation dates and degrees of indexation, it is possible to calculate contract-specific measures of unexpected price increases and unexpected real wage changes, and to estimate the separate effects of price surprises and real wage surprises. Variation in contract lengths and the staggering of expiration dates also make it possible to control for aggregate-level disturbances that affect all contracts at a point in time. Second, the analysis pays special attention to the issue of endogenous wage determination.[3] Even in a simple Fischer–Gray contracting framework this is a potentially serious problem, insofar as the bargaining parties have information on future employment demand that is unavailable to an outside data analyst. If predictable components of future employment demand affect wages, they create a simultaneity bias in ordinary least-squares estimates of the elasticity of employment with respect to realized wage rates.

To solve this problem, I use the unexpected component of real wages as an instrumental variable for the level of wages. By assumption, unexpected changes in real wages are correlated with wages but uncorrelated with information known at the negotiation date of the contract. Unexpected wage changes therefore form a valid instrumental variable for a structural analysis of employment demand. This procedure also provides a direct test of the role of nominal wage rigidities in generating employment responses to nominal shocks. The instrumental variables estimate of the elasticity of labor demand is nonzero if and only if employment is correlated with unexpected real wage changes.

The empirical results confirm the value of this approach. In ordinary least-squares regressions, changes in employment are only weakly related to changes in contract wages. When unexpected real wage changes are used as an instrumental variable, however, employment is found to be systematically negatively related to wages. This finding continues to hold when unexpected price changes are added directly to the employment demand equation. It is also robust to the addition of unrestricted dummy variables representing each year of the sample. I conclude that nominal wage contracts play an important role in determining the cyclical properties and persistence of employment in the union sector.

8.1. Employment and Wages in a Simple Contract Model
8.1.1. Interpreting the Correlation of Employment and Wages

This section outlines a simple model of long-term contracting in which nominal wages are predetermined and employment is set unilaterally by the firm after aggregate prices and firm-specific demand shocks are observed. Even in this simple model the interpretation of the partial correlation of employment and real wages is clouded by the fact that the contracting parties may have better information on future demand shocks than is available to an outside data analyst. To develop this point more formally, suppose that wages are negotiated in some base period (period 0) for a contract of duration T. Let $n(t)$ and $w(t)$ denote the logarithms of employment and real wages in period t of the contract, respectively, and assume that hours per worker are fixed. The notion of "nominal contracting" is captured by the assumption that the bargaining parties do not set $w(t)$ directly: rather, they establish a series of nominal wage increases from the start of the contract, possibly in conjunction with an indexation formula.[4] Let $w^*(t)$ represent the parties' expectation of $w(t)$, conditional on their information in the negotiating period, and let $u(t)$ represent the forecast error $w(t) - w^*(t)$. The distribution of $u(t)$ depends on the length of the contract and whether or not it contains a cost-of-living escalation clause.[5]

Assume that $n(t)$ is determined by an employment demand schedule of the form

$$(1) \qquad n(t) = \alpha z(t) + \beta w(t) + \varepsilon(t),$$

where $z(t)$ is a vector of observable variables shifting the demand for labor, β represents the elasticity of labor demand ($\beta < 0$), and $\varepsilon(t)$ is an unobservable component of employment variation. The specification of $z(t)$ and the corresponding interpretation of β are discussed in the next section. Note that supply considerations are explicitly ignored: there are assumed to be enough available workers to fill the firm's demand irrespective of the forecast error in real wages. This assumption is a plausible one in the context of the available data, which pertain to unionized manufacturing establishments.

This simple model is completed by a specification of the determinants of $w^*(t)$. Assume that the expected real wage rate in period t is determined at the negotiation date by variables known at that time, say $x(0)$, and by the parties' expectations of $z(t)$ and $\varepsilon(t)$, $z^*(t)$ and $\varepsilon^*(t)$, respectively:

$$(2) \qquad w^*(t) = az^*(t) + bx(0) + c\varepsilon^*(t).$$

The realized real wage rate in the tth period of the contract is therefore

$$w(t) = az^*(t) + bx(0) + c\varepsilon^*(t) + u(t).$$

The presence of simultaneity bias in ordinary least squares (OLS) estimates of the employment demand equation (1) depends on two factors. If $\varepsilon^*(t) = 0$, then the parties have no informational advantage and there is no simultaneity problem. Alternatively, if $c = 0$, negotiated wages are unaffected by expected employment demand and again there is no simultaneity problem. If the parties are better able to forecast employment demand than an outside observer, however, and if higher forecasted demand leads to an increase in negotiated wage rates, then real wage rates will be positively correlated with the error in the employment equation, leading to a positively biased estimate of the wage elasticity β.

Irrespective of the parties' wage setting behavior, the elasticity β may be consistently estimated by considering the correlation between unanticipated wage rates and employment outcomes. The forecast error $u(t)$ forms a natural instrumental variable for $w(t)$: by definition, it is correlated with wages but uncorrelated with information available to the parties at the time of their negotiations.[6] Additional instruments may also be available if there are determinants of negotiated wages that can be legitimately excluded from the employment demand equation (the variables denoted as $x(0)$ in equation (2) above).

There are two important caveats to this procedure. The first is the possibility that forecast errors in real wages are directly correlated with unobservable determinants of labor demand. Suppose for example that employment demand shocks are positively correlated with unexpected price increases.[7] Then unexpected real wage increases are negatively correlated with employment demand shocks, leading to a negative bias in the instrumental variables estimate of the wage elasticity β. A simple way to control for this possibility is to include unexpected consumer price increases directly in the employment equation and to use variation across contracts in the degree of indexation to separately identify the effects of unexpected wage changes and unexpected price changes. A complementary approach is to include dummy variables representing the year in which employment is measured. These year effects absorb any aggregate demand shocks (or supply-side shocks) that affect all contracts in any given year.

A second difficulty may arise if unexpected changes in real wages during the term of a contract are immediately offset in subsequent negotiations. If this is the case then unexpected changes in real wages are inherently short-lived, and the presence of adjustment costs will substantially dampen the employment responses to such changes.[8] In the empirical analysis reported below I investigate the effect of real wage surprises on subsequent wage negotiations, and find that real wage rates in the subsequent contract move in the same direction as unexpected wage changes occurring during the previous contract. Thus, unexpected changes in real wages generate persistent effects on the cost of contractual labor, and should be expected to generate significant employment effects if the wage elasticity β is nonzero.

251

8.1.2. Specification of the Employment Demand Function

This section discusses the specification of the employment demand function (1) introduced above. An important limitation of the contract-based data set used in the empirical analysis is the absence of firm-specific price or output data. Selling prices, intermediate input prices, and output indexes are only available at the three-digit industry level. Nevertheless, these industry-level data may be used as proxies for the underlying firm-specific variables. To derive an interpretation of the resulting specification, suppose that output is produced from three factors: labor, capital, and intermediate inputs (raw materials and energy). Ignoring firm-specific constants, assume that the logarithm of employment at a given firm in a particular industry in period t, $n(t)$ is related to the logarithm of firm-specific output, $y(t)$, the logarithm of firm-specific wages, $w(t)$, the logarithm of firm-specific nonlabor input prices, $v(t)$, the user cost of capital in period t, $r(t)$ (assumed to be constant across firms and industries), and an error term $\eta(t)$:

$$(3) \qquad n(t) = \beta_1 w(t) + \beta_2 v(t) - (\beta_1 + \beta_2)\, r(t) + \sigma y(t) + \eta(t).$$

This equation can be derived from an underlying Cobb–Douglas production function, or alternatively it can be interpreted as a loglinear approximation to an arbitrary employment demand equation. The restriction that the elasticities of employment demand with respect to the three factor prices sum to zero is a consequence of the homogeneity of the cost function. This restriction implies that the equation is invariant to the deflator used to index wages and other factor prices. The magnitude of the coefficient σ reflects the degree of returns to scale: constant returns to scale implies $\sigma = 1$.

Let $\bar{y}(t)$ represent the logarithm of industry output in period t, and let $\bar{w}(t)$ and $\bar{v}(t)$ represent weighted averages of wages and intermediate input prices in the industry. Ignoring constants, assume that the logarithm of the firm's relative share of industry output is given by

$$(4) \qquad y(t) - \bar{y}(t) = \gamma_1(w(t) - \bar{w}(t)) + \gamma_2(v(t) - \bar{v}(t)) + \phi(t).$$

This equation can be derived by assuming that firms with identical Cobb–Douglas production functions act as price takers with respect to firm-specific selling prices.[9] Alter natively, equation (4) can be interpreted as an approximation to the output share equation arising from a simple differentiated product oligopoly model. In either case, the error component $\phi(t)$ represents a mixture of firm-specific relative demand shocks and firm-specific productivity shocks.

The combination of equations (3) and (4) leads to an expression for firm-specific employment in terms of firm-specific wages, industry-level output and intermediate input prices, the aggregate cost of capital, and industry wages:

$$(5) \qquad n(t) = (\beta_1 + \sigma\gamma_1)w(t) + \beta_2\bar{v}(t) - (\beta_1 + \beta_2)r(t) + \sigma\bar{y}(t)$$

$$- \sigma\gamma_1\bar{w}(t) + (\beta_2 + \sigma\gamma_2)(v(t) - \bar{v}(t)) + \sigma\phi(t) + \eta(t).$$

Under the assumption that increases in marginal cost at a particular firm lead to decreases in its relative share of industry output, the co-efficients γ_1 and γ_2 are negative. Thus, the elasticity of employment with respect to firm-specific wages, holding constant *industry* output, is larger in absolute value than the elasticity holding constant *firm-specific* output. Under the assumption of price-taking behavior the elasticity holding constant industry output is the unconditional elasticity of employment with respect to wages, allowing for the effect of changes in wages on the output supply decision of the firm. Under these same assumptions the predicted elasticity of employment with respect to industry wages is positive, reflecting the fact that as industry wages increase (holding constant the firm's wage) the firm's share of industry output will increase.

8.1.3. Allowing for the Presence of Efficient Contracting

The specification of equation (5) assumes that employment levels are determined by the firm taking the realized real wage rate as given. Except under very special circumstances, however, unilateral employment determination by the firm fails to provide an efficient allocation of employment between contractual and extra-contractual opportunities.[10] For this reason, the empirical relevance of simple nominal contracting models has been sharply criticized (for example, see Barro 1977; Hall 1980). The efficient determination of contractual employment is formally addressed in the implicit contracting literature and also within the efficient contracting literature.[11] The point of both literatures is that a jointly optimal contract (i.e., one that maximizes profit subject to a utility constraint for workers) determines employment on the basis of a shadow wage that can differ from the contractual wage. A contracting model with homogeneous workers and unrestricted transfers between employed and unemployed workers implies that the appropriate shadow wage is the marginal productivity of workers in their best alternative job. Brown and Ashenfelter (1986) refer to this as the "strong form" efficient contracting hypothesis. Strong form efficiency implies that contractual wages (and contractual wage rigidities) are irrelevant for employment determination and serve only to transfer income between employers and employees.[12]

In light of the differing implications of efficient contracting models and models with unilateral employment determination, it is important to adopt an empirical framework that encompasses either possibility. In principle this can be accomplished by including a measure of the appropriate shadow wage of labor in the employment demand function. A convenient assumption is that the shadow wage in an efficient contract is a weighted average of the observed contract wage and some measured alternative wage.[13] This leads to a specification of employment demand that includes both the contract wage and the measured alternative wage. Even though this procedure cannot provide a definitive test against the efficient contracting hypothesis,[14] it can provide useful evidence for or against the unilateral employment determination model, when the alternative is a testable version of the efficient contracting hypothesis.

8.2. Data Description and Measurement Framework

The empirical analysis in this chapter is based on a sample of 1293 contracts negotiated by 280 firm and union bargaining pairs in the Canadian manufacturing sector.[15] The available information for each contract includes its starting (or effective) date, its ending (or expiration) date, and the base wage rate in each month of the contract.[16] The number of employees covered by the agreement is only available at renegotiation dates. I associate this level of employment with the expiring agreement. Thus, each sample point consists of an end-of-contract employment observation and a series of wages, including the beginning-of-contract and end-of-contract wage rates.

Table 8.1

Characteristics of Expiring Contracts by Year

Year	Number of contracts	Average duration	Percent with escalation clause	Real wage index[a] 1971 =100	Employment index[b] 1971 = 100	Average forecast error[c]	
						Prices	Real wages
	(1)	(2)	(3)	(4)	(5)	(6)	(7)
1968	5	11.2	0.0	87.6	104.4	-0.1	0.1
1969	23	21.9	0.0	89.5	101.8	-0.9	0.9
1970	87	26.9	12.6	94.1	108.0	-2.0	1.8
1971	68	29.0	17.6	100.0	100.0	-4.6	3.8
1972	76	26.3	14.5	104.6	103.6	-3.0	2.8
1973	90	28.9	11.1	104.8	103.3	1.1	-1.1
1974	82	29.4	28.0	104.5	110.4	7.1	-6.1
1975	92	26.9	32.6	106.2	105.9	7.0	-6.3
1976	104	25.6	52.9	115.2	108.1	1.9	-1.2
1977	113	23.7	50.4	118.9	105.7	-2.2	1.8
1978	134	22.1	27.6	118.5	105.6	0.1	-0.3
1979	81	22.7	34.5	118.2	112.8	1.1	-0.9
1980	114	24.8	37.7	117.8	112.1	1.9	-1.2
1981	64	25.9	40.6	115.9	109.9	4.5	-3.3
1982	85	27.4	38.8	119.1	111.7	4.9	-3.8
1983	75	28.5	65.3	122.2	104.6	-0.5	1.2
Overall	1293	25.9	32.9	–	–	1.2	-0.9

[a] Estimated wage index for level of real wages at the end of expiring contracts.

[b] Estimated employment index for level of employment at the end of expiring.

[c] Average percentage difference between price level (or real wage) at the end of contract and expected price level (or real wage) as forecast at the signing date of contract. See text.

Source: See data appendix in Card 1988.

Some summary characteristics of the sample are presented in Table 8.1. The expiration dates of the contracts span a 16-year period between 1968 and 1983, with relatively few contracts in the first 2 years. The average duration of the contracts is 26 months, al though durations vary somewhat by year, with relatively shorter contracts in the mid-1970s. The fraction of contracts with escalation clauses shows a steadily increasing trend until the mid-1970s and then varies erratically, with an overall average of 33 percent.

An indication of the trends in employment and wages in the sample is provided by the indexes in columns 4 and 5 of the table.[17] Real wage rates among expiring contracts show significant growth until 1977 and then remain relatively constant. Average employment shows no secular trend but reflects cyclical downturns in 1971, 1975, and 1983.

The empirical strategy of this paper is to fit regressions based on equation (5) to end-of-contract observations on employment and wages for each contract. Assuming that the employment demand function is homogeneous of degree zero in factor prices, the analysis is invariant to the choice of deflators for wages and intermediate

255

input prices. Given the nature of wage indexation clauses, however, it is particularly convenient to work with real wages deflated by the consumer price index. In the remainder of the chapter, wages and industry prices are therefore expressed as real variables, deflated by the consumer price index.

The real wage rate at the end of each contract is measured directly. This rate differs from its expectation as of the negotiation date of the contract by a component that depends on the indexation provisions of the contract and the deviation between actual and expected prices at the end of the contract. Following the notation above, let $w^*(T)$ represent the expected value of the logarithm of the real wage at the end of the contract. In a nonindexed contract, the logarithm of the actual real wage rate at the end of the contract, $w(T)$, is related to $w^*(T)$ by

$$(6) \qquad w(T) = w^*(T) - (p(T) - p^*(T)),$$

where $p(T)$ represents the logarithm of the consumer price index at the end of the contract, and $p^*(T)$ represents the parties' expectation of $p(T)$, formed T months ago at the negotiation date of the contract.

In an indexed contract, unexpected changes in prices generate unexpected changes in real wage rates only to the extent that indexation is incomplete. For example, if an escalation clause increases nominal wages by e percent for each one percent increase in the consumer price index, then $w(T)$ and $w^*(T)$ are related by

$$(7) \qquad w(T) = w^*(T) - (1 - e)(p(T) - p^*(T))$$

Although most escalation clauses in North American labor contracts do not specify a fixed elasticity of indexation, this equation is approximately correct when e is defined as the marginal elasticity of indexation evaluated at the expected level of prices at the end of the contract.

Given an estimate of the elasticity of indexation, $\hat{e}$, and an estimate of the parties' expected price level at the end of the contract, $\hat{p}(T)$, it is possible to decompose the real wage rate at the end of a contract into an estimate of its expected component, $\dot{w}(T)$, and an estimate of its unexpected component:

$$w(T) = \dot{w} + \dot{u}(T),$$

where

$$\dot{w}(T) \equiv w(T) + (1 - \hat{e})(p(T) - \dot{p}(T)).$$

Using the definition of $\hat{w}(T)$, the estimated unexpected component of real wages can be written as

$$\hat{u}(T) = u(T) + (\hat{e} - e)(p(T) - p^*(T)) + (1 - \hat{e})(\dot{p}(T) - p^*(T)).$$

This estimate differs from the true value $u(T)$ by two terms: one that depends on the difference between the actual and measured elasticity of indexation (and is therefore identically zero in a nonindexed contract), and another that depends on the difference between measured price expectations and the parties' true expectations. Provided that the measurement errors in the indexation elasticity and the expected price level are orthogonal to unmeasured components of employment demand, however, these errors do not preclude the use of $\hat{u}$ (T) as an instrumental variable for the level of wages at the end of the contract.

In this chapter, I use a naive forecasting model to form estimates of the expected price level at the end of the contract, based on the average rate of inflation over the 12 months prior to the negotiation date.[18] This model was selected by comparing the noncontingent wage increases in the first year of 24–36 month nonindexed contracts to alternative forecasts of the 12-month inflation rate formed at the negotiation date of the contract. I have also experimented with more sophisticated forecasting equations and found few differences in the results. Since the forecasts are only used to form instrumental variables, the choice of an inefficient forecasting model should not bias the empirical results.

The other ingredient in the calculation of unexpected real wage changes is the elasticity of indexation e. Precise information on the actual indexation formulas in the sample is not readily available. I therefore use the ratio of total escalated increases over the life of the contract to the total increase in consumer prices over the life of the contract as a rough estimate of e. This measure is reasonably accurate for contracts with no restrictions on the escalation formula. For contracts with restricted escalation formulas that delay the start of indexation or specify a maximum escalated wage increase, this measure introduces some noise into the calculation of $\hat{u}(T)$.

Column 6 of Table 8.1 reports the average forecasting errors in the end-of-contract price level. The average annual forecast error is 1.2 percent, but it varies considerably by year, ranging from 7.0 percent for contracts expiring in 1974 and 1975, to -4.5 percent for contracts expiring in 1971. As the formulas in equations (6) and (7) imply, forecasting errors in end-of-contract real wage rates are negatively correlated with the forecast errors in prices. The average forecast errors in real wages in column 7 of the table are close to mirror images of the associated price forecasting errors. Relative to the forecasting errors in prices, however, the forecast errors in real wages are dampened by the indexation provisions of the escalated contracts. The average estimated elasticity of indexation among indexed contracts is 0.50, implying that the forecast errors in real wages among these contracts are about one-half as large as the corresponding forecast errors in prices.[19]

The average forecast errors in end-of-contract real wages are also negatively correlated with the employment index in column 5: the correlation coefficient over 16 annual observations is -0.54, and the regression coefficient of the employment index on unanticipated real wage changes is -0.70, with a standard error of 0.27. This provides some evidence that contractual employment outcomes are negatively related to unexpected changes in real wages. By comparison, the employment index is positively correlated with the index of real wage levels in column 4.

Contract-specific correlations between employment and wages are reported in Table 8.2. All the data in this table are measured as changes from the expiration date of the previous contract, using the sample of negotiations described in Table 8.1. Also presented in the table are the correlations of employment and wages with two measures of outside wages: the average real wage rate in the same (two-digit) industry, measured in the expiration month of the contract, and the average real wage for unskilled nonproduction laborers in the same province, measured in the expiration year of the contract.[20] Finally, the last two rows of Table 8.2 present the correlations of employment and wages with contract-specific measures of unexpected price changes and unexpected real wage changes.

Table 8.2

Means and Correlation of Employment and Wage Changes
Between Consecutive Contract[a]

	Mean	Standard deviation	Employment (end of contract)	Real contract eage (end of contract)
1. Employment (end of contract)	-0.017	0.201	1.00	-0.07
2. Real contract wage (end of contract)	0.052	0.075	-0.07	1.00
3. Industry wage (expiration month)	0.045	0.056	-0.04	0.59
4. Provincial wage (Expiration year)	0.044	0.060	-0.07	0.51
5. Unanticipated change in real wages over contract [b]	-0.004	0.060	-0.12	0.45
6. Unanticipated change in consumer prices over contract [c]	0.006	0.069	0.13	-0.44

[a] Sample size is 1293. All variables are measured as changes in logarithms between expiration dates of consecutive contracts.
[b] Percentage difference between real wage at end of contract and expected real wage forecast at signing date of contract.
[c] Percentage difference between Consumer Price Index at end of contract and expected price index forecast at signing date of contract.

These simple correlations reveal three features of the contract-level data. First, changes in employment are only weakly negatively correlated with changes in end-of-contract real wage rates. Second, the correlations between employment and outside wages are of similar magnitude to the correlations between employment and contract wages. Third, changes in employment are more strongly negatively correlated with changes in the unexpected component of real wages. Thus, the OLS estimate of the elasticity of employment with respect to contract wages is much smaller in absolute value than the corresponding instrumental variables estimate formed using unexpected changes in real wages as an instrumental variable. The OLS estimate is -0.19, with a standard error of 0.08, while the instrumental variables estimate is -0.70, with a standard error of 0.18. As will be seen below, this pattern continues to hold when other covariates are added to the employment determination equation.

8.3. The Effect of Previous Wage Rates on Subsequent Wage Determination

As a preliminary step in the analysis of employment demand, this section presents a brief summary of estimated wage equations for the sample of collective bargaining contracts described above. The purpose of this analysis is to identify any "spillover" effect from real wage rates at the end of one contract to wage rates in the next contract. A finding of significant spillovers implies that unexpected changes in real wages have persistent effects on the cost of contractual labor. A finding of insignificant spillovers, on the other hand, implies that these unexpected changes are relatively short-lived. The degree of persistence in unexpected wage changes is important for assessing the magnitude of the effect that these changes will exert on employment determination.

The analysis is based on two alternative measures of negotiated wages: the real wage at the start of the contract and the expected average real wage over the term of the entire contract. In the presence of adjustment costs the wage at the start of the next contract is particularly relevant for employment setting behavior in the last few months of an existing agreement. The expected average real wage over the next contract gives a longer-term measure of the costs of contractual employment.

A convenient statistical framework for analyzing the determinants of wages is a simple components-of-variance model of the form

$$(8) \qquad w_{ij} = \theta_i + bx_{ij} + \lambda w(T)_{ij-1} + \xi_{ij},$$

where w_{ij} represents the measure of wages (either the real wage at the start of the contract or the expected average real wage over the life of the contract) for the jth contract of the ith firm, θ_i, represents a permanent firm-specific component of wage variation, x_{ij}, represents a vector of determinants of wages (measured at the negotiation date), $w(T)_{ij-1}$, represents the real wage at the end of the previous contract, and E represents a contract-specific component of variance. The parameters b and λ can be estimated by taking contract-to-contract first-differences:

$$(9) \qquad \Delta w_{ij} \equiv w_{ij} - w_{ij-1} = b\Delta x_{ij} + \lambda \Delta w(T)_{ij-1} + \Delta \xi_{ij}.$$

Ordinary least-squares estimates of this first-differenced wage equation may be inappropriate, however, if there is any correlation between the real wage at the end of the $(j - 1)$st contract and the error component $\xi_{ij} - \xi_{ij-1}$ in the first-differenced wage equation.[21] This problem is readily overcome by using instrumental variables for the lagged change in ending real wage rates. Suitable instruments include the first-difference in the unexpected component of ending real wages and any exogenous components of Δx_{ij-1}. First-differencing also introduces a moving average error component into consecutive wage observations from the same bargaining pair. The estimated standard errors and test statistics throughout this paper therefore allow for a first-order moving average error component among the observations from each bargaining pair, as well as for arbitrary conditional heteroskedasticity.

Estimation results for the first-differenced wage equation (9) are reported in Table 8.3. Columns 1–4 of the table report estimates using the real wage at the start of the contract as the measure of wage outcomes, while columns 5–8 report estimates using the first-difference of the expected average real wage rate over the life of the contract as the dependent variable.[22] The components of x_{ij} include the regional unemployment rate and the real wage rate in aggregate manufacturing (measured in the effective month of the contract), a province-specific real wage rate for unskilled workers (measured in the effective year of the contract), and a set of unrestricted year effects for the effective date of the contract. The year effects capture a number of omitted factors, including a period of wage-price controls between 1975 and 1978. Their addition provides a significant improvement in the fit of the wage equations, although they hardly affect the estimated coefficient of previous wages. I have also estimated wage equations that include industry-specific output and price variables. These are only weakly related to negotiated wages, however, and their inclusion has virtually no effect on the reported coefficients in Table 8.3.

Columns 1 and 5 of Table 8.3 report OLS estimates of equation (9) for the two alter native dependent variables, while columns 2 and 6 report instrumental variables (IV) estimates. These specifications suggest that negotiated wages are significantly positively related to the level of wages at the end of the preceding contract. The OLS estimates of the spillover coefficient λ (in row 6) differ somewhat between the two alternative measures of the dependent variable, although the IV estimates are closer together. The last row of the table reports overi-

Table 8.3

Estimated Wage Determination Equations

	Real wage at start of contract				Expected average real wage during contract			
	OLS	IV[a]			OLS	IV[a]		
	(1)	(2)	(3)	(4)	(5)	(6)	(7)	(8)
1. Year effects	Yes	Yes	Yes	Yes	Yes	Yes	Yes	Yes
2. Regional unemployment rate	-0.50	-0.45	-0.46	-0.46	-0.38	-0.44	-0.45	-0.47
	(0.12)	(0.12)	(0.12)	(0.12)	(0.12)	(0.13)	(0.13)	(0.13)
3. Real wage in manufacturing	0.04	0.11	0.11	0.10	0.40	0.30	0.31	0.26
	(0.10)	(0.11)	(0.11)	(0.12)	(0.11)	(0.12)	(0.12)	(0.12)
4. Real wage in region	0.02	0.04	0.04	0.03	0.04	0.02	0.02	0.01
	(0.05)	(0.04)	(0.04)	(0.05)	(0.05)	(0.05)	(0.05)	(0.05)
5. Real wage at end of previous contract	0.48	0.36	0.35	—	0.25	0.41	0.35	—
	(0.03)	(0.05)	(0.07)		(0.03)	(0.06)	(0.07)	
6. Expected real wage at end of previous contract	—	—	—	0.46	—	—	—	0.36
				(0.08)				(0.09)
7. Unexpected real wage at end of previous contract	—	—	—	0.41	—	—	—	0.43
				(0.06)				(0.07)
8. Change in prices during previous contract	—	—	-0.01	—	—	—	-0.05	—
			(0.03)				(0.03)	
9. Standard error	0.039	0.039	0.039	0.038	0.038	0.039	0.038	0.038
10. Overidentification text[b]	—	0.261	0.273	0.489	—	0.037	0.016	0.006

Note: Standard errors in parentheses. Sample size is 1,293. All regressions include a (first-differenced) linear trend. The mean and standard deviation of the dependent variable in columns 1–4 are 0.050 and 0.066. The mean and standard deviation of the dependent variable in columns 5–8 are 0.043 and 0.061. Standard errors are corrected for first-order moving average error component and heteroskedasticity.

[a] In columns 2, 3, 6, and 7, instrumental variables for real wage at the end of the previous contract include 18-year effects, the real wage in manufacturing at the start of the previous contract and the unanticipated change in real wages over the previous contract. In columns 4 and 8 instrumental variables for expected real wage at the end of the previous contract include 18-year effects, the real wage in manufacturing at the start of the previous contract, and the change in consumer prices during the previous contract.

[b] Probability value of test for orthogonality of residuals and instruments. The statistic is distributed as chi-squared with 19 degrees of freedom in columns 2, 3, 6, and 7, and with 18 degrees of freedom in columns 4 and 8.

dentification test statistics for the instrumental variables estimators. There is no evidence against the exclusion restrictions implicit in the IV procedure for the specification in column 2. The test statistic for the specification in column 6, on the other hand, presents mild evidence against these restrictions.

In columns 3 and 7 the change in prices over the preceding contract is introduced directly into the wage determination equation. This addition permits a test of the hypothesis that aggregate price movements affect future wage determination only to the extent that they affect the level of real wages at the end of the preceding contract. The estimated coefficients in row 8 of the table provide no evidence against this hypothesis. Finally, the specifications in columns 4 and 8 relax the assumption that the expected and unexpected components of the end-of-contract wage $w(T)_{ij-1}$ have the same effect on subsequent wages.[23] Perhaps surprisingly, there is no evidence against the restricted specification: the t-statistics for the hypothesis of equal coefficients for the expected and unexpected components are 1.32 in column 4 and 1.22 in column 8.

These results suggest that unexpected changes in wages have persistent effects on the costs of contractual labor. An unanticipated 10 percent decrease in real wages leads to an approximately 3 percent lower real wage throughout the following contract. Thus even in the presence of substantial adjustment costs, employment should be expected to respond to unanticipated changes in real wages, provided that the unilateral employment determination model is correct.

8.4. The Determinants of Contractual Employment

This section turns to estimates of the employment demand function (5). As in the previous section, the framework for the analysis is a components-of-variance model for the logarithm of end-of-contract employment in the jth contract of the ith firm (n_{ij}):

$$(10) \qquad n_{ij} = \psi_i + \alpha z_{ij} + \beta w(T)_{ij} + \varepsilon_{ij}.$$

In this equation, ψ_i represents a permanent firm-specific effect, z_{ij} represents a vector of determinants of employment, measured at the end of the contract, $w_{ij}(T)$ represents the real wage rate at the end of the contract, and ε_{ij} is a contract-specific disturbance. Assuming that industry output and prices are used as proxies for firm-specific output and price data, the wage elasticity β in equation (10) is related to the underlying parameters of the employment demand schedule (3) and the relative output equation (4) by $\beta = -(\beta_1 + \sigma\gamma_1)$. Note that β is assumed to be constant across industries. Although this is unlikely to be true, the relatively small number of contracts in each industry makes it difficult to estimate parameters other than the average demand elasticity across industries. Heteroskedasticity introduced by variation in β is taken into account in the calculation of the standard errors.

Again, a convenient method for eliminating the pair-specific effects is to take first differences between consecutive contracts, yielding

$$\text{(11)} \qquad \Delta n_{ij} = \alpha\Delta z_{ij} + \beta\Delta w(T)_{ij} + \Delta\varepsilon_{ij}.$$

In many previous studies, employment outcomes have been found to follow a partial adjustment equation of the form $n_{ij} = (1 - \mu)n_{ij}^* + \mu\, n_{ij-1}$, where n_{ij}^* represents the optimal level of employment in the absence of adjustment costs, as given by an equation such as (5). Partial adjustment is readily accommodated within the framework of equation (11) by the addition of a lagged dependent variable. In the present context, however, consecutive employment outcomes are 20–36 months apart. Thus, the extent of partial adjustment is likely to be much smaller than that observed in quarterly or annual data. This issue is addressed more thoroughly below.

Estimation results for the first-differenced employment equation are presented in Tables 8.4 and 8.5. Following the discussion in Section 8.1.2. the determinants of employment include the three-digit industry input price index (deflated by the consumer price index), industry-level real output, and the end-of-contract real wage rate. Specifications that add outside wage rates and a lagged dependent variable are presented in Table 8.5. The odd-numbered columns of Table 8.4 present estimated equations that include a linear time trend, while the even-numbered columns report estimates that include a set of unrestricted dummy variables for the different expiration years in the sample. I have not made any attempt to measure the user cost of capital. On the assumption that capital costs are constant across manufacturing industries, variation in the user cost of capital is absorbed by the trends and/or time effects in the empirical specification. The unrestricted year effects also capture any aggregate-level shocks (such as aggregate demand shocks or productivity shocks) that are shared by all contracts in a given year.

In an effort to capture partial adjustment effects, and also to control for the fact that industry output is measured annually, the employment equations in Tables 8.4 and 8.5 include industry output in both the expiration year of the agreement and the previous year. I have experimented with specifications that also include wage rates and input prices in the year prior to the expiration date, but the effects of these variables are always poorly determined and small in magnitude.

The first two columns of Table 8.4 present OLS estimates of the employment equation with and without dummy variables for the expiration date of the contract. Employment is positively related to intermediate input prices and current and last year's level of output. The elasticity of employment with respect to output (i.e., the sum of the coefficients of current and last years' output) is substantially less than unity, implying increasing returns to scale in the framework of equation (5). The addition of the year effects results in a relatively small improvement in the fit of the employment equations: the probability value of an exclusion tests for the year effects is reported in row 8 of the table. When the year effects are included, however, the estimated wage elasticity of employment demand falls to essentially zero.

The estimated wage elasticity is substantially larger (in absolute value) when the end-of-contract wage rate is instrumented by the unanticipated change in real wages over the term of the contract. The results of this exercise are reported in columns 3 and 4 of Table 8.4. Without year effects, the estimated elasticity rises from -0.15 to -0.28, although the estimated standard error rises proportionately. With year effects, the change in the point estimate is even more remarkable: from -0.02 to -0.45. Due to the imprecision of the IV estimators, however, tests of the difference between the OLS and IV estimates are insignificant in either case.

The specifications in columns 5 and 6 attempt to reduce this imprecision by expanding the list of instrumental variables for the end-of-contract real wage rate to include the level of real wages in manufacturing at the start of the contract and year effects for the signing date of the contract. The additional instrumental variables lead to a slight increase in the magnitude of the estimated wage elasticities and provide some increase in the precision of the estimates. Overi-

Table 8.4
Estimated Employment Determination Equations

	OLS		IVa		IVb			
	(1)	(2)	(3)	(4)	(5)	(6)	(7)	(8)
1. Year effects	No	Yes	No	Yes	No	Yes	No	Yes
2. Real industry input price	0.22	0.16	0.20	0.16	0.19	0.16	0.19	0.15
	(0.06)	(0.08)	(0.06)	(0.08)	(0.06)	(0.08)	(0.06)	(0.08)
3. Real industry output	0.20	0.29	0.22	0.28	0.23	0.28	0.23	0.28
	(0.07)	(0.09)	(0.07)	(0.09)	(0.07)	(0.09)	(0.07)	(0.09)
4. Real industry output (Previous Year)	0.17	0.10	0.15	0.11	0.14	0.11	0.14	0.10
	(0.06)	(0.07)	(0.07)	(0.07)	(0.06)	(0.07)	(0.07)	(0.07)
5. Real wage at end of contract	-0.15	-0.02	-0.28	-0.45	-0.39	-0.51	-0.42	-0.40
	(0.08)	(0.10)	(0.17)	(0.35)	(0.12)	(0.29)	(0.17)	(0.42)
6. Unexpected inflation during contract	—	—	—	—	—	—	—	—
7. Standard error	0.196	0.194	0.196	0.195	0.196	0.196	0.196	0.195
8. Test for exclusion of year effects (p-value)	—	0.003	—	0.006	—	0.004	—	0.004
9. Overidentification test [c]	—	—	—	—	0.76	0.97	0.74	0.96

Note: Standard errors in parentheses. Sample size is 1,293. All regressions include a (first-differenced) linear trend. The mean and standard deviation of the dependent variable are -0.017 and 0.201. Standard errors are corrected for first-order moving average error component and heteroskedasticity.

[a] Instrumental variable for real wage at end of contract is the unanticipated change in real wages during the contract.

[b] Instrumental variables for real wage at end of the contract include 18 year effects, the real wage in manufacturing at the start of the contract, and the unanticipated change in real wages during the contract.

[c] Probability value of test for orthogonality of residuals and instruments. The test statistic is distributed as chi-squared with 19 degrees of freedom in all cases.

dentification test statistics for the internal consistency of the instruments are reported in row 9 of the table. In all cases these are below conventional significance levels. I have also estimated employment equations that use only the additional instruments (i.e., excluding the unexpected change in real wages) to identify the effect of wages on employment. As the overidentification statistics suggest, these estimates are very similar to those in Table 8.4.

Table 8.5

Estimated Employment Determination Equations

		OLS		IV[a]			IV[b]	
		(1)	(2)	(3)	(4)	(5)	(6)	(7)
1.	Year effects	Yes	Yes	Yes	Yes	Yes	No	Yes
2.	Real industry input price	0.16	0.16	0.14	0.16	0.14	0.13	0.10
		(0.08)	(0.08)	(0.08)	(0.08)	(0.08)	(0.07)	(0.09)
3.	Real industry output	0.29	0.29	0.27	0.28	0.27	0.20	0.25
		(0.09)	(0.09)	(0.09)	(0.09)	(0.09)	(0.07)	(0.09)
4.	Real industry output	0.10	0.10	0.11	0.11	0.11	0.15	0.13
	(previous year)	(0.07)	(0.07)	(0.07)	(0.07)	(0.07)	(0.07)	(0.08)
5.	Real wage at end of	-0.03	-0.02	-0.56	-0.51	-0.56	-0.52	-0.58
	previous contract	(0.10)	(0.10)	(0.32)	(0.31)	(0.33)	(0.22)	(0.32)
6.	Real wage in industry	0.06	–	0.23	–	0.23	0.26	0.38
		(0.22)		(0.26)		(0.26)	(0.22)	(0.25)
7.	Real wage in region	–	-0.03	–	0.04	0.06	–	–
			(0.15)		(0.16)	(0.21)		
8.	Lagged dependent	–	–	–	–	–	-0.13	-0.08
	variable (instrumented)						(0.14)	(0.15)
9.	Standard error	0.194	0.194	0.196	0.196	0.196	0.193	0.194
10.	Overidentification text [c]	–	–	0.972	0.967	0.972	0.451	0.666

Note: See note to Table 8.4. Standard errors in parentheses.

[a] Instrumental variables for the real wage at the end of the contract include 18-year effects, the real wage in manufacturing at the start of the contract, and the unanticipated change in real wages during the contract.

[b] Estimated on subsample of 1,107 observations. Mean and standard deviation of the dependent variable are -0.015 and 0.0200, respectively. Instruments include the instrument set above plus the lagged value of industry output.

[c] Probability value of test for orthogonality of residuals and instruments. The test statistic is distributed as chi-squared with 19 degrees of freedom in columns 3–5, and 16 degrees of freedom in columns 6–7.

Even with the additional instrumental variables the estimated elasticity of employment demand in column 6 is only significantly different from zero at the 10 percent level. Nevertheless, a test of the difference between the estimated demand elasticities in columns 1 and 5 is significant at the 1 percent level, and a test of the difference between the estimated elasticities in columns 2 and 6 is significant at the 10 percent level. These results suggest that OLS estimates of the elasticity of employment demand are positively biased.

The final two columns of Table 8.4 present employment equations that include the unexpected change in consumer prices during the term of the contract as an additional explanatory variable. These specifications provide a simple check on whether unexpected price increases affect employment through the contractual wage, or whether there is a direct correlation between unexpected inflation and employment demand.[24] Neither specification provides any evidence of a direct role for unexpected price changes. Nevertheless, the standard errors of the wage and price terms in column 8 are sufficiently large that one cannot rule out a direct effect of inflationary surprises on employment demand.[25] Taken together with the other estimates in the table, however, I interpret the results in columns 7 and 8 as supporting the conclusion that price surprises affect employment determination solely through their effect on realized wages.

The effect of outside wage rates on contractual employment is addressed in Table 8.5. The theoretical analysis in Section 8.1. identifies two alternative routes for this effect. On the one hand, increases in average wages in the industry may have a positive effect on employment, reflecting the competitive advantage implied by higher costs elsewhere in the industry. On the other hand, increases in wage rates representing the alternative value of workers' time may have a negative effect if employment is influenced by efficient contracting considerations. In an effort to distinguish between these hypotheses, I have included the industry average wage in columns 1 and 3 of the table, and a province-specific wage for unskilled laborers in columns 2 and 4 of the table. Both wage measures are included in column 5.

The OLS estimates in columns1 and 2 of Table 8.5 show no evidence of a role for either outside wage measure. When the contract wage is instrumented, however, the point estimate of the effect of the industry-specific wage rises substantially, while the estimated effect of the regional wage measure remains close to zero. A similar pattern emerges in column 5 when both outside wage measures are included. Given the imprecision of the estimated elasticities it is difficult to draw strong conclusions from these results. Nevertheless, the estimates lend much stronger support to the view that outside wages belong in the employment equation as a proxy for the level of competitors' costs than to the view that outside wages belong in the employment equation as a proxy for the shadow value of employees' time.[26] If the former view is taken literally, the point estimates in column 3 suggest that the output-constant elasticity of employment demand with respect to wages is -0.33, while the elasticity of output supply with respect to an increase in wages is -0.70.[27] This estimate of the output-constant demand elasticity is in the midpoint of the range of estimates usually reported in the static employment demand literature (see Hamermesh 1986, pp. 451–454).

The question of whether the estimated employment equations are robust to the inclusion of lagged employment is explored in the last two columns of Table 8.5. Since the employment models are estimated in first-differences, and the covariance of consecutive changes in employment is biased downward by any measurement error, the lagged value of industry output is added to the list of instrumental variables, and lagged employment and real wages are treated as jointly endogenous. The results show no evidence of a role for lagged employment. As mentioned earlier, this probably reflects the 20–36 month interval between consecutive observations in the data set. Over two or three years the effects of partial adjustment are likely to be much smaller than over an interval of a quarter or year.[28]

The estimates in Tables 8.4 and 8.5 suggest two main conclusions. First, employment outcomes are negatively related to contractual wage rates. Although the simple correlation between end-of-contract wage rates and employment is small and statistically insignificant, this is apparently a consequence of simultaneity bias. When unanticipated real wage changes and/or other exogenous variables are used as instrumental variables for the end-of-contract wage, the estimated wage elasticity is consistently negative and stable in magnitude across alternative specifications. Second, there is no evidence that employment is related to outside wages in a manner consistent with simple efficient contracting models. Even though employment is uncorrelated with region-specific wage measures, it is weakly positively correlated with industry average wages. This positive correlation is consistent with the hypothesis that higher average industry wages lead to improvements in the firm's competitive position and increases in employment.

8.5. Conclusions

This chapter presents evidence on the role of nominal wage contracts in the union sector. An important feature of these contracts, emphasized by the simple macro models of Fischer (1977) and Taylor (1980), is the predetermined nature of nominal wages. Real wage rates at the end of a contract therefore contain unanticipated components that reflect unexpected changes in consumer prices and the degree of indexation in the contract. The empirical analysis, based on a large sample of indexed and nonindexed contracts, indicates that these unexpected real wage changes are associated with systematic employment responses in the opposite direction. This suggests that nominal contracts play a role in the link between aggregate demand shocks and real economic activity, at least in the part of the economy covered by explicit nominal contracts.

Three other findings emerge from the empirical analysis. First, the contract-level correlation between employment and wages apparently reflects both demand and wage-setting behavior. Similar simultaneity problems may arise in other studies of firm-specific employment and wage data. Second, unanticipated changes in prices are found to generate changes in real wages that spill over from existing labor contracts to subsequent agreements. Inflation surprises therefore have persistent effects on real wages in the union sector, in addition to their short-run effects on employment. Finally, the empirical results suggest that employment outcomes in union contracts are determined on a conventional downward-sloping demand schedule, taking the prevailing contract wage as given. There is no indication that employment is related to outside wages in a manner consistent with a simple model of efficient contracting.

Appendix

1. Contract Sample

The contract sample is derived from the December 1985 version of Labour Canada's Wage Tape. This tape contains information on collective bargaining agreements covering more than 500 employees in Canada. Starting from the 2,868 manufacturing contracts on the tape, I merged together contract chronologies between the same firm and union covering different establishments, and eliminated contracts from bargaining pairs with fewer than four contracts. These procedures yield a sample of 2,258 contracts negotiated by 299 firm and union pairs. Further information on the merging process and the characteristics of the resulting sample are presented in the data appendix to my 1988 paper and in tables 1 and 2 of that paper.

The employment data for this sample were then checked in two stages. First, the number of workers covered in each contract was compared to the number covered in the preceding and subsequent agreements. Second, in cases where the number of workers changed dramatically between contracts, the contract summaries in the appropriate issue of the Collective Bargaining Review were consulted. In 238 contracts, the employment counts recorded on the wage tape were found to be in disagreement with the counts reported in the Collective Bargaining Review. In these cases, counts from the published contract summaries were used. In cases for which the set of establishments covered by the contract changed over time, contracts with inconsistent coverage were deleted from the sample. Of the 2,258 contracts in the subsample of merged contracts, valid coverage data are available for 1,813 contracts (80.3%). Checking of the employment data was performed by Thomas Lemieux. I am extremely grateful for his assistance with these data.

In this chapter, employment at the end of a contract is measured by the number of workers covered by the subsequent agreement. Furthermore, the estimation procedures require information on employment and wage outcomes in the previous agreement and on various industry and aggregate data that are only available between 1966 and 1983. The sample of contracts used in this chapter therefore consists of the subset of contracts in the initial 2,258 contract merged subsample that satisfy the following criteria:

(a) Information on at least one previous contract is available in the sample.

(b) Information on at least one subsequent contract is available in the sample.

(c) The expiration dates of the current and previous contract are after January 1966 and before December 1983.

(d) Valid employment data are available for both the current and preceding contract (i.e., valid counts of workers covered are available for both the current and subsequent contracts).

2. Aggregate and Industry-Level Data

The following aggregate and industry-level data were merged to the contract sample.

a) Consumer price index, all items, 1981 = 100. January 1961 to November 1985: Cansim 0484000, from the 1985 Cansim University Base Tape. December 1985 to June 1986: from the *Bank of Canada Review,* November 1986.

(b) Average hourly earnings in manufacturing. January 1961 to March 1983: Cansim D1518, from the 1983 Cansim University Base Tape. April 1983 to December 1983: Cansim L5607, from the *Bank of Canada Review,* various issues. Data from April 1983 and later are multiplied by 1.04035 to correct for the revision in the establishment survey.

(c) Average hourly earnings of nonproduction production laborers, by province. Annual data on hourly earnings for selected occupations are available for major cities. I matched data for the following cities to their respective provinces: Halifax, St. John, Montreal, Toronto, Winnipeg, Regina, Edmonton, Vancouver. The wage rates used are listed as rates for "male general laborers" between 1966 and 1977, for "general laborers in service occupations" between 1978 and 1981, and for "nonproduction laborers" between 1982 and 1985. Data for 1966–1972 are from *Wage Rates, Salaries, and Hours of Labour,* 1966–1972 editions. Data for 1973–1986 are from *Canada Year Book,* various editions. For contracts that cover two or more provinces, I used a weighted average of Montreal, Toronto, and Vancouver rates with weights of 0.35, 0.55, and 0.10, respectively.

(d) Unemployment rates, seasonally adjusted. For contracts in Quebec, Ontario, and British Columbia, I used the province-specific unemployment rates for all workers. For contracts in other provinces, I used the national average unemployment rate. The series used were as follows: Quebec-Cansim D768478; Ontario-Cansim D7fi8648; British Columbia-Cansim D7fi9233; all others-Cansim 0767611. Data for January 1966 through November 1983 were obtained from the 1983 Cansim University Base. Data for December 1983 were taken from the *Bank of Canada Review,* November 1986.

(e) Industry selling prices, input prices, and output. Three-digit industry level annual data for 1961–1971 were taken from Statistics Canada, *Real Domestic Product by Industry* 1961–1971. These data are classified by 1960 standard industrial codes (SICs). Data on a 1971 SIC basis for 1971–1983 were taken from the 1978 and 1984 issues of Statistics Canada, *Gross Domestic Product by Industry.* The 1960 and 1971 SIC codes were then matched, and the price and output indexes spliced using the 1971 observations from the two sources. Of 65 three-digit industries represented in the contract sample, there were a total of 31 for which three-digit-level data were not available on a consistent basis. For these industries, two-digit-level data were used. The publications report the value of gross output and implicit price indexes for gross output and intermediate inputs. These data were used to construct the value of real gross output (the measure of "output" used in this chapter). Implicit price indexes for gross output and intermediate inputs were deflated by the annual average consumer price index to obtain real selling prices and input prices used in the paper.

(f) Industry average hourly earnings. Monthly two-digit industry-level average hourly earnings data for the period January 1961 to March 1983 were taken from the 1983 Cansim University Base. Earnings data are unavailable for two industries: knitting mills and miscellaneous manufacturing. For the former, I used earnings in clothing industries. For the latter, I used average earnings in all manufacturing. Wage rates for April through December 1983 were constructed by index-linking wage rates from the new establishment survey to the rates in the old survey using their values in March 1983. Earnings data from the new survey for March–December 1983 were taken from the 1985 Cansim University Base

IV

Concluding Thoughts

The chapters in this book document the evolution of our thinking in two important areas. They also illustrate a broader trend in the development of empirical research methods in labor economics. In the early 1980s empirical research methodology suffered a crisis of confidence. Influential papers by David Hendry (1980) and Edward Leamer (1983) called attention to the lack of credibility of the results in many empirical studies. The statistician David Freedman (1991) and others emphasized problems identifying causal effects from observational data. Robert Lalonde (1986) used data from a randomized experiment to evaluate existing program evaluation methods and showed the difficulty of choosing between methods that gave widely different estimates of the effectiveness of a training program. H. Gregg Lewis (1986), the doyen of empirical labor economics, concluded that estimates of the union wage effect based on state-of-the-art econometric methods were often unreliable and uninformative.

Over the next decade, empirical studies based on credible, transparent research designs – including natural experiments and randomized manipulations – gained much wider acceptance within labor economics. The research in these chapters was strongly influenced by the ideas behind this "credibility revolution," and by the desire to improve the standards of evidence in empirical microeconomics.

In retrospect, we believe these studies point to three important lessons. The first is the value of causal hypotheses derived from well-specified economic models. The human capital investment model, for example, elucidates a series of channels through which school quality affects earnings. The neoclassical labor demand model predicts a negative effect of an exogenously imposed wage increase on a firm's employment demand, and provides insights into the factors that determine the magnitude of the response; and the monopsony and search models provide well specified alternatives.

A second lesson is the value of an explicit research design in conducting empirical research. The designs used in the studies included in this book range from simple difference-in-differences to instrumental variables to randomized controlled trials. Each of these designs has limitations and no one method can be used to address every problem of interest. But the exercise of specifying and defending an explicit design can lead to more credible and ultimately more important findings.

A third lesson is the importance of high quality data. The validity of any empirical research depends first and foremost on the quality of the underlying data. Oftentimes, the construction of the appropriate data set – for example, our survey of restaurants in New Jersey and Pennsylvania – is the single most important step in a research project. A great benefit of the shift in empirical methods in labor economics since the early 1980s is the increasing range of data sets that have been assembled and even specially created to analyze the questions of interest, as well as a concern for the reliability of the data.

We are honored to have been able to contribute to the shift in empirical methodology in labor economics over the past two decades. We especially thank the many colleagues, co-authors, students, and friends who guided our thinking and helped us along the way.

Notes

Chapter 1

1   For example, the addition of test score information to the earnings models reported by Griliches and Mason (1972, table 3) improves the explanatory power of their models by less than one-half of a percentage point.

2   Our approach is conceptually similar to that of Behrman and Birdsall (1983), who relate the returns to schooling among young Brazilian men to the average years of education of teachers in each individual's region of residence.

3   We normalize the coefficients γ_{jc} and p_{rc} by setting $\sum_r f_{rc} p_{rc} = 0$, where f_{rc} is the fraction of cohort c living in one of the nine census regions.

4   Specifically, the models include linear and quadratic terms in potential experience, a dummy variable for being married with spouse present, a dummy variable for residence in an SMSA, and unrestricted dummy variables for residence in each of the 50 states. Additionally, dummy variables indicating state of birth were included if the sample combined observations from more than one state. The models are estimated on subgroups of the sample described in Appendix B.

5   Further details of our investigation, including tabulations of the estimated thresh-old points and education percentiles, are available on request. The 13 state groups include 11 individual states (California, New York, Ohio, Texas, Pennsylvania, Illinois, Michigan, New Jersey, Massachusetts, North Carolina, and Virginia) and two pairs of states (Alabama/Georgia and Kentucky/Tennessee).

6   The estimated coefficients suggest that rates of return to education vary across regions of residence by as much as 2 percent per year of education. Returns are lowest in the Mountain and Pacific regions and highest in the East–South Central and West–South Central regions. These patterns are consistent with those reported by Chiswick (1974) in an earlier analysis of the regional variation in returns to education.

7   An optimal second-step estimation scheme should take account of the covariances between the estimated returns for different states. We have experimented with such a procedure and found few differences from the simpler weighting scheme described in the text. The reason for this is that the estimated returns by state of birth are "almost" independent. The only source of covariation between them arises from the fact that the same regression parameters are used to adjust for other control variables in the first-stage regressions.

8   The R^2 coefficients in row 6 can be used to form χ^2 test statistics for the hypothesis that the included explanatory variables explain *all* the nonsampling variation in the state and cohort returns. The χ^2 test statistic for

the model in col. 1 is 1,164, with 144 degrees of freedom. On the other hand, the test statistic for the model in col. 10 is 165.5, with 93 degrees of freedom.

9   One possible difficulty with the term length variable is that teachers would prefer a shorter term. This suggests that teacher quality may decline with term length, with teacher wages held constant. We have reestimated the models in Table 1.3 using the teacher wage expressed in terms of days worked per year (using term length as days worked). This change has the effect of raising the coefficient on the term length variable by about 0.5, with little or no effect on the other coefficients in the model. Even with this adjustment, the term length effects in col. 10 are insignificantly different from zero.

10   These and subsequent covariates are described in Appendix A.

11   For example, across our three cohorts and 49 states of birth, the correlation between the fraction who completed high school and the pupil/teacher ratio is -.71.

12   Coleman, Hoffer, and Kilgore (1982) present data on standardized test scores that indicate higher achievement levels among students in private (mainly Catholic) schools. The interpretation of these data is an issue of some dispute: see Goldberger and Cain (1982), Murnane (1984), and San Segundo (1988).

13   Let p represent the pupil/teacher ratio for all students, p_1 the ratio in the public school system, p_2 the ratio in the private school system, and f the fraction of enrollment in private schools. Then $p \cong (1 - f) \cdot p_1 + f \cdot p_2$. Hence $p - p_1 = f \cdot (p_2 - p_1)$.

14   We also used the estimated P matrix to obtain estimated sampling variances for the corrected returns. These sampling variances were used to weight the regressions. A table containing these results is available on request.

Chapter 2

1   These and many other aspects of black economic progress since 1940 are described in Smith and Welch (1986, 1989).

2   See Freeman (1973) and Brown (1982). Ashenfelter (1970) presents evidence that part of the rise in black–white relative earnings measured in the Current Population Survey between 1966 and 1967 is attributable to a change in sampling and processing procedures.

3   Precise descriptions of the samples used to construct these averages are provided in the Data Appendix.

4   Unless the age distributions of the white and black labor forces are identical, this equation is not strictly correct. As the population shares in Table 2.1 suggest, however, the age distributions are fairly similar. We use the age distribution of all workers (white and black) in Table 2.2.

5   A similar decomposition is performed by Duncan and Hoffman (1983) using data on individuals in the Panel Study of Income Dynamics (PSID). Duncan and Hoffman conclude that about one half of the decline in the black–white wage gap (for southern-born and northern born-workers) between the late 1960s and the late 1970s is attributable to cohort effects.

6   Appendix B reports cohort-specific measures of relative earnings, schooling, and rates of return to schooling for whites and blacks born in the south.

7   Between 1970 and 1980 the return to education for white workers in the 21–30 age group fell dramatically, while the return to education for black workers was roughly constant. However, the change for whites was counteracted by a corresponding *increase* in the coefficient associated with the linear experience term.

8   These rates of return are estimated from linear regressions that contain the same control variables as used in the regressions underlying Table 2.4. Similar results are found for 1960 and 1970.

9   Starting in 1918, the data are available biennially. As noted in Anderson (1988), many counties in the deep south did not provide public high schools for black students until the mid-1920s: thus, our quality indicators, which pertain to publicly supported schools, may be mismeasured for higher-educated blacks born before 1915.

10   The eighteen states with available data are Alabama, Arkansas, Delaware, D. C., Florida, Georgia, Kentucky, Louisiana, Maryland, Mississippi, Missouri, North Carolina, Oklahoma, South Carolina, Tennessee, Texas, Virginia, and West Virginia. With the exception of Missouri these states comprise the Southern region as defined by the Bureau of the Census.

11   Data for some years are taken from periodic reports on black and white schools compiled by the Office of Education, e.g. Blose and Caliver (1936). A complete catalog of the sources used to collect the school quality data is available from the authors on request.

12   There is some reason for concern about the accuracy of the data in the early part of our sample. We have tried to eliminate obvious errors in individual reports and have cross-checked the data whenever possible. We have also compared reported teacher salaries with mean annual earnings by state and race for teachers in the 1940, 1950, and 1960 Censuses, and found very high correlations between the two series (e.g. 0.95 in 1940).

13   The estimates in the table are based on data from the National Survey of Black Americans (NSBA) and the General Social Survey (GSS). The NSBA survey is described in Jackson and Gurin (1987), and the GSS survey is described in Davis and Smith (1990). These tabulations are based on Southern-born men with the relevant level of schooling.

14   In the later years of our sample, some border states show substantial levels of racial integration. In these cases we have assigned white and black schools the same (overall) quality averages. Some states, including Mississippi and Louisiana, continued to publish school data by race until the mid-1960s. Whenever possible, we have used data from the state reports. Term lengths for black and white students were essentially equal by 1954; so we use the overall term length figures for whites and blacks.

15   Data for 1955–1957 are reported in SERS (1959). Data for later years appear in various issues of "Status of School Segregation and Desegregation in the Southern and Border States."

16   The underlying state-level data are weighted by enrollments to obtain the overall averages used in Figure 2.1.

17   There is a noticeable break in the relative teacher wage series for Mississippi in 1955. For other states, however, there is little indication of a trend shift after 1954.

18   It should be stressed that other dimensions of relative school quality may have lagged behind the measures that we concentrate on. Bond (1934, pp. 151–171) notes that expenditures on schoolhouses, equipment, and school buses for white students rose very quickly in the early 1930s, while similar expenditures for black students lagged.

19   West Virginia and Washington, D.C., were unusual for the quality of schools provided to blacks early in the twentieth century. The unique circumstances of the federal district (including the availability of federal funds) clearly affected the situation in D.C. See United States Commissioner of Education (1871, reprinted 1969) for a detailed survey of black schools in D.C. on the eve of the Civil War.

20   The same relationship was true across different counties within the southern states: see Bond (1934, pp. 238–245) and Margo (1990, p. 40).

21   The NAACP campaign was launched in 1934. In anticipation of a more favorable judicial reception in the border states, the first of these lawsuits were filed in Maryland and Virginia. See Bullock (1967) and Margo (1990, Chapter 4).

22	See, for example, the discussions by Griffith (1969, pp. 658–659) and Kirk (1969, p. 1129) of legislative actions in Mississippi and South Carolina to improve black schools in the early 1950s.
23	The states with over 30 percent black population in 1920 are Alabama, Florida, Georgia, Louisiana, Mississippi, and South Carolina.
24	Data in these figures were extended back to 1901 using information from the North Carolina and South Carolina State Reports of Education.
25	See, for example, Harlan (1958). This difference is perhaps partially a reflection of the higher fraction of blacks in South Carolina (58% in 1900 versus 33% in North Carolina), which itself is a legacy of the greater use of slave labor in cotton than tobacco farming (see Fogel and Engerman (1974), pp. 44–45).
26	We use state-of-birth and cohort-specific distributions of completed education among workers in the 1970 Census to form these weighted averages. In much of the analysis in Section 2.3., we limit the sample to individuals who were born in the south and moved north. Here we use distributions of completed education among workers who are observed in the relevant labor markets in 1970. The state-level quality averages differ very little between the entire sample of southern-born workers and the subsample of northern migrants.
27	In other work we have noted that the return to education is virtually zero until the grade attained by the second percentile of the education distribution, and is linear thereafter. Equation (4) ignores this nonlinearity. Nevertheless, the specification is approximately correct given the low levels of educational attainment among the cohorts of southern-born men analyzed here.
28	The sample restrictions imposed on individuals with allocated data or extreme values of wages described in Appendix A are also employed here.
29	These percentages are calculated for black men born 1910–1949, as of 1970. The sample sizes are presented in Appendix A.
30	On the other hand, we are aware that an objection could be raised that migrants are a nonrandom sample. Any bias from this nonrandomness must stem from a correlation between the propensity to migrate, unobserved school quality, and measured school quality in the state. Most research suggests that southern out-migrants were better educated than nonmigrants (e.g. Margo 1990). Thus, the most likely scenario would imply a downward bias in the estimated effect of school quality because, given a fixed school quality threshold for migration, the unobserved component of school quality for individuals in our sample will be negatively correlated with measured school quality in the state.
31	Notice that some of the parameters in the model could be freed up even further. For example, the state fixed effects could be allowed to differ by race. When we relax these restrictions, however, none of the main conclusions are altered.
32	The survey asks respondents to identify the place they lived the most between age six and sixteen; we use this as a measure of where they grew up.
33	Although the sample size is relatively small, we also computed the fraction of southern-born blacks observed living in the north at the time of the survey who report that they grew up in their state of birth. This fraction is 68 percent for individuals born between 1900 and 1949.
34	Assigning an individual the school quality in his state of birth leads to estimated state-specific returns that are weighted averages of the returns to education in the various states where an individual actually attended school, with weights equal to the probabilities of attending school in a state conditional on the state of birth. This then leads to a downward measurement-error bias in the estimated quality effects in the second-stage regression. Our analysis of returns to education for white men (Card and Krueger 1992a, see Chapter 1) suggests that the bias is on the order of 10 percent.

Notes

35   The quality index is the product of coefficient estimates of the effects of pupil–teacher ratio, term length, and teacher wage on the return to education for white men reported in Card and Krueger (1992), and the corresponding measures of school quality for black schools in each state.

36   We formed an estimate of the average pupil–teacher ratio for men from each state and race group using a simple average of the data for each of the three cohorts reported in Appendix C.

37   The dependent variables in Tables 2.7 and 2.8 differ from the returns reported in Table 2.6 only in that they are estimated separately for each ten-year birth group in the 1960, 1970, and 1980 Censuses. The second-step regressions are estimated by weighted least squares, using the inverse sampling variances of the estimated returns to education as weights.

38   We suspect that this apparent widening arises from the fact that we impose the same year effects on the return to education for all age groups. Relative returns to education for older cohorts of blacks rose between 1970 and 1980, but not for the youngest (1940–1949) cohort (see Appendix B). The regression model thus underpredicts the rate of return for blacks in the 1940–1949 cohort in 1980 and attributes part of the underprediction to a permanent cohort effect.

39   Although we believe that it is safe to take the pupil–teacher ratio as exogenously determined for blacks in the south for these cohorts, we have experimented with using the fraction of blacks in the state's population as an instrument for the pupil–teacher ratio. The instrumental variables estimates are very close to the OLS estimates reported in Table 2.7.

40   The F-statistic for a test of the joint significance of the state effects in column 3 is 2.29, with a probability value of 0.007.

41   A higher price for skill after 1980 is hypothesized by Juhn, Murphy, and Pierce (1991) to explain the widening of the black–white wage gap over the last decade.

42   The sample contains eighteen states and three cohorts (1910–1919, 1920–1929 and 1930–1939), for a total of fifty-four observations.

43   In this subsample the average black-white gap in the return to education closed by 1.61 percent between 1960 and 1980 (slightly more than in the overall sample).

44   Notice that the inclusion of the teacher wage variable by itself renders the state effects statistically insignificant

45   Notice that this differenced specification is equivalent to a model for the level of average wages that includes 180 state-by-year-by-cohort dummies.

46   None of the conclusions from this analysis is qualitatively altered if the underlying data are limited to the sample of men who moved to the nine Northern labor markets considered earlier.

47   The entries in Table 2.9 are formed as weighted averages of the cohort-year wage gaps for each state, using the inverse sampling variances of the cohort-year observations as weights.

48   The absence of teacher wage data forces us to drop all the observations from Kentucky, Missouri, and Tennessee in columns 3–7. The deletion of these states significantly curtails the range of variation in the relative school quality variables.

49   It is interesting to note that simultaneity effects might have been expected to create a positive bias in the estimated effect of the pupil–teacher variable. Holding constant the number of teachers, an increase in enrollment leads to an increase in the pupil–teacher ratio.

50   See Heckman and Payner (1989) for a study of changes in the racial composition of employment in the South Carolina textile industry.

Chapter 3

1   If *all* the estimates with unknown signs are counted as negative, the odds are still less than one in 100. On the other hand, Hanushek finds a much weaker pattern for the teacher–pupil ratio. But one must wonder whether some of these studies controlled for both the teacher–pupil ratio and expenditures per student in their estimating equations.

2   This model is developed formally in Card and Krueger (1996a). Also see Lang (1993) for a related model.

3   This analysis ignores any general equilibrium effects of changing the endowment of human capital. This assumption can be justified if the school system under consideration is small relative to the rest of the economy, so the price of human capital is set exogenously in the market.

4   Examples of this literature include Morgan and Sirageldin (1968), Johnson and Stafford (1973) and Rizzuto and Wachtel (1980). An example that found an insignificant positive effect of school resources is Ribich and Murphy (1975).

5   School spending per student in the NLS data pertains to the average secondary school in the district where the worker lived.

6   A seminal paper of this genre is by Behrman and Birdsall (1983), which studies school resources in Brazil. Because the emphasis in this chapter is on the United States, however, we do not describe their findings in detail.

7   By analogy, a high-quality undergraduate economics program is likely to have its most beneficial effect on students who continue on to graduate school. Would any department chair want his or her program evaluated on the basis of a sample that explicitly excludes students who continue on to graduate school?

8   Although Heckman, Layne-Farrar, and Todd (1996) find that school resources have a varying effect on the earnings–education slope across regions, in the average region, a smaller pupil–teacher ratio is associated with a higher payoff to additional education.

9   Betts (1995) does not adjust the standard errors of his estimates for the fact that there are as many as 10 wage observations per individual in the NLSY sample. Betts generously provided us with his data, and we have used his sample to calculate standard errors that account for the correlation across earnings residuals for the same individual over time. This adjustment raises the estimated standard errors by up to 100 percent.

10   These elasticities are calculated at the means of their respective data sets. The t-ratio of the Card and Krueger estimate reported in this paragraph is 6.2; for the Betts estimate, it is 1.7. However, both t-ratios are probably overstated because of multiple earnings observations per worker or per state. In specifications that include cumulative work experience rather than age, Betts finds a weaker effect of the teacher – pupil ratio. Because work experience may be influenced by educational attainment, which in turn may be influenced by school resources, we chose to hold constant age instead of experience in the reduced form models in Chapter 2.

11   The data used to construct this figure are taken primarily from the U.S. Office of Education's Biennial Survey of Education and from various state education reports.

12   Despite the 1954 Brown vs. Board of Education decision, substantial school integration did not begin until the mid-1960s.

13   Interestingly, the data show that South Carolina blacks in the earliest birth cohorts were more likely to move to higher wage urban areas outside the south than North Carolina blacks. Without any adjustment for region of residence, average wages of South Carolina blacks in the earlier cohorts are therefore quite similar to averages for North Carolina blacks.

14 The 12-student reduction in relative class size is roughly a 28 percent reduction; that is, average class size in North Carolina for the 1900–1909 cohort of blacks was 55.7, and for the 1940–1949 cohort, was 31.

Chapter 4

1 There is also debate over what should be the appropriate measure of school outputs (see Card and Krueger (1996a)). Whereas education researchers tend to analyze standardized test scores, economists tend to focus on students' educational attainment and subsequent earnings

2 Hanushek attributes this difference to omitted state-level variables that bias the state-level studies, although it is possible that endogenous resource decisions within states (e.g. assignment of weaker students to smaller classes as required by compensatory education) bias the within-state micro-data estimates, and that the interstate estimates are unbiased.

3 If a school had more than one small class, students could be moved between small classes.

4 This section draws heavily from Folger (1989) and Word et al. (1990).

5 Participating schools had an average per-pupil expenditure in 1986–1987 of $2,724, compared with the statewide average of $2,561.

6 The reason that regular classes often had a teacher aide is that the ethic underlying the study was that students in the control group (i.e., regular classes) would not be prevented from receiving resources that they ordinarily would receive.

7 The procedure for randomly assigning students was as follows, Each school prepared an alphabetized enrollment list. Algorithms were centrally prepared which assigned every kth student to a class type; the algorithm was tailored to the number of enrolled students. A random starting point was used by each school to apply the algorithm. The schools were audited to ensure that they followed procedures for random assignment.

8 I thank Jayne Zaharias for providing the enrollment sheets. The sample I analyze excludes twins; schools were allowed to assign twins to the same class if that was the school's ordinary practice.

9 To be precise, the fraction on free lunch actually measures the fraction who receive free or reduced-price lunch.

10 In two cases the p-value was less than 10. Third grade teachers assigned to small classes were less likely to have a master's degree or higher than were teachers assigned regular-size classes, and first grade teachers in small classes had two more years of experience than those in regular-size classes (although less experience than those in regular/aide classes).

11 Formally, denote the cumulative distribution of scores on test j (denoted T^j) of students in the regular and regular/aide classes as $F^R (T^j) = $ prob $[T^j_{Ri} < T^j] = y^j$. For each student i in a small class, we then calculated $F^R(T^j_{Si}) = y^j_{Si}$. Naturally, the distribution of y^j for students in regular classes follows a uniform distribution. We then calculated the average of the three (or two for BSF) percentile rankings for each student. If one subtest score was missing, we took the average of the two percentiles that were available; and if two were missing, we used the percentile score corresponding to the only available test.

12 Note that because we have averaged over three percentile scores, the distributions are not uniform for students assigned to regular classes.

13 The robust standard errors are about two-thirds larger than the OLS standard errors. The estimated standard deviation of the class effects (μ_{cs}) is about 8 in the models in column 4.

14 Ninety-nine percent of the students are white or black. The small number of

Asian students are included with white students in the analysis. The small number of hispanic students and others are included with the black students.

15   In the case of a student who left the sample but later returned, the average test score in the years surrounding the student's absence was used. Test scores were also imputed for students who had a missing test score but did not exit the sample (e.g. because they were absent when the test was conducted). This technique is closely related to the "last-observation-carry-forward" method that has been used in clinical studies.

16   The coefficient on the regular/aide initial assignment dummy is also quite similar if the model is estimated with or without the imputed data.

17   Because the teacher aide was found to have a small effect in Table 4.5, we do not hold constant the availability of an aide in equation (4). One could, however, add a dummy indicating the presence of a full-time aide to equation (4).

18   To interpret this model as yielding the causal effect of current class size on achievement, it is necessary to assume that initial class assignment only affects current test scores by affecting current class size. If previous class sizes affect current performance, initial assignment will be correlated with the error term in equation (4). Of course, in the kindergarten year this assumption is not controversial, but it may not hold in later grades.

19   The other covariates in this regression are the same as in column 3 of Table 4.9.

20   Inner-city schools were defined as schools in metropolitan areas in which more than half of students received free lunch; suburban was defined as the balance of metropolitan area schools; towns were defined as areas with more than 2500 inhabitants; and rural was defined as areas with fewer than 2,500 inhabitants.

21   To adjust for sampling variability in the coefficient estimates, the average squared standard error was subtracted from the variance of the estimated coefficients.

22   For an interesting study that finds little evidence of Hawthorne effects in the original Hawthorne experiments, see Jones (1992). One could argue in the current context that each individual teacher in small classes has an incentive to free ride rather than work extra hard.

23   The standard deviation of class size in the sample of students assigned to regular classes is 2.3, as compared with 4.1 among all students in the experiment.

24   These regression results are reported in table 12 of Krueger (1997).

Chapter 5

1   A classic example of this reasoning is the effect of the federal minimum wage in Puerto Rico. See Reynolds (1965).

2   Using the Consumer Price Index for all items, the real federal minimum wage in January 1950 was $4.08 (in 1990 dollars). It ranged between $3.64 (in 1954) and $6.00 (in 1968). Its value in 1989 was $3.53.

3   The widespread setting of state minimum wages above the federal rate was unprecedented. For example, Cullen (1960) observed that the federal minimum wage had served as a *ceiling* for state-specific minimum rates during the period from 1940 to 1960.

4   See Bureau of National Affairs (undated, 91: 14, 15–22).

5   A similar evaluation methodology figured prominently in many early studies of minimum wage laws (see especially Lester 1965: 518–523), but that approach has been largely supplanted in the literature by aggregate time-series studies (for example, Welch 1976; Brown, Gilroy, and Kohen 1982, 1983; Wellington 1991).

6   The Construction of the wage variable is explained below.

7   The Census Bureau allocates responses for individuals who do not answer the earnings questions in the CPS (about 3% of teenage workers). To avoid measurement error, I do not use the earnings data for these individuals.

8   To avoid problems posed by measurement error, I set the wage including tips equal to the reported straight-time hourly wage *unless* the difference between average weekly earnings including tips and the product of the straight-time wage and usual weekly hours is positive. The average wage measures in Table 5.1 also exclude individuals with reported or imputed wages less than $1 per hour or greater than $20 per hour.

9   Under the pre-1989 law, employers in retail trade, agriculture, and higher education were permitted to pay full-time students a subminimum wage 15% below the regular rate. The available evidence suggests that use of this exemption was relatively modest. Freeman, Gray, and Ichniowski (1981) estimate that only 3 percent of student hours in the late 1970s (when the minimum was relatively high) were worked under the subminimum provisions.

10   The standard errors of the 1989 and 1990 employment rates for all teenagers in the top row of Table 5.1 are both 0.4 percent. The standard error for the change in employment rates between 1989 and 1990 is 0.5 percent.

11   The regression is estimated with data for 1975–1989. The fitted equation is Teen Employment = Constant -0.86 * Trend +2.17 Overall Employment Rate, with an R^2 of 0.99.

12   If the prediction equation is re-estimated including the logarithm of the real value of the federal minimum wage (deflated by the Consumer Price Index), the estimated minimum wage coefficient is -2.5, with a standard error of L7. This coefficient implies that a 10 percent increase in the minimum wage will reduce teenage employment by 0.25 percent – a smaller effect than is usually estimated in the literature (Wellington 1991).

13   See Grossman (1983) for an earlier analysis of this spillover hypothesis.

14   The model is estimated on data for 1989 and 1990. The implied elasticity of the teenage employment rate with respect to the overall employment rate is 1.70 (with a standard error of 0.83).

15   I have weighted the regression model by the average CPS extract size for each state. Unweighted results are very similar.

16   One potential issue in the estimation of standard errors for the models in Table 5.4 is the presence of systematic correlation between the residuals of nearby states. This "spatial correlation" will tend to lead to understated standard errors. As a rough check, I computed the Durbin-Watson (DW) statistics for the residuals. If the states are sorted by region, this computation provides a test for spatial correlation. The DW statistics for both the wage and employment models are very close to 2, giving no evidence of spatial correlation.

17   The dependent variable in Table 5.5 is the state-specific change in the teenage employment rate between the last three quarters of 1989 and the last three quarters of 1990. The lagged change in the teenage employment–population ratio is based on data for all four quarters of 1988 and 1989.

18   A similar pattern for overall state-level employment is suggested by the results in Topel (1986).

Chapter 6

1   See Brown, Gilroy, and Kohen (1982, 1983) for surveys of this literature. A later update (Wellington 1991) concludes that the employment effects of the minimum wage are negative but small: a 10 percent increase in the minimum

2   is estimated to lower teenage employment rates by 0.06 percentage points.

2   At the time we were uncertain whether the $5.05 rate would go into effect or be overridden.

3   In a pilot survey Katz and Krueger (1992) obtained very low response rates from McDonald's restaurants. For this reason, McDonald's restaurants were excluded from Katz and Krueger's and our sample frames.

4   The sample was derived from white-pages telephone listings for New Jersey and Pennsylvania as of February 1992.

5   Copies of the questionnaires used in both waves of the survey are available from the authors upon request.

6   Response rates per call-back were almost identical in the two states. Among New Jersey stores, 44.5 percent responded on the first call, and 72.0 percent responded after at most two call-backs. Among Pennsylvania stores 42.2 percent responded on the first call, and 71.6 percent responded after at most two call-backs.

7   As of April 1993 the store closed because of road construction and one of the stores closed for renovation had reopened. The store closed by fire was open when our telephone interviewer called in November 1992 but refused the interview. By the time of the follow-up personal interview a mall fire had closed the store.

8   We discuss the sensitivity of our results to alternative assumptions on the measurement of employment in Section 6.3.3.

9   These programs offer current employees a cash "bounty" for recruiting any new employee who stays on the job for a minimum period of time. Typical bounties are $50–$75. Recruiting programs that award the recruiter with an "employee of the month" designation or other noncash bonuses are excluded from our tabulations.

10   These restaurants were interviewed twice because their phone numbers appeared in more than one phone book, and neither the interviewer nor the respondent noticed that they were previously interviewed.

11   Similar reliability ratios for very similar questions were obtained by Katz and Krueger (1992).

12   A probit analysis of the probability of closure shows that the initial size of the store is a significant predictor of closure. The level of starting wages has a numerically small and statistically insignificant coefficient in the probit model.

13   An alternative possibility is that seasonal factors produce higher employment at fast-food restaurants in February and March than in November and December. An analysis of national employment data for food preparation and service workers, however, shows higher average employment in the fourth quarter than in the first quarter.

14   To investigate the cyclicality of fast-food restaurant sales we regressed the year-to-year change in U.S. sales of the McDonald's restaurant chain from 1976–1991 on the corresponding change in the unemployment rate. The regression results show that a 1-percentage-point increase in the unemployment rate reduces sales by $257 million, with a t statistic of 3.0.

15   A regression of the proportional wage change between waves 1 and 2 on has a coefficient of 1.03.

16   In a regression model without other controls the expected attenuation of the GAP coefficient due to measurement error is the reliability ratio of GAP (γ_o), which we estimate at 0.70. The expected attenuation factor when region dummies are added to the model is $\gamma_1 = (\gamma_o - R^2)/(1 - R^2)$, where R^2 is the R-square statistic of a regression of GAP on region effects (equal to 0.30). Thus, we expect the estimated GAP coefficient to fall by a factor of $\gamma_1/\gamma_o = 0.8$ when region dummies are added to a regression model.

17   These specifications are reported in table 4 of Card and Krueger (1993).

18   The proportional change in employment is defined as the change in

employment divided by the average level of employment in waves 1 and 2. This results in very similar coefficients but smaller standard errors than the alternative of dividing by wave 1 employment. For closed stores we set the proportional change in employment to -1.

19   Analysis of the 1991 Current Population Survey reveals that part-time workers in the restaurant industry work about 46 percent as many hours as full-time workers. Katz and Krueger (1992) report that the ratio of part-time workers' hours to full-time workers' hours in the fast-food industry is 0.57.

20   We also added dummies for the interview dates for the wave 1 survey, but these were insignificant and did not change the estimated minimum-wage effects.

21   Assuming average employment of 20.4 in New Jersey, the 14.92 GAP coefficient in row 1, column 2 implies an employment elasticity of 0.73.

22   The "070" three-digit zip-code area (around Newark) and the "080" three-digit zip-code area (around Camden) have by far the largest numbers of stores among three-digit zip-code areas in New Jersey, and together they account for 36 percent of New Jersey stores in our sample.

23   In the other 19 percent of stores, full-time workers are paid more, typically 10 percent more.

24   Within New Jersey, the fraction of full-time employees increased about as quickly at stores with higher and lower wages in wave 1.

25   In wave 1, the average time to a first wage increase was 18.9 weeks, and the average amount of the first increase was $0.21 per hour.

26   Katz and Krueger (1992) report that a significant fraction of fast-food stores in Texas responded to an increase in the minimum wage by raising wages for workers who were initially earning more than the new minimum rate. Our results on the slope of the tenure profile are consistent with their findings.

27   According to the McDonald's Corporation 1991 Annual Report, payroll and benefits are 31.3 percent of operating costs at company-owned stores. This calculation is only approximate because minimum-wage workers make up less than half of payroll even though they are about half of workers, and because a rise in the minimum wage causes some employers to increase the pay of other higher-wage workers in order to maintain relative pay differentials.

28   The effect is attributable to a 2.0 percent increase in prices in New Jersey and a 1.0 percent decrease in prices in Pennsylvania.

29   Direct inquiries to the chains in our sample revealed that Wendy's opened two stores in New Jersey in 1992 and one store in Pennsylvania. The other chains were unwilling to provide information on new openings.

30   We used the 1986 Current Population Survey (merged monthly file) to construct the minimum-wage variables. State minimum-wage rates in 1990 were obtained from the Bureau of National Affairs Labor Relations Reporter Wages and Hours Manual (undated).

31   The employment rate of individuals age 25 and older fell by 2.6 percent in New Jersey between 1991 and 1992, while it rose by 0.3 percent in Pennsylvania, and fell by 0.2 percent in the United States as a whole.

32   Daniel G. Sullivan (1989) and Michael R Ransom (1993) present empirical results for nurses and university teachers that suggest monopsony-like behavior of employers.

Chapter 7

1   In the March 1995 version of their paper, NW relied exclusively on 71 observations collected by EPI. Subsequent versions have also included information from their supplemental data collection.

2	The ES-202 data are also known as the Business Establishment List.
3	The first question on the Pennsylvania form requests the "Total covered employees in pay period md. 12th of month." Employers are asked to report employment for each month of the quarter. A copy of these forms is available from the authors on request. Other points to note about the ES-202 data include: they are not restricted to employers with any minimum number of employees, or to employees who have earned any minimum pay in the pay period; there is no information on hours of work; the pay period may vary across employers, or within employers for different workers; employees on vacation or sick leave should be included if they are paid while absent from work.
4	For confidentiality reasons, BLS has requested that we not reveal the identity or number of these chains. We can report, however, that there are fewer than 10 chains in the sample.
5	We reached this conclusion by comparing the distribution of restaurants by three-digit zip code and chain in the two data sets.
6	Additionally, to ensure that the sample consisted exclusively of restaurants (as opposed to, e.g. headquarters or monitoring posts), the authors restricted the sample to establishments with an average of five or more employees in February and March 1994, and average monthly payroll per employee below $3,000 in 1992:Ql and 1992:Q4. These restrictions eliminated 17 observations from the original sample of 704 observations.
7	An interviewer visited all of the nonresponding stores in both states to determine if they were closed in our original survey.
8	In one case, employment was zero in March 1992, so the February figure was used.
9	This approach differs from Card and Krueger (1994, see Chapter 6 in this volume), which weights part-time workers by 0.5 to derive full-time equivalent employment.
10	Although Neumark and Wascher (2000, footnote 9) argue that variability in employment growth should be smaller for fast-food restaurants in a small geographic area than in a sample such as Davis, Haltiwanger, and Schuh (1996) set of manufacturing establishments, it should be noted that gross employment flows are considerably higher in the retail trade sector than in the manufacturing sector (see Lane, Stevens, and Burgess 1996).
11	The proportionate employment change was calculated as the change in employment divided by the initial level of employment. We use total number of full-time and part-time workers in our data for comparability to the BLS data. Neumark and Wascher (2000) show that some other wags of measuring the proportionate change of employment (e.g. using average employment in the denominator) and some sample restrictions (e.g. eliminating closed stores from the sample) increases the dispersion in our data relative to theirs.
12	Observations that are not reported as subunits of multiunit establishments are either part of a multiunit reporting firm or the only restaurant owned by a particular reporting unit.
13	Because, in principle, the BLS sample contains the population of fast-food restaurants in the designated chains, an argument could be made that the OLS standard errors understate the precision of the estimates. Nonetheless, throughout the chapter we rely on conventional tests of statistical significance.
14	Large negative employment changes are more likely because of restaurant closings.
15	The BNW data that we analyze were downloaded from www.econ.msu.edu in November 1997.
16	A referee pointed out to us that Neumark and Wascher (2000, appendix A) offers a different rationale for taking over the data collection, namely, "to get data on all types of restaurants represented in CK's data."
17	The most recent version of NW's data set at the time the paper on which this

chapter is based first appeared includes an indicator variable for restaurants collected by EPI, This variable shows a total of 81 restaurants in the EPI sample, representing the 72 restaurants in the original Berman sample and the 9 restaurants which were provided directly to EPI after March 1995.

18   Neumark and Wascher's letter to franchisees stated that they planned to "reexamine the New Jersey-Pennsylvania minimum-wage study" and emphasized that they were working "in conjunction with ... a restaurant-supported lobbying" organization. This lead-in may have affected response patterns for restaurants with different employment trends in New Jersey and Pennsylvania, accounting for their low response rate. We asked David Neumark if he could provide us with the survey form that EPI used to gather their data, and he informed us, "To the best of my knowledge there was no form; this was all solicited by phone" (e-mail correspondence, December 8, 1997).

19   BNW's sample universe covers a broader region of eastern Pennsylvania than ours because BNW define their geographic area based on our three-digit zip codes. These zip codes encompass 19 counties, although our sample universe only included restaurants in 7 counties.

20   Among the subset of stores that reported nonmanagement employment, the difference-in-differences in average payroll hours/35 is -0.43, with a standard error of 0.55. Thus, there is no strong difference between relative payroll hours trends in the pooled BNW sample and among the subset of restaurants that reported nonmanagement employment.

21   To compare relative changes in hours and employees it is convenient to work with logarithms, so scaling is not an issue. For the sample of 55 observations that reported both numbers of employees and hours, the difference-in-differences of log payroll hours is -0.018; the difference-in-differences of log nonmanagement employees is 0.066; and the difference-in-differences of log employees minus log hours is 0.084 (t-ratio = 2.28). Thus, the apparent opposite movement in hours and employees is statistically significant for this small sample.

22   In view of this fact, we disagree with Neumark and Wascher's (2000) assertion that because they collected hours worked for a "well-defined payroll period (which is specified as either weekly, biweekly or monthly)" the BNW data set should provide a more reliable measure of employment changes than our survey data. Because Neumark and Wascher failed to collect the dates covered by their payroll periods, or the number of days the store was in operation during their payroll periods, there are potential problems such as the correlation between employment growth and the reporting interval that cannot be explained in their data.

23   These factors are unlikely to be a problem in our original survey data or in the BLS data because the number of workers on the payroll should be unaffected by temporary shutdowns, and because the BLS consistently collected employment for the payroll period containing the 12th day of the month. It is possible that weather and holiday factors account for the contrasting results discussed previously for hours versus number of workers in the BNW data set.

24   This franchisee supplied data on 23 restaurants (all in Pennsylvania) to the original Berman/EPI data-collection effort, and on three additional restaurants (all in New Jersey) to NW's later sample.

25   The first three digits of the postal zip code do not correspond to any conventional geographic entity.

26   The situation is more complex if the BNW data are treated as a noisy measure of the truth, e.g. because of sampling or nonsampling errors. In particular, let λ_j represent the reliability of the observed employment changes (by zip code and chain) in survey j ($j = 1, 2$). In this case, if the measurement errors in the two surveys are uncorrelated, the probability limit of the regression

coefficient from a linear regression of the employment change in survey 1 on the change in survey 2 is λ_2 (the reliability of the second survey), and the probability limit of the R^2 is $\lambda_1 \cdot \lambda_2$ (the product of the reliability ratios).

27   Only the subsample of cells with nonmissing data in both cell-level data sets was used in the analysis.

28   At the restaurant level this proportionate gap is defined as the difference between the new minimum wage and the restaurant's starting wage in wave 1 divided by the starting wage in wave 1. (The gap is set to zero if the starting wage is above the new minimum wage.) The *GAP* measure in our regressions is the weighted average of the restaurant-level proportionate gaps, where the weights are the number of restaurants in the cell.

29   The wage-gap variable was assigned a value of zero for all Pennsylvania restaurants. Including dummy variables that indicate whether restaurants are located in Pennsylvania or New Jersey thus completely absorbs interstate variability in the wage-gap variable.

30   The BLS-790 data are revised after their initial release. We are uncertain of when Neumark and Wascher assembled their data set; however, their data for 1982–1994 are identical to the data available as of January 1999. The data we used for the estimates in the table are the final BLS employment estimates, and not subject to revision.

31   Similarly, using the revised data affects their estimates based on December-to-December changes. The minimum-wage coefficient from the model in panel A, column 4, of their Table 10 falls to -0.12 (standard error 0.08) with the revised data.

32   Again, a similar pattern is found using the December-to-December changes in the BLS-790 data also analyzed by Neumark and Wascher. In particular, the estimated coefficient of the minimum-wage variable falls to -009 (standard error 0.07) controlling for December-to-December changes in unemployment.

Chapter 8

1   See the survey of implicit contracting models by Sherwin Rosen (1985). A concise summary of the implications of these models from a macroeconomic perspective is presented by Stanley Fischer (1987, pp. 42–50).

2   Much of the earlier literature on nominal contracting models focuses on their implications for aggregate price and wage dynamics: see Taylor (1980) and Orley Ashenfelter and David Card (1982). A study by Shaghil Ahmed (1987) correlates the degree of wage flexibility in an industry, measured by the elasticity of indexation among indexed labor contracts, with the slope of the industry-specific Phillips curve. Ahmed's measure of wage flexibility is based on a sample of only 98 contracts in 20 industries, and fails to take into account any of the characteristics of the nonindexed contracts in an industry. Furthermore, his measure of flexibility only pertains to workers in large union contracts and ignores variation across industries in the extent of unionization or the share of large firms. Thus, I do not interpret his findings as strong evidence for or against the hypothesis that nominal contract rigidities are important. The approach taken by Mark Bils (1989) is perhaps most similar to that in this chapter. He compares the variability of industry employment growth in months with a significant number of contract negotiations to the variability in other months.

3   John Kennan (1988) presents an illuminating analysis of the difficulties that arise in the interpretation of aggregate employment and wage data when the data are generated by a simple model of demand and supply.

4   The nature of typical indexation formulas in North American labor contracts

Notes

is described in my 1983 paper. The only case in which the real wage is set directly by the parties is the case of a contract in which nominal wages are indexed to the consumer price level with a formula that increases the wage by one percent for each percentage point increase in prices. Such formulas are rare, particularly in the manufacturing sector of the United States and Canada.

5   This point is made by Wallace E. Hendricks and Lawrence M. Kahn (1987).

6   It is interesting to compare this procedure to the one suggested by Bennett T. McCallum (1976) for the estimation of a structural equation that contains the expected value of a future endogenous variable. McCallum's procedure replaces the expected future value by its actual value and uses the predicted value (from a linear forecasting equation) as an instrumental variable. His procedure therefore eliminates simultaneity bias induced by a correlation between the dependent variable and the unexpected component of the explanatory variable. In the present context, the simultaneity bias arises from a correlation between the dependent variable and the expected value of the explanatory variable. Hence, the proposed instrument is the unexpected component of the explanatory variable.

7   This may arise if employers have imperfect information on their relative demand shocks.

8   Unexpectedly low real wage rates could induce an increase in overtime hours, however.

9   Specifically, the Cobb–Douglas assumption implies that the output supply equation of the ith firm can be written as

$$y(t) = \gamma_1 w(t) + \gamma_2 v(t) + \gamma_3 r(t) - (\gamma_1 + \gamma_2 + \gamma_3)\, q(t) + \theta(t).$$

where $q(t)$ is the selling price for the output of the firm and $\theta(t)$ represents a total factor productivity shock. Define industry output as a geometric weighted average of the outputs of the individual firms in the industry. Then aggregate output follows a similar equation, and equation (4) can be derived directly, with

$$\phi(t) \equiv \theta(t) - \bar{\theta}(t) - (\gamma_1 + \gamma_2 + \gamma_3)(q(t) - \bar{q}(t)).$$

10   See Robert E. Hall and David Lilien (1979).

11   The implicit contracts literature is reviewed by Sherwin Rosen (1985). See Ian M. McDonald and Robert M. Solow (1981) for a theoretical treatment of efficient contracting and James N. Brown and Orley Ashenfelter (1986) for a concise summary of the empirical implications of simple efficient contracting models.

12   See John M. Abowd (1989) for an attempt to test this hypothesis using stock market data on negotiating firms.

13   This hypothesis can be motivated formally by assuming that employees' preferences are represented by a Cobb–Douglas utility function defined over employment and the difference between the contractual wage and the alternative wage: see Brown and Ashenfelter (1986, p. S54).

14   See Thomas E. MaCurdy and John H. Pencavel (1986), especially p. S13.

15   The data set only includes contracts with 500 or more workers. The sample is drawn from a public use tape distributed by Labour Canada. A complete description of the sample and its derivation is presented in the Data Appendix. Louis N. Christofides and Andrew J. Oswald (1987) have also analyzed employment and wage data drawn from this source.

16   The base wage rate is typically the wage paid to the lowest-skill group covered by the collective bargaining agreement. An important assumption for the analysis in this chapter is that variation over time in intracontract wage differentials is small enough to be safely ignored.

17   The wage and employment indexes represent estimated year effects from

regression equations for contract-to-contract percentage changes in end-of-contract wages and employment. These indexes therefore control for the composition of the set of expiring contracts in each year.

18   The forecasting equation predicts the one-year ahead inflation rate at the negotiation date t as $0.0144 + 0.7858 \, DP(t - 12)$, where $DP(t - 12)$ is the actual percentage change in prices over the preceding 12 months. The two- and three-year-ahead inflation rate forecasts generated by this equation are $0.021 + 0.693 \, DP(t - 12)$, and $0.026 + 0.6135 \, DP(t - 12)$, respectively.

19   The forecast error in end-of-contract real wages is $-(1 - e)\rho$, where ρ is the forecast error in end-of-contract prices, and e is the elasticity of indexation. The average forecast error in real wages is therefore $-(1 - \bar{e})\bar{\rho} + \text{covariance}(e, \rho)$, where $\bar{e}$ is the average elasticity of indexation and $\bar{\rho}$ is the average forecast error in prices.

20   The provincial wage is measured from data collected annually by Labour Canada in its area wage survey. Data in this survey is collected by city. I have used the wage rate for the largest city in each province as a measure of the province-specific wage. See the Data Appendix.

21   This problem is similar to one of estimating the effect of a lagged dependent variable in a panel data model: see Douglas Holtz-Aitken, Whitney Newey, and Harvey S. Rosen (1988).

22   The expected average real wage in each month of the contract is estimated by formulas analogous to equations (6) and (7), using estimates of the expected price level in that month and estimates of the elasticity of indexation as described above. The expected average real wage is an unweighted average of expected monthly rates sampled at six-month intervals throughout the contract period, starting in the first month of the contract.

23   These equations are estimated using the change in prices over the previous contract, the manufacturing wage at the effective date of the previous contract, and year effects for the effective date of the previous contract as instrumental variables for the expected and unexpected components of real wages at the end of the previous contract.

24   It is worth pointing out, however, that aggregate demand shocks (or any other variables that affect all contracts at a point in time) are absorbed by the year effects included in columns 4 and 6.

25   At the suggestion of a referee, I estimated an employment equation that includes unexpected price increases (and year effects) and excludes wages. In this specification the estimated elasticity of employment with respect to unanticipated price increases is 0.23, with a standard error of 0.14.

26   My 1986 paper and that of Stephen I. Nickell and Sushil Wadhwani (1987) report employment specifications that show a positive effect of outside wages, while Brown and Ashenfelter (1986) report positive effects in more than one-half of their specifications.

27   Recall from equation (5) that the elasticity of employment with respect to wages is $-(\beta_1 + \sigma\gamma_1)$, while the elasticity of employment with respect to industry average wages is $\sigma\gamma_1$. An estimate of σ from column 3 of Table 8.5 is 0.39 (the sum of the coefficients of current and last year's output). Using the other estimated coefficients from this equation leads to the estimates of β_1 and γ_1 reported in the text.

28   In principle, the coefficient of the lagged dependent variable will differ, depending on the duration of the previous contract. In view of the imprecision of the estimated partial adjustment coefficients in Table 8.5, however, I have not attempted to address this issue.

References

1. Introduction by the Editors

Blaug, M., Vane, H. R. (Eds.) (2003). Who's Who in Economics, Cheltenham: Edward Elgar Publishing Ltd, 137-38 and 470-71.

Card, D. (1990). The Impact of the Mariel Boatlift on the Miami Labor Market, in: Industrial and Labor Relations Review, 43(2): 245-57.

Card, D., Krueger, A. B. (1994). Minimum Wages and Employment: A Case Study of the Fast-Food Industry in New Jersey and Pennsylvania, in: American Economic Review, 84(4): 772-93. [Chapter 6 in this volume]

Card, D., Krueger, A. B. (1996). School Resources and Student Outcomes: An Overview of the Literature and New Evidence from North and South Carolina, in: Journal of Economic Perspectives, 10(4): 31-50. [Chapter 3 in this volume]

Card, D., Krueger, A. B. (2000). Minimum Wages and Employment: A Case Study of the Fast-Food Industry in New Jersey and Pennsylvania: Reply", in: American Economic Review, 90(5): 1397-420. [Chapter 7 in this volume]

Eichhorst, W., Zimmermann, K. F. (2007). And Then There Were Four ... How Many (and Which) Measures of Active Labor Market Policy Do We Still Need?, in: Applied Economics Quarterly, 53 (3): 243-72.

IZA Compact, Special Issue (November/December 2002). An Improved Economic Framework for Increased Employment – Seven Proposals for a Modern Labor Market Policy in Germany.

IZA Compact, Special Issue (December 2008). Full Employment is not a Utopia – IZA Labor Market Program.

Kennan, J. (1995). The Elusive Effects of Minimum Wage, in: Journal of Economic Literature, 33(4): 1950-65.

Krueger, A. B. (1999). Experimental Estimates of Education Production Functions, in: Quarterly Journal of Economics, 114(2): 497-532. [Chapter 4 in this volume]

Neumark, D., Wascher, W. (2000). Minimum Wages and Employment: A Case Study of the Fast-Food Industry in New Jersey and Pennsylvania: Comment, in: American Economic Review, 90(5): 1362-96.

Schmidt, C. M., Zimmermann, K. F., Fertig, M., Kluve, J. (2001). Perspektiven der Arbeitsmarktpolitik. Internationaler Vergleich und Empfehlungen für Deutschland, Berlin: Springer.

Zimmermann, K. F. (Ed.) (2003). Reformen jetzt! So geht es mit Deutschland wieder aufwärts, Wiesbaden: Gabler.

Zimmermann, K. F. (Ed.) (2006). Deutschland – was nun? Reformen für Wirtschaft und Gesellschaft, München: dtv.

Zimmermann, K. F., Schneider, H., Eichhorst W., Hinte, H., Peichl, A. (2009). Vollbeschäftigung ist keine Utopie: Arbeitsmarktpolitisches Programm des IZA, IZA Standpunkte No. 2., Bonn: IZA.

2. Bibliography Sections II-IV

Abowd, J. M. (1989). The Effect of Wage Bargains on the Stock Market Value of the Firm, in: American Economic Review, 79(4): 774-800.

Ahmed, S. (1987). Wage Stickiness and the Non-Neutrality of Money: A Cross-Industry Analysis, in: Journal of Monetary Economics, 20(1): 25-50.

Akin, J. S., Garfinkel, I. (1980). The Quality of Education and Cohort Variation in Black-White Earnings Differentials: Comment, in: American Economic Review, 70(1): 186-91.

Altonji, J., Dunn, T. (1996). Using Siblings to Estimate the Effect of School Quality on Wages, in: Review of Economics and Statistics, 87(4): 665-71.

Anderson, J. D. (1988). The Education of Blacks in the South, 1860-1935. Chapel Hill: University of North Carolina Press.

Angrist, J., Krueger, A. B. (1991). Does Compulsory Schooling Affect Schooling and Earnings?, in: Quarterly Journal of Economics, 106(4): 979-1014.

Angrist, J. Lavy, V. (1999). Using Maimonides' Rule to Estimate the Effect of Class Size on Children's Academic Achievement, in: Quarterly Journal of Economics, 114(2): 533-76.

Ashenfelter, O. C., Krueger, A. B. (1994). Estimates of the Economic Return to Schooling from a New Sample of Twins, in: American Economic Review, 84(5): 1157-73.

Ashenfelter, O. C., Card, D. (1982). Time-Series Representations of Economic Variables and Alternative Models of the Labour Market, in: Review of Economic Studies, 49(5): 761-82.

Ashenfelter, O. C. (1970). Changes in Labor Market Discrimination over Time, in: Journal of Human Resources, 5(4): 403-30.

Bank of Canada Review (various issues). Ottawa: Bank of Canada.

Barro, R. J. (1977). Long Term Contracting, Sticky Prices, and Monetary Policy, in: Journal of Monetary Economics, 3(3): 305-16.

Behrman, J. R., Birdsall, N. (1983). The Quality of Schooling: Quantity Alone Is Misleading, in: American Economic Review, 73(5): 928-46.

Berman, R. (1995). The Crippling Flaws in the New Jersey Fast-Food Study, Washington, DC: Employment Policies Institute.

Betts, J. R. (1995). Does School Quality Matter? Evidence from the National Longitudinal Survey of Youth, in: Review of Economics and Statistics, 77(2): 231-50.

Betts, J. R. (1996). Is There a Link Between School Inputs and Earnings? Fresh Scrutiny of an Old Literature, in: Burtless, G. (Ed.), Does Money Matter? The Effect of School Resources on Student Achievement and Adult Success, Washington, DC: Brookings Institution, 141-91.

Blanchard, O. J., Summers, L. H. (1986). Hysteresis and the European Unemployment Problem, in: Fischer, S. (Ed.), NBER Macroeconomics Annual, Cambridge: MIT Press, 15-78.

Blanchard, O. J., Summers, L. H., Kiyotaki, N. (1987). Monopolistic Competition and the Effects of Aggregate Demand, in: American Economic Review, 77(4): 647-66.

Blose, D. T., Caliver, A. (1936). Statistics of the Education of Negroes, Washington, DC: Government Printing Office.

Bond, H. M. (1934). The Education of the Negro in the American Social Order, New York, NY: Prentice Hall.

Boozer, M., Krueger, A. B., Wolkon, S. (1992). Race and School Quality since Brown vs. Board of Education, in: Baily, M. N., Winston, C. (Eds.), Brookings Papers on Economic Activity: Microeconomics, Washington, DC: Brookings Institution, 269-326.

Brown, C. (1982). The Federal Attack on Labor Market Discrimination: The Mouse that Roared?, in: Polacheck, S. W. (Ed.), Research in Labor Economics, Vol. 5, Greenwich, CT: JAI Press, 33-68.

Brown, C., Gilroy, C., Kohen, A. (1982). The Effect of the Minimum Wage on Employment and Unemployment, in: Journal of Economic Literature, 20(2): 487-528.

Brown, C., Gilroy, C., Kohen, A. (1983). Time Series Evidence on the Effect of the Minimum Wage on Youth Employment and Unemployment, in: Journal of Human Resources, 18(1): 3-31.

Brown, J. N., Ashenfelter, O. C. (1986). Testing the Efficiency of Employment Contracts, in: Journal of Political Economy, 94(3): 40-87.

Bullock, H. (1967). A History of Negro Education in the South: From 1619 to the Present, Cambridge, MA: Harvard University Press.

Burdett, K., Mortensen, D. T. (1989). Equilibrium Wage Differentials and Employer Size, Center for Mathematical Studies in Economics and Management Science Discussion Paper No. 860.

Bureau of National Affairs (undated). Labor Relations Reporter Wages and Hours Manual, Washington, DC: Bureau of National Affairs.

Bureau of National Affairs (1990). Daily Labor Report,Washington, DC: Bureau of National Affairs.

Bus, M. (1989). Testing for Contracting Effects on Employment, NBER Working Paper No. 3051.

Canada Department of Labour (various issues). Wage Rates, Salaries and Hours of Labour, Ottawa: Information Canada.

Card, D. (1983). Cost of Living Escalators in Major Union Contracts, in: Industrial and Labor Relations Review, 37(1): 34-48.

Card, D. (1986). Efficient Contracts with Costly Adjustment: Short Run Employment Determination for Airline Mechanics, in: American Economic Review, 76(5): 1045-71.

Card, D. (1988). Strikes and Wages: A Test of a Signaling Model, NBER Working Paper No. 2550.

Card, D. (1990). Unexpected Inflation, Real Wages, and Employment Determination in Union Contracts, in: American Economic Review, 80(4): 669-88. [Chapter 8 in this volume]

Card, D. (1992a). Using Regional Variation in Wages to Measure the Effects of the Federal Minimum Wage, in: Industrial and Labor Relations Review, 46(1): 22-37. [Chapter 5 in this volume]

Card, D. (1992b). Do Minimum Wages Reduce Employment? A Case Study of California, 1987- 89, in: Industrial and Labor Relations Review, 46(1): 38-54.

Card, D. (1995). Schooling, Earnings and Ability Revisited, in: Polachek, S. W. (Ed.), Research in Labor Economics, 14, Greenwich, CT: JAI Press, 23-48.

Card, D., Krueger, A. B. (1992a). Does School Quality Matter? Returns to Education and the Characteristics of Public Schools in the United States, in: Journal of Political Economy, 100(1): 1-40. [Chapter 1 in this volume]

Card, D., Krueger, A. B. (1992b). School Quality and Black-White Relative Earnings: A Direct Assessment, in: Quarterly Journal of Economics, 107(1): 151-200. [Chapter 2 in this volume]

Card, D., Krueger, A. B. (1993). Minimum Wages and Employment: A Case Study of the Fast Food Industry in New Jersey and Pennsylvania, NBER Working Paper No. 4509.

Card, D., Krueger, A. B. (1994). Minimum Wages and Employment: A Case Study of the Fast-Food Industry in New Jersey and Pennsylvania, in: American Economic Review, 84(4): 772-93. [Chapter 6 in this volume]

Card, D., Krueger, A. B. (1995). Myth and Measurement: The New Economics of the Minimum Wage, Princeton, NJ: Princeton University Press.

Card, D., Krueger, A. B. (1996a). Labor Market Effects of School Quality: Theory and Evidence, in: Burtless, G. (Ed.), Does Money Matter? The Effect of School Resources on Student Achievement and Adult Success, Washington, DC: Brookings Institution, 97-140.

Card, D., Krueger, A. B. (1996b). School Resources and Student Outcomes: An Overview of the Literature and New Evidence from North and South Carolina, in: Journal of Economic Perspectives, 10(4): 31-50. [Chapter 3 in this volume]

Card, D., Krueger, A. B. (1997). A Reanalysis of the Effect of the New Jersey Minimum Wage Increase on the Fast-Food Industry with Representative Payroll Data, Industrial Relations Section Working Paper No. 393.

Card, D., Krueger, A. B. (2000). Minimum Wages and Employment: A Case Study of the

Fast-Food Industry in New Jersey and Pennsylvania: Reply, in: American Economic Review, 90 (5): 1397-420. [Chapter 7 in this volume]

Chain Operators Guide (various issues).

Chiswick, B. R. (1974). Income Inequality: Regional Analyses within a Human Capital Framework, New York, NY: Columbia University Press.

Christofides, L. N., Oswald, A. J. (1987). Efficient and Inefficient Employment Outcomes: A Study Based on Canadian Contract Data, Oxford Institute of Economics and Statistics, Applied Economics Discussion Paper No. 37.

Coleman, J. S., Campell, E. Q., Hobson, C. L., McPartland, J., Modd, A. M., Weinfeld, F. D., York, R. L. (1966). Equality of Educational Opportunity, Washington, DC: Government Printing Office.

Coleman, J. S., Hoffer, T., Kilgore, S. (1982). High School Achievement: Public, Catholic, and Private Schools Compared, New York, NY: Basic Books.

Cullen, D. E. (1961). Minimum Wage Laws, Bulletin 43, New York State School of Industrial and Labor Relations, Cornell University.

Davis, J. A., Smith, T. W. (1972-1990). General Social Surveys, Chicago, IL: National Opinion Research Center, Producer, 1990; Storrs, CT: The Roper Center for Public Opinion Research, University of Connecticut, Distributor.

Davis, S. J., Haltiwanger, J. C., Schuh, S. (1996). Job Creation and Destruction, Cambridge, MA: MIT Press.

Donohue, J. J., Heckman, J. J. (1991). Continuous Versus Episodic Change: The Impact of Affirmative Action and Civil Rights Policy on the Economic Status of Blacks, in: Journal of Economic Literature, 29(4): 1603-43.

Duncan, G. J., Hoffman, S. D. (1983). A New Look at the Causes of the Improved Economic Status of Black Workers, in: Journal of Human Resources, 18(2): 268-82.

Ehrenberg, R., Marcus, A. J. (1980). Minimum Wage Legislation and the Educational Outcomes of Youth, in: Ehrenberg, R. (Ed.), Research in Labor Economics, Vol. 3, Greenwich, CT: JAI Press, 61-93.

Electric Utility Week (1992). Two-Day 'Nor'easter' Cuts Power to Nearly 2 Million in Northeast, December 21st, 1992, 7.

Finn, J. D., Achilles, C. M. (1990). Answers and Questions about Class Size: A Statewide Experiment, in: American Educational Research, 27(3): 557-77.

Fischer, S. (1977). Long-Term Contracts, Rational Expectations, and the Optimal Money Supply Rule, in: Journal of Political Economy, 85(1): 191-206.

Fischer, S. (1987). Recent Developments in Macroeconomics, NBER Working Paper No. 2473.

Fogel, R., Engerman, S. (1974). Time on the Cross, Boston, MA: Little Brown.

Folger, J. (1989). Editor's Introduction: Project STAR and Class Size Policy, in: Peabody Journal of Education, 67(1): 1-16.

Folger, J., Breda, C. (1989). Evidence from Project STAR about Class Size and Student Achievement, in: Peabody Journal of Education, 67(1): 17-33.

Folger, J., Parker, J. (1990). The Cost-Effectiveness of Adding Aides or Reducing Class Size, Nashville, TN: Vanderbilt University.

Freedman, D. (1991). Statistical Models and Shoe Leather, in: Sociological Methodology, 21: 291-313.

Freeman, R. B. (1973). Changes in the Labor Market for Black Americans, 1948-72, in: Brookings Papers on Economic Activity, 4(1): 67-132.

Freeman, R. B. (1976). Black Elite: The New Market for Highly Educated Black Americans, New York, NY: McGraw-Hill.

Freeman, R. B., Gray, W., Ichniowski, C. E. (1981). Low Cost Student Labor: The Use and Effects of the Youth Subminimum Provisions for Full-Time Students, in: Report of the Minimum Wage Study Commission, Vol. 5., Washington, DC: Government Printing Office, 305-35.

Geary, P. T., Kennan, J. (1982). The Employment - Real Wage Relationship: An International Study, in: Journal of Political Economy, 90(4): 854-71.

Glass, G., Smith, M. L. (1978). Meta-Analysis of Research on the Relationships of Class Size and Achievement, ERIC Document Reproduction Service No. ED 168 129.

References

Goldberger, A. S., Cain, G. G. (1982). The Causal Analysis of Cognitive Outcomes in the Coleman, Hoffer and Kilgore Report, in: Sociology of Education, 55(2-3): 103-22.

Gray, J. A. (1976). Wage Indexation: A Macroeconomic Approach, in: Journal of Monetary Economics, 2(2): 221-35.

Gray, J. A., Spencer, D. (1990). Price Prediction Errors and Real Economic Activity: A Reassessment, in: Economic Inquiry, 28(4): 658-81.

Griffith, R. W. (1969). Mississippi, in: Pearson, J., Fuller, E. (Eds.), Education in the States: Historical Development and Outlook, Washington, DC: National Education Association of the United States.

Griliches, Z. (1977). Estimating the Returns to Schooling: Some Econometric Problems, in: Econometrica, 45(1): 1-22.

Griliches, Z. (1986). Economic Data Issues, in: Griliches, Z., Intriligator, M. D. (Eds.), Handbook of Econometrics, Vol. 3, New York, NY: North-Holland, 1465-514.

Griliches, Z., Mason, W. M. (1972). Education, Income, and Ability, in: Journal of Political Economy, 80(3): 74-103.

Grogger, J. (1996). School Expenditures and Post-Schooling Earnings: Evidence from High School and Beyond, in: Review of Economics and Statistics, 78(4): 628-37.

Grossman, J. B. (1983). The Impact of the Minimum Wage on Other Wages, in: Journal of Human Resources, 18(3): 359-78.

Hall, R. E. (1980). Employment Fluctuations and Wage Rigidity, in: Brookings Papers on Economic Activity, 11(1): 91-142.

Hall, R. E., Lilien, D. (1979). Efficient Wage Bargains under Uncertain Supply and Demand, in: American Economic Review, 69(5): 868-79.

Hamermesh, D. S. (1986). The Demand for Labor in the Long Run, in: Ashenfelter, O. C., Layard, R. (Eds.), Handbook of Labor Economics, Amsterdam: North- Holland, Chapter 8.

Hanushek, E. A. (1986). The Economics of Schooling: Production and Efficiency in Public Schools, in: Journal of Economic Literature, 24(3): 1141-77.

Hanushek, E. A. (1996a). School Resources and Student Performance, in: Burtless, G. (Ed.), Does Money Matter? The Effect of School Resource on Student Achievement and Adult Success, Washington, DC: Brookings Institution, 43-73.

Hanushek, E. A. (1996b). A More Complete Picture of School Resource Policies, in: Review of Educational Research, 66(3): 397-409.

Hanushek, E. A. (1998). The Evidence on Class Size, W. Allen Wallis Institute of Political Economy, Occasional Paper No. 98-1.

Hanushek, E. A., Rivkin, S., Taylor, L. (1996). The Identification of School Resource Effects, unpublished paper, University of Rochester.

Hanushek, E. A., Taylor, L. (1990). Alternative Assessments of the Performance of Schools, in: Journal of Human Resources, 25(2): 179-201.

Harlan, L. R. (1958). Separate and Unequal: Public School Campaigns and Racism in the Southern Seaboard States 1901-1915, Chapel Hill, NC: University of North Carolina Press.

Harnon, C., Walker, I. (1995). Estimates of the Economic Return to Schooling for the United Kingdom, in: American Economic Review, 85(5): 1278-86.

Heckman, J. J. (1995). Lessons from the Bell Curve, in: Journal of Political Economy, 103(5): 1091-20.

Heckman, J. J., Polachek, S. W. (1974). Empirical Evidence on the Functional Form of the Earnings-Schooling Relationship, in: Journal of the American Statistical Association, 69(346): 350-54.

Heckman, J. J., Payner, B. (1989). Determining the Impact of Federal Antidiscrimination Policy on the Economic Status of Blacks: A Study of South Carolina, in: American Economic Review, 79(1): 138-77.

Heckman, J. J., Layne-Farrar, A., Todd, P. (1996). Does Measured School Quality Really Matter? An Examination of the Earnings-Quality Relationship, in: Burtless, G. (Ed.), Does Money Matter? The Effect of School Resources on Student Achievement and Adult Success, Washington, DC: Brookings Institution, 192-289.

Hedges, L. V., Stock, W. (1983). The Effects of Class Size: An Examination of Rival Hypotheses, in: American Educational Research Journal, 20(1): 63-65.

Hedges, L. V., Laine, R., Greenwald, R. (1994). Does Money Matter? A Meta-Analysis of Studies of the Effects of Differential School Inputs on Student Outcomes, in: Education Researcher, 23(3): 5-14.

Hendricks, W. E., Kahn, L. M. (1987). Contract Length, Wage Indexation, and Ex Ante Variability of Real Wages, in: Journal of Labor Research, 8(3): 221-36.

Hendry, D. F. (1980). Econometrics – Alchemy or Science?, in: Economica, 47(188): 387-406.

Holtz-Eakin, D., Newey, W., Rosen, H. S. (1988). Estimating Vector Autoregressions with Panel Data, in: Econometrica, 56(6): 1371-98.

Jackson, J., Gurin, G. (1987). National Survey of Black Americans, 1979- 1980, Inter-university Consortium for Political and Social Research, No. 8512.

Johnson, G. E., Stafford, F. P. (1973). Social Returns to Quantity and Quality of Schooling, in: Journal of Human Resources, 8(2): 139-55.

Jones, S. (1992). Was There a Hawthorne Effect?, in: American Journal of Sociology, 98(3): 451-468.

Juhn, C., Murphy, K. M., Pierce, B. (1991). Accounting for the Slowdown in Black-White Wage Convergence, in: Kosters, M. H. (Ed.), Workers and Their Wages: Changing Patterns in the United States, Washington, DC: AEI Press.

Kane, T., Rouse, C. (1993). Labor Market Returns to Two- and Four-Year Colleges: Is a Credit a Credit and Do Degrees Matter?, Working Paper No. 311, Princeton University, Industrial Relations Section.

Katz, L. F., Krueger, A. B. (1992). The Effects of the Minimum Wage on the Fast Food Industry, in: Industrial and Labor Relations Review, 46(1): 6-21.

Kennan, J. (1988). An Econometric Analysis of Fluctuations in Aggregate Labor Supply and Demand, in: Econometrica, 56(2): 317-34.

Kirk, F. M. (1969). South Carolina, in: Pearson, J., Fuller, E. (Eds.), Education in the States: Historical Development and Outlook, Washington, DC: National Education Association of the United States.

Krueger, A. B. (1997). Experimental Estimates of Education Production Functions, Princeton University, Industrial Relations Section Working Paper No. 379.

Krueger, A. B. (1999). Experimental Estimates of Education Production Functions, in: Quarterly Journal of Economics, 114 (2): 497-532. [Chapter 4 in this volume]

Kydland, F. E., Prescott, E. C. (1982). Time to Build and Aggregate Fluctuations, in: Econometrica, 50(6): 1345-70.

Labour Canada (various issues). Collective Bargaining Review, Ottawa: Labour Canada.

LaLonde, R. J. (1986). Evaluating the Econometric Evaluations of Training Programs with Experimental Data, in: American Economic Review, 76(4): 604-20.

Lane, J., Stevens, D., Burgess, S. (1996). Worker and Job Flows, in: Economics Letters, 51(1): 109-13.

Lang, K. (1993). Ability Bias, Discount Rate Bias and the Return to Education, unpublished paper, Boston University.

Leamer, E. E. (1983). Let's Take the Con Out of Econometrics, in: American Economic Review, 73(1): 31-43.

Lester, R. A. (1960). Employment Effects of Minimum Wages, in: Industrial and Labor Relations Review, 13(2): 254-64.

Lester, R. A. (1964). Economics of Labor, New York, NY: Macmillan.

Lewis, H. G. (1986). Union Relative Wage Effects, Chicago, IL: University of Chicago Press.

Link, C., Ratledge, E., Lewis, K. (1980). The Quality of Education and Cohort Variation in Black-White Earnings Differentials: Reply, in: American Economic Review, 70(1): 196-203.

Machin, S., Manning, A. (1994). The Effects of Minimum Wages on Wage Dispersion and Employment: Evidence from the U.K. Wage Councils, in: Industrial and Labor Relations Review, 47(2): 319-29.

MaCurdy, T. E., Pencavel, J. H. (1986). Testing Between Competing Models of Wage and Employment Determination in Unionized Markets, in: Journal of Political Economy,

References

94(3): 3-39.

Mankiw, N. G. (1985). Small Menu Costs and Large Business Cycles: A Macroeconomic Model of Monopoly, in: Quarterly Journal of Economics, 100(2): 529-39.

Margo, R. (1990). Race and Schooling in the South, 1880-1950: An Economic History, Chicago, IL: University of Chicago Press.

McCallum, B. T. (1976). Rational Expectations and the Natural Rate Hypothesis: Some Consistent Estimates, in: Econometrica, 44(1): 43-52.

McDonald's Corporation (1991). Annual Report, Chicago, IL.

McDonald, I. M., Solow, R. M. (1982). Wage Bargaining and Employment, in: American Economic Review, 71(5): 896-908.

McGiverin, J. D., Gilnan, D., Tiflitski, C. (1989). A Meta-Analysis of the Relation Between Class Size and Achievement, in: Elementary School Journal, 90(1): 47-56.

Mincer, J., Leighton, L. (1981). The Effects of Minimum Wages on Human Capital Formation, in: Rottenberg, S. (Ed.), The Economics of Legal Minimum Wages, Washington, DC: American Enterprise Institute, 155-73.

Minimum Wage Study Commission (1981). Report of the Minimum Wage Study Commission; Washington, DC: Government Printing Office.

Morgan, J. N., Sirageldin, I. (1968). A Note on the Quality Dimension in Education, in: Journal of Political Economy, 76(5): 1069-77.

Mortensen, D. T. (1988). Equilibrium Wage Distributions: A Synthesis, Center for Mathematical Studies in Economics and Management Science Discussion Paper No. 811.

Mosteller, F. (1995). The Tennessee Study of Class Size in the Early School Grades, in: The Future of Children: Critical Issues for Children and Youths, 5(2): 113-127.

Murnane, R. J. (1984). A Review Essay-Comparisons of Public and Private Schools: Lessons from the Uproar, in: Journal of Human Resources, 19(2): 263-77.

Murnane, F., Willett, J. B., Levy, F. (1995). The Growing Importance of Cognitive Skills in Wage Determination, in: Review of Economics and Statistics, 77(2): 251-66.

National Center for Education Statistics (1996). Digest of Education Statistics, Table 166, Washington, DC: Government Printing Office.

Neumark, D., Wascher, W. (1995). The Effects of New Jersey's Minimum Wage Increase on Fast-Food Employment: A Re-Evaluation Using Payroll Records, unpublished manuscript, Michigan State University.

Neumark, D., Wascher, W. (2000). Minimum Wages and Employment: A Case Study of the Fast-Food Industry in New Jersey and Pennsylvania: Comment, in: American Economic Review, 90(5): 1362-96.

Nickell, S. J., Wadhwani, S. (1987). Financial Factors, Efficiency Wages and Employment: Investigations Using U.K. Micro-Data, in: London School of Economics, Center for Labour Economics Working Paper No. 993.

Nye, B., Zaharias, J., Fulton, B. D., Achilles, C. M., Hooper, R. (1994). The Lasting Benefits Study: A Continuing Analysis of the Effect of Small Class Size in Kindergarten through Third Grade on Student Achievement Test Scores in Subsequent Grade Levels, in: Seventh Grade Technical Report, Nashville, TN: Center of Excellence for Research in Basic Skills, Tennessee State University.

Phelps, E. S., Taylor, J. B. (1977). Stabilization Powers of Monetary Policy under Rational Expectations, in: Journal of Political Economy, 85(1): 163-90.

Prais, S. J. (1996). Class-Size and Learning: The Tennessee Experiment – What Follows?, in: Oxford Review of Education, 22(4): 399-414.

Ransom, M. R. (1993). Seniority and Monopsony in the Academic Labor Market, in: American Economic Review, 83(1): 221-33.

Reynolds, L. G. (1965). Wages and Employment in the Labor Surplus Economy, in: American Economic Review, 55(1): 19-39.

Ribich, T. I., Murphy, J. L. (1975). The Economic Returns to Increased Educational Spending, in: Journal of Human Resources, 10(1): 56-77.

Rizzuto, R., Wachtel, P. (1980). Further Evidence on the Returns to School Quality, in: Journal of Human Resources, 15(2): 240-54.

Rosen, S. (1985). Implicit Contracts: A Survey, in: Journal of Economic Literature, 23(3): 1144-76.

San Segundo, M. J. (1988). Do Private Schools Make a Difference?, Working paper, Southern European Economics Discussion Series, Leioa (Vizcaya): Instituto de Economía Pública.

Sander, W. (1993). Expenditures and Student Achievement in Illinois: New Evidence, in: Journal of Public Economics, 52(3): 403-16.

Sipe, C. L., Grossman, J. B., Milliner, J. A. (1988). Summer Training and Education Program (STEP): Report on the 1987 Experience, Philadelphia, PA: Public/Private Ventures.

Smith, J. P. (1984). Race and Human Capital, in: American Economic Review, 74(4): 685-98.

Smith, J. P., Welch, F. (1986). Closing the Gap: Forty Years of Economic Progress for Blacks, Santa Monica, CA: The RAND Corporation.

Smith, J. P., Welch, F. (1989). Black Economic Progress after Myrdal, in: Journal of Economic Literature, 27(2): 519-64.

Southern Education Reporting Service (1959). Southern Schools: Progress and Problems, Nashville, TN: SERS.

Southern Education Reporting Service (1965). A Statistical Summary, State by State, of School Segregation-Desegregation in the Southern and Border Area from 1954 to the Present, Nashville, TN: SERS.

Statistics Canada (various issues). Information Division, Canada Year Book, Ottawa: Statistics Canada.

Statistics Canada (1984). Industry Product Division, Gross Domestic Product by Industry, Ottawa: Statistics Canada.

Statistics Canada (1977). Real Domestic Product by Industry 1961-1971, Ottawa: Statistics Canada.

Stigler, G. (1946). The Economics of Minimum Wage Legislation, in: American Economic Review, 36(3): 358-65.

Sullivan, D. G. (1989). Monopsony Power in the Market for Nurses, in: Journal of Law and Economics, 32(2): 135-78.

Summers, A. A., Wolfe, B. L. (1977). Do Schools Make a Difference?, in: American Economic Review, 67(4): 639-52.

Topel, R. H. (1986). Local Labor Markets, in: Journal of Political Economy, 94(3): 111-43.

United States Commissioner of Education (1969). History of Schools for the Colored Population, originally published by United States Office of Education, in: Special Report of the Commissioner of Education on the Improvement of Schools in the District of Columbia, Washington, DC: Government Printing Office (1871), New York, NY: Arno Press.

U.S. Census Bureau (1996). Historical Income Tables, Washington, DC: Government Printing Office, Table P25.

U.S. Department of Commerce (1987). Census of Retail Trade: Miscellaneous Subjects, Washington, DC: Government Printing Office.

U.S. Department of Labor, Bureau of Labor Statistics (various years). Geographic Profiles of Employment and Unemployment, in: Bulletin Nos. 2327, 2361, 2381. Washington, DC: Government Printing Office

Vroman, W. (1974). Changes in the Labor Market Position of Black Men Since 1964, in: Industrial Relations Research Association, Proceedings of the Twenty-Seventh Winter Meeting, 294-301.

Wachtel, P. (1976). The Effects on Earnings of School and College Investment Expenditures, in: Review of Economics and Statistics, 58(3): 326-31.

Welch, F. (1966). Measurement of the Quality of Schooling, in: American Economic Review, 56(2): 379-92.

Welch, F. (1967). Labor-Market Discrimination: An Interpretation of Income Differences in the Rural South, Journal of Political Economy, 75(3): 225-40.

Welch, F. (1973a). Black-White Differences in Returns to Schooling, in: American Economic Review, 63(5): 893-907.

Welch, F. (1973b). Education and Racial Discrimination, in: Ashenfelter, O. C., Rees, A. (Eds.), Discrimination in Labor Markets, Princeton, N.J.: Princeton University Press,

References

43-81.

Welch, F. (1976). Minimum Wage Legislation in the United States, in Ashenfelter, O. C., Blum, J. (Eds.), Evaluating the Labor Market Effects of Social Programs, Princeton, NJ: Princeton University Industrial Relations Section.

Wellington, A. J. (1991). Effects of the Minimum Wage on the Employment Status of Youths: An Update, in: Journal of Human Resources, 26(1): 27-46.

Word, E., Johnston, J., Pate-Bain, H., Fulton, B. D., Boyd-Zaharias, J., Achilles, C. M., Lintz, M. N., Folger, J., Breda, C. (1990). The State of Tennessee's Student/Teacher Achievement Ratio (STAR) Project: Technical Report 1985-1990, Nashville, TN: Tennessee State Department of Education.

Index

Index

About the Authors...

 **David Card** is Professor of Economics at the University of California, Berkeley, Director of the Center for Labor Economics at the University of California, Berkeley, and Director of the Labor Studies Program at the National Bureau of Economic Research. He received his B.A. in 1978 at Queen's University (Kingston) and his Ph.D. at Princeton University in 1983. He was Associate Editor of the Journal of Labor Economics (1988-1992), Co-editor of Econometrica (1993-1997), and Co-editor of the American Economic Review (2002-2005). He is currently on the editorial board of various scientific journals. David Card joined IZA as a Research Fellow in 1999.

 **Alan B. Krueger** is the Bendheim Professor of Economics and Public Affairs at Princeton University and has been nominated to chair the Council of Economic Advisers to the President of the United States. He previously served as Assistant Secretary for Economic Policy at the U.S. Department of the Treasury (2009-2010) and as Chief Economist of the Department of Labor (1994-1995). Krueger is also the Founding Director of the Princeton University Survey Research Center and a Research Associate of the National Bureau of Economic Research. In addition he was on the editorial board of Science (2001-2009), Editor of the Journal of Economic Perspectives (1996-2002), and Co-editor of the Journal of the European Economic Association (2003-2005). Alan Krueger joined IZA as a Research Fellow in 2000.

David Card and **Alan B. Krueger** were jointly awarded with the IZA Prize in Labor Economics in 2006.

...and the Editors

Randall K. Q. Akee is Assistant Professor of Economics at Tufts University. He completed his Ph.D. at Harvard University in June 2006. Prior to his doctoral studies, he earned a master's degree in International and Development Economics at Yale University and also spent several years working for the State of Hawaii Office of Hawaiian Affairs Economic Development Division.  His main research interests are Labor Economics, Economic Development, and Migration. From August 2006 until August 2009 he was a Research Associate at IZA, where he also served as Deputy Program Director for Employment and Development.

Klaus F. Zimmermann has been Full Professor of Economics at the University of Bonn and Director of the Institute for the Study of Labor (IZA Bonn) since 1998. From 2000 until 2011 he was President of the German Institute for Economic Research (DIW Berlin). Zimmermann is Honorary Professor of Economics at the Free University of Berlin (since 2001) and  Honorary Professor at the Renmin University of China (since 2006). He is also Chairman of the Society of the German Economic Research Institutes (ARGE) (since 2005), and a member of the German Academy of Sciences Leopoldina (since 2001), the World Economic Forum's Global Agenda Council on Migration (since 2009) and the Academia Europaea (since 2010).

Printed and bound by CPI Group (UK) Ltd, Croydon, CR0 4YY